One Shot Hitchcock

One Shot Hitchcock

A Contemporary Approach to the Screen

Edited by

LUKE ROBINSON AND MELANIE ROBSON

OXFORD

UNIVERSITY PRESS

OXFORD
UNIVERSITY PRESS

Oxford University Press is a department of the University of Oxford. It furthers
the University's objective of excellence in research, scholarship, and education
by publishing worldwide. Oxford is a registered trade mark of Oxford University
Press in the UK and certain other countries.

Published in the United States of America by Oxford University Press
198 Madison Avenue, New York, NY 10016, United States of America.

Library of Congress Cataloging-in-Publication Data
Names: Robinson, Luke (Film theorist), editor. | Robson, Melanie, editor.
Title: One shot Hitchcock : a contemporary approach to the screen /
edited by Luke Robinson and Melanie Robson.
Description: New York, NY : Oxford University Press, 2024. |
Includes bibliographical references.
Identifiers: LCCN 2023057306 (print) | LCCN 2023057307 (ebook) |
ISBN 9780197682883 (paperback) | ISBN 9780197682876 (hardback) |
ISBN 9780197682906 (epub)
Subjects: LCSH: Hitchcock, Alfred, 1899–1980—Criticism and interpretation. |
Framing (Cinematography)
Classification: LCC PN1998.3.H58 O54 2024 (print) | LCC PN1998.3.H58 (ebook) |
DDC 971.4302/33092—dc23/eng/20240108
LC record available at https://lccn.loc.gov/2023057306
LC ebook record available at https://lccn.loc.gov/2023057307

DOI: 10.1093/oso/9780197682876.001.0001

Paperback printed by Marquis Book Printing, Canada
Hardback printed by Bridgeport National Bindery, Inc., United States of America

Contents

Acknowledgments

One morning Luke awoke with a title in his head—*One Shot Hitchcock*. It was early, the sun was out, he felt he was on to something. He texted the title to Melanie. It was way too early to be texting on a Saturday, but Luke couldn't wait. "Yes!" was Melanie's reply! And with those initial texts, their project began. We were very fortunate that many of the best film scholars also took to our idea and wanted to be included in the book. We would therefore first like to thank all the authors in the volume whose passion for the project has made it a joy to do. Special thank you to Noa Steimatsky, who introduced us to Tom Gunning, and to Bruce Isaacs for reading and editing our proposal and synopsis before we submitted it to Oxford University Press. Thank you also to Bruce for introducing us to our OUP editor. We would also like to thank Jodi Brooks, Jane Mills, and George Kouvaros for their support of our book and us as film scholars. We would also like to thank our editor Norman Hirschy at Oxford University Press and our title manager and project editors Paloma Escovedo and Zara Cannon-Mohammed.

Luke would like to thank his parents Jude Robinson and Colin Campbell Robinson, and his partner Enrico Gentalia, for their love and support. Thank you also to Enrico for making him laugh when the editing processes got a little too heady and serious! Luke would also like to thank the University of New South Wales, especially the Graduate Research School and the Faculty of Arts, Design & Architecture, for providing resources and funding during his PhD candidature. Thank you also to the Australian Federal Government for providing Luke with the Australian Government Research Training Program Scholarship while he was completing his PhD. And the biggest thank you to Melanie Robson for being the best coeditor one could ask for, and for being such a beautiful friend.

Melanie would like to thank her parents, Charmaine and William Robson, and her sister, Amelia, for their love and support through this project. Thank you to the School of the Arts and Media at the University of New South Wales for their provision of resources via an Adjunct Lectureship, which helped support this project. Finally, Melanie would like to thank Luke for being a wonderful coeditor and writing partner. Our meetings to work on this volume have been as productive as they have been enjoyable conversations about film.

Contributors

Born during World War II, **Charles Barr** became one of the first generation of university film teachers, working mainly in England at the University of East Anglia, but also in the United States and Ireland. His publications include books on *Ealing Studios* (1977; rev. ed. Cameron & Hollis, 1999), and three on Hitchcock, including the BFI Classic on *Vertigo* (2002; rev. ed., 2012). He tries to stay active in retirement, his latest book being *A Very Short Introduction to British Cinema* (Oxford University Press, 2022).

Jodi Brooks is a Senior Lecturer in Film Studies in the School of the Arts & Media, University of New South Wales (Australia). Her work has been published in journals such as *Camera Obscura*, *Feminist Media Studies*, *Continuum*, *Screen*, *Screening the Past*, *Writings on Dance, Art & Text*, and *Senses of Cinema*, and in various edited collections.

Megan Carrigy is the author of *The Reenactment in Contemporary Screen Culture* (Bloomsbury, 2021). Her research interests include national, transnational, and First Nations media, re-enactment, virtual reality, spectatorship, and film theory. Megan has spent her career working in research, education, and public programming roles and is currently Public Programs Manager for the National Gallery of Australia. Previously, she was Associate Director for Academic Programs at New York University's Sydney campus. She is also a former programmer for Queer Screen and the Mardi Gras Film Festival, where she spent four years building partnerships with local and international distributors, filmmakers, festivals, and community organizations.

Tom Gunning is Professor Emeritus in the Department on Cinema and Media at the University of Chicago. He is the author of *D. W. Griffith and the Origins of American Narrative Film* (University of Illinois Press, 1986) and *The Films of Fritz Lang; Allegories of Vision and Modernity* (British Film Institute, 2000), and over a hundred and fifty articles on early cinema, film history and theory, avant-garde film, and film genre. With André Gaudreault he originated the theory of the "Cinema of Attractions." In 2009 he was awarded an Andrew A. Mellon Distinguished Achievement Award and in 2010 he was elected to the American Academy of Arts and Sciences.

Helen Hughes is Senior Lecturer in German and Film Studies at the University of Surrey. Her research has engaged with documentary studies, German-language cinema, and environmental humanities. She is the author of *Radioactive Documentary* (Intellect, 2021), *Green Documentary* (Intellect, 2014), coeditor of *Documentary and Disability* (Palgrave Macmillan, 2017), and co-translator of Kluge and Negt's *History and Obstinacy* (Zone Books, 2014), and she has also published several chapters and articles in journals such as *Screen*, *Continuum*, and the *Historical Journal of Film, Radio and Television*. She is currently working on a project about the GDR filmmaker Annelie Thorndike with the working title *Red Documentary*.

Bruce Isaacs is Associate Professor in Film Studies at the University of Sydney. He has published extensively on classical and post-classical American cinema and is the author of *The Art of Pure Cinema: Hitchcock and His Imitators* (Oxford University Press, 2020) and *The Orientation of Future Cinema: Technology, Aesthetics, Spectacle* (Bloomsbury, 2013).

Julian Murphet is Jury Professor of English Language and Literature at the University of Adelaide. He is the author of *Modern Character, 1888–1905* (Oxford University Press, 2023) and *Prison Writing in the Twentieth Century: A Literary Guide* (Edinburgh University Press, 2023), among other publications.

Luke Robinson teaches film and media studies at the University of New South Wales (UNSW) and University of Technology Sydney. He completed his PhD in film studies at the UNSW with a thesis on "Facing Erasure: The Disappearing Faces of 1940s Hollywood Gothic Cinema." His first coedited book *Sound Affects: A User's Guide* (Bloomsbury, 2023) examines how sounds produce affects and the ways that affects can operate as sound. He has published and given papers on teaching pedagogy for film and media studies, and he is a video artist working with Move in Pictures (https://www.move-in-pictures.com).

Melanie Robson is an adjunct lecturer at UNSW Sydney. She teaches film at UNSW and Australian Film Television and Radio School (AFTRS). Her doctoral thesis focuses on the long take in contemporary European cinema through the works of Theo Angelopoulos, Bela Tarr, Michael Haneke, and Alexander Sokurov. She has published on horror film and television, and the aesthetics and form of modernist cinema in *MAI: Feminism & Visual Culture*, *Refractory*, *Studies in European Cinema*, and *Mise-en-scène*. Her current research project investigates the long take as a transnational modernist tradition across contemporary film and television.

Martin P. Rossouw is head of the Department of Art History and Image Studies, University of the Free State in Bloemfontein, South Africa, where he teaches as Senior Lecturer in Film and Visual Media. He is the author of *Transformational Ethics of Film: Thinking the Cinemakeover in the Film-Philosophy Debate* (Brill, 2021) and coeditor, with Julian Hanich, of *What Film Is Good For: On the Values of Spectatorship* (University of California Press, 2023). His most recent essay publications are in *Literature/Film Quarterly*, *Short Film Studies*, *Akademisk Kvarter*, *Image & Text*, and *New Review of Film and Television Studies*.

Sebastian Smoliński is a film critic, scholar, and lecturer. He is the coauthor of several books, including the Spanish-language monograph *La doble vida de Krzysztof Kieślowski*, a book about African American cinema, and a bilingual (Polish/English) monograph of David Lynch. He was a recipient of the 2019/2020 Kosciuszko Foundation scholarship for teaching a history of Polish film at Cleveland State University in Ohio. He is preparing his PhD dissertation about US film criticism and the construction of national identity at the University of Warsaw. He is one of the co-hosts of the *Foreign Correspondents: Deeper into Hitchcock* podcast.

Noa Steimatsky is author of the award-winning *The Face on Film* (Oxford University Press, 2017), of *Italian Locations* (University of Minnesota Press, 2008), as well as of numerous articles. She was recipient of a Guggenheim Foundation Fellowship, an NEH Fellowship, an ACLS Senior Fellowship, the American Academy in Rome Prize, a Getty Grant, and a Fulbright Award. She was faculty member at Yale, tenured at the University of Chicago, and guest professor at Stanford, University of California–Berkeley, and Sarah Lawrence College. Her work on Cinecittà's hidden history inspired a documentary film and is being expanded into a book. She lives and writes in Rome.

Sarah Street is Professor of Film at the University of Bristol, UK. She has published extensively on British cinema and on aspects of film color. Her books include *Colour Films in Britain: The Negotiation of Innovation, 1900–85* (Bloomsbury, 2012) and, more recently, *Chromatic Modernity: Color, Cinema, and Media of the 1920s* (coauthored with Joshua Yumibe, Columbia University Press, 2019), winner of the Katherine Singer Kovács Book Award for 2020 and the Michael Nelson Book award (IAMHIST) for 2021; and *Colour Films in Britain: The Eastmancolor Revolution* (coauthored with Keith M. Johnston, Paul Frith, and Carolyn Rickards, Bloomsbury, 2021).

Domietta Torlasco is a filmmaker, critical theorist, and Professor of Cinema and Comparative Literature at Northwestern University. She is the author of three books: *The Time of the Crime: Phenomenology, Psychoanalysis, Italian Film* (Stanford University Press, 2008), *The Heretical Archive: Digital Memory at the End of Film* (Minnesota University Press, 2013), and *The Rhythm of Images: Cinema beyond Measure* (Minnesota University Press, 2021). Her video essays have screened at national and international venues, including the Galerie Campagne Première in Berlin, the Walker Art Center in Minneapolis, the Pacific Film Archive in Berkeley, and the Museum of Contemporary Art in Los Angeles.

Susana Viegas is a Researcher in Philosophy of Film and a full member of IFILNOVA, Universidade NOVA de Lisboa. She received her PhD in Philosophy (Aesthetics) from the Universidade NOVA de Lisboa in 2013 with a doctoral thesis on Gilles Deleuze's philosophy of film, and a FCT PhD Studentship during the years 2007–2011. She was a Postdoctoral Research Fellow at the University of Dundee and Deakin University with the project "Rethinking the Moving Image and Time in Gilles Deleuze's Philosophy" (2014–2019) and is currently working on philosophy's relation to painting, film, and death.

1

One shot

Hitchcock's crime scenes

Luke Robinson and Melanie Robson

. About halfway through *Vertigo* (1958), John "Scottie" Ferguson (James
Stewart) dashes up the stairs of a church bell tower in pursuit of the mysterious Madeleine Elster (Kim Novak). Losing sight of her, he pauses on the
stairs and nervously looks around a pillar and over the handrail. An eyeline
match accounts for his uneasy disposition: a bird's-eye view shot looks down
through the center of the square staircase to the ground. A moment later, a
dolly-zoom shifts the shot's perspective, and the floor seems to drop swiftly
away from the camera (see Figure 1.1). This dolly-zoom shot is one of Alfred
Hitchcock's most famous shots and has come to be known as the Vertigo
Shot. For the casual twenty-first-century viewer, it is already familiar, having
been repeated, referenced, and parodied countless times. Considered within
Hitchcock's oeuvre, however, it speaks to a characteristic at the heart of every
shot examined in this volume: it is layered and meaningful in several regards
beyond its striking aesthetics. First, the shot represents a character's point of
view with which we have been aligned throughout the film. In this regard, it
also has narrative value since Scottie's vertigo has rendered him unable to act
previously. Second, the shot not only signals that Scottie is experiencing vertigo, but also creates the experience of it for the viewer, thereby contributing
to the film's affect. Third, despite the prolonged recognition of this shot as
pioneering and as a signature of *Vertigo*, Hitchcock had tried to perfect the
Vertigo Shot since at least as early as *Rebecca* (1940), rendering the shot
Hitchcockian in a deeper sense than is normally acknowledged.[1] And fourth,
since this vertigo shot takes place shortly before the true Madeleine (Jean
Corbett) is pushed to her death by her husband, this vertigo shot is one where
issues of narration, affect, auteurism, and gendered politics all intersect.

This collection is a volume about Hitchcock, but it also reveals the value of
analyzing the single shot. Encapsulated within this small, cinematic unit is a

Luke Robinson and Melanie Robson, *One shot* In: *One Shot Hitchcock*. Edited by: Luke Robinson and Melanie Robson,
Oxford University Press. © Oxford University Press 2024. DOI: 10.1093/oso/9780197682876.003.0001

Figure 1.1 A point-of-view shot is enhanced by the dolly-zoom effect in Alfred Hitchcock's *Vertigo* (1958).

code that unlocks a series of revelations about, broadly, cinema as an artistic practice and a theoretical study, and, specifically, the filmmaker's choices. The word "shot" is used in both a literal and a metaphorical sense: to refer to the cinematic shot under investigation, and to evoke the scrutinizing eye of the camera lens, which has the capacity to reveal something unseen before. In Tom Gunning's *The Films of Fritz Lang: Allegories of Vision and Modernity*, he argues the filmmaker is "imprinted" within the form of the film. Their labor's

> existence is indicated by the films themselves; a source we find only by reading backward from them, as though the films, or our careful viewing of them, created the figure of Lang as much as vice versa. In what way did Lang imprint himself in his films, or . . . in what ways do Lang's films imprint him on the audience, on film history?[2]

Taking this question as inspiration, this collection posits that the value of Hitchcock's shots is that they are always more than meets the eye. While he is often discussed in terms of his signature ("Hitchcockian"), something more profound is revealed when locating the "imprint" he leaves in each shot. This methodology is akin to unpacking a Russian doll: each shot reveals something about the film, which tells us about its historical and cultural context, and in turn about Hitchcock as a filmmaker. This Russian doll layering is central to each chapter in this collection as it speaks to the central goal: not only to further Hitchcock scholarship, but also to shed light on the shot as something that is simultaneously singular and multiple.

Among the many book-length works on Hitchcock in recent years there has been substantially limited engagement with or analysis through a formalist approach. For a director so revered as one of the most important in twentieth-century Hollywood, it is strange that there are not many studies interrogating single shots from his films, particularly given that they represent such highly recognizable moments and cinematic gestures so central to his popularity. Addressing this absence in Hitchcock scholarship, *One Shot Hitchcock* uses close formal analysis to interrogate key single shots from across the director's long career that spans American, British, and German production. In his essay "Some Hitchcockian Shots," Murray Pomerance categorizes repeated shots from across Hitchcock's films. While he, like us in this volume, is dedicated to giving Hitchcock's shots serious scholarly attention, in this single essay Pomerance discusses nine types of shot and with each type he provides numerous examples from Hitchcock's films.[3] In contrast to Pomerance's essay, in *One Shot Hitchcock* each chapter is devoted to a single shot from a film directed by Hitchcock, offering an increased focus on the shot in question. If Hitchcock is known as a director of suspense films, and films about murder, the shots discussed in *One Shot Hitchcock* are his crime scenes: these are the shots that resist being forgotten, these are the shots that repeatedly demand to be investigated, these are the shots in which Hitchcock's influence on aesthetics and culture is at its most acute.

The one shot approach

In this coedited collection, we propose a method—the one shot approach. And, with the assistance of our authors, we demonstrate the value of this approach by examining films directed by Alfred Hitchcock. With this aim in mind, there are three questions that are guiding us in writing this introduction: What is a shot? Why examine a single shot? And why examine single shots of Alfred Hitchcock's films? To answer these questions, we turn to film scholarship and the films and writings of Hitchcock himself.

Shots can be static, they can move, and they can be very short or very long in duration. In film studies we often describe shots in relation to what they are doing—we might refer to a tracking shot or a pan, or our discussion of a shot might refer to the spatial distance between the camera's lens and the main subject; for example, we might say a shot is a facial close-up or an establishing shot of a specific location. So, what precisely is a shot? A shot is a technical term in film studies that refers to two different things. When used to describe what is being recorded on set, or on location, a shot, or a *take*, begins after the camera begins to roll (when the director says "action") and before the camera is turned off (when the director calls "cut"). When used to describe a unit of a completed film, a shot refers to an uninterrupted duration of time between two edits, be it a cut, a wipe, or a fade to black.[4] A shot, or a take, initially determines what is recorded by a camera or, in the case of some digital cinema, including animation, a computer. In the form of rushes, what is recorded can be repeatedly viewed by the production team, by the film editor, by an historian who watches pre-cut material, or even, in some cases, a film viewer. In terms of the completed film, the beginnings and ends of a recorded shot are often trimmed during the post-production process. In addition to the framing of the shot, these edits contribute to what can, and cannot, be seen by a viewer when the film is projected or illuminated on a screen. Considering these points, we define a shot as *a unit of visuality that takes place in duration*.

A shot might be a single unit, but it is a unit that is composed of many elements (performers, props, lighting, sound) that together create this unity. When we study a single shot, we are studying not only the elements that create this shot, but also the elements that, more often than not, are used to create the film as a complete picture. Gilles Deleuze makes an argument about cinematic movement that has inspired our conception of a shot and its relationship to the completed film—to be clear, we are not adopting the concepts he uses, rather we are adopting the structural logic of his argument. For him: "the shot indeed has a unity. It is a unity of movement, and it embraces a correlative multiplicity which does not contradict it."[5] He also argues: "The shot is the movement-image. In so far as it relates movement to a whole which changes, it is the mobile section of duration."[6] For us, when we study a single shot, we are being attentive to both the unity of the shot and the correlative multiplicity that contributes to the dynamics of this shot. In turn, we argue that the study of single shot can not only reveal something about the dynamics of the shot being studied, but that it also can reveal something about the dynamics of the film as a whole.

For most of us it is only the completed film that we can access. It is therefore not surprising that most of the chapters in this volume conceptualize a shot as being what takes place between two edits of a completed film. However, even if this is a guiding principle for our authors, some of our authors also complicate this definition of a shot. For example, both Tom Gunning's and Noa Steimatsky's essays take what would for some be an edit between two shots—an "overlap dissolve" in Gunning's essay on *The Manxman* (1929) and a "superimposition" in Steimatsky's chapter on *The Wrong Man* (1956)— and conceptualize it as a type of an internal edit within a single larger "shot." Similarly, Bruce Isaacs chooses to discuss the long tracking shot toward Manderley that opens *Rebecca*. This shot does not constitute a single re- cording of film but is instead a sequence of independent takes that have been invisibly spliced together to create a single shot. In an endnote to his essay, Isaacs positions his approach: "I do want to emphasize that the traditional language of 'shots' and 'cuts' is often inadequate to the task of describing cinematic images in montage. Thus, I argue throughout this piece that the several shots encompass and contain a continuous thematic and formal compositional whole." Isaacs's argument is also true of many of the essays in this volume, including those by Gunning, Steimatsky, and, in a different way, Sarah Street. Street's essay is on the Technicolor of *Rope* (1948), osten- sibly a single shot film, but which is in fact a film composed of multiple long takes where the cuts are masked by brief moments of blackness. In her essay, Street focuses on separate sections of one of the final long takes in *Rope* to show how the film's overwise muted color design is "is broken by the intru- sion of a striking color effect which intensifies the drama's closing action." So, while edits can determine the duration of a shot—and therefore determine what is visible in the shot over the course of its duration—edits can also be internal to a "shot" without fully dividing the shot into two or more shots. While Gunning, Steimatsky, Isaacs, and Street complicate the notion of a shot as occurring between two edits, all the authors in this volume, in some way, identify and describe a unit of duration that is visually or thematically unified. For this reason, all the chapters in this volume are embracing what we are calling *the one shot approach*.

The focus on the single shot brings significant contemporary relevance to the collection. With the increasing reliance on digital resources in both the tertiary classroom and newer forms of fandom, the single shot has been fre- quently extracted from seminal cinematic works and proliferated through platforms such as YouTube and Vimeo. It has become a new focus of filmic analysis and the method by which students learn to recognize directorial signatures. Hitchcock foreshadows the changing contemporary relationship between viewer and screen in *Rear Window* (1954). In Martin P. Rossouw's chapter in this collection he observes, "the wheelchair-bound Jeff looking out his window becomes a metaphor for what *we* do. He is essentially a 'spectator' in front of a 'screen.' " Jeff's (Jimmy Stewart) position reminds us of the increasingly fragmented way in which screen content is consumed, and how the shot—the singular unit of film, akin to the vignette framed in the window across the courtyard—has adopted its own independent meaning. *One Shot Hitchcock* perpetuates a developing methodology of filmic interpretation increasing in popularity among both scholars and students.[7] It is thus a *contemporary* approach in all senses of the word. But why put together a book that focuses specifically on single shots from Hitchcock's films?

Hitchcock's shadow

Hitchcock is a director who people feel they know something about. For anyone who has taught on Hitchcock and his films, we learn from our students that he is the "master of suspense," that he thinks of his stars and actors as "cattle," and that his favorite type of female star is an ice-cold blonde. Even though since at least the 1930s Hitchcock has been seen as a director who "hates women,"[8] more recently, after the Me Too (#MeToo) movement, students have also come to associate Hitchcock with poor misogynist treatment of his female stars. Speaking to these concerns, Julian Murphet's and Jodi Brooks's chapters in this collection reflect on the revelation by Donald Spoto, in particular, of Tippi Hedren's treatment by Hitchcock in their respective discussions of *The Birds* (1963) and *Marnie* (1964). As a director of classical Hollywood films, Hitchcock is also known as someone who looked for ways to have control over the style of his films, either by making films with his own production companies or by directing scenes with such economy that the shots had to be edited together the way he envisioned them.[9] Everyday viewers and students see Hitchcock as casting various shadows over his films. In addition, film scholarship on Hitchcock has also cast its own shadow on him as an auteur. Examining single shots from his films offers a way of testing what we think we already know about this director. At the same time, since Hitchcock is a director many know so well, with his name lending itself to a specific style of film—"Hitchcockian"—he is a good figure to test how effective the one shot approach is for offering new perspectives on the films that many have seen so often.

People might know something of Hitchcock, but we should nonetheless give him some introduction. Over the course of his fifty-odd year career, Hitchcock directed fifty-five feature films and many shorts. He was a known director before Hollywood, and in Hollywood, with his name used to publicize films before the concept of an auteur became fashionable in French criticism in the 1950s.[10] Hitchcock is also cited as arguing for the director as the main creative influence, and the most important focus for marketing of a film, since the mid-1920s.[11] While Hitchcock liked to brand himself as the key creative influence of a film, he in fact worked with many collaborators, with his closest collaborator being the film editor and screenwriter Alma Reville (who was also his wife).[12] Another collaborator of note was the screenwriter and producer Joan Harrison, who in addition to working with Hitchcock on his last British film (*Jamaica Inn*, 1939) and his first Hollywood films (*Rebecca, Foreign Correspondent*, 1940; *Suspicion*, 1941; *Saboteur*, 1942) oversaw the production and stylization of the television series *Alfred Hitchcock Presents*.[13] As Patricia White argues in regards to *Rebecca*, and Tania Modleski argues in her discussion of *Rebecca* and other examples,[14] there were many women who were crucial for creating the image of Hitchcock as a director and who, as screenwriters, editors, creative producers, and stars, were also part of creating the "Hitchcockian" style that we often attribute to his, and also some other directors' films. Therefore, while we might be studying single shots from films directed by Hitchcock, we need to be mindful of the many women who contributed to what each of the authors identify as a Hitchcockian shot.

Because of the collection's focus on film form, it is the female protagonist and star that authors are most often attentive to in this volume. In addition to Murphet's and Brooks's essays on Hedren, Megan Carrigy's chapter juxtaposes two shots of a heroine's scream, one by Jill Lawrence (Edna Best) from the 1934 version of *The Man Who Knew Too Much* and one from Josephine "Jo" Conway McKenna (Doris Day) from its 1956 remake. Through this juxtaposition she demonstrates how their screams, in different ways, disrupts the narrative of the films, and the narrative surrounding Hitchcock as an auteur. Luke Robinson's essay on *Frenzy* (1972) concludes this volume with a discussion of a facial close-up of Babs Milligan (Anna Massey) where, unbeknownst to her, she is being targeted by a serial killer to be his next victim. For him this close-up virtually, if not actually, pulls focus "between the close-up of Babs's face, and the agency that she has, and the face of death that threatens her life and her agency as a thinking, self-determining woman." So, even though this book is called *One Shot Hitchcock*, in these and in other essays in this volume, the women of "Hitchcock" films are very much in the picture.

Individual shots have been identified by film scholars as being Hitchcockian, but Hitchcock himself often stated that individual shots were in themselves not that important as a unit of a film. For example, in a 1963 interview on his directing style from *Cinema*, Hitchcock calls a shot a "cut": he says, "Every time I use the word cut . . . I mean a shot, a separate piece of film."[15] For Hitchcock "a separate piece of film"—a worthy, if a little uninspiring, description for a shot—is given a term that is normally used to describe a film transition—a "cut." Perhaps, then, this volume should be titled: *One Cut Hitchcock* and not *One Shot Hitchcock*. But even if we did give this book this alternative title, we would still encounter a problem since in the same interview Hitchcock argues: "Oh, well a cut is nothing. One cut of film is like a piece of mosaic. To me, pure film, pure cinema is pieces of film assembled. Any individual piece is nothing. But a combination of them creates an idea."[16] A shot is a cut, and a cut is . . . "nothing." For Hitchcock it is the combination of cuts (i.e., shots) that makes what he calls a "pure film" or "pure cinema"—it is the combination of shots that creates an idea. Though Hitchcock makes this argument about the shot being "nothing," and while he argues for the importance of montage and editing for the creation of a pure cinema,[17] there are some examples of single shots that Hitchcock discusses that exemplify his idea of a pure cinema. One of the most frequently discussed types of shots that Hitchcock refers to in his own writings and interviews when discussing his concept of a pure cinema is that of the facial close-up. Perhaps fittingly, the facial close-up is also one of the most discussed types of shots in the individual essays in *One Shot Hitchcock*.

Hitchcock argues that a good example of pure cinema is when a face in close-up reacts to something off-screen. In his discussion of *Rear Window*, which for him exemplifies his idea of pure cinema,[18] Hitchcock describes the situation of the film as follows: "Mr. Stewart is sitting looking out of the window. He observes. We register his observations on his face. We are using the visual image now. We are using the mobility of the face, the expression as our content of the piece of film."[19] As we have seen, for Hitchcock a "cut" is "a separate piece of film,"[20] and in his description of *Rear Window* a facial expression, and its reaction to something off-screen, constitutes the content of this film segment. When we consider that for Hitchcock a facial expression is a reaction to something and that this something is inscribed within the expression produced, we can understand that for Hitchcock a shot is not something singular, it is rather something double, or even multiple, since, like the multiple windows that Jeffries views in *Rear Window*, the face might be registering many different "shots" that are in its view.

It is this singularity of the multiple and the multiplicity of the singular that attracts us to look closely at individual shots from Hitchcock's films, from a director who is often argued to be invested (if not obsessed) with ideas of the double and the serial, with repetition and return—so many potentially poisoned glasses of milk in his films, so many spaces that Rebecca or other women haunt. In terms of studies of cinematic form, of all Hitchcock's films it is the shower *sequence* of *Psycho* that is most remembered, imitated, studied, and quoted, and when we say quoted, we mean in scholarly and popular essays and books, in student presentations and essays, and in films and contemporary art. It is also a sequence that has been remediated in various forms, including by Gus Van Sant in his 1997 shot-by-shot remake, by Douglas Gordon in his *24 Hour Psycho* (1993), and also by students when they create their own GIFs.[21] As our emphasis on the term sequence implies the shower sequence of *Psycho* is usually considered and/or reimagined as a sequence, with the individual shots of Janet Leigh as Marion Crane showering before—and as a corpse after—she is cut to death by a silhouette in the shape of "Mrs. Bates." If we were to take one shot from the shower scene of *Psycho* to stand in for the whole sequence (an approach that we have not taken in *One Shot Hitchcock*), then it would most likely be the image of Marion with wet hair screaming at someone or something off-screen. However, this common, highly memorable image of Marion screaming, one that often appears doing an image search for *Psycho* in Google—and one that her daughter and star of the slasher film *Halloween* (1978) Jamie Lee Curtis recreated—is in fact a publicity still for the film, and not a shot from *Psycho* itself. Often publicity stills stand in for, or act as representations of, a film as a whole. However, for us, singling out a shot does more than stand in for, or act as a representative of, a film since shots are always part of an ongoing dialogue with the film that it is featured in.

If we were to choose one shot from *Psycho* as representative of the scream, we face a difficulty anyway since the shot of the "scream" is in fact three intensified facial close-ups. The scream begins with a medium close-up of Marion's face, followed by a close-up, and then an extreme close-up of Marion's mouth, sliced together by two jump cuts (see Figures 1.2–1.4). Since the sequence is edited together with such speed, to identify these

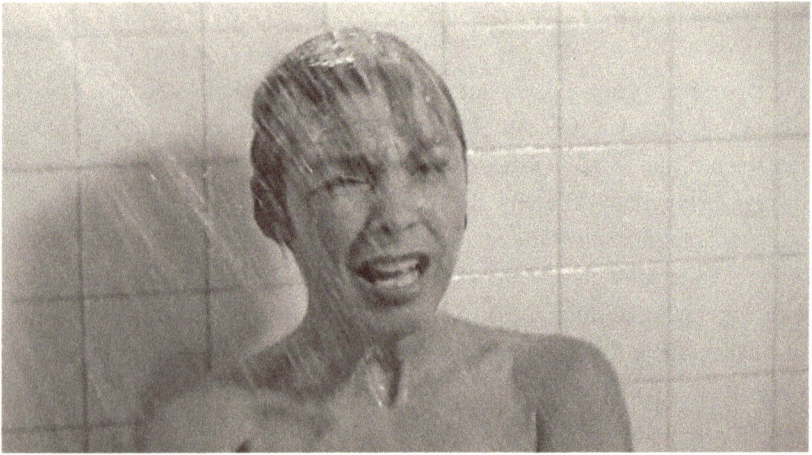

Figure 1.2 The first of three screaming shots of Marion Crane (Janet Leigh) in Alfred Hitchcock's *Psycho* (1960).

Figure 1.3 The second of three screaming shots of Marion in *Psycho*.

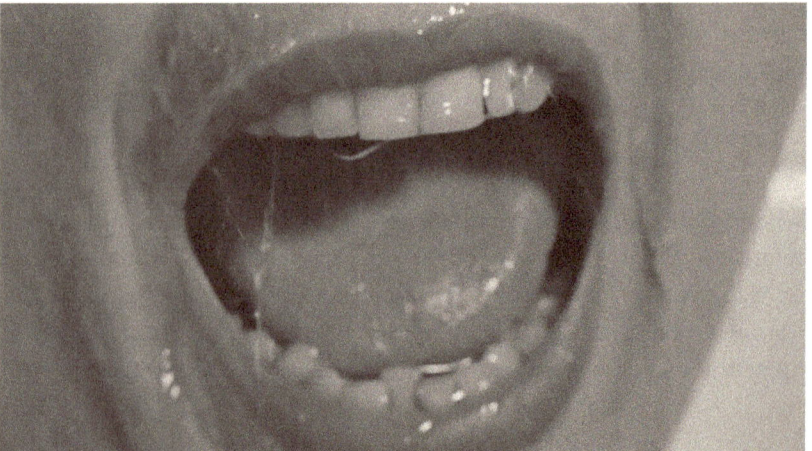

Figure 1.4 The third of three screaming shots of Marion in *Psycho*.

three shots, we had to slow the sequence down and then pause on each one. The act of slowing or pausing a film does more than allow one to identify shots, since, as Laura Mulvey argues, it can give the viewer some access to temporality of the profilmic event.[22] By slowing down and pausing a film, it is thus possible for a viewer and a film scholar to access two different types of shot: the shot of the completed film within two edits, and the shot of the original recording. With Mulvey's arguments about pausing and slowing down film in mind, it is possible for each shot of a completed film to grant us access to another type of shot within it, much as a Russian doll has a smaller doll inside a larger one (and vice versa). For example, when we pause the three shots of the scream from *Psycho*, we can spend time focusing on the shape and texture of the tiles. We can also make note of the direction of the lighting and the way Marion's shadow is cast to the left. We can also see how the face is slightly out of focus in the second shot, which, if we know something about cinematography, draws our attention to how the focus puller is working in this shot. Creating a contrast, we can also be attentive to the clarity of vision in the final shot of Marion's mouth, a shot that is lit far brighter than the previous two shots. Because *Psycho* was shot on analogue film, each of these details point to, and are indexical of, the space and time of the production of the shot. Slowing down and pausing the shower sequence of *Psycho* provides us with some details about the production and recording of the sequence, details that can then be used to write about the shot or sequence.

While we gain something by pausing and slowing a film, we also lose something. Crucially, for a sequence that features a scream, when we pause or slow a film, we can no longer hear its soundtrack. This is because, as Michel Chion argues, the trajectory of sound "has its own temporal dynamic."[23] So after pausing and slowing down a film, we need to watch the sequence again, listening and noting the sounds that we hear. When we listen to the sound of Marion's diegetic scream we see and hear that it is bridging all three shots. The commonplace notion of a shot as being between two edits is therefore complicated by our close engagement with the visuals, edits, and sounds of the shower scene from *Psycho*. The scream unifies the three shots together visually at the same time that the visuals—the increasing close shots of Marion's face and mouth, and the user of jump cuts—intensify the sound of the scream. Here we again turn to Chion, who argues: "sound shows us the image differently than what the image shows alone and the image likewise makes us hear sound differently."[24] It is the relation between visuals and sound that means that the three shots of Marion screaming are *a unit of vis-uality that takes place in duration*. However, while many might think of the scream from *Psycho* when they hear the title of our collection, the shot that most directly represents Hitchcock's signature is his cameo.

The cameo

This introduction began by considering Gunning's provocation, questioning how a filmmaker "imprints" himself on his films, and in turn, on the audience and film history.[25] As well as marking particular shots as identifiably Hitchcockian in terms of style and affect, Hitchcock imprinted himself on singular shots in his films and television series in the form of on-screen cameos. By the time *Alfred Hitchcock Presents* (1955–1962) aired its first episode in 1955, Hitchcock's cameos were an established feature of his films. And yet, the television series' title sequence and introduction—in which he appears in the form of a line drawing, a silhouette, and finally in his usual likeness directly addressing the audience—cemented Hitchcock's image in the public consciousness. As well as his regular appearances in the opening and closing of all 268 episodes (and each of the 77 episodes of the 1985–1989 remake series) of *Alfred Hitchcock Presents*, he also made appearances in 36 of his 53 feature films. These cameos adopt a particularly interesting role in the experience of viewing his films. Surprisingly little has been written on Hitchcock's cameos, and yet they form a significant mo-ment of recognizability and a stamp of authorship for each film. They have also become an important part of contemporary Hitchcock fandom: a brief search on YouTube yields several supercuts of his cameos from across his career. What is so significant about these cameos, for this edited collection, is that, if noticed and recognized by the viewer, they solidify the shot they appear in as remarkable, and they inextricably link the film to Hitchcock as director.

   Looking across Hitchcock's career at each of his cameos, it is evident that they evolved over time. His early cameos were not intended to be remark-able, nor was he meant to be recognized. In some of his earliest cameos, even to a current viewer who is familiar with Hitchcock's appearance, he is difficult to notice. He often appeared facing away from the camera or as a face in a crowd, as he does in his two cameos in *The Lodger: A Story of*

London Fog (1927). In *Murder!* (1930), *Easy Virtue* (1928), and *The Man Who Knew Too Much*, he walks between the protagonist and the camera, side on and with his face barely visible. As his directorial style developed throughout his career, so did the style of his cameos. In later cameos, he deliberately frames himself frontally to the camera and often devises a way of drawing attention to himself through both comedy and overt interaction with other characters in the frame. As early as *Blackmail* (1929), a child sitting next to Hitchcock on a train takes his hat and he gestures to the boy's mother to discipline him. In *Shadow of a Doubt* (1943), he appears again on a train, playing cards with a couple sitting opposite who say to him, "you don't look very well either." In *Stage Fright* (1950), as Jane Wyman walks toward the camera along the street, Hitchcock walks past her in the opposite direction, and then stops, turns and looks at her, revealing his face to the camera. The only time Hitchcock's cameo motivates the camera movement is in *To Catch a Thief* (1955), when during a shot of the backseat of a bus, Cary Grant is framed next to an elderly woman, with a birdcage between them. After a few seconds, the camera pans to the right and reveals Hitchcock sitting next to Grant (see Figure 1.5). In these latter instances in particular, Hitchcock's proximity to the shot's action make his appearances more than just cameos; rather, he becomes an integral and irreplaceable part of the film's diegesis.

Figure 1.5 (See also Plate 1)   Alfred Hitchcock's cameo in his film *To Catch a Thief* (1955).

While each of these instances offers a brief moment of levity in otherwise macabre-themed films, they also offer a new meaning upon repeat viewings and draw subtle connections between his films and to his authorship. For Noa Steimatsky, in her chapter in this volume, Hitchcock's appearance imbues the film with legitimacy. She discusses Hitchcock's cameo in *The Wrong Man* (1956) as making "a remarkable statement on veracity and authenticity" as he appears frontally to the camera and addresses the viewer in voiceover. For Michael Walker, the particular timing and placement of these cameo shots in the film are significant. Many of Hitchcock's cameos, Walker argues, occur at a moment of transition in the film, during which "the protagonist is crossing a threshold and Hitchcock's cameo is like a coded signal."[26] Starting in a place of innocence, the cameo marks the moment in the film when "the protagonist will be precipitated into the chaos world. The literal intrusion of the director into the diegesis could thus be seen as a mark of Hitchcock's self-conscious control over the narrative."[27] It is not always the case that he marks such a moment, but Walker's observation holds increasingly true through Hitchcock's latter films. He appears outside Marion's office just as she collects the money she later decides to steal in *Psycho*; he also boards the train in *Strangers on a Train* (1951) where Guy and Bruno's deal is struck. These shots mark not only a moment to recognize the director but also a moment for him to mark his intervention.

This intervention points to another value of the single shot, in that each of these cameos rewards more attentive viewing. Without these shots in which Hitchcock's cameos appear, the narrative would be unchanged. But with their inclusion, they enhance the film's meaning on two levels: first, they offer viewers a playful recognition of a prominent director, whose recognizability was ostensibly tied to the increasing prominence of the auteur framework. Second, upon repeat viewing, they offer an opportunity to examine the specific narrative placement and actions of Hitchcock's on-screen character. They cement the idea that individual shots can form patterns of style and performance not only within films, but across films, too. To return to our crime scene analogy, these are moments that demand and reward repeat investigation. Further, such brief moments act as a reminder of the director's control (or perceived control) over the narrative. To the uninformed viewer, these shots would go by unnoticed, but to the viewer familiar with Hitchcock's overt control over his narratives, they contribute to a career-long narrative woven together by his cameos and leave an indelible mark of his directorial contribution.

The collection

In a growing field of Hitchcock scholarship, *One Shot Hitchcock* marks its impact in two different ways: first, by examining the specific operation of the shot; and second, by furthering scholarship on the relevant theoretical lenses (gender, sexuality, philosophy) through which each chapter examines its selected shot. Each chapter reflects this duality in its approach, by using such a lens to discover something new about Hitchcock, and using Hitchcock to discover something new about the operations of cinema. Chapters were commissioned in two stages: first, through invitation of a range of internationally leading scholars who either were renowned for their Hitchcock scholarship, or whose writing sensibilities were well matched to the aims of this volume; second, a call for papers was distributed to selectively address particular perspectives, films, or eras in Hitchcock's career not already covered by the existing authors. The result of this dual approach is a collection of authors whose varying approaches to scholarship demonstrate the highly creative potential of examining cinema through the single shot. In this volume, specialists in film philosophy, such as Susana Viegas, are brought into conversation with key scholars of national cinema and historical approaches, such as Charles Barr and Tom Gunning, and with theorists of gender and sexuality, such as Jodi Brooks. At the same time, a range of well-established scholars are brought together with emerging scholars. The intention of bringing different theoretical lenses into dialogue is to circumvent the well-trodden paths of Hitchcock scholarship and to establish connections between his work and other frameworks of analysis, for example, gender, race, technology, and remake scholarship.

The films chosen for discussion in this collection represent the full span of Hitchcock's career. Existing scholarship on Hitchcock's work tends to focus only on the more well-known or commercially successful films from the middle of his career, for example, *Psycho* and *Rear Window*. In commissioning chapters, we did not prescribe films or eras; each author chose a film that spoke to them and their research interests. Similarly, we did not prescribe particular shots. It was important, however, that both Hitchcock's very early and very late career be represented. By starting with *The Lodger*, this collection affirms the importance of Hitchcock's oft-neglected silent film career. In Sebastian Smoliński's chapter, he observes that this early film already evidences Hitchcock's burgeoning transnational influences and complicates its assumed British identity. Further, the choice of both British and American films for inclusion in this collection brings to the fore consideration of the rigid structures of the Hollywood system under which Hitchcock worked through his mid-career and how this structure impacted upon formal decisions. And by ending with *Frenzy*, a bookending of Hitchcock's career is offered, showing how his directorial style developed across six decades, as well as how vast industrial shifts across the same period impacted cinema aesthetics. By way of emphasizing this evolution, the chapters are ordered chronologically.

Given the innovative nature of examining a director through single shots, it is particularly interesting that the authors in this collection generally use the single shot in two different ways. Some authors use the shot to illuminate theoretical, industrial, and aesthetic trends and frameworks external to the film. Susana Viegas uses the philosophy of Stanley Cavell to consider how the shot of a kiss between John Robie (Cary Grant) and Frances Stevens (Grace Kelly) during a fireworks show in *To Catch a Thief* can "inspire significant philosophical and moral questions that echo other questions about social and economic class related to love and marriage, untrustworthiness and de-lusion, and the struggle to create a new woman/human." Domietta Torlasco uses the shot of Scottie watching Madeleine in the museum in *Vertigo* to question the nature of watching, and what the film can tell us about "our cur-rent predicament as screen viewers." Helen Hughes holds up the moment in which the bus explodes in *Sabotage* (1936) as exemplifying both a cru-cial step in Hitchcock's refinement of suspense and a confronting image that speaks to a growing visual landscape of terrorist acts. Charles Barr argues the French-language propaganda film *Aventure Malgache* (1944) marks both a return to Europe for Hitchcock and one of the few times the repre-sentation of race comes to the fore in his films. Other authors in this col-lection, however, use the single shot to exemplify themes that occur across the film. Tom Gunning's chapter examines an unusual shot—a lap dissolve of Kate drowning in the harbor—in *The Manxman*, by way of redeeming the oft-neglected early film as one that anticipates some of Hitchcock's most complex visual and narrative tropes. Melanie Robson marks a climactic dinner table shot from *Shadow of a Doubt* as a turning point in the villainous Charles's concealment of his identity, to open up a discussion about facades and performance in Hitchcock's films. In doing so, each chapter contributes uniquely to the Russian doll analogy described earlier. Analysis of the single shot allows for the outer layers to be peeled back and to reveal how Hitchcock casts his shadow over not just the film itself, but over a particular way of screen storytelling.

Notes

1. François Truffaut and Helen G. Scott, *Hitchcock* (London: A Panther Book, 1969), 307–308.
2. Tom Gunning, *The Films of Fritz Lang: Allegories of Vision and Modernity* (London: BFI Publishing, 2000), 3.
3. Murray Pomerance, "Some Hitchcockian Shots," in *A Companion to Alfred Hitchcock*, ed. Thomas Leitch and Leland Poague (Chichester: Wiley-Blackwell, 2011), 237–252.
4. For a less detailed description of the shot or "take" of a film's recording, see David Bordwell and Kristin Thompson, *Film Art: An Introduction*, 5th ed. (New York: McGraw Hill, 1997), 481.
5. Gilles Deleuze, *Cinema 1: The Movement-Image*, trans. Hugh Tomlinson and Barbara Habberjam (Minneapolis: University of Minnesota Press, 1986), 27.
6. Deleuze, *Cinema 1*, 22.
7. One such publication that uses this methodology is *Peephole Journal*, which "features short essays on single shots of film, television and other screen media" and is edited by Whitney Monaghan, Belinda Glynn, and Kate Warren. For more information see "About," *Peephole Journal*, http://peepholejournal.tv/about/.
8. Alfred Hitchcock and Barbara J. Buchanan, "Women Are a Nuisance: An Interview with Barbara J. Buchanan (1935)," in *Hitchcock on Hitchcock: Selected Writings and Interviews*, ed. Sidney Gottlieb (Berkeley: University of California Press, 1997), 79.
9. See, e.g., Donald Spoto, *The Life of Alfred Hitchcock: The Dark Side of Genius* (London: Collins, 1983), 218.
10. Joe McElhaney, "Hitchcock, Metteur-en-scène: 1954–60," in *A Companion to Alfred Hitchcock*, ed. Thomas Leitch and Leland Poague (Chichester: Wiley-Blackwell, 2011), 229. On Hitchcock and the *Cahiers du cinéma* auteur critics, also see Pam Cook and Mieke Bernink, eds., *The Cinema Book*, 2nd ed. (London: BFI Publishing, 1999), 246.
11. Janet Staiger, "Creating the Brand: The Hitchcock Touch," in *The Cambridge Companion to Alfred Hitchcock*, ed. Jonathan Freedman (New York: Cambridge University Press, 2015), 40. Also see Spoto, *The Life of Alfred Hitchcock*, 73.
12. See Tania Modleski, "Suspicion: Collusion and Resistance in the Work of Hitchcock's Female Collaborators," in *A Companion to Alfred Hitchcock*.
13. Thomas Schatz, "Hitchcock and the Studio System," in *The Cambridge Companion to Alfred Hitchcock*, 35.
14. Patricia White, *Rebecca*, BFI Film Classics (London: British Film Institute, 2021), 51–52; Modleski, "Suspicion."
15. Alfred Hitchcock, "On Style (1963)," in *Hitchcock on Hitchcock: Selected Writings and Interviews*, ed. Sidney Gottlieb (Berkeley: University of California Press, 1997), 286.

16. Hitchcock, "On Style," 288.

17. Hitchcock, "On Style," 288. For others on Hitchcock and montage and pure cinema, see Bruce Isaacs, *The Art of Pure Cinema: Hitchcock and His Imitators* (New York: Oxford University Press, 2020), 19–23.

18. Hitchcock, "On Style," 289. Also see Isaacs, *The Art of Pure Cinema*, 1–2.

19. Hitchcock, "On Style," 289.

20. Hitchcock, "On Style," 286.

21. On the remake of *Psycho* (1997) see Megan Carrigy, "Re-Staging the Cinema: *Psycho*, Film Spectatorship and the Redundant New Remake," *Screening the Past*, 34 (2012), http://www.screeningthepast.com/issue-34-untimely-cinema/re-staging-the-cin ema-psycho-film-spectatorship-and-the-redundant-new-remake/. Alfred Hitchcock's *Psycho* and Gus Van Sant's remake are frequently the source material for student-made GIFS in Jodi Brooks's course *Contemporary Approaches to Cinema* taught at the University of New South Wales.

22. Laura Mulvey, *Death 24x a Second: Stillness and the Moving Image* (2006; London: Reaktion Books, 2007), 30.

23. Michel Chion, *Audio-Vision: Sound on Screen*, trans. Claudia Gorbman and with a foreword by Walter Murch (New York: Columbia University Press, 1994), 10.

24. Chion, *Audio-Vision*, 21.

25. Gunning, *The Films of Fritz Lang*, 3.

26. Michael Walker, *Hitchcock's Motifs* (Amsterdam: Amsterdam University Press, 2005), 91.

27. Walker, *Hitchcock's Motifs*, 92.

2

The Lodger (1927)

Contaminating British silent cinema

Sebastian Smoliński

Charles Barr, in his 1999 book *English Hitchcock*, felt obliged to defend the director's English pedigree: "The book's title is intended to serve as a reminder, and a claim, about the identity of the man and of the work."[1] Barr, one of the most distinguished Hitchcock scholars, argues that "British" is too broad a category when discussing the director's pre-Hollywood works. He instead suggests we should refer to the lively film culture of southern England. Most of his British films were shot in southern England, and almost all the novelists Hitchcock refers to as being his major sources of inspiration are English. The exception was John Buchan, a Scot, whose *The 39 Steps* Hitchcock adapted in 1935. However, as Barr is quick to add, the film "does not have much of a Scottish feel."[2] Although Barr acknowledges several important sources of the director's narrative and aesthetic style (including German Expressionism and Soviet montage), he builds his book around the idea of Hitchcock's essential "Englishness"—Hitchcock's reliance on English locations, literature, culture, and collaborators in the first two decades of his career. We should note that Barr does not want to "deny the cosmopolitanism of his cinema in a spirit of cultural nationalism," but rather he wants "simply to redress a balance."[3] My aims are similar—"to redress a balance"—but focused in the opposite direction: I would like to highlight the international dimensions of Hitchcock's early work, *The Lodger: A Story of the London Fog* (1927) in particular.

Part of the impetus behind Barr's Anglocentric argument seems to come from the decades-long struggle of British cinema to gain proper recognition as one of the major cinematic forces.[4] Until the mid-1980s, British silent cinema had often been critically neglected, largely unknown, and considered inferior to French, American, or German films of the period.[5] In his book-length interview with Hitchcock published in 1966, François Truffaut formulated a notorious claim that England is profoundly "anticinematic,"

Sebastian Smoliński, The Lodger *(1927)* In: *One Shot Hitchcock.* Edited by: Luke Robinson and Melanie Robson, Oxford University Press. © Oxford University Press 2024. DOI: 10.1093/oso/9780197682876.003.0002 citing "the English countryside, the subdued way of life," "the weather," and the "understatement" of "British humor" as some of the key "national characteristics."[6] Truffaut's subjective and, admittedly, indefensible notion was part of the discussion of national cinemas and their supposed national identities. Barr's book, along with such studies as Tom Ryall's 1986 volume *Alfred Hitchcock and the British Cinema*, served as counter-arguments to Truffaut's and other critics' observations, defending Hitchcock as a local artist—not so much British, but predominantly English, based in London before the war and more interested in continental Europe than in other parts of the United Kingdom. The distinction between "Britishness" and "Englishness" is an important one, especially given the historically grounded "collision of Englishness—defined in terms of rural localities—and Britishness—defined in imperial and urban industrial terms."[7] As Rebecca Langlands argues, "a more fluid or 'fuzzy' relationship between Englishness and Britishness exists, in part, because the centre of economic, political and ideological power in Britain is London (and so England)."[8] Exploration of *The Lodger* would therefore require crossing the local "Englishness" in order to investigate the "British Hitchcock"—and beyond.

A figure on the threshold: "Englishness" of *The Lodger* and beyond

Arguments about Hitchcock's "Englishness" vs. "Britishness," or efforts to contextualize his work using the framework of national cinemas, become more complicated when we try to address and unpack the identity of his earliest silent films. For example, *The Pleasure Garden* (1925), Hitchcock's London-set debut feature, was shot in Germany as a British-German co-production. It is difficult to establish a moment when the "Englishness" emerges in his filmography. Should we consider *The Lodger* a breakthrough, since it is the first film that Hitchcock made in England? Can we pin a "national identity" on to some of Hitchcock's most iconic early images? We may try to answer these questions by looking at a famous shot from *The Lodger*, a shot that I am calling the threshold shot. As a whole, *The Lodger* is considered by many, including the director himself, to be "the first true 'Hitchcock movie.'"[9] This film adaptation of the novel by Marie Belloc Lowndes is one of the most eerie and unsettling silent films ever made. It is also, on many levels, an international endeavor, beginning with its diverse crew and bold stylistic choices, through the editing strategy and reception. *The Lodger* epitomizes what we can call an artistic "contamination." I borrow the term contamination from Bo Florin's revealing book *Transition and Transformation: Victor Sjöström in Hollywood 1923–1930*. The author quotes the interview with actor Conrad Nagel, who said that with their working methods Victor Sjöström and other artists who immigrated to California "contaminated the whole of Hollywood."[10]

The notion of contamination—not really developed by Florin, but used as a metaphor for that stage of Sjöström's career—with its negative connotations of impurity, pollution, or even something poisonous and deadly, is especially striking, suggesting a virus that is spreading without control or recognition. The idea of contagion implies the resentment or feeling of uncertainty when dealing with changes and foreign influences. *The Lodger* is also about spreading and contaminating in the literal sense: it tells the story of a serial killer called "The Avenger" who spreads fear and insecurity in the community and makes Londoners terrified of their own city. In the same vein, Richard Dyer suggests, referring to the film's full title (*The Lodger: A Story of the London Fog*), that "fog has geohistorical connotations, of Britain as notoriously damp, of industrialisation and pollution, and these have had their role in the promulgation of Jack the Ripper as peculiarly British."[11]

Given that it is a silent film made by the young director with European training, its "Englishness" is also uniquely "contaminated" on the level of film style and visual echoes that resonate through the narrative and make *The Lodger* part of transnational silent cinema. The point where many of these inspirations and foreign cinematic "dialects" come together is a shot in which The Landlady (Marie Ault) meets the prospective lodger played by Ivor Novello at a doorway.[12] This threshold shot constitutes a few seconds of a visually intense meeting between the two strangers.

What is so special in hindsight about this threshold shot is that we can see it as the first iconic Hitchcock image: the very first, chronologically speaking, that achieved a life of its own and became the singular picture associated with the director's silent films (except for, arguably, some images from the 1929 *Blackmail*, which exists in both silent and sound versions). It comes exactly fifteen minutes into the movie and is part of a rapidly edited scene in which The Lodger appears in front of the house of the film's protagonists and knocks on the door. Interestingly, we see The Lodger approaching the door from his perspective, in one of Hitchcock's ominous point-of-view shots. When The Landlady opens the door, however, the perspective is reversed: we are no longer seeing what the mysterious Lodger is seeing. Instead we look at him from the other side of the threshold—he is outside, ready to enter, while we are deep inside, looking at the stairs, The Landlady and The Lodger's silhouette surrounded by the thick fog (this shot proves that the film truly deserves its full title).

We will focus on this single moving image, a threshold shot, but it will be useful to build the context by listing several shots surrounding it:

1. Long shot: The Landlady starts opening the door;
2. Medium shot: a closer look at The Landlady's back and a figure behind the slowly opening door; we do not see his/her face yet;
3. Long shot: back to the camera setup from Shot 1. A balanced, rich composition showing the stairs on the left (occupying approximately one third of the frame); the Landlady, the door, the entrance, and The Lodger in the middle, and a piece of the wall and a house plant on the right side of the frame. This is the iconic shot from *The Lodger* (see Figure 2.1);

Figure 2.1 The iconic threshold shot from Alfred Hitchcock's *The Lodger: A Story of the London Fog* (1927).

4. Medium close-up: The Landlady looks at the newcomer with fear visible on her face;

5. Medium close-up: The Lodger, with the scarf on his mouth, looks at The Landlady intensely, his eyes shining uncannily (see Figure 2.2).

This list of shots is only a part of a longer, more elaborate sequence, but these five shots are distinct and disturbing and confuse the initial identification we could have established with The Lodger knocking at the door. Structurally, the key wide threshold shot (Shot 3, Figure 2.1) is bracketed by the two shots preceding it and two shots following it. The five shots are different from the subsequent ones in that they constitute a moment of terror and silence, as The Landlady and The Lodger have not yet started to speak to each other. Thus, they operate on a purely visual level; they convey the simplest of situations: two people looking at each other, trying to recognize and decipher each other's faces, trying to discover each other's identity.

Coming back to the discussion of Hitchcock's "Englishness," let us ask what is the identity of this shot? Can we locate something (trans)national about Hitchcock's iconic shot and, by extension, about *The Lodger* itself? This

Figure 2.2 Medium close-up of Ivor Novello's mysterious face in *The Lodger*.

question has already been partly answered by several Hitchcock scholars. Let us begin, however, with the source novel by Lowndes published in 1913. By comparing Lowndes's description of The Lodger/The Landlady encounter with the Hitchcock version, we can clearly see the ways in which the adaptation departs from the book.

At the beginning of Chapter 2 of Lowndes's novel, Mrs. Bunting reacts to the knocking she has just heard:

> Slowly she opened the front door.
>
> On the top of the three steps which led up to the door, there stood the long, lanky figure of a man, clad in an Inverness cape and an old-fashioned top hat. He waited for a few seconds blinking at her, perhaps dazzled by the light of the gas in the passage. Mrs. Bunting's trained perception told her at once that this man, odd as he looked, was a gentleman, belonging by birth to the class with whom her former employment had brought her in contact.[13]

Their meeting, as described by Lowndes, is an innocent one. It does not suggest the fear experienced by The Landlady in the Hitchcock film. Moreover, roles are reversed: it is the man at the door who is "blinking" and "dazzled"; it is his face that, as far as the reader can tell, registers emotions and reacts to the situation. In the novel, the focal point is the landlady Mrs. Bunting; there is no disconcerting change of perspective that the adaptation provides. The newcomer is not a sinister, suspicious figure: he is "a gentleman," a person that can be approached with a considerable level of trust. The very "British" thing in this otherwise generic situation is the Inverness cape, which we see in the iconic shot from The Lodger as well. Interestingly, this recognizable sign of Britishness cannot be reduced to an item synonymous with English culture: it is a piece of clothing that most probably originated in Scotland in the late 1850s and is associated with the culture of the Scottish Highlands.[14] The other British landmark, of course, is the Welsh composer and actor Novello, whose body and half-covered face was recognizable to the local audiences.[15]

Comparison of the 1913 source novel with Hitchcock's 1927 film adaptation allows us to formulate two arguments. Although the Hitchcock version is anchored in the literary original, it radically changes the tone, style, meanings, and atmosphere of this moment in the narrative. The lighthearted paragraphs of the novel are transformed into a scene imbued with tension. Even though, on the surface, the Lowndes text and the Hitchcock text tell the same "story," the plot and the chain of events are less important than the questions of style and visual imagination. Barr's emphasis on the English sources of Hitchcock's films was essential in his project to "redress a balance" and put the word "English" before the name of Hitchcock (presumably: again, bringing Hitchcock closer to his roots). It is true that the vast majority of Hitchcock scholars do not even try to compare literary sources with Hitchcock's early films.[16] However, as the example above indicates, sometimes such a comparison may only highlight the disparity between the novel/play and Hitchcock's images that transform it.

Inverness cape revisited: The unstable identity of the threshold shot

Returning to a discussion of the Inverness cape, it may offer a starting point in the investigation of the national identity of Hitchcock's iconic shot from *The Lodger*. The Inverness cape is mentioned several times in the novel as part of the protagonist's clothing. Hitchcock and his crew decided to stick to the source and prepared a necessary costume for Novello. A Welsh actor wearing a Scottish cape: this shot is certainly not purely "English." Scanning the frame and looking for similar clues may seem a tiresome task; the identity of a given film is not a simple sum of objects and people visible on the screen. That said, *The Lodger*—and the threshold shot—is a special case: it was Hitchcock's breakthrough film and is often analyzed as the cornerstone of his art. The image of Novello coming to us from the fog complicates even the "Englishness" vs. "Britishness" opposition (The Lodger may represent here the non-English British subject visiting the house of the properly English Landlady). The shot is, in miniature, representative of the forces that were shaping the transnational silent cinema at the time.

The Lodger is Hitchcock's founding myth: the film in which, as the story goes, Hitchcock the artist established his style, themes, obsessions, and rituals (including his personal cameo). Much has been written about the fusion of national styles evident in the film as a whole and in specific scenes, including the one we are discussing. Robin Wood claims that the influence of both German Expressionism and Soviet montage can be traced back to *The Lodger*, noting cannily that Hitchcock "perverted both" traditions, as he devoted himself to "the creation of popular bourgeois entertainment."[17] Barr, among others, adds other ingredients, noting Hitchcock's evident indebtedness in American cinema and "the contemporary English stage and novel."[18] In the footnote to his essay on the roots of Hitchcock's films, Barr regrets that he had not enough space to discuss Swedish and American films by Sjöström: "Whether or not Hitchcock saw them in London, as he certainly had the chance to, they have an abundance of instructive parallels."[19] In his introduction to *Framing Hitchcock: Selected Essays from the Hitchcock Annual*, Sidney Gottlieb argues that we need to look for how other national cinemas impacted Hitchcock's style, adding that "closer examination of the French influence on Hitchcock" is needed to better understand director's visual experiments.[20] A French influence on Hitchcock had already been established by Tom Ryall, who compares René Clair's *Entr'acte* (1924) to the famous shot with the plate glass ceiling from *The Lodger*. In the shot from *The Lodger*, a family downstairs hears—and thanks to the special effects, "sees"—The Lodger walking in the room above them.[21] A considerable portion of the scholarship on Hitchcock also places *The Lodger* in the context of 1920s national cinemas and refers to specific, mostly German titles like Robert Wiene's *The Cabinet of Dr. Caligari* (1920), Arthur Robison's *Warning Shadows* (1923), and Paul Leni's *Waxworks* (1924). It is this German influence on Hitchcock's style in *The Lodger* that is most frequently commented on, although there are other ways we can trace the influence of Expressionist filmmaking on Hitchcock's 1927 film.

The one connection that is rarely acknowledged in the scholarship on *The Lodger*, even in the most detailed and penetrating studies of the film, is the film's Italian cinematographer: Baron Gaetano di Ventimiglia. He photographed the first three features directed by Hitchcock. Ventimiglia's work on the set of *The Lodger* is worth noting because he started his career in the Italian film industry in the 1910s.[22] Like the inclusion of the Inverness cape and the Welsh matinée idol in the film's mise-en-scène, the presence of the Italian-born artist behind the camera contributes to the dazzling tapestry of nationalities and cultural signs that constitute the unstable identity of the iconic shot from *The Lodger*. The Italian-trained cinematographer apparently had no problems in assimilating Expressionist-like style into his work, which may prove Barry Salt's statement that "chiaroscuro lighting styles and pronounced camera angles" did not necessarily have a direct connection with the Expressionist style developed in the two German films *Warning Shadows* and *Waxworks*. Rather, the Expressionist style was part of an international language of silent film that appeared "well before the 20s in American and Danish cinema."[23]

Bringing these disparate influences together, we can create a cluster of styles, schools, physical items, people, and ideas that contributed to the eclectic form of *The Lodger*. In addition to what I have discussed, there is also the supposed Soviet influence and strong inspiration coming from the American continent. However, not all these references are equally convincing or can stand the test of archival fact-checking since, in many cases, Hitchcock scholars only assume that the director himself had watched, or was familiar, with a given film or a cinematic phenomenon. There is, for example, a level of uncertainty regarding Hitchcock's familiarity with Soviet cinema of the 1920s and the Soviet theory of montage at the time when he was making *The Lodger*.[24] For many years it was believed that Ivor Montagu, who according to many sources re-edited the movie after its supposedly poorly received studio screening and later translated Soviet writings on cinema, was, in fact, the vital force behind the film's Eisensteinian touches. The scene set at the threshold of *The Lodger* that I have been discussing has been interpreted as an example of editing that owes a lot both to the Soviet filmmakers Lev Kuleshov and Sergei Eisenstein.[25] In 1930, Hitchcock claimed that the only Soviet film he had watched was *Battleship Potemkin* (1925).[26] Such biographical detective work—looking for evidence of which artist might have seen or read what at a given point in time—seems to be a highly imperfect way of establishing influences and stylistic crosscurrents: it relies heavily on the belief in intentional and controlled exchange of artistic ideas, is centered on individuals and not the social and cultural environment that shapes them, and ultimately will always be insufficient because of the lack of information and available primary resources. Henry K. Miller, author of the recent, and in many ways revelatory, book-length study of *The Lodger*, convincingly refutes this oft-circulated claim about the film being inspired by Eisenstein. Carefully unpacking the myth surrounding the film's production and distribution, he states that Montagu's creative involvement has often been exaggerated and that "there was nothing Soviet about *The Lodger*'s montage. It came out of all that Hitchcock had learned of cinema as a viewer and as a filmmaker."[27]

It is safe to say, however, that *The Lodger* is a highly contaminated work of art, absorbing, assimilating, changing, and translating a number of cultural signs and cinematic styles. In this case, contamination is a very productive metaphor. Since the raison d'être of the threshold shot from *The Lodger*—which makes a mysterious figure finally visible—is to introduce an ambiguous character in a visually arresting way, we may look at it as one of a series of shots from German films that defined European horror cinema of the

Figure 2.3 Another threshold shot: Max Schreck in F. W. Murnau's *Nosferatu: A Symphony of Horror* (1922).

1920s. F. W. Murnau's *Nosferatu: A Symphony of Horror* (1922) and Leni's *Waxworks* both feature shots of protagonists or antagonists standing in the background, looming ominously over the space from a doorway and walking closer and closer to the camera as if they were in a trance (see Figures 2.3 and 2.4).

Nosferatu, a film about a vampire and which features shots of rats, can especially be read as a story about contamination. Here my reading is inspired by J. Hoberman, who asks in his recent essay on the film: "What does this fear of contamination tell us?" He also argues: "more than a prime example of the Weimar imaginary, Nosferatu illuminates a primal fear—that of foreign contagion."[28] Perhaps, since the threshold shot from *The Lodger* is visually comparable to a shot of The Nosferatu from Murnau's film, we can consider Hitchcock's shot to be one that could also have provoked viewers to react against "foreign contagion." If so, then the stakes of thinking of the threshold shot as an international or transnational shot, rather than an instance of English cinema, becomes clear. The shot represents, and at the same acts as a reflective commentary on, the fear of contagion of England by "foreign"

Figure 2.4 And another: Conrad Veidt in Paul Leni's *Waxworks* (1924).

cultures circulating at the time. Moreover, the static nature of these shots—there is no camerawork involved—and the staging that situates protagonists at a considerable distance from the camera and the viewers, adds to the hypnotic quality of these images. Visually, they echo one another, which only points toward the idea of certain shared stylistics of transnational silent film.

The Lodger and vernacular modernism

If British silent cinema had indeed been undervalued and forgotten, the antidote for this state of affairs, I argue, should not be a retreat to the relatively insular notion of English cinema. Following Miriam Bratu Hansen's theoretical framework centered on the idea of "vernacular modernism," we could position *The Lodger*—and the iconic shot with its ambiguous identity—on a transnational map, highlighting the negotiations between various national cinemas and treating local film cultures as inescapably connected to each other.[29] To this end, we should also study "actual processes of transfer and translation, circulation and reception": that is, the ways in which different film cultures were engaged with the experience of modernism and modernity.[30] Writing in the context of Chinese and Japanese cinema of the 1920s and 1930s, Hansen describes how the filmmakers needed to navigate "between competing models of national culture and creative appropriations of the globalizing vernaculars of Hollywood, European, Soviet, as well as Japanese cinemas."[31] Similar dynamics, I argue, are demonstrative in the threshold shot from *The Lodger*. The shot is an example, in miniature, of how conflicting and interlocking cultural practices come together and are successfully resolved, forging, perhaps, a British version of cinematic vernacular modernism.

In the last part of the essay, I would like to look at the contaminated qualities of the threshold shot from another angle, the one that is more grounded in the historical circumstances surrounding the production. The iconic shot from *The Lodger* serves as a useful metapicture, a concept defined by W. J. T. Mitchell in *Picture Theory*. For Mitchell, metapictures are: "pictures about pictures—that is, pictures that refer to themselves or to other pictures, pictures that are used to show what a picture is."[32] Novello as The Lodger standing at the doorstep waiting to be admitted to a home belongs to a specific class of Mitchell's metapictures, that is, dialectical images characterized by: "the co-existence of contrary or simply different readings in the single image, a phenomenon sometimes called 'multistability.'"[33] Classic examples of dialectical metapictures, most famously "The Duck-Rabbit" and "My Wife and My Mother-in-Law," can be found in early psychology textbooks. These metapictures make it impossible for our minds to settle on a single, definite reading of an image—they are contaminated, "impure" phenomena par excellence. For example, if we read a version of the drawing "The Duck-Rabbit" from the left to the right then the drawing looks like it is of a duck, but, if we read the image from the right to the left the image looks like a rabbit. Such a dialectical metapicture therefore comments upon the shifting identity of pictorial representations.

The shot from *The Lodger* is a metapicture on many levels. Its multistability has to do with the actor's appearance—is this man with a face half-covered with the scarf Novello or not? Stylistic borrowings—is this German Expressionist film or not? And national identity—does the Inverness cape make the image less English? But there is a set of other unstable meanings that may be decoded from this shot. Many of these meanings appear a posteriori—as they can be more clearly identified by contemporary viewers and critics and most probably could not be inferred by the film's 1920s audience. However, their emergence allows us to use the threshold shot as a tool for rethinking the relation between the present and the future of British cinema.

Mitchell observes that dialectical metapictures are sometimes associated with "'liminal' or threshold experiences."[34] Let us examine how visual ideas from *The Lodger* reflect and allude to this liminality. Most obviously, the shot represents the literal threshold experience of a figure standing in front of the house and waiting to cross the line separating the outside—the street and city—from the inside—cozy interiors of the London house. Novello's character is literally caught in-between in this shot, existing in the intermediary space that is both recognizable and alien.

The self-reflexive quality of the image may be said to illuminate the trajectory of Hitchcock's career. Describing this shot as a metapicture is also, in a way, an effort to decipher its unconscious—remembering that these readings will remain more or less convincing assumptions. However, it is essential to look at Hitchcock's iconic shot from many perspectives to at least approach an explanation of its enduring power. Although Hitchcock's earlier film *The Pleasure Garden* already features self-reflexive images—for example, in the very first scene where a male character's gaze is centered on women performers on stage (a shot that is self-reflexive about the nature of male spectatorship in the cinema)—it is in *The Lodger* that Hitchcock's predilection for self-reflexivity is imbued throughout the film. Not unlike famous examples ranging from *Rear Window* (1954) to *Psycho* (1960), *The Lodger* is deeply interested in investigating its own mode of storytelling and representation. However, why does this picture, and not any other, have such a lasting appeal? This is an important question since chronologically it is the first Hitchcock film that a broader public associate with Hitchcock's cinema.[35] It is also the first Hitchcock film that features predominantly in this volume on single shots from Hitchcock's films.

I have addressed these questions herein, by showing the stylistic complexity of the shot and the variety of national/transnational signs that it weaves together. Treated as a metapicture, the shot may also testify to authorial anxieties: it may be, quite simply, an image of Hitchcock the artist standing on the threshold. Hitchcock was at that time in a liminal state: *The Lodger* was his first film shot in England. Hence, the image of Novello materializing out of the fog and waiting to be admitted to a London household is in this sense a visual equivalent of the director who came back home and made the first feature on his native soil. Novello's figure is framed by the door frame—he exists in a picture within a picture, doubling the film's self-reflexive intuitions. Moreover, through the deliberate staging and mise-en-scène, the threshold shot highlights the phantom presence of the foreign protagonist, meaning that the shot functions as a specter of Expressionism haunting British cinema.

However, there are two other dimensions in which the shot seems prophetic. They take us beyond the questions of authorship, back to the contaminated cultural landscape of mid-1920s Britain. First is the introduction of the 1927 Cinematograph Films Act, commonly known as the Quota Act, which was designed to foster domestic production and facilitate competition with Hollywood, which had since the end of the First World War drastically dominated the UK market. Although not necessarily considered a success, the Cinematograph Films Act was an important step in creating an institutionalized national cinema. Sarah Street summarizes the changes introduced by the legislation: "The Act imposed a statutory obligation on renters and exhibitors to acquire and show a quota of British films. In the first year the renters' quota was 7.5 per cent and the exhibitors' was 5 per cent (the renters' was higher so that exhibitors would be able to exercise an element of choice)." These quotas were designed to gradually reach 20 percent in 1936. The act also specified, among other issues, that a British film was the "one made by a British subject or company," and that "all studio scenes had to be shot within the Empire." Street also emphasizes that "the Act attempted to abolish blind and block booking."[36]

The Lodger, then, is a film standing on the threshold—it was shot in 1926, one year before the implementation of the regulations that gave birth to the phenomenon of quota quickies and impacted Hitchcock's career. The film occupies a liminal space in which there are no new regulations regarding the production and distribution yet, but they are just about to appear and change the course of British cinema.

Another—even more groundbreaking—transformation was about to take place. *The Lodger* premiered in 1927, the year of Alan Crosland's *The Jazz Singer* and the beginning of the sound revolution in Hollywood. The talkies changed the paradigm of cinema production and consumption, and they further contributed to the development of national cinemas and the differentiation of film cultures. The transnational silent film gave way to local languages, stars, and modes of production. Like Buster Keaton/Clyde Bruckman's *The General* (1926), Murnau's *Sunrise* (1927), and Fritz Lang's *Metropolis* (1927), Hitchcock's *The Lodger* is an example of silent cinema at its height. Indifferent as the filmmakers might have been to the technological change on the horizon, *The Lodger* includes a premonition shot of things to come—the door will have to be opened for sound, the introduction of which would ultimately bury the silent film culture.

Even if they were at a certain point indifferent to them, though, industry professionals were certainly not unaware of these changes. As Miller's study of *The Lodger* makes clear, both the transition to sound and, especially, the Cinematograph Films Act were important topics for the filmmakers, the producers Michael Balcon and C. M. Woolf in particular.[37] Miller states that in 1927, the year of its premiere, "*The Lodger* was already a relic. It had been made at the end of one epoch and was released at the beginning of a new one."[38] Once again, the contaminated identity of the threshold shot seems to provide a visual equivalent of this changing situation, of standing in-between the two distinct cinematic eras.

Hitchcock was to revisit and restage threshold shots several times throughout his career. Whether it is Joan Fontaine's heroine entering the late Rebecca's bedroom (only to be surprised by the eerie presence of Mrs. Danvers a moment later) in *Rebecca* (1940), Hitchcock's first Hollywood film, or Lars Thorwald paying an unexpected visit to L. B. Jefferies in *Rear Window*, there is something both casual and frightening about Hitchcock's doors as common liminal spaces of everyday life. Opening the door and looking out—or in—is a risky business in a Hitchcock film, especially if the protagonists, like Fontaine's unnamed character and James Stewart's nosy photographer, are unable to curb their deepening curiosity. The basic molecule of a Hitchcock thriller is already in place in *The Lodger*: not only because it employs the theme of "an innocent man wrongly accused," but also because of the ambiguity that it bestows upon the safety of a home and a conception of a home territory. In *The Lodger*, Hitchcock appears to be saying that there are very few places in which a person can truly feel secure and sheltered. In this regard the threshold shot, its contaminated nature notwithstanding, bears a clear Hitchcock signature.

The anxiety associated with entering a new space or leaving it is a constant element of the director's visual and narrative language, and was equally intense in his later works. *The Birds* (1963) ends, famously, with a family leaving the home by a door that in previous sequences was an object of severe bird attacks. The most significant counterpoint of the threshold shot, however, can be found in Hitchcock's penultimate film *Frenzy* (1972), which features an extraordinary long take in which the film's heroine and villain, a serial killer, disappear from our sight. While the camera in Hitchcock's films often provides us with the most convenient and exciting point of view, in this film it decides to pull back and go down the stairs onto the street. The camera moves away from a door that leads to an upstairs apartment rather than crossing the threshold with the characters to enter a new domestic space. The horror of what will happen—the serial killer enters the apartment accompanied by his victim who is unaware of his true identity—is left to our imagination. We might not see the murder, though this device is as cruel as Hitchcock's more literal representations of murders in *Frenzy* since we do have an unsettling impression that no one around the murderer and victim really cares about the violence happening behind closed doors. The Covent Garden street that the camera retreats back to is busy, teeming with life and oblivious to the unseen tragedy that is happening upstairs.

Widely copied and circulated, the threshold shot from *The Lodger* is the quintessential image from Hitchcock's silent period. Given the longevity of this metapicture, we can argue that the film is unique not only because it delineates Hitchcock's thematic preoccupations, but also because for the first time in his career it successfully integrates film styles and cultural references to offer a contaminated, rich, and fascinating version of British cinema. Maybe when we are calling Hitchcock's earliest silent films English, we should add a qualification. They are English, but they are also so much more. The identity—be it national, stylistic, or authorial—of the shot is complex and, after all, it is just a few dozen frames out of a feature film. It offers, however, a poignant visual metaphor for Hitchcock buffs and other viewers. It indirectly, and metaphorically, represents the transnational silent cinema itself standing on the threshold—a quintessentially modern phenomenon that, somewhat unexpectedly, was soon to become a mere phase in cinema's—and Hitchcock's—twentieth-century expansion.

Notes

1. Charles Barr, *English Hitchcock* (Moffat: Cameron & Hollis, 1999), 6.
2. Barr, *English Hitchcock*, 6.
3. Barr, *English Hitchcock*, 14.
4. Barr himself summarized this problem in 1997: "To most people other than specialist academics and historians, British silent cinema is an unknown country. No British feature films from the silent era belong to an internationally known repertoire, or

to a national tradition that is absorbed by, or at least known to, later generations of film-makers and cinephiles. Our film culture has no roots in, and no memory of, the formative silent period. For a country which was to become a major producer in the sound period, this is extraordinary." Twelve years later, Barr added a postscript in which he wrote that the "rediscovery and reassessment" of British cinema's early decades were in progress. Charles Barr, "Before *Blackmail*: Silent British Cinema," in *The British Cinema Book*, ed. Robert Murphy (London: British Film Institute, 2009), 145–154.

5. The extensive and critical analysis of this problem can be found in Charles Barr's introduction to British Film Institute's *All Our Yesterdays: 90 Years of British Cinema*. Barr quotes Gilbert Adair's observation that "the history of the British cinema is that of the inferiority complex." Charles Barr, "Amnesia and Schizophrenia," in *All Our Yesterdays: 90 Years of British Cinema*, ed. Charles Barr (London: British Film Institute, in association with The Museum of Modern Art, New York, 1986), 2.

6. François Truffaut with Helen G. Scott, *Hitchcock*, rev. ed. (1966; New York: Touchstone, 1985), 124. It is a bit puzzling that Truffaut made his claims as late as in 1962, when he was recording his conversations with Hitchcock. The British New Wave was well under way with landmark films like *Saturday Night and Sunday Morning* (1960) and *A Taste of Honey* (1961) having already been released.

7. Rebecca Langlands, "Britishness or Englishness? The Historical Problem of National Identity in Britain," *Nations and Nationalism* 6, no. 1 (1999): 64.

8. Langlands, "Britishness or Englishness?," 64.

9. Truffaut and Scott, *Hitchcock*, 43.

10. Conrad Nagel, quoted in Bo Florin, *Transition and Transformation: Victor Sjöström in Hollywood 1923–1930* (Amsterdam: Amsterdam University Press, 2013), 37.

11. Richard Dyer, *Lethal Repetition: Serial Killing in European Cinema* (London: British Film Institute, 2015), 133.

12. "The Landlady" and "The Lodger" are the names given in the credits.

13. Marie Belloc Lowndes, *The Lodger* (Chicago: Academy Chicago Publishers, 2010), 19.

14. Norah Waugh, *The Cut of Men's Clothes* (New York: Theatre Arts Books, 1964), 143. Waugh's book does not explain the origins of the piece of clothing's name. Waugh states only that: "The Inverness cape appeared in the late '50's and was a very popular type of overgarment until the end of the century."

15. Richard Allen, "*The Lodger* and the Origins of Hitchcock's Aesthetic," *Hitchcock Annual* 10 (2001): 58. Allen writes: "The presence of Novello in the scene further contributes to its staging for the spectator (in contrast to Mrs. Bunting). By the time he made *The Lodger*, Novello was well established as a matinee idol."

16. A book entirely devoted to investigating the relationship between Hitchcock's films and their literary sources is Mark Osteen, ed., *Hitchcock and Adaptation: On the Page and Screen* (Lanham, MD: Rowman & Littlefield, 2014).

17. Robin Wood, *Hitchcock's Films Revisited* (New York: Columbia University Press, 2002), 208.

18. Barr, *English Hitchcock*, 14.

19. Charles Barr, "Hitchcock and Early Filmmakers," in *A Companion to Alfred Hitchcock*, ed. Thomas Leitch and Leland Poague (Chichester: Wiley-Blackwell, 2011), 65.

20. Sidney Gottlieb, "Introduction," in *Framing Hitchcock: Selected Essays from the Hitchcock Annual*, ed. Sidney Gottlieb and Christopher Brookhouse (Detroit: Wayne State University Press, 2002), 19.

21. Tom Ryall, *Alfred Hitchcock and the British Cinema* (London: Athlone Press, 1996), 25.

22. There is, as far as I could find, not a single study devoted to Ventimiglia in English and there are few facts about the first years of his career known.. For some information about Ventimiglia see Duncan Petrie, "Innovation and Economy: The Contribution of the Gainsborough Cinematographer," in *Gainsborough Pictures*, ed. Pam Cook (London: Continuum, 1997), 122; and Henry K. Miller, *The First True Hitchcock* (Oakland: University of California Press, 2022), 86.

23. Barry Salt, "From Caligari to Who?," *Sight and Sound* 48, no. 2 (1979): 120, quoted in Ryall, *Alfred Hitchcock*, 25.

24. Richard Allen argued: "The influence of Soviet montage and in particular, Eisenstein, upon Hitchcock is less direct than German expressionism, but equally significant. Hitchcock probably read about the Kuleshov effect in the writings of Pudovkin on film that were translated into English in 1928 by Ivor Montagu, the young cineaste and founding member of the London Film Society, and Hitchcock's thoughts upon the idea of 'pure cinema,' first articulated in the early 1930s, clearly demonstrate his indebtedness to Eisenstein's early essays on film. However, Hitchcock could not have had access to these texts before he made *The Lodger* in 1926." Allen, "*The Lodger*," 54–55.

25. Allen, "*The Lodger*," 56–57.

26. O.B., "Advance Monologue," *Close Up* 7, no. 2 (August 1930): 146–147.

27. Miller, *The First True Hitchcock*, 125.

28. J. Hoberman, "The Twinned Evils of *Nosferatu*," *Tablet*, May 19, 2020, https://www.tabletmag.com/sections/arts-letters/articles/nosferatu-hoberman-murnau.

29. Miriam Bratu Hansen, "The Mass Production of the Senses: Classical Cinema as Vernacular Modernism," *Modernism/Modernity* 6, no. 2 (1999): 59–77.

30. Miriam Bratu Hansen, "Vernacular Modernism: Tracking Cinema on a Global Scale," in *World Cinemas, Transnational Perspectives*, ed. Natasa Ďurovičová and Kathleen A. Newman (New York: Routledge, 2010), 293.

31. Hansen, "Vernacular Modernism," 295.

32. W. J. T. Mitchell, *Picture Theory* (Chicago: University of Chicago Press, 1994), 35.

33. Mitchell, *Picture Theory*, 45.

34. Mitchell, *Picture Theory*, 46.

35. Contemporary articles popularizing the film, for example published on the British Film Institute website in 2014 and 2018, use a frame taken from this shot as accompanying visual material. See Svet Atanasov, "The Lodger: A Story of the London Fog / Downhill Blu-ray Review," Blu-ray.com, May 27, 2017, https://www.blu-ray.com/movies/The-Lodger-A-Story-of-the-London-Fog-and-Downhill-Blu-ray/122277/#Review. The iconic image reappeared recently due to the release of the

film, together with Hitchcock's subsequent silent feature *Downhill* made in the same year, on Blu-ray by the Criterion Collection in 2017. The review of this edition on a popular website also features The Lodger on the threshold as the main image.

36. Sarah Street, *British National Cinema* (New York: Routledge, 2009), 9.

37. Miller, *The First True Hitchcock*, 177.

38. Miller, *The First True Hitchcock*, 179.

3

The Manxman (1929)

Written on the water: Hitchcock's dissolving ink

Tom Gunning

Only a skillful director could have devised from a story of this kind a picture of such remarkable power and interest.[1]

In spite of his dismissal of the film in his interview with François Truffaut, Alfred Hitchcock's last silent film, *The Manxman* (1929), offers one of his most complex explorations of passion in conflict with both personal loyalty and class hierarchy.[2] Set on the very traditional and rather isolated Isle of Man, the film's main character Philip Christian (Malcolm Keen) must balance his love for Kate Cregeen (Anny Ondra) with his friendship with the fisherman Peter Quiliam (Carl Brisson), who loves her as well. Peter travels to South Africa to make his fortune so he can marry Kate whom he leaves in the care of Philip. However, it is reported that Peter has died abroad, and during his absence Kate and Philip fall in love. Following family tradition, Philip is destined to become a "Deemster," a judge on the island, and his family disapproves of his courting of Kate, daughter of a mere publican. Peter returns unexpectedly, his reported death an error. He and Kate marry, Peter unaware she is pregnant with Philip's child. Kate tries to love her new husband but finally confesses to him that the child is not his and she loves an unnamed other man. However, when she goes to him, Philip hesitates to claim her and the child due to his newly achieved status as judge. Distraught, friendless, Kate decides to commit suicide.

The shot I will analyze is a complex one, including an overlap dissolve blending two shots into one. After three shots that show Kate's leap into the harbor, this shot opens with bubbles rising to the surface of dark water, presumably from Kate's submerged body. As this image dissolves, a large pointed

Tom Gunning, The Manxman *(1929)* In: *One Shot Hitchcock.* Edited by: Luke Robinson and Melanie Robson, Oxford University Press. © Oxford University Press 2024. DOI: 10.1093/oso/9780197682876.003.0003 object enters the frame and penetrates into the dark liquid. A camera movement out reveals the black liquid to be ink and the object to be a pen in Philip's hand as he writes, in his official role as Deemster. Vividly, the shot dissolves from a scene animated by female despair to one portraying the rigidity of male law. This highly expressive and compressed image demonstrates Hitchcock's mastery of images that could carry metaphoric meanings as well as the striking visual power of the image known as *photogénie*.[3]

Hitchcock may be the filmmaker must easily recognized by both critics and audiences as an "auteur," a director with a consistent style and series of themes. The auteur theory situates films in relation to a larger corpus; inevitably this logic makes early work seem to prefigure later ones. The undeniable power and inventiveness of Hitchcock's silent film *The Lodger: A Story of the London Fog* (1927) and his part-talkie *Blackmail* (1929) demonstrate both the power and the limitations of such contextualization. As an auteur, Hitchcock became identified with a specific genre—the thriller—which formed the center of his oeuvre. In fact, Hitchcock's work exceeds the genre that eventually defined it. Hitchcock's cinema stylistics and thematic obsessions offered more than lessons in suspense—as masterful as those were. If Hitchcock's signature blossomed under the aegis of the thriller, nonetheless the non-thrillers of his early career provided a seedbed of devices and themes that ultimately redefined his chosen genre.

While I acknowledge that Hitchcock achieved his greatest work in his sound and Hollywood films, careful analysis of his British and silent films highlights the deep currents that underlie the Hitchcock thriller. As Leslie Brill (as well as Hitchcock's signature composer, Bernard Herrmann) has stressed, Hitchcock's thrillers are in fact complicated romances.[4] Of course, most classical Hollywood films included a romantic couple but, from *The Lodger* and *Blackmail* on, deeply conflicted desires motivate rather than decorate the Hitchcock thriller. *The Manxman* explores such intertwining of guilt and desire outside the thriller. The eloquent and insightful commentator on *The Manxman*, Canadian critic Maurice Yacowar, even described the film as "a fuller realization of human nature than his subsequent thrillers."[5] In contrast, Hitchcock dismissed *The Manxman* as a "banal picture" in spite of Truffaut's attempt to defend it and indicated the limitations he felt inherent in its source, Hall Caine's novel. Hitchcock claimed, "The novel had quite a reputation and it belonged to a tradition. We had to respect that reputation and that tradition."[6] Presumably the tradition is that of the popular, but somewhat scandalous, Victorian novel of adultery (Caine was one of the most popular British authors of best sellers of the late nineteenth and early twentieth centuries). Charles Barr, the most thorough critic of Hitchcock's British films, also thinks highly of *The Manxman* and finds Hitchcock's dismissal of it surprising, speculating it was due to his discomfort in working in the shadow of a well-known novel or perhaps coming from his impatience to make the transition to sound film.[7] Hitchcock's earliest serious critics, Eric Rohmer and Claude Chabrol, and his best known interpreter, Robin Wood, praise *The Manxman*, although their comments remain fairly brief. For Wood the film's romantic triangle anticipates *Under Capricorn* (1949), while the public confession that forms its climax recalls *The Scarlet Letter* (1926).[8] Rohmer and Chabrol are especially eloquent in their praise of the film's ambiguous morality, its recognition of the tragic consequences for sympathetic victims of human desire and social constraint.[9] More recently, Belgian philosopher Laurent Van Eynde opens his book on Hitchcock, *Vertige de l'image*, with a detailed discussion of *The Manxman*, seeing it as a culmination of the *cinéma pur* Hitchcock admired from the silent era.[10] This film is now available in excellent quality prints and digital versions, and I feel it possesses unheralded richness that merit a rediscovery. I think the shot I will explore demonstrates this.

"Fear death by water"

The shot, or dissolve, I have chosen to discuss was first highlighted by Yacowar in his pioneering account of the film (see Figure 3.1). The description he gives offers a compressed but rich analysis:

> When Kate tries to drown herself, Hitchcock dissolves from the close-up of the water, the ripples, her air bubbles, to a close-up of another dark pool, the inkwell into which Deemster Christian dips his pen to write a sentence. The dissolve anticipates the one to Janet Leigh's eye from bath drain in *Psycho*. The pool that has all but overwhelmed the girl and can yet doom her to a life more miserable than death is under Philip's control both as judge and lover. As Judge Christian can sentence Kate to imprisonment, either in jail or with her husband. As lover, he can again reject her or embrace her. Plunging his pen into the ink is both sexual and jurisprudent. The girl's water is dark because Phillip became a judge. He gave her up for the profession of inkwells and verdicts.[11]

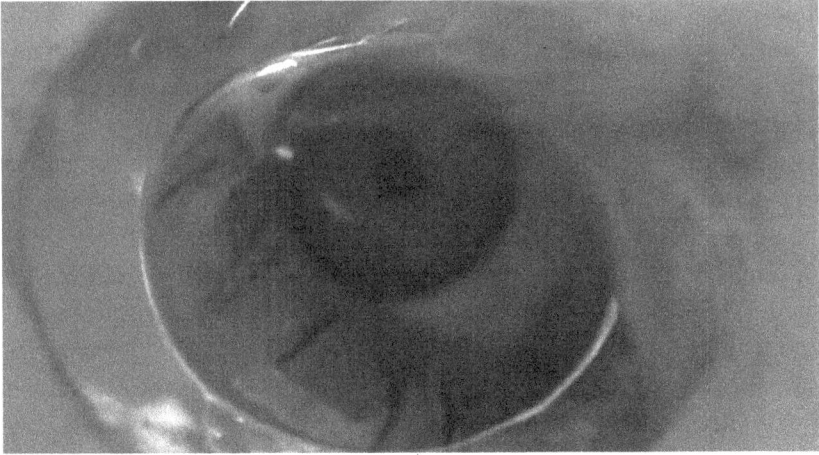

Figure 3.1 Blood circles down the drain after the shower murder in Alfred Hitchcock's *Psycho*.

Barr (who includes three frames from the dissolve in his text) acknowledges Yacowar's commentary and especially endorses the comparison to the eye/drain dissolve in *Psycho* (1960). Barr underscores that the dissolve accomplishes a transition in space and situation as well as a thematic contrast. "A woman's life has been (apparently) wiped out and the camera pulls back into an unfeeling world." He adds, "A woman's emotions become something to just dip a pen into."[12] While the dissolve functions as a rich metaphor, its more prosaic syntactical function of marking an ellipsis and providing a transition to another scene and location needs to be examined as well. Through this dissolve Hitchcock moves us from an (attempted) suicide to the Deemster's courtroom where he will hear Kate's case for attempting the unlawful act of self-murder. This ellipsis interrupts the narrative flow, suspending, for the moment, the outcome of Kate's leap into the harbor, the bubbles rising to the surface hinting that she has drowned.

Before we pursue the meanings generated by this dissolve, I want to linger over its starkly defamiliarizing visual effect. Interrupting our intense emotional and narrative involvement in Kate's plight, the image that appears on the screen is visually ambiguous. We scrutinize the dark water, searching for signs of life (or death). But in place of a dead body—or an act of rescue—an alien form overwhelms the frame. A pull-back of the camera reveals a circular form, which we eventually identify as an ink pot, that encloses the fluid blackness. More than *cinéma pur*, this startling visual transformation provides an instance of *photogénie*. French filmmakers and theorists of the 1920s—including Louis Delluc, Jean Epstein, and Germaine Dulac—described *photogénie* as the effect cinema has on objects filmed, transforming them through the visual devices of the motion picture. These visual devices include especially the mysterious power of magnification of a close-up.[13] *Photogénie* exceeds photography's ability to reproduce the familiar world, achieving what the Russian critic Viktor Shklovsky called *defamiliarization*: what is seen suddenly appears strange, renewing the viewer's perception with a shock. Therefore, along with its metaphoric and syntactical roles, this dissolve has a visceral effect; it disorients and surprises us. For an instant the fabric of narrative space has been sundered by this nearly abstract ambiguous image. Epstein felt *photogénie*—and especially the close-up—often worked against the narrative flow, the continuity of storytelling.[14] Yet in this instance it feels as though an excess of dramatic emotion forces this fissure. The image following Kate's apparent death may seem abstract, but this abstract enlargement reinforces the emotional impact and shock of her suicide attempt—expressing its violence in a new register, like a scream, or a fateful irony that intervenes as an overt authorial touch.

The shot that follows this dissolve, while still a rather extreme close-up, returns us to the recognizable world of the narrative. Abstract shapes become concrete objects and we become situated in a more stable space: we see the pen writing in a large ledger. As the camera rises and widens its frame to a medium shot, we recognize Philip with his Deemster's robe and wig and we enter firmly into a setting. The next shot dissolves quickly to a long shot of the courtroom in which quotidian legal action takes place. A court official asks, "His Honor to dispose of a minor charge, a case of attempted suicide." Philip is told "the prisoner refuses her name." After we watch Philip blow his nose, Kate is brought in, her head bowed and her face concealed by a shawl. Philip asks, "My poor woman is there no one here who can answer for you?" At this point Kate (in close shot) looks up, her gaze directly confronting the camera—and Philip—who, in reverse shot, gives a start of recognition. Kate very subtly raises a finger to her lips, requesting his silence.

The opening dialogue of this scene (conveyed, of course, by intertitles) translates the results of Kate's tragic action, so compressed and visually striking in the dissolve, into cold legal and literal terms that resonate with the drama to this point. Philip had already disposed of Kate as "a minor case" by abandoning her in preference to his career and status. She has "refused

her name" both in the sense of refusing to give it to the court and in her refusal of the name her husband has given her. Philip's question whether anyone can answer for her rebounds upon himself as he recognizes the woman
he has betrayed, refused, and driven to suicide. The question becomes, Who
can answer for him and his treatment of her? And what answer can be given?
Kate's shy, pathetic gesture, asking for silence, visualizes the way she has
been disposed of in this realm of male-dominated justice. Kate's appearance
and the account the policeman gives of her rescue fills in the narrative ellipsis of her suicide attempt, resolving its suspense. But what the sequence
in court initially enacts is her legal erasure, her fate worse than death via
non-recognition.

As Rohmer and Chabrol claimed, Hitchcock's morality here is more complex than a simple melodramatic victimization of the innocent. It is crueler
than that, because no one remains untouched by guilt. As the French critics
put it:

> The situation in *The Manxman* is sublime because it is insoluble and rejects
> all artifice. It is insoluble because it does not depend on the evilness of the
> characters or the relentlessness of fate. Hitchcock gave himself up to a mi-
> nute complete and unflinching description of the moral conflict opposing
> three people whose behavior is practically beyond reproach. Their failing is
> the failing of all human beings.[15]

Although I would hardly agree that Philip's behavior is "beyond reproach,"
Hitchcock explores the dire effect of his decisions on him as well as on Kate.
He is extremely culpable, but he is not a heartless melodramatic seducer and
villain of the sort D. W. Griffith portrayed in *Way Down East* (1920).

Introduced by our dissolve, this courtroom drama forms the penultimate
scene and dramatic climax of the film, revealing Hitchcock's complicated reworking of the logic of melodrama. It enacts the final public sorting out of
the signs of guilt and innocence that melodrama aspires to. But as Rohmer
and Chabrol indicate, Hitchcock does not show the law as aligning with what
Peter Brooks called the "moral occult."[16] This courtroom cannot serve as the
final arbiter of this woman's tragedy. In response to Phillip's question whether
anyone can answer for Kate and her own gesture imploring silence, her loyal
and simple husband Peter arrives in court and proclaims, "Phil—Phil! Let
me speak for her." Peter pleads, "I'll take her back, sir. Please Phil let her go,"
as if it were his place to forgive her. Within this triangle of love and betrayal,

it is perhaps Peter who plays the innocent, but less in the moral sense of lack of culpability than in the sense of a naïve, even a bit of a holy fool. As if concluding a bargain between men, Philip grants Peter's plea, declaring, "The prisoner is discharged and free to return to her husband." If this were a drama of conventional morality, this hypocritical judgment might lead to a reconciliation between husband and wife, but Hitchcock's morality demands a further settling of accounts.

Kate, who has been the silent pivot of the editing during this verbal exchange between men, abruptly refuses the judgment, declaring: "I am not going back!" with an icy stare at the camera. At this point the legal protocol of the courtroom breaks down, as Kate's father, a mere spectator rather than a sworn witness (as Peter had been), rises to denounce the Deemster as Kate's betrayer and betrayer of Peter's marriage and friendship. Kate stares at the camera in silence as her father makes the traditional melodramatic gesture of the outstretched finger pointing out the guilty one. He demands, "Can't you see, Pete—can't you see?" Philip rises from the bench as Hitchcock cuts to a wide shot of the assembled courtroom, their eyes riveted on him. The Deemster declares, "He speaks the truth," and, confessing his "sin against God and Man," resigns his post, as he slips off his official wig. Peter, the naïve, registers disbelief, then disillusionment. As Philip steps down from the bench, Pete grabs him in fury. Kate comes forward, the three characters forming a triangular tableau displaying Pete's anger, Philip's guilt, and Kate's compassion, as she says, "Pete, we too have suffered."

It is this recognition of mutual suffering rather than simply the judging of guilt and innocence that forms Hitchcock's version of the "moral occult." The film's brief coda visualizes this shared burden of loss, as Kate and Philip leave the village with their child, jeered at by the villagers, followed by a close-up of Pete, back on his fishing boat, staring blankly at the camera with grief and incomprehension. Only the end of *Vertigo*, as Scottie gazes into the abyss that has swallowed his dead love, matches this ending in bitterness.

The domain of vertigo

It is as though I were walking down a long corridor that once was mirrored, and fragments of mirror still hang there, dark, and shadowy [. . .]. At the end of the corridor there is nothing but darkness, and I know when I walk into the darkness, I'll die.

—Madeleine, in *Vertigo* (1958)

It is striking that in 1957, one year before Hitchcock completed and released his masterpiece, *Vertigo*, Rohmer and Chabrol wrote of *The Manxman*: "For the first time. Hitchcock penetrated into a domain that has since become dear to him—vertigo."[17] Unfortunately, as evocative as this claim is, the authors do not detail what they think the domain of vertigo might be, although the statement occurs in the context of their comments about the film's moral ambiguity quoted above. The term "vertigo" resounds with multiple connotations, evoking not only a world of uncertain motivations and conflicting drives, but a general sense of the dizziness and lack of balance. *The Manxman*'s courtroom climax lays bare these conflicting emotional dynamics through a dense weave of exchanged looks and spoken revelations. But I think Rohmer and Chabrol would agree that vertigo (or the *vertigineux*, as in the French original) in Hitchcock possesses a visual and even visceral effect: a feeling of falling into unplumbed depths, a sinking into darkness. In *The Manxman* the dissolve that merges two realms of black liquids serves as its emblem.

As I mentioned, Yacowar, seconded by Barr, compared the dissolve in *The Manxman* to the famous shot in *Psycho* in which the bloody water spiraling down the shower drain merges with Marion Crane's open, but sightless, eye (see Figure 3.2). I find this a brilliant association. Most immediately the two dissolves show a formal similarity: the round shape of the inkwell superimposed over the dark bubbly liquid recalls the circular bath drain. In *Psycho*, the mini-whirlpool of the drain and the rotating camera movement on the eye aligns with the spiral motif often noted in Hitchcock's films and most fully explored through numerous images in *Vertigo*: the tree rings of the sequoia cross-section; the spiral staircase in the bell tower; Madeleine's twisted hairdo; and, especially, the animated spirals of the opening credit sequence and Scottie's nightmare where the motif evokes (and even induces) a sense of dizziness. In *The Manxman*, the close-up of Kate, closing her eyes before she throws herself into the water, portrays her suicide attempt as a vertiginous loss of consciousness, more a collapse than a leap. The shot of the bubbles rising to the surface of dark water seems initially to indicate death by drowning. The motif of a revolving cycle appears in *The Manxman* as well: the grindstone within the mill where Philip and Kate first make love and Pete and Kate hold their wedding feast; the turning millwheel outside it; and the rotating beam of the lighthouse that sweeps through the port. More than vertigo, these circular elements evoke a sense of the cycles of fate (connotations of the motifs in *Vertigo* and *Psycho* as well). Yacowar sees the mill in *The Manxman* as an emblem of "wheels turning wheels turning wheels," paralleling the triangle of interlocking love and betrayal that entraps

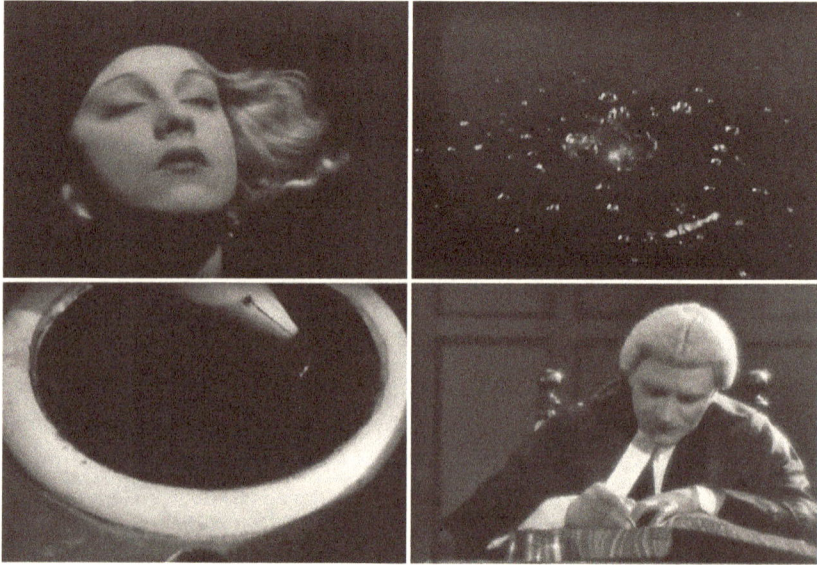

Figure 3.2 The dissolve from Kate's (Anny Ondra) attempted suicide to Philip (Malcolm Keen) dipping his pen into ink as he writes in Alfred Hitchcock's *The Manxman* (1929).

our characters.[18] Present in most night scenes in the port, the revolving lighthouse beam finally flashes across Kate as she stands at the wharf, gazing into the water and then disappears into it.

As a dissolve merging two shots into one, our shot presents a double image.[19] Its two-part structure sutures two extremely different locations, as well as contrasting two actions, asking the viewer to discover the significance of their union. The first element of the dissolve—the bubbling water—visualizes despair and death and the vertigo that preceded Kate's leap. This image, while dire, is not unfamiliar and is fairly easily readable: death by drowning. But the second part of the image that overwhelms this dark bubbling water strikes a different tone. As a defamiliarized image, it appears ambiguous, almost unreadable. What are we seeing here? The rather phallic shape—a fingernail? An oar? Perhaps some sort of life preserver?—that invades the dark background only becoming fully recognizable retrospectively, after the following shot clearly defines it as a pen, and abruptly pulls us out of the harbor location to land us in the stolid courtroom scene. The black liquid of death has been confined and rendered seemingly harmless, redefined as ink in a small container rather than the dark sea of oblivion. The shot that reveals the object as a pen in the Deemster's hand establishes a certain stability and for the moment submerges the image of death. But I find it impossible to see this second part of the diptych as simply reassuring. The persistent darkness of the image, the unexpected difficulty in identification and the radical change of scale, all shock us even more than the image of death by water.

As mentioned, the radical transition between the two images performs an abrupt narrative interruption. Whether Kate has died is suspended. But this ellipsis in action, while it interrupts the narrative flow, shifts our attention to another register. The Deemster's act of writing does not result from Kate's action, does not complete the narrative arc of her leap into the water. Rather, we could say, it shows the *cause* of her action. Kate has been abandoned by her lover because he prioritizes his traditional social role over his love for her. This secure and brightly lit realm of thick books, pens and ink, the act of writing and laying down the law, has not only caused her suffering, but ultimately has chased her from the world, blotted out her existence and her love, disposed of her as "a minor case." In effect, what the Deemster writes is Kate's death sentence. This act of inscribing the letter of the law seeks to cover over that dark space of death and betrayal. But we could also reverse this effect and see Kate's act as opening a dark abyss in the center of traditional law and order. She emerges from this darkness to destroy the appearance of authority in the courtroom scene. This is the nature of Hitchcock's vertigo: a black abyss that suddenly tears the surface of order, revealing not simply a sudden intrusion, but a history of deceit and passion that prompted this spiral of loss.

Continuity and its discontents

Somewhere in here I was born, and there I died. For you it was only a moment [. . .] you took no notice.

—Madeleine, in *Vertigo*

Ultimately I feel this dissolve, as pregnant with resonances vital to the characters and narrative of *The Manxman* as it may be, goes beyond a thematic interpretation. This complex shot carries lessons about the nature of Hitchcock's cinematic and narrative style, lessons that also reflect on the one aspect Hitchcock was willing to praise about the film—its role as his last silent film, its place in the history of film style. This dissolve, as we have seen, seems to pull us out of the narrative action for an instant justifying the assumption of this anthology: that single shots in Hitchcock films possess a certain degree of autonomy. Is the shot in a Hitchcock film simply a unit within an edited continuity, like the bricks forming a wall or links in a chain described by V. I. Pudovkin, whose book on film style greatly influenced Hitchcock?[20] Or does the shot at points in Hitchcock assert its independence, becoming not simply an element in a seamless succession, but introducing a moment of interruption, a radical act of rupture?

As a filmmaker Hitchcock represents simultaneously a mastery of the classical style of film narration based in continuity *and* a testing of the limits of this system. Although definitions of the classical style are numerous and often debated, I think a few basics are agreed upon.[21] Classical film style primarily delivers a narrative—it tells a story, channeling narrative action by placing it within a stable space and time. However, this continuity of space and time is based on a systematic breakdown into individual shots, whose articulation serves to detail actions and reveal emotions and motivations. The courtroom climax of *The Manxman* exemplifies this classical style and shows Hitchcock's subtle mastery of its elements at the end of the silent era. The space of the courtroom location is clearly established, as well as articulated dramatically. The ebb and flow of emotions and interaction between characters are not only orchestrated by cutting between them, but by the classical system, which orients the exchange of looks and dialogue, tying characters together in a consistent setting. Space and time hang together, even as the emotions that surface threaten this unity with tension and rupture.

The establishment of feature-length films around 1917 (the date that David Bordwell, Kristin Thompson, and Janet Staiger credibly assign for the beginning of the classical era in Hollywood)[22] marked a moment when this continuity editing system gained a stability that arguably lasted for decades. But within this stability distinct periods exist. During the later 1920s, when Hitchcock's style was forming, Hollywood and much of Western European filmmaking introduced an increase in the number of shots within a heightened sense of continuity, breaking down action into significantly closer shots. This new style focused on articulating details, both significant objects and reactions of characters. Its visual specificity and wit was especially evident in what Lea Jacobs has termed the "sophisticated comedies" of the twenties directed by Cecil B. DeMille, Ernst Lubitsch, Monte Bell, and Harry d'Abbadie d'Arras.[23] Jacobs describes this sophisticated style as "a

rather complex system of narration, which limited use of subtitles and employed devices such as point-of view editing and motivic scene construction to convey characters' state of mind."[24] Hitchcock emerged as a director
at the point where this new mode of filmmaking was being introduced by
filmmakers and praised by critics. More than the influences on Hitchcock
traditionally noted by historians—Griffith, German Expressionism, and
Russian montage—I believe Lubitsch and DeMille exemplified the up-to-
date style that the young Hitchcock aspired to. *The Farmer's Wife* (1928),
filmed the year before *The Manxman*, most closely resembles these sophisticated comedies and shows Hitchcock's mastery of the use of patterns of repetition and significant objects that Jacobs discusses. Certainly the grim ending
and general sense of guilt and betrayal in *The Manxman* forbid approaching
it as a comedy, sophisticated or otherwise. But we can see Hitchcock adopting
the new subtle, highly visual, and character-based style Jacobs describes to
rework what could have been an old-fashioned melodrama into a demonstration of the power of cinema to explore emotions without exaggeration or
simple moral polarities.[25]

But if the courtroom climax shows Hitchcock as an up-to-date classical
filmmaker of the late silent era, the dissolve that introduces the scene reveals
a filmmaker who pushes the classical style to its limits and challenges its stability. The rituals of the law, the location of the courtroom, and the protocols
of classical shot/counter-shot—all these root the film's climax in a scenog-
raphy that allows the revelation of truth and confrontations of guilt and suffering to emerge. However, as we have already seen, the dissolve threatens the
classical principles of continuity and stability. It is disruptive; its objects difficult to identify; and it abruptly switches both location and scale. If Hitchcock
is a master of what Bordwell calls the "straight corridor" of classical filmmaking, his straight corridors become fractured by shattered mirrors.[26] The
dissolve in *The Manxman* poses one of those fragmented images that lead us
into darkness. It embeds a moment of *photogénie* with its visual intensity and
ambiguous significance into the heart of a classical narrative.

This contrast between two different modes of filmmaking not only shows
Hitchcock's originality and versatility at this early stage in his career but
provides a key to the dialectic of his style. At the end of the 1920s, Hitchcock
was able to adopt a new modern style of classical continuity and at the same
time to draw on the elements of 1920s avant-garde filmmaking. Clearly, both
Weimar stylistics and Soviet montage inspired Hitchcock; this dissolve, with

its play on scale and form, draws especially on French avant-garde film-making and its concept of *photogénie* where the sudden unfamiliarity of the filmic image releases a sense of animism, an almost irrational power, a feeling akin to vertigo. Even if Hitchcock tests the limits of the classical style, he remains within its paradigm because he in effect "narrativizes" the disruptions he introduces. These moments do not overwhelm or subvert the narrative into which they intrude, but rather they become expressive of the forces of violence within the story. Rather than distractions from his stories, these elements of pure cinema become the combustion motors that drive them. Thus our dissolve conveys the shock and violence of Kate's suicide attempt and the powers of repression that have led her to it.

This may sound too simple, reducing Hitchcock's disruptions to simply a symbolic function. Symbolic significance they may have, but it is their affective power that impresses us. At these moments of intensity, Hitchcock not only employs the powers of cinema but comes close to short-circuiting them, calling the foundations of cinematic representation into question. Here darkness overwhelms the screen, and one form seems to dissolve into another in a world where objects seen through cinema expose unexpected dimensions. Although the de-familiarizing dissolve eventually yields recognizable objects (pen and inkwell) followed by a recognizable action (writing in a ledger) and then becomes contextualized as a recognizable place (the courtroom) with its established roles and protocols, I experience the scene less as a progression to stability than as a seeping of the dark liquid of annihilation into the activities of seemingly rational order.

Yacowar's comparison of our shot to the dissolve that ends the shower murder in *Psycho* prompts a further consideration of Hitchcock's portrayal of cinematic violence—both on screen and, I might say, *to* the screen. The enormous impact of the shower sequence relies most obviously on its extreme violence—its combination of surprise, sexuality, and vulnerability. But every commentator (including Hitchcock) on this sequence has also described it as an exemplary instance of the power of cutting. The violence of the scene occurs on two levels: the knife slicing into flesh and the editor splicing celluloid. The eye/drain dissolve brings the shower sequence to an imagistic climax. The visual match between circular forms creates an eerie sense of the process of vision and death, as dark liquid spirals into an invisible depth, down the drain, dissolving disparate elements into an uncanny unity. The effect of the shower sequence also sends us back to the very elements of Hitchcock's medium, his conditions of filmic representation. Hitchcock threatens the viewer with the very dangers he portrays, challenging the basic ontological division between artifice and diegesis on which fiction relies. If this sounds a bit too theoretical and deconstructive (or even far-fetched), my thought is rooted in the way the screenplay for *Psycho* describes the shower murder:

> A hand comes into the shot. The hand holds an enormous bread knife. The flint of the blade shatters the screen to an almost total, silver blankness.
> THE SLASHING
> An impression of the knife slashing, as if tearing at the very screen, ripping the film.[27]

Interestingly, the text of this script (signed by Joseph Stefano but undoubtedly the product of discussions between Hitchcock and the scriptwriter) does not describe the eye/drain dissolve. But I would claim that the characterization of the cutting in the shower attack as directed against the film and the screen (and implicitly the viewer) reveals the disruptive power of the image in Hitchcock. The violence suffered by Marion Crane seems to emerge from the screen, breaching it in the process. The open drain and the dead eye, like the dark liquid abyss of Kate's demise and the Philip's deadly inkwell ("for the letter killeth," as Paul says in II Corinthians), image not only death but the darkness that lies beyond the screen, the vortex into which all things vanish. *Psycho*, as a culminating work of Hitchcock's maturity goes further than *The Manxman* and, true to its thriller genre, descends into more extreme violence. "As if tearing at the very screen, ripping the film"—describing Norman Bate's slicing knife as a threat to the screen and the images it bears recalls Stanley Cavell's understanding of the film screen not only as a surface for the projection of the film's images, but as a barrier between audience and action, between a primal violence that remains virtual and the bodily spectator who becomes potentially (if only in affect) vulnerable.[28] The screen, Cavell claims, protects us from what we see; but here Hitchcock threatens to pierce that veil and release the darkness we fear. Like Marion Crane's blank but gaping eye, Hitchcock's image envisions the overwhelming blindness of an eye that can no longer see, emerging from the swirling vertigo of the loss of consciousness. Everything solid dissolves. . . .

Notes

1. "*The Manxman*," *Bioscope*, January 1929, 38.
2. François Truffaut, *Hitchcock/Truffaut: The Definitive Study of Alfred Hitchcock*, rev. ed. (New York: Simon & Schuster, 1984), 61.
3. Theorists of late silent cinema, especially in France, used the term "*photogénie*" to stress the ability of the photographic image to reveal aspects of the world otherwise not noticed. I will discuss this further later in this essay.
4. Lesley Brill, *The Hitchcock Romance: Love and Irony in Hitchcock's Films* (Princeton, NJ: Princeton University Press, 1988). See Herrmann's comment: "Most people think of Hitchcock as a master of mystery and suspense. Although this is fundamentally true, he is also a great romantic director, his films allowing enormous scope for sensual and lyrical musical treatment." Liner notes from album *Music from the Great Movie Thrillers* (1969), also quoted in Steven C. Smith, *A Heart at Fire's Center: The Life and Music of Bernard Herrmann* (Berkeley: University of California Press, 2002), 293.
5. Maurice Yacowar, *Hitchcock's British Films*, 2nd ed. (Detroit: Wayne State University Press, 2010), 75.
6. Truffaut, *Hitchcock/Truffaut*, 61.
7. Charles Barr, *English Hitchcock* (Moffat: Cameron & Hollis, 1999), 67.
8. Robin Wood, *Hitchcock's Films Revisited* (New York: Columbia University Press, 1989), 333.
9. Eric Rohmer and Claude Chabrol, *Hitchcock: The First Forty-Four Films,* trans. Stanley Hochman (New York: Frederick Unger, 1979), 17.
10. Laurent Van Eynde, *Vertige de l'image: L'esthétique reflexive d'Alfred Hitchcock* (Paris: Presses Universitaires de France, 2011), 29–43.
11. Yacowar, *Hitchcock's British Films*, 69–70.
12. Barr, *English Hitchcock*, 75.
13. See the excellent summary of this concept in Richard Abel, *French Film Theory and Criticism*, Vol. 1: *A History/ Anthology 1907–1939*, 2 vols. (Princeton, NJ: Princeton University Press, 1993), 107–111, 204–215.
14. See especially Jean Epstein, "Magnification (1921)" and "The Senses 1(b) (1921)," in Abel, *French Film Theory and Criticism*, I: 235–241; 241–246.
15. Rohmer and Chabrol, *Hitchcock*, 18.
16. Peter Brooks, *The Melodramatic Imagination: Balzac, Henry James, Melodrama and The Mode of Excess* (New Haven, CT: Yale University Press, 1976), 5–7.
17. Rohmer and Chabrol, *Hitchcock*, 18. The original French text says, "*Pour la première fois, Hitchcock pénétrait dans un domaine qui lui est devenu cher, celui du vertigineux.*" Rohmer and Chabrol, *Hitchcock* (Paris: Classiques du cinéma, 1957), 42. Dash in the original.
18. Yacowar, *Hitchcock's British Films*, 71.
19. As Luke Robinson has pointed out to me, this double image anticipates the more elaborate superimposition in Hitchcock's *The Wrong Man* from 1956, which reveals the true identity of the robber, brilliantly analyzed by Noa Steimatsky in her book *The Face on Film* (New York: Oxford University Press, 2017), 173–176.

20. V. I. Pudovkin, *Film Technique*, trans. I. Montagu, 2nd ed. (London: Geo. Newnes, Ltd., 1933). See Hitchcock's comment in *Hitchcock/Truffaut*, 214.

21. The primary sources are David Bordwell, Kristin Thompson, and Janet Staiger, *The Classical Hollywood Cinema: Film Style and Mode of Production to 1960* (New York: Columbia University Press 1985), 1–74; and David Bordwell, *Narration in the Fiction Film* (Madison: University of Wisconsin Press, 1985), 156–204. I have relied on these for my summary. The focus of these accounts are Hollywood, but the principles had an international scope.

22. In Part 1 by Bordwell he defines the concept and justifies the date. See Bordwell, Thompson, and Staiger, *Classical Hollywood Cinema*, 1–70.

23. Lea Jacobs, *The Decline of Sentiment: American Film in the 1920s* (Berkeley: University of California Press, 2008).

24. Jacobs, *The Decline of Sentiment*, 125.

25. Jacobs has pointed out that the classical style was also perceived in the 1920s as innovative and modern; "The emphasis on simplicity and economy was perceived as distinctive, efficient, and stream-lined, a departure from more old-fashion ways of making movies." *The Decline of Sentiment*, 276.

26. David Bordwell, "Classical Hollywood Cinema: Narrational Principles and Procedures," in *Narrative, Apparatus, Ideology: A Film Theory Reader*, ed. Philip Rosen (New York: Columbia University Press, 1986), 18.

27. Joseph Stefano, *Psycho* (1959), *Screenplays for You*, https://sfy.ru/?script=psycho.

28. Stanley Cavell, *The World Viewed: Reflections on the Ontology of Film*, enlarged ed. (Cambridge, MA: Harvard University Press, 1979), 24.

4

Sabotage (1936)

A thriller and its aftereffects

Helen Hughes

The shot depicted in Figure 4.1 appears some 56 minutes into Alfred Hitchcock's British film *Sabotage* (US title *The Woman Alone*, 1936). A London double-decker bus has been destroyed from the inside by a terrorist bomb while making its way from the Lord Mayor's Show parade outside the Royal Courts of Justice in the Strand, to the Underground station at Piccadilly Circus. It is a fictional scene, and an adaptation of Joseph Conrad's 1907 novel *The Secret Agent*. Conrad's bleak story is based on an historical event, the "Greenwich bomb outrage" of 1894, in which an anarchist device exploded in the parkland outside the Greenwich Observatory, killing only its bearer, Martial Bourdin. Conrad turned the historical figure, an unemployed French tailor, into a disabled young man, and then alienated his readers by killing him, the only sympathetic character in the entire novel. In Conrad's story, the Observatory on the Prime Meridian became a symbol of the global status of British infrastructure and the target of terrorism. Hitchcock and Charles Bennett, on the other hand, turned Conrad's Bourdin-turned-Stevie (Desmond Tester) from an adult with a cognitive disability into an easily distracted schoolboy. The film includes the London icons listed in Stephen Tallents's public relations pamphlet of 1933: Piccadilly, Big Ben, the Lord Mayor of London, the Metropolitan Police, the London Omnibuses, and the Underground.[1] The London bus becomes in *Sabotage* an everyday symbol of modern England, alongside Piccadilly, the target of attack, and the Lord Mayor's show. When the bus explodes, we find that Hitchcock has blown up a symbol, a schoolboy, a friendly conductor, a stylish old lady, and a cute little dog, making the world a hostile place, and the London bus a vulnerable form of carriage.

When I first saw *Sabotage*, quite by chance, in 2021, I was startled by the way it brought back strong memories of the site of the Aldwych bus bombing in

Helen Hughes, Sabotage *(1936)* In: *One Shot Hitchcock.* Edited by: Luke Robinson and Melanie Robson, Oxford University Press. © Oxford University Press 2024. DOI: 10.1093/oso/9780197682876.003.0004

Figure 4.1 The scene blends to the site of the explosion. The dust rises above the wreck of the bus in Alfred Hitchcock's *Sabotage* (1936).

London in 1996, as well as the July 7 bombing on Southampton Row in 2005. Both locations are close by the place referenced by this fictional scene, which captures the feel of a violently disrupted city center in a visceral way. Following up on this unexpected encounter, I went on a search to find out what the reaction to this film had been and whether my sense of shock at this image had been explored in the scholarship on Hitchcock. This essay is a report on what I discovered about the response to *Sabotage* over time. For me, two questions about Hitchcock's narratives came to the fore. The first question concerns narrative suspense and Hitchcock's mastery of the relationships between suspense and other narratively induced emotions such as surprise, dread, and pleasure. All newspaper reviews of the film on its release mentioned suspense, most of them positively,[2] and sometimes as the redeeming feature of an otherwise poor film. The other question has concerned the ethics of the portrayal of violent killing, and the idea that a director has a responsibility to an audience. This debate was initiated by the well-known film reviewer C. J. Lejeune.[3] Through its brutal use of suspense the film opens up an immediate historical and contextual dimension to the representation of London as a vulnerable city.

Somewhat surprisingly, the initial confrontation between director and critic over what was permissible in popular crime fiction in 1936 has led scholars to formal rather than thematic questions about narrative. These have remained at the center of critical analyses of *Sabotage* to the exclusion of engagement with the effects and affects of terrorism on the streets of London. Already at the press viewing on the launch of the film in 1936, Hitchcock was persuaded by the critic Lejeune of the *Observer* that he had committed a *faux pas* with the film, and, as late as 1976, in response to a question about which of his films had taught him the most about the audience, Hitchcock recalled Lejeune—livid and with her fists raised at him—and replied it was *Sabotage* from which he had learned his biggest lesson. In Hitchcock's words: "If you get the suspense from an audience from a thing like a bomb, it mustn't go off. It's got to be discovered and thrown out of the window. You've got to relieve that suspense in other ways."[4]

Understanding the narrative functions of hope

In an effort to bring my report on this formal discussion together with an interpretation of the thematic significance of the film, I will begin with a reference to Tarja Laine's book *Feeling Cinema* and her theorization that historicizes the thriller as a film genre. Laine argues that hope is a key feeling common to traditional (Hitchcockian) and more recent (existential) thrillers. For Laine, there has been a change in the genre from thrillers where suspense is built up through identification with a heroic and sympathetic character, to thrillers in which the resolution of suspense is complicated by forced identification with unsympathetic characters through complex narrative puzzles and shared perspectives. In the latter, a clash between dislike of morally dubious character and the human desire not to see someone harmed is created by a context of "(hopeless) hope" in which information about what is happening is distributed in the film in complex ways.[5] Echoing Hitchcock's idea that the audience likes to "play God," Laine writes that thrillers "put the spectator into a 'clairvoyant,' although not omniscient, position. The viewer is confronted with a dilemma: will they prefer the satisfaction of their aesthetic desire or the satisfaction of their moral desire?"[6]

Laine's readings of late twentieth-century films indicate a parallel development in the spectators and producers of thriller films. She finds that both are concerned with the orchestration of affective and formal narrative issues rather than with the interaction between story and historical context.

The reception history of Sabotage confirms that the strategies of more recent thrillers could not, it seems, have worked in 1936 when, as we saw, Hitchcock accepted that his film violated existing narrative conventions and developed his art accordingly.

The critic Lejeune referred to herself as an injured fan of crime fiction. It is worth here going into some more detail about what happens in Sabotage to understand her objection. At the beginning of the film a mysterious political agent named Karl Anton Verloc (Oskar Homolka) switches off London's lights through an act of sabotage, but the city is hardly affected. The pragmatic Londoners merely laugh off the incident and its temporary inconvenience so that the saboteur's handlers demand something more spectacular. Verloc, who lives with his wife (played by Sylvia Sidney) and her schoolboy brother Stevie, and runs a cinema, must blow up the underground station at Piccadilly Circus. A sequence of events leads the saboteur to give the bomb to Stevie to take to its destination. The lad cheerfully travels on the bus in his cap and blazer not knowing he is carrying a fully primed explosive device.

In Sabotage the possibility that the bomb carried by Stevie might explode—first as the boy gets distracted by the Lord Mayor's show, and then as he rides the bus—is made constantly present to the spectator through a number of cuts to different clocks as the time counts down to the planned ignition. At the same time, the scene inside the bus develops the characters, increasing spectator engagement with them. There is the kindly conductor who lets the boy on the bus despite the fact he believes he is carrying two cans of film—a highly flammable material; the elderly lady who lets the boy pet her dog; and the boy himself, a lively presence as he impatiently looks out of the window. The accumulation of these narrative events increases anxiety for the characters' safety, but all of this detail points to the expectation—in terms of the thriller genre in the 1930s—that the bomb will not explode on the bus even if Stevie does arrive too late. How will this plausibly be achieved? In actually allowing the bomb to explode on the bus, Lejeune complains, Hitchcock goes against the conventions of crime fiction and upsets the audience. Putting it in Laine's terms, the aesthetic outcome—the unlikely delivery to the left-luggage locker at Piccadilly at the right time—and the moral outcome—the rescue of all passengers in transit—are both thwarted. Curiosity about how the story will unfold from this point is also abruptly terminated.

In his contemporary review of the film, Webster sees the intense suspense and shock that Hitchcock achieves in this sequence as rescuing the film from a banal cast and a thin plot.[7] In contrast, in her attempts to explain her sense of disgust, Lejeune's words condemn the film for its abrupt reminder of the brutality of random violence. However, both point to narrative convention as the point of contention. As Lejeune puts it: "As a detective fan and an inveterate reader of thrillers I suggest that this is the sort of thing that should get a fellow blackballed from the Crime Club. Discreet directors don't kill schoolboys and dogs in omnibuses."[8] I would suggest that Lejeune's condemnation is important because it not only asks questions about suspense and narrative pleasure, but also poses an ethical problem inherent in the representation of violence. What is the director's responsibility for the well-being of the spectator? In turbulent times, what are the limits to the representation of violence?

Defending *Sabotage*

Other contemporary reviewers of the film, as well as more recent scholarly readings, have noted that Hitchcock's narrative violence is taken from the novel on which it is based. Indeed, as the screenwriter Charles Bennett points out, the death of the boy was more or less dictated by the novel.[9] The fact that the film is a literary adaptation, if only a loose one, is the starting point for Paula Cohen's analysis of the film, which defends it by thinking comparatively. Cohen argues that the intensified suspense and surprising brutality of the film *Sabotage* came about through a conscious attempt to develop the cinematic art as a serious form distinct from the literary. In this experiment, the historical context lurks in the background in the form of Hitchcock's use of crowds as a "lever for an emotional response."[10] It is an argument that turns the problematically harsh scene in which the bus is blown up into an exemplary moment when Hitchcock is pitching patriarchal, family values against this representation of the harsh ideological pursuit of social revolution, making it keenly felt in the moment of brutal violence.

Comparing the novel and the film, Cohen argues that Conrad's direct and satirical literary description—portraying all his characters as excessively lazy and selfish and engaged in generally mean thoughts—is a modernist vision in which every citizen is morally compromised, whether engaged in maintaining or disrupting the establishment. Hitchcock, on the other hand, says Cohen, working in the cinematic medium, uses intellectual montage to present the same British public as pragmatic but also understatedly heroic. Cohen's argument rests on the study of the internal organization of the film and the way in which it replaces the literary device of telling the audience what they should think about the characters with cinematic juxtaposition and analogy. For example, after Verloc has explained the death of Stevie on the bus, Hitchcock has his sister enter the cinema where the animated Disney film *Who Killed Cock Robin* (1935) is being projected. This mise-en-abyme creates a comparison between the jolly cartoon depiction of killing and the tragic and senseless death of Stevie. Cohen argues that Hitchcock is here portraying the mass cinema-going public of the interwar years as one that is robust in its attitude toward terrorist attacks, with a capacity to laugh off threats of violence.

A key point is the contrast between the cinematic opening of the film, which portrays London ablaze with light temporarily darkened by the sabotage at the power station, and Conrad's negative literary passage portraying London as a "cruel devourer of the world's light."[11] This first sabotage leads to a scene in which the mass audience (and by analogy the film viewer) is introduced within the film as a point of identification for the spectator. Conrad's view of British society as essentially selfish is transformed by Hitchcock into a portrait of the ordinary citizen as a benign force that resists the attempt of sabotage by downplaying it. Cohen argues: "In place of psychological desire, Hitchcock substitutes the possibility of controlled feeling—salvation from the outside rather than the inside. The mass audience, in this context, is the human embodiment of the outside. It serves both as the rationale for a simplification of meaning and as the raw material for it."[12] Hitchcock's formal preference for aesthetic control is at one with the values expressed in the film, and the terrorist act, as an experience of shock, is diminished. Does this argument about the meanings emerging from juxtaposition rescue the film itself from the accusation of callousness, however? There is still, after all, a gulf between the two kinds of cinematic death.

In his chapter on Hitchcock's adaptation, Matthew Carlson expresses a rather different view that takes more account of the idea that the reaction to the film was one of distaste. He interprets the placement of the word "sabotage" as a dictionary entry at the very beginning of the film as a clue to reading the film itself, seeing it as a self-reflexive statement. The film itself engages in "the wilful destruction of buildings or machinery with the object of alarming a group of persons or inspiring public uneasiness."[13] Both the novelist Conrad, and the filmmaker Hitchcock, are, according to Carlson, engaged in an attempt to alarm a wide audience. Carlson takes the saboteur, Verloc, to be an "artist surrogate," who is compelled by circumstances to move from a comic and ineffective act of sabotage—which merely puts out

London's lights—to a tragic intervention in which innocent bystanders are murdered. Verloc, Conrad, and Hitchcock all first please and then upset the audience: "each artist, in his own distinctive way, uses the opportunity to do both at the same time and with great style."[14] Carlson's interpretation brushes over the sensitivities of the explosion on the bus and instead focuses on the killing of Verloc toward the end of the film, seeing it as fulfilling the desire of the budding genre fan to murder the director.

Like Cohen, Carlson ultimately displaces the shock of the explosion on the bus onto a broader strategy in which the disgust of the spectator is a price paid for a more general message about violence. Neither argument defending the film is ethically convincing, however, unless it is felt that that its strategies—celebrating the thick skin of Londoners or developing the cinematic art—override the "sense of disgust" expressed by Lejeune. Interestingly, Mark Osteen proposes a different set of arguments that focus particularly on the distaste of the spectator, arguing that she is being punished for her love of thrillers.

Osteen argues that the spectator's feeling of shock at the explosion is not because of the vulnerable family at home, but the result of the buildup to it through repeated shots of ticking clocks and by the constant comedic delays, writing:

> the power and horror of the sequence are largely the result of this brilliant montage by Hitchcock and editor Charles Frend, but derive also from Hitchcock's canny use of the puppy and the old woman in her fur coat (two more animals) to heighten our sympathy. Yet our response is complex: as the scene proceeds, we don't really believe that the boy and the dog will be blown to bits, even though the rising tension (emphasized by the ominous music) forecasts that outcome.[15]

Osteen goes on to argue that the viewer actively desires the explosion. For him "the degree to which we are drawn into the suspense [of the scenes] is precisely the degree to which we also desire this violent cataclysm; indeed, we need it, or the scene will fizzle out anticlimactically, leaving our emotions with no place to go."[16]

Osteen's argument that the audience "needs" the explosion is interesting, as it suggests the idea that *Sabotage* is in fact more like the existential thriller as described by Laine, rather than a traditional one. Laine, we can recall, sees an historical development in the genre from the Hitchcockian suspenseful drama in which the spectator expects the worthy or innocent character to survive all hazards, to the modern thriller in which a complex plot ends up saving a morally compromised protagonist. Osteen's analysis places *Sabotage* perhaps between the two types of thriller handling character identification in the traditional way, precisely so that the framework can situate the audience as vulnerable and easily seduced into moral ambiguity. The explosion is then "artistically fulfilling,"[17] because for the spectator it draws attention to those interpretations that link the film to Conrad's novel and its modernist deconstruction of the British. The sophistication of the adaptation is the reward. Osteen describes the film as ruthless, and his conclusion refuses the idea of the audience as in need of protection. Instead, *Sabotage* "explodes the conventions of cinematic response almost as definitively as it blows up the Bijou. And we, like Hitchcock and the other bombers, must consider our own responsibility as we depart the theater."[18]

Osteen paints a picture of Hitchcock as a tough rather than cynical director, experimenting with the emotions of his audience, learning gradually to gain the kind of control that later paid such dividends in the case of the film *Psycho* (1960). Linda Williams, using her own memories of seeing that film, has demonstrated Hitchcock's tightening of the cinema experience beyond the space of the screening room into the street and the queue outside.[19] Hitchcock's conclusions about the negative audience reaction to *Sabotage* demonstrate a thought process that understands emotional as well as intellectual responses as integral to the creation of a successful film. Hitchcock does not, however, conclude that the answer is to step outside the fictional into the historical world. Rather, he concludes that the conventions must be upheld, and that the bomb should not go off in the fictional world.

From fiction to actuality

Each of the three readings of the film discussed in this report has approached it in a relatively abstract way, perhaps led by Hitchcock's later commentary on suspense, fear, and excitement in the cinema. They have also all constructed immanent readings taking in the relationship of the film with the novel, but neither the historical context for Conrad's story nor the references within *Sabotage* to contemporary London are considered. The spectator response to suspense is studied as part of narrative structure. Shock involves an abrupt detachment from immersive engagement in the

story, and a moment when the spectator questions the motivation or purpose of the storyteller. A legitimate question for narratology would be to ask
whether there is something consistent about such shocks. Hitchcock's discussion has directed the focus to the narrative experiment itself rather than
the wider historical context in which cinematic tales are embedded. Why
is it that no reference is made to anarchy or to ideological conflict or to the
violent political events taking place in London and other cities in the early
twentieth century?

Laine, in her discussion of the thriller genre, extends the exploration of
suspense and the internal coherence of a film with her analysis of George
Sluizer's film *Spoorlos* (1988). This film has been called a copybook exploration of Hitchcock's technique.[20] Laine describes Sluizer's film as disturbing,
comparing it with Hitchcock's *North by Northwest* (1959), but, as mentioned
above, she also brings in a different discussion about hope as a wider emotional context. Laine discusses the paradox that the narrative makes the sad
disappearance of one of the characters inevitable in the same way that the
death of Stevie becomes inevitable, but that the spectator still hopes for another resolution. The final disappearance provokes, for Laine, anxiety but
also "a tiny sense of relief, as the outcome we have anticipated so nervously
is finally over and done with."[21] In this way, the channeling of emotion into
expectations of a disaster should make the explosion in *Sabotage* a relief, as
Osteen suggests, even though there is also shock.

Hitchcock famously said that suspense is created when the spectator knows
what the characters do not know. Playing God, for Hitchcock, is responding
to this knowledge by attempting to predict what will happen.[22] Such a technique maintains a focus on the text as an internally coherent construction
and discourages the idea that a fiction film might refer to contemporary affairs through interruption or other forms of estrangement. Although the
emotions provoked by the explosion in *Sabotage* might be channeled by a
subsequent scene into eventual revenge on the saboteur Verloc, there is an
argument that the image of the shattered bus also has enough resonance to
take it outside the film to London in 1936. In the course of the film, the story
has shown the public resist an act of sabotage. The characters have carried on
daily life, going to Lyons Corner teashop on the Strand, which we pass on the
bus. There have already been the fictional scenes of the Lord Mayor's show
with an image of the Royal Courts of Justice back-projected. The fronts of
the buildings behind the exploded bus have reconstructed the relationship
between the office, the commercial premise, and the busy road exactly. The

global city in all its energy has been resisting the possibility of catastrophe, but now it has become vulnerable to it in 1936 and again in the twenty-first century.

Perhaps it is the experience of watching a digital reproduction of the film on a computer screen that encourages such a dialectical moment. As Laura Mulvey puts it in *Death 24x a Second*, where she considers the effects of digitization on the experience watching of old films made on celluloid:

> The time of the film's original moment of registration can suddenly burst through its narrative time. Even in a Hollywood movie, beyond the story is the reality of the image: the set, the stars, the extras take on the immediacy and presence of a document and the fascination of time fossilized overwhelms the fascination of narrative progression. The now-ness of story time gives way to the then-ness of the time when the movie was made and its images take on social, cultural or historical significance, reaching out into its surrounding world.[23]

In her discussion of the paradox of suspense as desiring and not desiring the explosion, Laine argues for a distinction "between the affective appraisal and the emotional evaluation of a cinematic event." For Laine the difference between the affective response and the emotional response explains the importance of suspense to the thriller genre. She connects her remarks to the work of Antonio Damasio, who distinguishes between emotions or "extended consciousness," where there is access to memory and reasoning, and affect, which, as Laine puts it, "takes place on the level of core consciousness that is not depending on memory or reflective reasoning."[24] Laine translates these categories into "pre-reflective consciousness" and "reflective consciousness" or "awareness of being aware."[25] Affect is experienced more quickly than emotion and, more important, is not protected from error. "It would seem that suspense in cinema is always 'fresh' since at the suspenseful moment core consciousness outweighs extended consciousness so that we feel the tension intensely even the second time around."[26]

The buildup to the explosion on the bus, and the shock of it actually occurring, works every time on the level of affect, despite the knowledge that the director has already made the decision to blow it up. It works also emotionally, however, as stepping outside the narrative in this case takes the emotional evaluation of the film beyond the immediate question of what happens to Stevie. It is not only the conventions of crime fiction that come into question. The vulnerability of the human spectator to the tricks of cinema are also evidenced. Again, as Mulvey puts it:

> Human consciousness creates ordered time to organize the rhythms of everyday life according to the demands of society and economy, but also in recognition of the intractable nature of time itself. For human and all organic life, time marks the movement along a path to death, that is, to the stillness that represents the transformation of the animate into the inanimate. In cinema, the blending of movement and stillness touches on this point of uncertainty so that, buried in the cinema's materiality, lies a reminder of the difficulty of understanding passing time and, ultimately, of understanding death.[27]

Damasio's ideas are controversial within the field of memory studies because of the difficulty in repeating his laboratory experiments.[28] As can be seen from Laine's equivalent terms, however, the ideas are already present in critical approaches to film spectatorship. Most events—film events included— are embedded in a structure that is based on knowledge and memory so that even though a shock might feel detached it is in fact already structured by what has come before. Like Cohen, Laine argues that the spectator of the film can come to understand the explosion as provoking unpleasant emotions as a punishment for the less reflexive enjoyment that is the initial affect. For Laine, discussing *Spoorlos*, the spectator is afflicted with the unpleasant feeling as a punishment for morbid curiosity. In *Sabotage*, Cohen argues that the punishment is for enjoying the feeling of peril—exemplified by the audience laughing in the Walt Disney film.

Although Laine does not consider why a film might take up the morality of the narrative situation of suspense, her arguments point to some ways in which the image of the aftermath of the explosion in *Sabotage* might connect narrative displeasure not only with the morality of storytelling itself but also with contemporary history. Taking the debate in this direction connects it with the Brechtian idea of the cinematic as an educational experience, as a positive rather than negative guide to modern life. This is explored by Miriam Bratu Hansen in *Cinema of Experience*, where she reflects on the role of cinema as a modernist medium for mass cultural development.[29] Reflecting on the work of the social theorists Siegfried Kracauer, Walter Benjamin, and Theodor Adorno, Hansen argues that cinema in the early twentieth century took on the role of creating and exemplifying new social behaviors in the modern world. How to engage in friendship, romance, collective protest, even work could be seen and evaluated through the big screen. Following in her spirit, *Sabotage* can be understood as a film about individual and collective reactions to terrorism. At first the robust response of laughter to sabotage exemplifies the kind of spirit that became famous during the Blitz in the Second World War. The death of Stevie, however, does not create a template for a response. The characters and the audience are shown as powerless.

Immediately after the expected and yet unexpected explosion on the bus, which at first is portrayed very briefly and dynamically in an obscured view of bursting flames, the film incongruously cuts to a scene where the saboteur Verloc, his wife, and a police detective are all laughing. "Well, now everything seems to be alright," says Verloc, who had given the bomb to Stevie to carry to its destination at Piccadilly Underground. The detective is, however, called away to speak on the telephone with his station, which the spectator knows must have something to do with the explosion. After he has listened, he tells the couple "a whole bus load of people has been blown up in the West End." The scene is then faded back to the scene of the crime and the shot that is shown in the figure that opened this chapter.

Figure 4.2   A crowd gathers around the scene of the explosion in *Sabotage*.

As can be seen on the reproduced frame in Figure 4.1, the cloud of dust is still rising over a crowd, an ambulance, the fire service, and police. As can be seen in the figure, people on the site are engaged in putting out the fire. The labor involved in creating a scene like this is indicated in an essay by Hitchcock called "Looking for the Sun," published in the *New York Times* in February 1937.

> Out in a field near Harrow, "London" stands. It is a complete replica of a London street scene, built for my new Gaumont-British thriller, *Sabotage*. Fully equipped shops, trams, buses traffic lights, beacons, overhead railway, and hundreds of pedestrians are there but nothing is happening. The cameras are covered up, the microphone is shrouded, the crowd stands huddled against the shops.[30]

The ethics of labor involved in creating a shot that describes the spectacle of death became a key subject for film criticism after an article by Jacques Rivette, "On Abjection," was published in *Cahiers du cinéma* in 1960.[31] This article was a critique of the film *Kapò* (1960) directed by Gillo Pontecorvo about the concentration camps created in Europe during the Second World War. Rivette attacks the approach of the film to its subject by describing a single shot. Rivette calls for a greater engagement with ethics in the composition of such shots, writing emotionally:

> Look, however, in *Kapò*, at the shot where Riva kills herself by throwing herself on an electric barbed-wire fence; the man who decides, at that moment, to have a dolly in to tilt up at the body, while taking care to precisely note the hand raised in the angle of its final framing—this man deserves nothing but the most profound contempt.[32]

In contrast, in *Sabotage*, Hitchcock's scene portrays the aftermath of the moment of death and there are no bodies to be seen. Nevertheless, like in *Kapò*, the shock of the sequence has the potential to shift attention from the narrative and how it will unfold onto the *mise-en-scène*. The shot that follows of Londoners looking on the scene reinforces the doubled sense of the London location violated by the attack in the story and demeaned by the detail of the set: the various parts of the bus scattered across the road, the service vehicles, the journalist in his typical rain coat and trilby hat.

From this point on, the film shows how Stevie's sister, Verloc's wife, comes to realize that it was her brother who was carrying the bomb and her husband who planted it. This film, like Hitchcock's 1942 film *Saboteur* set in an American factory attacked by a fascist organization, played to audiences' experience of contemporary violence, one in the post-revolutionary period after the First World War and the other during the Second World War.

As a twenty-first-century digital viewer of this film made on celluloid, I see this shot not as a stage in a linear narrative that celebrates the London citizens who continue to ride the Clapham omnibus despite the threat of sabotage. Rather, slowing down the film and noticing the cloud of dust rising in the center of the image, I can pick up on Brian Massumi's exploration of the digital arts of affect in his *Parables for the Virtual*. Taking some time to settle, the dust creates a momentary lack of focus, allowing for a delayed affective acknowledgment of the explosion. Obscured by the cloud, the emerging image of the destroyed bus then accidentally creates a different point of departure. Before it can be attached to the crowd and the police, investigators and journalists gathered around with the buses lined up behind them, there is a chance for an autonomous synaesthetic, physically open affective response. Massumi describes:

> the simultaneous participation of the virtual in the actual and the actual in the virtual, as one arises from and returns to the other. Affect is this two-sidedness, *as seen from the side of the actual thing*, as couched in its perceptions and cognitions. Affect is *the virtual as point of view*, provided the visual metaphor is used guardedly.[33]

The human figures—the silhouetted hats at the bottom of the image, the individuals in mackintoshes looking down at the wreckage in the center, and the group that has gathered and been confined to the pavement back right and left—seem to be witnesses to London as the site of violent spectacle at several different times in its history. Both Conrad in 1907 and Hitchcock in 1936 underline their portrayal of London as a city under attack by killing an innocent and in so doing refer to a historical reality that the audience is aware of. The Greenwich Outrage, which was the source of Conrad's story, is sometimes claimed as the first terrorist incident in the city connected to the "first globalization" between the 1870s and the start of the First World War. What is known of the background to the apparently anarchist bombing incident, and its consequences for the otherwise largely peaceful refugees from France,[34] is narrated by Vlad Solomon in his survey of policing counterterrorism in Britain in the late nineteenth and early twentieth centuries: "Around 4.50 p.m. a loud boom, slightly less powerful than a cannon's report, was heard all throughout the park and as far away as Stockwell Street. Rushing towards the place of the explosion, a park-keeper found Bourdin kneeling in a pool of blood at the first bend in the uphill pathway. He was half eviscerated and his left hand had been completely blown off."[35] This explosion scene, then, is entirely different from that of Hitchcock's film. It is still not clear whether it was actually intended as an attack on that particular location. What it created was, as Solomon puts it, a sense of outrage from the general public and the policing agencies: "his lasting legacy . . . besides inspiring one of the twentieth-century's first great spy novels, was the embarrassment caused to authorities by his gruesome demise."[36]

Hitchcock's film thus transposes this story of an accidental anarchist bombing in the park in 1894 into a bomb intended for the London Underground and diverted onto a London bus in 1936. This idea was not unheard of, as the Fenian dynamite campaign during the 1880s included bombs left in station spaces such as Victoria Station, Paddington, and Ludgate Hill. Attempts, however, to connect the film with a point of view with respect to the politics of 1936 come up against the lack of statements from Hitchcock about how his films relate to contemporary themes.[37] All that can be said is that he regretted the explosion scene and explained the response of shock as the result of a breach of trust on the part of the director.

In the twenty-first century, the image is available to renewed shock, not as the starting point for an analysis of narrative technique, but as a provocative expression of something beyond the control of the director and the viewer of the film. Via Massumi's work, the particular significance of the cloud of dust thrown up over the image can also be drawn out as something that might provide clues as to why the clarity of twentieth- and then twenty-first-century realist images often fail to signify the death of innocent victims in an acceptable way. In his explorations of the place of affect in the perception of art, Massumi argues that the artist working with light, the "brightness confound"—the emergence of luminosity and color into shape—must "yield to its self-activity."[38] This point can turn film as a visual art into "more an experimental tweaking of an autonomous process than a molding of dumb matter."[39] That is, in allowing the cloud to develop over the scene, Hitchcock, together with his set designer and his cinematographer, also allowed, in a most un-Hitchcockian way, the emergence of "a whole world captured at the moment of its emergence from the unform," Massumi, *Parables for the Virtual*, 173. here the whole being the world created by the first globalization, with its hectic pace, its malcontents, and its push toward total war.

The isolation of the thriller from reality

The explosion scene is fictional. It is a mock-up of the effects of a fictional bomb in a fictional city. Understanding the relationship between director and audience as one of trust, Hitchcock became eloquent about the workings of narrative empathy, suspense, and terror, but he did not enlarge on any relationship between those and historical reality. The fault, if there is one, is in having allowed for such a relationship to develop at all. For Lejeune in 1936 this explosion scene at the center of the film did not retain the trust of the audience in the director to keep reality at bay. Her point was that she had a small boy at home. The success of the films that followed—the literary adaptation of the Gothic novel *Rebecca* (1940), the horror-thriller *Psycho* (1960), and the self-reflexive study of desire *Vertigo* (1958)—have eclipsed the popular failure of this one made in London between the wars. And yet there is an argument to make that, of all of Hitchcock's films, this one expresses most eloquently the state of things in the twentieth- and the twenty-first-century city. Its focus on the importance of maintaining the infrastructure for the hustle and bustle of mass urban living, its exposure of the vulnerability of all to the machinations of one, and above all its icy exploration and countdown through the clock of the city and the emotions and affects involved in intimate human betrayal—all borrowed from Conrad's famous tale—make it a significant and still relevant London film.

Notes

1. The civil servant and public relations pioneer Stephen Tallents did not approve of crime films for the projection of England to the world. The list of icons was intended for prestige film projects. Stephen Tallents, "The Projection of England," in *Public Relations and the Making of Modern Britain*, ed. Scott Anthony (Manchester: Manchester University Press, 2012), 206–235.
2. See, e.g., Walter Webster, "Bombs and Villainy in London," *Sunday Pictorial*, December 6, 1936, London edition, 16.

3. C. J. Lejeune, "One for All, and All for One," *Sunday Observer*, December 6, 1936, London edition, 14. The local and national newspapers did not echo her sentiments. A. T. Borthwick goes in for many spoilers before declaring it "An unlikely tale with artfully human touches to make it grip." *Daily News*, December 3, 1936, London edition, 9.

4. Anthony Macklin, "'It's the Manner of Telling': An Interview with Alfred Hitchcock [1976]," in *Hitchcock on Hitchcock: Selected Writings and Interviews*, Vol. 2, ed. Sidney Gottlieb, 2 vols. (Berkeley: University of California Press, 2015), 55–56.

5. Tarja Laine, *Feeling Cinema: Emotional Dynamics in Film Studies* (London: Continuum, 2011), 9.

6. Laine, *Feeling Cinema*, 9.

7. Webster, "Bombs and Villainy in London," 16.

8. Lejeune, "One for All, and All for One," 14.

9. See Charles Bennett, *Hitchcock's Partner in Suspense: The Life of Screenwriter Charles Bennett* (Lexington: University Press of Kentucky, 2014).

10. Paula Marantz Cohen, "The Ideological Transformation of Conrad's *The Secret Agent* into Hitchcock's *Sabotage*," *Literature Film Quarterly* 22, no. 3 (1994): 206.

11. Cohen, "The Ideological Transformation," 201.

12. Cohen, "The Ideological Transformation," 206.

13. Matthew Carlson, "Conrad's *The Secret Agent*, Hitchcock's *Sabotage*, and the Inspiration of 'Public Uneasiness,'" in *Hitchcock and Adaptation: On the Page and Screen* ed. Mark Osteen (Lanham, MD: Rowman & Littlefield, 2014), 111.

14. Carlson, "Conrad's *The Secret Agent*," 116.

15. Mark Osteen, "'It Doesn't Pay to Antagonize the Public': Sabotage and Hitchcock's Audience," *Literature and Film Quarterly* 28, no. 4 (2020): 263.

16. Osteen, "'It Doesn't Pay to Antagonize the Public,'" 263.

17. Osteen, "'It Doesn't Pay to Antagonize the Public,'" 265.

18. Osteen, "'It Doesn't Pay to Antagonize the Public,'" 266.

19. Linda Williams, "Discipline and Fun: *Psycho* and Postmodern Cinema," in *Alfred Hitchcock's Psycho: A Casebook*, ed. Robert Kolker (Oxford: Oxford University Press, 2004), 164–204.

20. Wear, review of *The Woman Alone*, directed by Alfred Hitchcock, *Variety*, March 3, 1937, 14.

21. Laine, *Feeling Cinema*, 35.

22. Alfred Hitchcock, "Let 'Em Play God [1948]," in *Hitchcock on Hitchcock: Selected Writings and Interviews*, ed. Sidney Gottlieb (London: Faber & Faber, 1995), 113–115.

23. Laura Mulvey, *Death 24x a Second: Stillness and the Moving Image* (London: Reaktion Books), 30–31.

24. Laine, *Feeling Cinema*, 35.

25. Laine, *Feeling Cinema*, 148n12.

26. Laine, *Feeling Cinema*, 35–36.

27. Mulvey, *Death 24x a Second*, 31–32.

28. See Jan Plamper, *The History of Emotions: An Introduction*, trans. Keith Tribe (Oxford: Oxford University Press, 2017), 214–218.

29. Miriam Bratu Hansen, *Cinema and Experience: Siegfried Kracauer, Walter Benjamin, Theodor Adorno* (Berkeley: University of California Press, 2012).

30. Alfred Hitchcock, "Search for the Sun [1937]," in *Hitchcock on Hitchcock*, 250–252.

31. Jacques Rivette, "De l'abjection," *Cahiers du cinéma* 120 (June 1961): 54–55. A translation by David Phelps with the assistance of Jeremi Szaniawski can be found at http://www.dvdbeaver.com/rivette/ok/abjection.html.

32. See also the discussion in Daniel Fairfax, *The Red Years of Cahiers du Cinéma (1968–1973)*, Vol. II: *Aesthetics and Ontology*, 2 vols. (Amsterdam: Amsterdam University Press, 2021), 799–801.

33. Brian Massumi, *Parables for the Virtual: Movement, Affect, Sensation* (Durham, NC: Duke University Press, 2002), 35. Italics in the original.

34. See Constance Bantman, *Jean Grave and the Networks of French Anarchism, 1854–1939* (London: Palgrave, 2021).

35. Vlad Solomon, *State Surveillance, Political Policing and Counter-Terrorism in Britain 1880–1914* (Woodbridge: Boydell Press, 2021), 145–146.

36. Solomon, *State Surveillance*, 146.

37. Ina Rae Hark attempts to see the films of the period as political but does not include *Sabotage* in her discussion of the films. See "Keeping Your Amateur Standing: Audience Participation and Good Citizenship in Hitchcock's Political Films," *Cinema Journal* 29, no. 2 (1990): 8–22.

38. Massumi, *Parables for the Virtual*, 173.

39. Massumi, *Parables for the Virtual*, 173.

5

Rebecca (1940)

The impure object of vision

Bruce Isaacs

The opening sequence of Hitchcock's *Rebecca* (1940), the elaborate introduction to Manderley, opens not with an image of the estate—as one might expect from the voice-over prompt, "Last night I dreamt I went to Manderley again"—but with an image of a bank of fog moving slowly across a full moon hanging low in the sky (see Figure 5.1).[1] Emerging from the credit sequence, we enter into a single shot of some duration, holding the distinct shape of the moon as the voice-over commences. The shot is an explicit marker of time (of nighttime, or the gray shade of dusk), place (the metonymic Manderley that will stand in for the psychic dramas that structure the story), and diegetic setting. Whether the association is intentional or not, in the conspicuousness of the shot of the moon—set apart from any relationship to the physical site of the building and its surrounds, holding the image of Manderley at abeyance as if to build the spectator's anticipation of the reveal—one cannot but see the image of the moon cut by a layer of cloud in Luis Buñuel and Salvador Dalí's *Un Chien Andalou* (*The Andalusian Dog*, 1929) (see Figure 5.2). Buñuel and Dalí first screened their hugely influential surrealist film in Paris in 1929, at much the same time that Hitchcock was developing a philosophy of film form, which he termed "pure cinema," following in the footsteps of the European avant-garde film artists. The notion of a pure cinema ethos, which I will attempt to read in Hitchcock's construction of the opening sequence of *Rebecca*, grew swiftly out of a creative sojourn in Europe, where he spent some time with the Expressionist experimental filmmaker F. W. Murnau and other artistic and philosophical thinkers working in the film medium.[2]

The same diegetic content—a moon suspended in the sky as clouds obscure it—is framed somewhat differently in *Un Chien Andalou*. In Buñuel and Dalí, the moon is more overtly expressive in design, bearing that aesthetic artifice that marked a great deal of surrealist art of the period. And

Bruce Isaacs, Rebecca *(1940)* In: *One Shot Hitchcock*. Edited by: Luke Robinson and Melanie Robson, Oxford University Press. © Oxford University Press 2024. DOI: 10.1093/oso/9780197682876.003.0005

Figure 5.1 The moon behind the clouds in the opening shot of Alfred Hitchcock's *Rebecca* (1940).

Figure 5.2 Luis Buñuel's *Un Chien Andalou* (*The Andalusian Dog*, 1929).

yet, intriguingly, the two sequences are strikingly similar. The moon is vertically centered in each frame (with *Un Chien Andalou*'s moon in the left third) rather than placed in the upper third, as would be more commonplace in a traditional exterior establishing shot. This is to say that for both films, one a surrealist experiment with psychic ideas and counter-narrative impulses, the other a fairly conventional, story-based suspense melodrama, these are not *establishing shots.* They are not merely, or exclusively, deictic signifiers but mark something more than time, place, and diegetic information. Against the convention of most opening shots establishing a diegetic frame for the spectator, rather than pointing *to something*—that is, to story, or character, or the time and place of setting—they reflect back upon themselves, upon the creation of the artistic form and representation, pointing reflexively to the site of the work of art as a formal experiment.

In each sequence, the moon within the frame is designed to function as the object of the gaze of the spectator, set in some relief from the movement of the cloud. Each sequence depicts the movement of cloud from right to left, cutting across the face of the moon. While the framing differs in notable ways—shot scale, the clarity of the moon against the cloud, and so on—each sequence exists to partially obscure the central object of vision: the illuminated moon. Both films, in more pervasive thematic and philosophical terms, are about conjuring presences out of the ephemera of past lives, and it becomes clear that these opening sequences are metonymic compositions signifying vision's essential opacity, or vision's incapacity to "see."

Buñuel and Dalí's famous image carried the weight of symbolism of the surrealist movement; the modernist artist's mission to challenge the nature of perception itself is neatly encapsulated in the suture of a moon sliced by cloud to an eyeball sliced by a razor. Hitchcock is less shocking in the cut to the front entrance of Manderley and the momentarily deferred entry to the estate, but this obfuscation of the object of vision as a formal and philosophical idea—and as a formal visual trope that would come to take on great significance for both the surrealists and Hitchcock—is as much an aesthetic and philosophical principle in the Manderley sequence as it is in *Un Chien Andalou.* The moon illuminates the estate and its looming structure, catching it in that liminal space between day and night. But the moon also illuminates a visual field prior to our encounter with Manderley that places the spectator in the liminal space of "being there"—being steadfastly in place—while also being imagined or subjectively perceived. While Hitchcock permits us to enter the estate and move along its winding path to center our gaze upon Manderley, that visual itinerary is interceded by surreptitious and shifting shadows, mist, fog, and densely hanging cloud, while the desired object of the gaze is at every turn barred by gates, trees, and thick foliage.

From literary and cinematic images

One way of thinking about the obfuscation of the object of vision as a reflexive stylistic trope is to read it in contradistinction to the corresponding passage of Daphne du Maurier's novel, published in 1938. The novel carries the formal characteristics of both melodrama and Gothic horror in which a protagonist-subject (the wanderer-subject of Rebecca's dream) "is dwarfed by a colossal space that engulfs and imprisons her."[3] Such structures tend to grossly exaggerate the effect of space on the subject, which gives the Gothic genre its layers of symbolic charge. This dwarfing of the woman further diminishes the woman as subject within her own paranoia. The narrator's dreaming of Manderley (the dream is in this sense a paranoid, spatially distorted projection) could explain the apparitional quality Hitchcock brings to the mise-en-scène of the film sequence; that is, we are supposed to take Manderley as part of the narrator's dream, and thus as part of a paranoid, debilitating fantasy.[4]

But we need to make a further distinction between the thematic of gothic melodrama that Hitchcock appropriates from du Maurier (one would not be able to adapt the novel without appropriating the narrative and visual tropes of the gothic genre) and the visual compositional form we see in the film sequence, which I am suggesting is a filmic experiment that radically departs from du Maurier's literary precedent. It is true that du Maurier casts the image of Manderley as part of a dream: "I called in my dream to the lodgekeeper"; and "Then, like all dreamers, I was possessed of a sudden with supernatural powers and passed like a spirit through the barrier before me."[5] Hitchcock actually uses this literary image as a way into the film sequence, which provides him with the potential for an innovative camera maneuver: as the camera moves toward the gate, approximating the smooth gait of a dreamer, it "passes like a spirit" through the gate and into the winding pathway. Christina G. Petersen describes such a visual effects trope as a physical impediment to the heroine's subjective development or self-realization.[6] Orson Welles would use a similar technique a year later to barricade the young Charles Foster Kane from Mr. Thatcher in an early sequence of *Citizen Kane* (1941).

Reading du Maurier's first chapter, which describes the narrator's dream of returning to Manderley, I'm struck by the crispness and concreteness of du Maurier's depiction of the estate: "No smoke came from the chimney, and the little lattice windows gaped forlorn"; "I bent my head forward to avoid the low swinging branch of a tree"; "The woods . . . crowded, dark and uncontrolled, to the borders of the drive. The beeches with white, naked limbs leant close to one another, their branches intermingled in a strange embrace, making a vault above my head, like the archway of a church."[7] As the novel's narrator wanders along the path, she is precise in her description of what she sees; objects are brought into relief from their surroundings or stand out from a play of light and shadow, and from the heavy bank of fog that one might imagine looming over the estate if one had seen Hitchcock's film before reading du Maurier's novel. Of the object of vision in its stunning literary revelation, the narrator provides the starkest visual description: "There was Manderley . . . the grey stone shining in the moonlight of my dream, the mullioned windows reflecting the green lawns and the terrace."[8] Yes, these are dreamed images, but they are also the perfectly composed images of a narrator seeing the place in its uncontaminated, uncompromised, and coherent *fullness*. If the dream is a projection, it is a projection through the literary mechanics of solid, crystalline, demarcated word-images—which is to say that du Maurier's narrator, while dreaming her return to Manderley, has no difficulty in seeing the place for what it is.

For Hitchcock, the dreamed estate of Manderley has none of the literary narrator's clarity of vision. After our surrealist moment with the image of the moon and all it promises about the obscurity of vision, the film image pauses on a medium-long shot of the gates of Manderley. The image holds on the gates as a shadow is slowly lifted from the frame; that is, the gates are revealed, and materialize, out of the shadows. For du Maurier's narrator, there is immediately the visual acuity to perceive "a padlock and a chain upon the gate."[9] Hitchcock's narrator does not have such visual acuity within the filmic mise-en-scène. In the subjective storytelling mode of the literary sequence, point of view is fixed. But as is common with the expressive modes of cinematic storytelling we see in the surrealist tradition and a great deal of Hitchcock's cinema of this period, the subjective point of view of the narrator is conflated with the point of view of the camera, which has the effect of configuring a mode of vision radically out of joint. We open with a medium-long shot of the gates. As the image comes to life, attempting to contrive the dream-movement of the narrator, the camera setup destabilizes the viewing position, crudely shifting the camera view to the left (my guess would be that this was an unintentional jitter brought about by the weight of the rig in its initial movement), which immediately configures a non-human, technological gaze. As the gaze moves through the gates and along the path, in addition to the obscurity of vision, Hitchcock's narrator is a cinematic, rather than strictly literary, "seer."

The lifting of the shadow presaging the movement toward the gate resembles the raising of curtains, a commonplace trope of the cinematic experience in the early 1940s. I can't help seeing this lifting of the shadow as the reflexive raising of the curtains of the simulacral cinematic frame,[10] a stylistic reflexivity Hitchcock almost certainly appropriated from the European avant-garde cinemas, and which we see again in some of his most famous films, such as *Rope* (1948) and *Rear Window* (1954). The framing of the gates is a striking deep-focus composition, with gates in foreground (revealed only at the instant of the curtain raise), an undefined darkness in midground, and the solid bank of fog that marks the majority of space contained within the expansive depth of field. The composition is designed to submerge the visual object beneath a pall of imperceptible visual fields. Du Maurier's literary framing in close-up—"a padlock and a chain upon a gate"—is eschewed for the impressionistic, surrealist imagery of an impure visual form. These are not indistinct wide shots as much as varying shot scales of objects beyond the capacity of the gaze of the narrator and spectator. The suggestion of a surrealist aesthetic sensibility is also apt, I would suggest, in the context of Hitchcock's fascination with surrealist art and representation, and his explicit rendering of surrealist images in films such as *Spellbound* (1945), *Vertigo* (1958), and *Marnie* (1964).

The narrator's curiously disembodied movement along the path (conjuring the surrealist excess that overwhelms the natural movements of du Maurier's narrator) is again plagued by imperfect vision of the objects within the frame. The image is composed through sudden alterations in focal depth and peripheral shadows to shift objects in and out of visual fields; that is, the path and its surrounds move in and out of vision, taking form only momentarily, and then obliquely, before again dissolving into the frame with a shift in focal length or an intensification of shadow. The shadow cast by the moon as the cloud passes over its visage is replicated in the shadows that move over the path, bringing a sudden darkness to any part of the frame that threatens illumination. The fixed, steadfastly embodied gaze of du Maurier's narrator—"and it was only when I bent my head" or "I stood, my heart thumping in my breast, the strange prick of tears behind my eyes"[11]—is dissolved in a visual perception that desires form and order but must settle for the inadequacies of visual form and perception.

When the narrator comes upon Manderley, the film's visual itinerary breaks most forcefully from du Maurier's literacy precedent. Du Maurier's "perfect symmetry of form" captured in the narrator's words cannot match the disjointed striatic images that mark Hitchcock's Manderley. du Maurier's narrator describes an image untainted by time, place, and subjective viewpoint: "time could not wreck the perfect symmetry of those walls."[12] In encountering the image of Manderley for the first time in Hitchcock's *Rebecca*, we see that there are no perfect symmetries in the expressive composition of the filmic image. The matte image sutures material to non-material objects, rendering the space through miniatures, models, and drawings of ephemeral shapes, lines, and patterns. Whether intentional or not, there is a brief moment toward the conclusion of the sequence in which it appears that one shot has been sutured to another to artificially contrive the flow and fluidity of an uninterrupted shot. But even with this intention to establish the clarity of the gaze of du Maurier's narrator, in the cinematic rendering of space, the fleeting dissolve only renders the whole further from the spectator's perceptual grasp.

Reflexive visual form: Miniatures and mattes

Aggravated by David O. Selznick's micromanagement of the production,[13] Hitchcock ultimately regarded *Rebecca* as a minor work within his oeuvre. In his estimation, *Rebecca* does not shirk its literary formalism, and he certainly never accorded it a special status as "pure cinema"; I'll return to this notion of pure cinema in the final part of this chapter. But *Rebecca* is notable because it is the one film that marks a decisive break from the British cinema. There are experimental moments throughout Hitchcock's work in Britain, and the visual effects Petersen identifies in *Rebecca* are part of a larger stylistic ethos at least as early as *The Lodger: A Story of the London Fog* (1927). But my sense is that the Manderley sequence represents a departure from the British-era formalism in the elaborateness of its design, in its willingness to break from source material, and most significant, in its explicit, in its reflexive meditation on cinematic vision. I've noted several markers of cinematic reflexivity in this opening sequence alone, some explicit, some more subtle, such as the association between Hitchcock's film and Buñuel and Dalí's *Un Chien Andalou.* I've further argued that Hitchcock's image of Manderley was reflexively cinematic in its formal obscurity and deliberate obfuscation of the object of vision; in contrast, du Maurier's literary image is marked by the clarity of its subjective vision, even if that subjectivity is compromised by trauma.

This distinction between cinematic and literary images also marks a distinction between cinematic and literary modes of subjective seeing. We could say that there can exist no cinematic seeing that operates purely within a diegetic world, that is, the hermetic story-world of the film. The cinematic gaze is necessarily a technological way of seeing and feeling; I would argue that this principle applies to any form of technologically produced image of movement. In stark contrast to the technologically produced cinematic image, subjective seeing within a novel such as du Maurier's *Rebecca* rarely breaks out of a literary diegesis. Characters conventionally see within a world, ordered by the structure of story, character, and the subjective perceptions that make narration possible. Words are the component elements that create larger units of representation, such as clauses, sentences, and so on, but they do not produce visual perception in the literal sense. This ontological capacity of the cinematic image (and cinematic vision) to break from the essential reality-index of an image would obsess Hitchcock for the remainder of his filmmaking life, and it is explored with greater confidence as he becomes increasingly ensconced in the American studio system.[14] *Rebecca* is therefore the moment of rupture from the British era because the formulaic template of the Hollywood melodrama accommodates a distinctive, experimental, reflexive filmic idiom. This synthesis of experimental visual style and the mechanics of classical narrative form would have a lasting impact on post-classical American cinemas.

Another way of illustrating this ontological chasm between the novel and film is to remind oneself, when watching the film, that the entire construct of Manderley in this opening sequence is an intricate assemblage of miniatures that emerge from a wider matte composition, and that Hitchcock used matte composition for several elaborate façades of the structure.[15] The miniature and matte composition lends itself to the artifice of technologically produced images. In essence, from a compositional point of view, a matte is "any form of artwork or photographic element designed to prevent exposure in a selected area of a photographic image."[16] In the classical era of

Hollywood, with a limited range of effects compositional tools (relative to the 1970s, 1980s, and beyond), a matte enabled a form of design "layering," that is, building whole or complete visual fields through the assemblage of multiple image fields. There are various approaches to the use of mattes as compositional tools, but this principle remains: a matte enables a full image to be produced out of component parts or visual field fragments. The conventional use of the matte provides the visual impression of depth of field such that all objects situated within the frame compose a harmonious whole, with each object within the frame in harmonious relationship to every other object. The dominant aesthetic impulse when using mattes during the classical era was the production of perceptual realism, and Hollywood production was extraordinarily successful at producing realistic mattes through visual effects photography.[17] As Keil and Whissel argue, the rise in the use of matte drawings in the classical era was driven both by the desire for an increased perceptual reality emanating from the image, and by a clearer, more precise synchronization with the recorded soundtrack.[18]

However, the matte is also part of another aesthetic and philosophical trajectory that tends toward formal visual fragmentation. This is to say that, in terms of its ontological basis, a matte is a compositional assemblage of parts that may obfuscate but never entirely do away with its fragments. While the seams within the matte composition are commonly elided, there is nothing within compositional capacity that determines that all images should be designed that way. The matte composition might also reveal holistic composition as a design composite, a stitching together of multiple parts within a rationalizing process of assemblage. There is therefore an important distinction between the use of the matte as segmented framing and the use of the matte as a focalized depth of field, containing all objects within the image. I would argue that this distinction is equivalent to the distinction between a mise-en-scène founded upon the fragment of an image (which we see, e.g., in a matte process), and a mise-en-scène founded upon the image as an uncontaminated, photographic whole. Hitchcock made extensive use of mattes, miniatures and models, rear projection, and other assemblage effects throughout his long career. There are expressive moments in Hitchcock's British and American cinema in which complex depth-of-field components hold in duration, revealing the fragmented composition of the frame. Again locating *Rebecca* as a seminal moment in Hitchcock's aesthetic and philosophical development of the image, we see in the façade of Manderley (in brief moments of the opening sequence but more explicitly in the final sequence of the film) a striking compositional matte that formally breaks from the classical harmonious narration of du Maurier's literary image of the mansion.

The film's narrator presents the mansion as if it is revealed in its fullness, without impediment to our seeing: "And finally, there was Manderley." The description of the structure emphasizes the abstract, expressionistic form, seen through shadow and half-light. The narrated description resorts to abstract cues, such as the question of "symmetry" or the play of light on walls. In du Maurier's novel, the narrator confidently moves from the abstract to the detail of figuration: "the grey stone shining," "the mullioned windows reflecting." However, this perceptual detail is not rendered in the technological gaze of the film; that is, Hitchcock's composited Manderley is thus explicitly abstracted from the concreteness of du Maurier's literary figurative form.

Matte composition in Hitchcock's framing of the structure of Manderley is better thought of as the imperfect assemblage of compositional fragments, set into imperfect relation, and contriving an elemental impurity of the cinematic visual field. The cinematic gaze has thus far wandered along the path leading from the gate, undulating with the uneven terrain of the path, contriving what I have called a cinematic subjectivity. The unsteady gaze pauses as Manderley is revealed in a shadowy long shot, holding on the façade of the building. The shot now transitions to a closer perspective of the figuration of the structure, emerging out of a slow dissolve (the transition between shots), conjuring the dream-like, apparitional quality the narrator attaches to the experience. This movement is in large part adapted faithfully from the prompts of du Maurier's literary narrativization. The slow dissolve traditionally contrives a sense of flow, or fluidity, and therein, some vague perception of spatial and temporal continuity.

However, we need to see the function of the cinematic dissolve separately from the literary narrational marker insofar as the dissolve is also a highly expressive mode of montage and renders excessively visible the compositional form that contains the image. That is, the dissolve brings the fragmented seams within the composition into a starker relation to the compositional whole. The frame configures the following visually fragmented parts: at the extreme foreground of the image, the limbs of a tree (likely a matte addition) cut the visual field with stark black lines, some thick, others thin and spindly. The tree limbs are part of the compositional whole, that is, part of the visual field composition that denotes the structure of Manderley in its surroundings (see Figure 5.3). However, the limbs clearly also point to the cinematic

Figure 5.3 The opening shot of *Rebecca*: Manderley in a surrealist dreamscape.

(viewing) frame that conjures a second order signification, or what I've suggested is a reflexive cinematic gaze. The camera then moves past the tree limbs to gaze with greater clarity on the façade of the building, shifting from left to right within the frame in a continuous movement. In a long shot, the image maintains some semblance of the whole, and some reassurance for the spectator of what André Bazin called an "aesthetic of reality."[19] But as the cinematic gaze moves in, it perceives with greater detail and greater specificity the composition in miniature. This is not the detail of du Maurier's literary subjectivization; there is in effect nothing to "see" in this façade of Manderley apart from the expressive façade itself and the markers of its compositional artifice: the fragmented assemblage of material and non-material forms that configure a filmic version of Manderley. I therefore agree with Petersen in her excellent reading of the function of such effects over and above the function of narration. Of the structure in miniature, she writes: "In this sense, the perfect miniature, such as those of Manderley . . . further encouraged the viewer's hesitation between the real and unreal elements of the text and an appreciation for the image as a representation rather than a reproduction of space."[20] Still, I think we can take this notion of a distinction between representation and reproduction further. I would argue that the image is neither purely denotative nor connotative (a representational signifier), but nearer to an onto-logical reproduction of the formal properties of image fragments contained within the miniature and matte configuration. If we take the image at façade value—that is, to see it for what it is—our gaze of the object is imperfect, and the object in its compositional frame impure in the visibility of its artifice.

In this composition, Hitchcock configures the Manderley façade as a graphic assemblage of forms. This is the kind of graphic effects practice that marked the history of visual effects production within the Hollywood system but remained a subterranean aesthetic impulse in a system that was revered primarily for its capacity to reproduce, with stunning fidelity, perceptual realism. It is curious though understandable that, with greater and greater tools for image manipulation at its disposal, the dominant aesthetic tendency within the classical Hollywood studio cinema leaned away from the artistic and philosophical possibilities of graphic rendering, abstract composition, and an emphasis on the building blocks of image form—line, shape, pattern, symmetry, space, and so on—such as we see in a film like *Rebecca*, or even more emphatically in Hitchcock's American films of the late 1940s, 1950s, and 1960s.

Pure and impure cinema

This chapter is an attempt to think through and tentatively suggest a resolution to the paradox of what Hitchcock described as a form of cinematic vision, or perhaps better, cinematic *perception*. Hitchcock often meditated on what he called "pure cinema," or a "purely cinematic film," and he recalled this idea in his interviews and writing throughout most of his filmmaking career.[21] As early as 1937, in a brief reflection on the directorial process, he already evinces cinematic form as a process of assemblage, a collating and patterning of fragments rather than a reproduction of an a priori whole: "I want to put my film together on the screen, not simply to photograph something that has been put together already in the form of a long piece of stage acting. This is what gives an effect of life to a picture—the feeling that when you see it on the screen you are watching something that has been conceived and brought to birth directly in visual terms."[22] This is a fascinating and complex statement about the elemental parts of cinematic form. We can distill a great deal of Hitchcock's approach to the visual image in attaching this statement to the Manderley composition. My sense is that there is a great deal of misunderstanding in what Hitchcock meant by the phrase "pure cinema." Pure cinema for Hitchcock was essentially a philosophical disposition toward the material to be captured on film. But underpinning this philosophical disposition is a way of thinking about the ontological properties of the image. Hitchcock's images desire a pure reproduction of reality as whole in only the most literal and banal sense. That is to say that, working within the realist-oriented industry of classical Hollywood in the 1940s, 1950s, and 1960s, all of Hitchcock's films are marked by a foundational fidelity to realistic narrative form; and realist narrative design requires compositional coherence (or continuity) for sense-making.

In this examination of the opening sequence of *Rebecca*, I have to tried to demonstrate a point of origin of an experimental mode of filmmaking Hitchcock introduced into the studio system. At the basis of this experimental mode is a philosophical disposition toward the impurity of visual form. Like Bazin, Hitchcock seems to attach some greater significance to the aesthetic and philosophical potential of the image than to the aesthetic potential of the real in its ideal form. Oddly enough, Hitchcock and Bazin seem closely connected in their address of the possibilities of cinematic form to make something more of the raw materials of experience, and each frequently spoke, wrote, and meditated on the creative potential of film images to do this. It is unfortunate that Hitchcock called what he attempted to understand "pure cinema," which connotes problematic and somewhat paradoxical values of fidelity to reality, truth, and harmonious form. Hitchcock's films—and most especially the fleeting avant-garde experimentation we see in sequences in films such as *The Birds* (1963) and *Marnie* (1964)—did not seek the reproduction of an a priori realism or classical form. In this sense, the 1940 composition of Manderley should be seen as a stunning aesthetic and philosophical break from a classical aesthetic norm.

Notes

1. In this chapter, I address the film's entry to Manderley in terms of several discrete shots that comprise a long duration coverage of the path that leads to the estate, and the reveal of the estate itself. However, I do want to emphasize that the traditional language of "shots" and "cuts" is often inadequate to the task of describing cinematic images in montage. Thus, I argue throughout this piece that the several shots encompass and contain a continuous thematic and formal compositional whole.

2. Sidney Gottlieb, "Early Hitchcock: The German Influence," in *Framing Hitchcock: Selected Essays from the Hitchcock Annual*, ed. Sidney Gottlieb and Christopher Brookhouse (Detroit: Wayne State University Press, 2002), 35–58.

3. Christina G. Petersen, "Impossible Spaces: Gothic Special Effects and Feminine Subjectivity," in *Gothic Heroines on Screen: Representation, Interpretation, and Feminist Inquiry*," ed. Tamar Jeffers McDonald and Frances Kamm (London: Routledge, 2019), 57.

4. In her seminal study of 1940s Hollywood "women's films," including *Rebecca*, Mary Ann Doane reads the representation of female desire as a paranoid form of the female gaze. See Mary Ann Doane, *The Desire to Desire: The Women's Film of the 1940s* (Bloomington: Indiana University Press, 1987). For a provocative reading of the repression of the lesbian gaze in the figuration of the Manderley estate, see Annamarie Jagose, *Inconsequence: Lesbian Representation and the Logic of Sexual Sequence* (Ithaca, NY: Cornell University Press, 2002), 109–111.

5. Daphne du Maurier, *Rebecca* (London: Penguin Books, 2007), 5.

6. Petersen, "Impossible Spaces," 58–59.

7. Du Maurier, *Rebecca*, 5.

8. Du Maurier, *Rebecca*, 6.

9. Du Maurier, *Rebecca*, 5.

10. Bruce Isaacs, *The Art of Pure Cinema: Hitchcock and His Imitators* (New York: Oxford University Press, 2020), 2.

11. Du Maurier, *Rebecca*, 5, 6.

12. Du Maurier, *Rebecca*, 6.

13. François Truffaut with Helen G. Scott, *Hitchcock*, rev. ed, (1966; New York: Simon & Schuster, 1985), 127.

14. The most famous examples of "cinematic perception" in Hitchcock's corpus include the "Vertigo Shot" (*Vertigo*, 1958) and the subjective camera gaze deployed throughout his later masterpiece, *Frenzy* (1972). For an extended analysis of cinematic perception in Hitchcockian cinema, see Isaacs, *The Art of Pure Cinema*.

15. Truffaut and Scott, *Hitchcock*, 132. For a useful discussion of the importance of matte and miniature effects in *Rebecca*, see Craig Barron, "New Interview with Craig Barron on *Rebecca's* Visual Effects," *Rebecca* (Sony Criterion Collection Blu-ray, 2017).

16. Mark Sawicki, *Filming the Fantastic: A Guide to Visual Effects Cinematography* (Waltham, MA: Focal Press, 2011), 43.

17. See Barron. For an historical overview of the relationship between visual effects production and the realist aesthetic, see Julie Turnock, *Plastic Reality: Special Effects, Technology, and the Emergence of 1970s Blockbuster Aesthetics* (New York: Columbia University Press, 2015), especially the introduction and chapter 1.

18. Kristen Whissel and Charlie Keil, "Introduction," in *Editing and Special/Visual Effects*, ed. Kristen Whissel and Charlie Keil (New Brunswick, NJ: Rutgers University Press, 2016), 17–18. For a multilayered historical reading of the interrelationship of digital effects and photography, Stephen Prince, *Digital Visual Effects in Cinema: The Seduction of Reality* (New Brunswick, NJ: Rutgers University Press, 2012).

19. André Bazin, "An Aesthetic of Reality: Cinematic Realism and the Italian School of Liberation," in *What Is Cinema?*, trans. and ed. Hugh Gray, 2 vols. (Berkeley: University of California Press, 1967), 2:16–40.

20. Petersen, "Impossible Spaces," 60.

21. Truffaut and Scott, *Hitchcock*, 214.

22. Alfred Hitchcock, "Direction (1937)," in *Hitchcock on Hitchcock: Selected Writings and Interviews*, ed. Sidney Gottlieb (Berkeley: University of California Press, 1997), 255–256.

6

Shadow of a Doubt (1943)

Performing a murder(er)

Melanie Robson

"What's worrying you?" asked Hitch.

"I've never played a murderer before, and here I am looking in the mirror at one who's nationally known as The Merry Widow Murderer."

"And you want me to tell you how a murderer behaves," stated Hitch.

"You're the expert," I said.[1]

This exchange is part of a conversation between Alfred Hitchcock and Joseph Cotten, recounted in the latter's autobiography. Cotten recalls the meeting he had with Hitchcock to discuss his character, Charlie Oakley, in the then-upcoming film *Shadow of a Doubt* (1943). According to Cotten, Hitchcock invited him to take a stroll down Rodeo Drive in Los Angeles and asked him to comment when they passed someone who he thought looked like a murderer. After observing one man walking down the street with "shifty eyes," and Claudette Colbert emerging from a car, neither of whom the men could be certain was a murderer, Cotten began to understand Hitchcock's exercise. "What you're trying to say," Cotten remarked to Hitchcock, "[is] that a murderer looks and moves just like anyone else."[2] Cotten's revelation in that moment speaks to the heart of the construction of his character in the film, as well as the crux of this chapter. In examining a single shot from *Shadow of a Doubt*, this chapter draws on two key ideas that emerge from this exchange between Cotten and Hitchcock. First and most important, the character of Oakley essentially comprises two personas—a murderer and a loving family man—the latter of whom is used as a façade to conceal the former. His ability to blend into average American suburbia without his nefarious alter ego

Melanie Robson, Shadow of a Doubt *(1943)* In: *One Shot Hitchcock*. Edited by: Luke Robinson and Melanie Robson, Oxford University Press. © Oxford University Press 2024. DOI: 10.1093/oso/9780197682876.003.0006 being detected is central to the film's plot and character development, and this dimension was intentional, evidenced by Hitchcock's Rodeo Drive exercise. Second, Cotten's status as an experienced actor but a novice in playing murderers assists in developing a particular kind of performance and viewer engagement that will be further examined in this chapter.

Shadow of a Doubt is Hitchcock's thirtieth feature film, and was arguably his favorite.[3] Set in Santa Rosa, California, it is about an "average family," the Newtons, of which the eldest daughter, also named Charlie (Teresa Wright), is feeling disillusioned by her dull life and is "waiting for a miracle."[4] When her namesake, Uncle Charlie, spontaneously arrives in town, her spirits are lifted by the close familial bond they share. When two detectives posing as journalists also arrive in pursuit of Uncle Charlie, young Charlie's suspicions are aroused about whether her uncle is the sweet, innocent man she presumed he was. Uncle Charlie, it appears, is responsible for a slew of murders of middle-aged widows in northeast United States. Of particular interest to this chapter is the way in which Uncle Charlie transforms from his façade of family man to his inner self as a murderer, principally through a combination of Cotten's performance and Hitchcock's framing. To avoid confusion between the names of the two characters, I will adopt the designations used by William Rothman of Charles to refer to Uncle Charlie and Charlie to refer to his niece.[5]

The specific shot at the focus of this chapter occurs about two-thirds of the way through the film. The scene in which the shot appears is the final of three scenes in which the Newton family sit around a dinner table eating, always with Charles at the head, his sister Emma (Patricia Collinge) at the other end, her children Ann (Edna May Wonacott) and Roger (Charles Bates) between them, and their father, Joe (Henry Travers), and Charlie on the other side. By this point, Charlie has developed strong suspicions of her uncle's murderous past, after becoming more acquainted with one of the detectives and doing some research at the local library. In this scene, she appears almost fearful of Charles, while her family continue to playfully banter with him, entirely unaware of any question over his devious past. Joe's friend, Herb (Hume Cronyn), has impolitely interrupted dinner to continue indulging Joe in his obsession with true crime. Herb is perched on a seat nearby and the camera frames a two-shot of him and Joe quietly discussing murder. The particular shot of interest begins with a sound bridge: Charlie exclaims, "oh, what's the matter with you two? Do you always have to talk about killing people?" A wide shot

Figure 6.1 Conversations about murder around the family dinner table in Alfred Hitchcock's *Shadow of a Doubt* (1943).

captures the whole dinner table, with Charlie now standing (see Figure 6.1). Charlie's misdirected rage stems from her suspicions about Charles and her discomfort at sitting with him on her left while murder is being discussed to her right. She storms out of the house, and instead of following her, the camera hurriedly tracks toward Charles's face and rests on a medium close-up (see Figure 6.2). He reassures the family he'll "catch up with her," as he stands up, and the camera continues to follow him out the door.

This shot continues a pattern of close-ups of Charles's face that confirm that the viewer's scrutiny of his innocence is equally important as his family's. Each prior close-up has revealed two distinct characters in Charles's face: a friendly, smiling face when his family are looking at him, and a deadpan, cold stare when they look away. The shot under interrogation in this chapter is the first time we see this duality of character merge into one. His smile has faded, and the double meaning of his words ("I'll catch up with her") invoke both the sense of potential assault and concern for a loved one. In this chapter I will investigate the way the film's suspense and the viewer's suspicion are

Figure 6.2 Charles Oakley's (Joseph Cotten) cold stare betrays his murderous past in *Shadow of a Doubt*.

manipulated by Cotten's shifting facial expressions by focusing on the moment his character shifts from loved uncle to manipulative murderer. To achieve this, I also consider the casting of Cotten in this role, and how the film draws on expectations of his typical character as being a kind, respectable figure. Such expectations are, at first, confirmed, but ultimately denied by scrutinizing Cotten's facial expressions in moments like this shot.

Façades

The driving force behind *Shadow of a Doubt*'s plot is the construction, maintenance, and dissolving of façades to conceal corruption and deviance. Charles's relationship with the Newton family is predicated on his façade of a loving, friendly, and trustworthy uncle. Through the early part of his visit to Santa Rosa, his close relationship to both his sister, Emma, and his niece, Charlie, is frequently emphasized through physical affection, gleaming smiles across the dinner table, and reminiscences of childhood. This façade substantially differs from the man he is revealed to be as the film proceeds, and this is reflected in his changing behavior around and toward the Newton family. Particularly crucial to the shot under investigation is that it marks the specific moment when this façade is entirely dissolved, at least in terms of Charles's presentation to his family.

The concept of façades extends, however, beyond performance and behavior and is signaled initially in the mise-en-scène. Numerous critics have observed the significance of the film's principal setting in Santa Rosa. Rothman names it a "storybook American town," representing "the cheery world of sentimental Americana."[6] It is a setting out of place in Hitchcock's oeuvre, contrasting with his more typically expressionistic mise-en-scène, but highly reflective of the world conjured by the film's screenwriter Thornton Wilder in his most famous play *Our Town* (1938). Santa Rosa is introduced via a series of shots of streetscapes. Hitchcock emphasizes the apparent innocence of the town through a low-angle shot of a smiling policeman assisting with traffic control and children riding by on bicycles. The Newton's house is presented as a typical American two-story weatherboard on a leafy Californian street. James McLaughlin observes that by characterizing Santa Rosa in this way, it operates in stark opposition to the truth about Charles's criminal past. He states, "the façade of the Newton family home . . . is composed of sweetness and sunshine; behind it, however, lies, in the words of Uncle Charlie, 'a foul sty.'"[7] The literal façade of the house stands in for the façade Charles presents to the Newton family, of kindness and innocence.

The specific way in which each of the Charlies is introduced to the viewer also reaffirms the idea of concealment. We first meet both of them through montages of the city and town where they respectively live, and then subsequent shots moving in closer reveal them lying in bed in their respective bedrooms. At the beginning of the film, Charles is in Philadelphia, living in a boarding house. He is introduced through a series of shots depicting the gritty urban landscape of the city: a bridge in an industrial area, an abandoned, dismantled car, and rowdy children playing ball in the street. The subsequent shots cut in ever closer to a boardinghouse room until Charles is revealed lying in the dark on a bed. Following the presentation of Santa Rosa's streetscape, young Charlie is also introduced through a series of shots—starting with the Newton's house on its suburban street, to a closer, low-angle shot of a small balcony, to a tracking shot inside Charlie's bedroom to reveal her also lying on her bed. For McLaughlin, Hitchcock's strategy of introducing both Charlies by tracking in from outside the house into the bedroom "creates suspicions of illegitimacy . . . that the two houses are hiding something vaguely sinister, which must be explored."[8] From the outset, before we even learn the similar names of these two characters, these montage sequences establish their connection to each other, as well as the tension that will develop throughout the film between presentation (façade) and inner truths.

Hitchcock employs a similar strategy on at least two other occasions in his work. In *Rebecca* (1940), the opening sequence, which is examined by Bruce Isaacs in this collection, begins with a shot of the front gate of Manderley and tracks in closer to the house, thereby hinting at the way in which the opulent façade of the house belies the tragedy and anguish experienced by the characters inside. Even more similar to *Shadow of a Doubt* is the opening of *Psycho* (1960), in which a panning shot of the skyline of Phoenix, Arizona, dissolves into a series of cuts moving closer to a particular window of a building, and into a bedroom to reveal (and introduce) Marion Crane and Sam Loomis half-dressed after sleeping together. Perhaps the opening sequence of *Rear Window* (1954), examined in this collection by Martin P. Rossouw, could be considered a reverse of this strategy, while still performing the same function, as the camera moves from inside Jefferies's living room out into the courtyard to present the various windows in which the film's action will take place. It should be noted that the camera's tracking movement in these examples is largely only implied by each subsequent shot framing an insert of the shot before it, since technology did not exist to allow Hitchcock to move the camera through windows.[9]

On the surface, each of these examples appears to be merely presenting an establishing shot to contextualize the action before tracking in to introduce the character and commence the narrative. However, it is the implied tracking motion that adds a particular layer of meaning to each of these moments and that helps illuminate the shot at the focus of this chapter from *Shadow of a Doubt*. In each instance—*Rebecca*, *Psycho*, and *Rear Window*—the camera's movement inward toward the action implies a stripping back of layers; just as McLaughlin points out about the Newton's house, it suggests the existence of a façade or a surface that needs to be removed and delved into. Each of these façades, with the exception perhaps of *Rebecca*, suggests a kind of innocence, which starkly contrasts with what lies within. This strategy, therefore, also suggests that the viewer's initial perception of the character we are about to meet might be shifted throughout the film as their true, inner self rises to the surface.

If such a strategy reveals a duality in the character, or the existence of deceptive surfaces, by moving from the wide to the close-up, then the shot under investigation in this chapter mobilizes the same strategy, albeit on a smaller scale. The wide framing on which the shot begins (see Figure 6.1) reveals almost the whole dinner table and the family gathered around it. The wide-angle frames Charles in the context we have been encouraged to think of him throughout the film: as an integral part of the family. Only Herb sits outside the circle of the dinner table. Charles's position at the head overtly positions him as included in the family unit. At this point in the narrative, Charlie's suspicions of her uncle's transgressions have been made known to the viewer, and at this particular dinner scene, her discomfort at sitting next to him is made palpable. But the remainder of the family are still fooled by his façade of innocence, and the opening frames of the shot suggest as much. When the camera tracks in toward Charles's face after Charlie leaves the table, however, we see the person behind the façade. The duality of his character is finally revealed in the same shot. The close-up isolates him and unveils the specifics of his emotional state: cold, determined, and perhaps a mild panic at the fear of his cover being blown. The juxtaposition of these two framings operates like a complex version of the Kuleshov effect: considered separately, the wide-angle and the close-up do not carry significant meaning, but placed sequentially (and connected by a dolly in, rather than montage), a transformation from one Charles to another is unveiled.[10] This duality is not a revelation to the viewer, since the cold stare captured in Figure 6.2 has made numerous earlier appearances in the film. Rather, what is significant about this shot is that it displays this duality for the first time to the whole family and marks the moment at which Charles's façade is stripped away for them.

Two faces

Given the film's opening sequences, which establish a duality in Charles (and Charlie), *Shadow of a Doubt* maintains a tension between wanting to reveal Charles's otherness to the viewer, while concealing it from his family. It achieves this by making overt to the viewer the way Charles constructs a performance to the Newtons, and suggests the high stakes in his behavior and facial expressions in adhering to a particular image they have of him. The shot under investigation in this chapter operates as a climax in the deconstruction of Charles's secret because several moments in the film prior to

Figure 6.3 Charles's serious expression as Charlie Newton (Teresa Wright) inspects the ring in *Shadow of a Doubt*.

this one closely resemble it, but diverge in their outcome. They are moments in which the camera observes both Charles's identities expressed on his face, but other characters in the room only see one. Charles's performance as a good man is kept intact for the Newtons, but comes close to being discovered. The first time this occurs is around 26 minutes into the film, when Charles and Charlie are standing in the kitchen after the former has given gifts to the whole family. Charlie receives a ring and she immediately notices it has an inscription inside: "TS from BM." Evidently, this is a ring stolen from one of Charles's many victims and it presents the very first opportunity for him to switch between performative-Charles and murderer-Charles. One frame shows Charles next to Charlie as she inspects the ring, with the same cold, panicked expression we see repeated later at the dinner table (see Figure 6.3). As soon as she turns to face him, he smiles and becomes affectionate, pretending he absent-mindedly bought a second-hand ring (see Figure 6.4). Soon after, Charlie grabs a pot from the counter, walks out of frame, and says to Charles, "you bring the coffee." As Charlie leaves the room, Charles turns back toward the camera and his serious expression appears again (see

Figure 6.4 Charles shifts to a smile as Charlie looks at him in *Shadow of a Doubt.*

Figure 6.5), as a lap dissolve reintroduces the dancing couples, earlier seen at the beginning of the film, accompanied by Franz Lehár's "Merry Widow Waltz." Hitchcock's framing in this scene very clearly evidences the intentional performance Charles exhibits for his family and, perhaps more important, it demonstrates the overt revelation of Charles's secret and his duality to the viewer. The viewer witnesses two different men here, but Charlie only sees one.

Charles's face as a surface on which we can read his performance of his two identities is also evident in a scene about a third of the way through the film. Charles is in bed, and Emma comes into the bedroom to serve him breakfast. Their conversation is playful, as Emma ribs Charles for being "the only person in this town to have breakfast at 10:30." Charles smiles as Emma begins unpacking his suitcase for him and telling him that the whole family are going to be interviewed for the newspaper by a man named Graham. In a single shot on Charles's face, we witness a transformation during the revelation of this information. His expression shifts dramatically from the playful smile he wore while Emma was looking at him, to a serious deadpan grimace

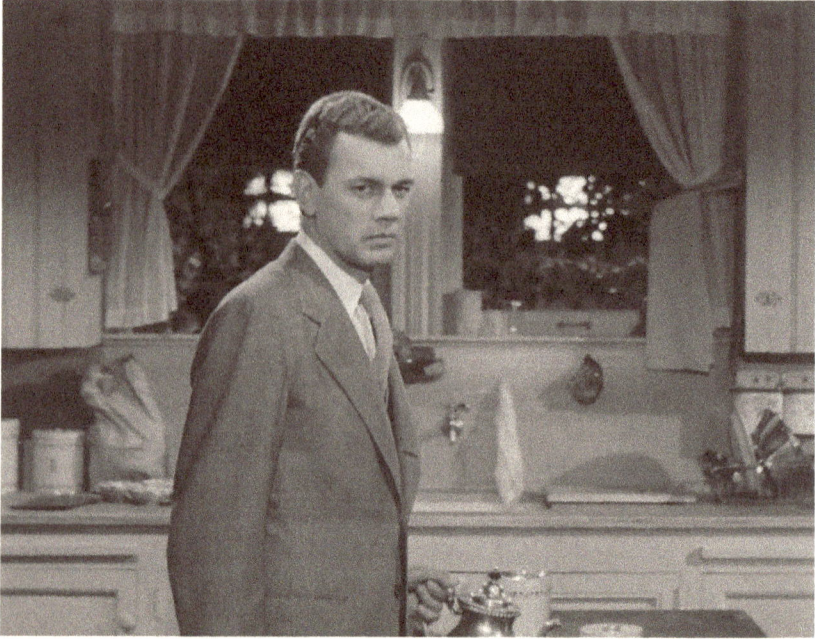

Figure 6.5 Charles returns to his cold stare after Charlie leaves the room in *Shadow of a Doubt.*

while her back is turned. He tries to quickly correct his reaction before she notices, by pretending to be worried that the newspapermen will be a nuisance, as opposed to revealing his true fear that his criminal past will be unearthed. Once again, just like Charlie in the kitchen, Emma fails to note Charles's friendly façade drop away, but Hitchcock's framing confirms that it is the viewer's testimony that counts. We witness his performance of Uncle Charlie dissolve into murderer-Charlie, and this transformation is precisely what cements the existence of Charles's two identities.

In the lead-up to the shot of this chapter's focus, these two scenes serve to mark Charles as a villain for the viewer. In doing so, the camera is imbued with a particular quality—a knowingness—that is absent from the other characters. Charlie develops this knowingness through her discussions with Graham, but her revelations only have high stakes because the viewer is already privy to the secret. For Rothman, this knowingness of the camera where villainous characters are concerned is a hallmark of Hitchcock's films. He draws on Peter Brooks's discussion of the theatrical melodrama, in which the villain nominates themselves as occupying such a role—"the villain, who at some point always bursts forth in a statement of his evil nature and intentions."[11] Rothman argues, however, that film characters, at least in their realist midcentury classical Hollywood form, "do not have the authority to 'nominate' themselves, to declare their moral identity, for they are always also the camera's subjects."[12] It is unlikely that that villains of cinema even see themselves as such, perhaps electing to justify their villainous actions, as Charles does with his widow murders explicitly in *Shadow of a Doubt*. It is, therefore, the director—and by extension, the camera—who must nominate the villain as villainous to the viewer.

Hitchcock approaches the act of nominating the villain using several strategies through his oeuvre. *Suspicion* (1941) and *Psycho* offer particularly interesting points of comparison. *Suspicion* narratively mirrors *Shadow of a Doubt* quite closely, in the sense that Johnnie Aysgarth (Cary Grant) appears to have a dual personality: the charming, doting husband to Lina (Joan Fontaine) and the increasingly evident suggestions of his villainous behavior as he gambles their furniture away and his best friend dies under mysterious circumstances. Like Charlie, Lina develops a knowingness—and an anxiety—about the possibility of Johnnie being a murderer, even though many of her suspicions turn out to be unfounded. Where *Suspicion* differs from *Shadow of a Doubt*, however, is that the camera does not operate as a witness to Johnnie's villainy. Not only does it not explicitly show any criminal acts, it also does not bear witness to a different version of Johnnie than Lina sees. There are no shifts in facial expression staged only for the camera. Rather, the camera is aligned with Lina's perspective, and the viewer's suspicions of Johnnie's villainous character are only aroused as Lina learns about his behavior from friends and family. Conversely, in *Psycho*, the camera more explicitly nominates Bates as the villain, which grants the viewer access to knowledge the other characters do not possess. Rothman uses the example of the peephole scene to demonstrate this act.[13] Here, an extreme close-up reveals Norman Bates watching Marion Crane in her motel room through a peephole, and then shows us his point of view. While the viewer does not yet know Bates is a murderer, this morally dubious act is the first hint of his villainous nature. As Rothman observes, "this is not an example of a villain's self-nomination, as in theatrical melodramas. Unbeknownst to him, this villain is 'nominated' by the camera, which links his villainy to his—and our—act of viewing."[14] By witnessing Bates commit a villainous act, the viewer is also implicated in his villainy and it colors our ongoing perception of the character's actions.

For *Shadow of a Doubt*, the scenes in the kitchen and the bedroom are precisely the equivalent of this peephole scene in the process of villain nomination. Hitchcock uses careful blocking and framing to conceal Charles's grimace from Charlie and Emma respectively. Hitchcock's act of cutting away from the scene's central action in both instances—either following Charlie to the dining room, or staying framed on Emma as she talks about the newspapermen—is further evidence of Hitchcock tipping his hand to the viewer. The camera trails behind and remains in the kitchen longer than expected to ensure the viewer sees Charles's smile fade rapidly to a cold stare (see Figure 6.5): this is Hitchcock marking his intervention in overtly nominating Charles as villain (or, at least, villainous). Hitchcock's intervention results in the camera's knowingness—its ability to work against conventional editing logic and, for example, not follow Charlie into the dining room. This strategy is in part explained by David Bordwell's discussion of spectator address. Bordwell discusses the "perspectival eye for the camera," which he argues has historically been an overused and frequently misunderstood concept, originating with V. I. Pudovkin and developing in complexity alongside twentieth-century film theory.[15] In Pudovkin's formulation, the cinema camera replicates the vision of an ideal, invisible observer and, as Bordwell describes, "could mimic ordinary experience."[16] Bordwell argues, however, that this concept of the camera standing in for an invisible witness is problematic because the camera often "violate[s] plausible viewer positions."[17] Furthermore, it overlooks both the artistry and logistics of staging a scene for the camera. It cannot, for example, "explain how action develops to prolong maximum visibility," or why characters might be arranged in front of the camera in a way that emphasizes power and social hierarchies.[18] Bordwell argues rather than thinking of film staging as an event observed by the camera, it is instead more productive to consider mise-en-scène as deliberately "addressed to the spectator."[19] In *Shadow of a Doubt*, this address becomes much more overt in the moments discussed thus far. The camera's positioning is such that it privileges the revelation of Charles's secret to the viewer. It establishes this relationship as central to the experience of viewing and to the unfolding of the narrative. More specifically, it maintains a tension between observing both identities at play, akin to an inside joke with the viewer.

Contrary to these earlier scenes, the shot at the focus of this chapter takes place around a dinner table, at which each person is on display to every other. In this sense, it is more substantially burdened with distinguishing between

Charles's performance of innocence to his family and Hitchcock's revelation of his villainy to the camera. Hitchcock frames these dinner table scenes as presentational and performative as he moves around the table and offers a close-up of each character, as though scrutinizing their true identity. This positioning offers an ideal scenario for Charles to play the role of the kindly uncle, as the close-ups of him mostly reveal his face in a grin, entertaining his nieces and nephew seated near him, and being watched with adoration by his sister at the other end of the table. But this positioning is also revealed to present a problem for Charles's dual identity: his face is too easily able to be scrutinized, which makes him vulnerable to his family's probing questions. Here, it is on display not just for the camera, but for his family, who are all permanently transfixed by his presence and his stories.

We see Charles's expression begin to shift a number of times when the family's conversational subject matter edges too close to his murderous past, and Hitchcock reveals the stakes in these shifts. During the second dinner table scene earlier in the film, Charlie sits down to eat dessert, humming the "Merry Widow Waltz," and proceeds to discuss the phenomenon of having a song in one's head. She then begins considering, with her mother, what the tune in question might be. As they identify it as a waltz, a medium close-up of Charles shows a dark expression on his face, looking downward and mildly worried. Charlie's dominance of the conversation has distracted the family's attention from Charles, but the camera ensures the viewer bears witness to this shift. Charles tries to delay his sister from identifying the tune, by initially saying he doesn't know what the tune is, and then falsely naming it "The Blue Danube." When Charlie realizes this is incorrect and begins considering other options, Charles deliberately tips over his glass, which causes the family to leap up and fuss over the spilled water. Such a scene reveals that Charles's identity as murderer is always concealed just below the surface. Even the most tangential of conversations, such as identifying a waltz, threaten to reveal this secondary identity on his face. Just as the viewer can read it, Hitchcock shows us that his family can, too.

During the shot at the focus of this chapter, the conversation again moves too close towards the subject of murder. While discussion of the "Merry Widow Waltz" had earlier prompted Charles to become nervous about the similarity of the song's subject matter, so too does Herb and Joe's discussion of true crime. When Charlie leaps up out of her chair, marking the beginning of the shot, yelling, "Do you always have to talk about killing people?" Her father responds, "we're not talking about killing people. Herb is talking about killing me and I'm talking about killing him," after they had been discussing, in hypothetical terms, how they would commit the perfect murder on each other. Unlike the previous dinner table conversation, when Charles was the only one in possession of his secret, and could distract from the conversation by spilling his water, this time both Charlie and the viewer are privy to it as well. Charlie is already quite certain that Charles is a murderer, having been tipped off by the detectives and conducting her own newspaper research in the library.

The true significance of this moment, however, is that this is the first time Charles's shift in facial expression risks being witnessed by the Newtons. Although his face is now on display for the family around the table, it is only the camera that observes the shift. Once again, Charles's shift between identities is performed as a direct address to the camera, but this is the first time in the film it has also been on display to other characters. This is not achieved through a cutaway, as in the kitchen or bedroom scenes, but this time via a track into Charles's face to a medium close-up. It is in the close-up that his cold stare is made evident, and this speaks to Béla Balázs's observations about a particular quality of the close-up. In *Theory of the Film*, he notes, "The close-up can show us a quality in a gesture of the hand we never noticed before when we saw that hand stroke or strike something [...]. The close-up shows your shadow on the wall with which you have lived all your life and which you scarcely knew."[20] The close-up does not just show us something larger, but reveals detail and draws attention to something we could not otherwise see. Balázs continues, "a good film with its close-ups reveals the most hidden parts in our polyphonous life."[21] For Balázs, therefore, the camera has a special ability to reveal that which is invisible to the naked eye. It can reveal detail to the viewer that is unavailable to the characters in the diegesis.[22] This is precisely what occurs in this shot from *Shadow of a Doubt*: Hitchcock's sudden track in toward Charles's face shows the viewer what is not plainly obvious in the wide-angle or to the other characters around the table. As well as his cold stare becoming more evident, this camera movement into a close-up also isolates and frames his face in a way that signals its meaningfulness.

While the shot makes clear the duality within Charles, it also perpetuates the duality of Charles and Charlie. Both their physicality shifts at this moment, but the camera's positioning evidences that Hitchcock's principal interest is interrogating Charles's shifting facial expression and movement. Charlie's physicality, up to this point, has been calm, graceful, and even playful in the presence of her uncle. For the first time, her face is full of worry and she storms out of the dining room and leaves via the front door angrily and quickly. Just as the camera trailed behind in the kitchen earlier to catch Charles's response, here it remains in the dining room and hurriedly tracks into Charles's face. It tilts up to follow his rising from the table, and then tracks behind him as he follows in Charlie's footsteps through the living room (see Figure 6.6). Charles has also presented as relaxed and graceful in his physicality up to this point. His hurried movement in this shot, however, suddenly imbues his character with a sense of panic that has been absent thus far. While the camera has only allowed Charles's secondary identity to emerge in his facial expressions earlier in the film, at this point it is evident in his physical movements too. The camera doubles this shift in physicality. Immediately after saying, "I'll catch up with her," the camera follows very closely behind his back as he walks toward the front door, akin to tracking a predator hunting its prey. This overt shift in pacing, physicality, and emotion, which signals clearly to the viewer that Charles is involved in something sinister, is contrasted by the diegetic off-camera dialogue of Emma saying,

Figure 6.6 Charles chases after Charlie to suppress his secret in *Shadow of a Doubt*.

"what's wrong with her?" indicating her continued ignorance as to Charles's secret.

Playing a murderer

Much of this chapter thus far has focused on the revelation the central shot makes for both the narrative and Charles's position within it. However, this shot also carries extradiegetic significance. In the Rodeo Drive exercise Hitchcock conducted with Cotten in preparation for the role, the intended key takeaway for the actor was that a murderer "moves and looks like anyone else." Evidently, this philosophy was integral in the choice to cast Cotten as Charles Oakley. Although Cotten was still early in his career at the time of *Shadow of a Doubt*'s production and release, even his minor reputation and star image in Hollywood was not that of a villain. On the contrary, Cotten's only earlier film roles had been either best friend or romantic interest characters, therefore Charles represented a notable shift in the role for the actor. Lesley L. Coffin discusses Hitchcock's original intention to cast William Powell, who had frequently played a "very suave villain indeed" early in his career but whose "likable qualities slowly but surely dominated his screen characterizations."[23] Coffin argues Cotten was ultimately cast because "he entered *Shadow of a Doubt* without an established public image that could dramatically influence the way audiences would view Uncle Charlie."[24] While this may be the case from the perspective of contemporary audiences of the film's release, it is difficult to ignore the explicit way in which Cotten's role as villain unequivocally contradicts the image of his earlier roles. Taking this further, I argue in the shot in question, Charles's transformation into murderer-Charles is particularly palpable not only because his performance to the Newtons has been so different earlier in the film, but also because it thwarts any expectations of Cotten as performer that had been satisfied by his performance as Uncle Charlie.

This contradiction is particularly notable given Hollywood's prevailing star system through the classical period. Alongside the economic dimension of the system, there is also an element of consistency in style and genre largely adhered to by the star. "The star system is based on the premise," Thomas Harris explains, "that a star is accepted by the public in terms of a certain set of personality traits which permeate all of his or her film roles."[25]

Harris offers the examples of Grace Kelly and Marilyn Monroe, for whom a consistent star image can be tracked not only across their roles, but in their publicity strategies, too. The idea of the consistent star image illuminates Hitchcock's casting strategy. He deliberately cast against type in order to establish expectations and then disarm the viewer. *Shadow of a Doubt* was not the only Hitchcock film to utilize this strategy. We can again return to a comparison with *Suspicion*. Due to the casting of Cary Grant, Johnnie's villainy is unexpected, and his suspected guilt is easy to deny for the viewer. Coffin argues he maintains the "carefree, comic charms" of his earlier starring roles that likely satisfies the viewer's expectations of Grant.[26] For John Ellis, the film's construction relies on the viewer's misguided expectations "in order to render Joan Fontaine's suspicions incongruous at first, and then increasingly irrefutable even to the most incredulous audience as the 'evidence' mounts . . . *Suspicion* needs the star image of Cary Grant in order to function at all."[27] Unlike *Shadow of a Doubt*, however, the ambiguous—perhaps even happy—ending of *Suspicion*, in which Lina's suspicions are explained as a misunderstanding, attempts to depict Grant as innocent in order to satisfy his star image.

In *Shadow of a Doubt*, however, the casting of Cotten offers a far greater challenge to the expected consistency of the star image. Although Cotten was not as well known as Grant, the film ends unambiguously, and the viewer is asked to fully believe that the affable Uncle Charlie truly is a murderer. This may have been more possible because Cotten, like Hitchcock, was on loan to Universal Pictures from Selznick International Pictures. By 1943, Cotten had played only three film roles, each of which had called for a similar kind of performance and had begun to establish a distinct star image. His first role, emerging out of a long professional relationship with Orson Welles, was as the principled and loyal Jedediah Leland in *Citizen Kane* (1941); his second role was as the kind and romantic love interest Michael Fitzpatrick in *Lydia* (1941); and his third role was as the loyal and downtrodden Eugene Morgan in *The Magnificent Ambersons* (1942). In *Citizen Kane* and *The Magnificent Ambersons*, especially, his character is more victim than villain, as his loyalty is betrayed by Charles Foster Kane, and he is rejected by Isabel Minafer respectively.[28] His performance in each of these films is distinguished by his unique warm smile and a friendly disposition. This distinctive performance style reappears in *Shadow of a Doubt* during his initial arrival at the train station, and each subsequent time he is observed in proximity to the Newtons. His façade as Uncle Charlie, therefore, undeniably satisfies expectations of

Cotten's typical performance, considering his earlier roles and his established star image.

This image of Cotten allows him (as Charles) to sustain two distinct identities in *Shadow of a Doubt*. Although his villainy is suggested in the introductory sequence, and subsequently each time the camera catches his cold stare, his overall adherence to the expected and typical Cotten performance perpetually allows the viewer to delay acceptance of Charles as the murderer. In this way, the viewer is at once privy to his secret through the camera angles and editing choices outlined in the previous section, and is also able to suspend their suspicions of his villainy, just as the Newtons do through most of the film. As long as his performance style forms a continuous pattern with his previous roles, those roles continue to inform the viewer expectations of Charles. In the moments immediately prior to the shot in question, Charles's playful discussion with Emma about wine sustains the connection between Charles as character and Cotten as performer. As soon as the shot begins, the viewer witnesses another shift in Charles, alongside those already discussed: at the start of the shot, he is relaxed in his chair with a calm, neutral expression on his face (see Figure 6.1). As Joe says "killing him," Charles moves backward in his chair, tenses his arms on the armrests, and adopts the iconic cold stare. As well as his character's façade being dropped in this instance, so too is the familiarity of Cotten's performance. For the first time, in any sustained fashion, he no longer resembles or conjures the character of his previous roles. It is for this reason that Hitchcock's casting of an actor who had "never played a murderer before" was crucial. The shift in character from Uncle Charlie to murderer-Charles is made more palpable and meaningful by the simultaneous shift from familiar performance to performing a murderer.

Notes

1. Thanks to Charmaine Robson for providing feedback on this chapter, and for sharing her love of Joseph Cotten. I would also like to thank Luke Robinson for his keen editor's eye and for providing feedback on this chapter. Joseph Cotten, *Vanity Will Get You Somewhere: An Autobiography*, 2nd ed. (San Jose, CA: toExcel, 2000), 63–64.
2. Cotten, *Vanity Will Get You Somewhere*, 64.
3. In a 1964 interview with Fletcher Markle, Markle states, "most critics have always considered *Shadow of a Doubt,* which you made in 1943 as your finest film,"

Hitchcock replies, "me too." Markle confirms, "that is your opinion of it still?" to which Hitchcock agrees with, "no question" ("A Talk with Alfred Hitchcock," *Telescope*, CBC, 1964). In his well-known interview with François Truffaut, however, he states, "I wouldn't say *Shadow of a Doubt* is my favourite picture; if I've given that impression, it's probably because I feel that [t]here [*sic*] is something that our friends, the plausibles and logicians, cannot complain about." (François Truffaut, *Hitchcock*, rev. ed. [New York: Simon & Schuster, 1984], 151). Thanks to Luke Robinson for alerting me to this latter discussion.

4. "Average family" and "waiting for a miracle" are both phrases used by members of the Newton family in *Shadow of a Doubt*.

5. William Rothman, *Hitchcock: The Murderous Gaze*, 2nd ed. (Albany: State University of New York Press, 2014), 191.

6. Rothman, *Hitchcock*, 188.

7. James McLaughlin, "All in the Family: Alfred Hitchcock's *Shadow of a Doubt*," in *A Hitchcock Reader*, ed. Marshall Deutelbaum and Leland Poague (Malden, MA: Wiley-Blackwell, 2009), 145.

8. McLaughlin, "All in the Family," 145.

9. This technological hinderance is corrected in Gus Van Sant's remake of *Psycho* (1998), in which his introduction to Marion Crane takes place via a smooth camera movement tracking from outside the building in through the window.

10. Thanks to Luke Robinson for this observation.

11. Peter Brooks, *The Melodramatic Imagination: Balzac, Henry James, Melodrama, and the Mode of Excess*, 2nd ed. (New Haven, CT: Yale University Press, 1995), 37.

12. William Rothman, *The "I" of the Camera: Essays in Film Criticism, History, and Aesthetics*, 2nd ed. (Cambridge: Cambridge University Press, 2004), 259.

13. Rothman, *The "I" of the Camera*, 259.

14. Rothman, *The "I" of the Camera*, 259.

15. David Bordwell, *Narration in the Fiction Film* (London: Routledge, 1987), 9.

16. Bordwell, *Narration in the Fiction Film*, 9.

17. Bordwell, *Narration in the Fiction Film*, 9.

18. Bordwell, *Narration in the Fiction Film*, 11.

19. Bordwell, *Narration in the Fiction Film*, 11.

20. Béla Balázs, *Theory of the Film: Character and Growth of a New Art* (New York: Dover, 1970), 55.

21. Balázs, *Theory of the Film*, 55.

22. See Luke Robinson's chapter in this volume for further discussion of the facial close-up using the work of Balázs.

23. Lesley L. Coffin, *Hitchcock's Stars: Alfred Hitchcock and the Hollywood Studio System* (Lanham, MD: Rowman & Littlefield, 2014), 40–41.

24. Coffin, *Hitchcock's Stars*, 42.

25. Thomas Harris, "The Building of Popular Images," in *Stardom: Industry of Desire*, ed. Christine Gledhill (London: Routledge, 2005), 41.

26. Coffin, *Hitchcock's Stars*, 31.

27. John Ellis, quoted in Coffin, *Hitchcock's Stars*, 31.

28. Although later than *Shadow of a Doubt*, this victimhood (as a direct result of his loyalty to the protagonist) can be seen in his role as Holly Martins in *The Third Man* (1949), again playing opposite Welles. Prior to his film career, Cotten had also taken on several similar loyal sidekick roles to Welles's lead in the latter's produced radio plays. This further cements the consistency in Cotten's roles and the building of audience expectation.

7

Aventure Malgache (1944)

French colonial tensions

Charles Barr

The long-held static image in Figure 7.1 forms a flattened isosceles triangle, creating a strong dramatic tension between its three points. The tension resonates at various levels, compositional, national, historical, authorial. One reason for choosing this shot is that it comes from such an obscure production. Obscure corners of a career can be revealing—sometimes especially so, as I will argue in relation to this film, and this image. *Aventure Malgache* (1944) must be the least known and least shown of all the films directed by Alfred Hitchcock, even including the second of his features, *The Mountain Eagle* (1927). That film, a German-British co-production, was screened and reviewed at the time in both countries and beyond before being, like so many titles from the 1920s, lost and forgotten when the industry converted to sound—lost and not yet found, though new finds are always possible.[1]

In contrast, *Aventure Malgache*, though never lost, failed to reach, in 1944, even the audience at which it was aimed: an audience limited in range—French territories after Liberation—and limited in time, since it was designed, like so many wartime short films, to do an immediate job of propaganda, in this case by celebrating the bravery of the French Resistance movement. It is one of a pair of French-language films that Hitchcock traveled from America late in 1943 to make at Welwyn Studios, near London, early in 1944—only his second return to his native country since he left for America in March 1939 to take up his contract with David O. Selznick. Its twin film, *Bon Voyage* (1944), was also forgotten for decades, but was shown widely in France at the time, and had a gratifyingly positive response. Its 23-minute narrative tells the story of a British pilot brought back successfully from occupied France by the heroic efforts of Resistance workers, in defiance of a network of undercover Gestapo agents.

Charles Barr, Aventure Malgache *(1944)* In: *One Shot Hitchcock*. Edited by: Luke Robinson and Melanie Robson, Oxford University Press. © Oxford University Press 2024. DOI: 10.1093/oso/9780197682876.003.0007

Figure 7.1 A triangle produced through staging creates tension in Alfred Hitchcock's *Aventure Malgache* (1944).

Aventure Malgache, running 6 minutes longer, is very different. Its location is less familiar, the island of Madagascar, a now-former French colony off the southwest coast of Africa—hence the title[2]—and the struggle is not between heroic French and sinister Germans, but between different factions within the community, bold resisters and equally determined Vichyite collaborators. The role of the British in the story is likewise ambivalent: islanders initially express a distrust of Britain's colonialist history and are reluctant to see them as more immediately attractive allies than the Germans. In the event, resisters and British will be shown, in mid-war, to cooperate and to succeed, but the story is clearly much less palatable, to French and British authorities alike, than that of *Bon Voyage*. The film was, predictably, suppressed, and the ban would stay in place for half a century: partly, it was claimed, because of the fear of libel actions that might have been brought by survivors from among the collaborators whose real-life activities were drawn upon.[3] The twin shorts were so closely linked at the time of their production that they have tended to be conflated, in historical retrospect, as little-seen failures; while this is inaccurate, it does make sense to link the two films in a compare-and-contrast way, formal aspects included.

In the frame-still, the man on the right is the film's protagonist, the Resistance organizer Clarus, reprising his own recent real-life Madagascar role. Facing him across the table is a lawyer who pretends sympathy, but whom he knows to be in league with the Vichyite governor of the island—we don't, however, learn the full extent of the lawyer's deviousness until after the scene ends, and Clarus lets off steam. The guard at the apex of the triangle contributes nothing except his presence, which becomes all the more eloquent in historical retrospect. In 1947 this French colony would be the site of a major uprising, ahead of the achievement of independence in 1960. So the image from 1944 encompasses, in its highly topical tight triangle, the past of Vichy, the present of the Liberation, and the decolonization that lies in the then indefinite, but foreseeable, future.

Hitchcock himself is at a tense moment in his career, subject in his own person to a triangle of forces. Most obviously in geography, Britain, America, Europe, his three major reference points from the 1920s onward, all of them acutely in play in this current enterprise; but also in terms of a trio of producers, Michael Balcon, Selznick, and Sidney Bernstein, representing respectively his own past, present, and future.

Balcon's support in the 1920s, and then, after a gap, in the 1930s, was indispensable to the launch and development of Hitchcock's directing career, but the pair had been alienated since the start of the war in Europe, when Balcon attacked him as a "deserter."[4] Selznick still had him under contract in Hollywood, but this relationship too had become difficult. It is Bernstein, in his wartime role working for the British Ministry of Information, who brought his old friend over to England to make these two films; Selznick could not object to such a worthy war-effort enterprise, but he was well aware that the two men had plans to develop a more serious commercial partnership as soon as Hitchcock was free, and he suspected that they may already have been working on these plans on his, Selznick's, time. As indeed they were, the result being their company Transatlantic Pictures, whose first production, *Rope*, Hitchcock would begin shooting in early 1948, soon after completing his final contractual commitment to Selznick, *The Paradine Case* (1947).

It would be facile to suggest any kind of match between the three on-screen *Malgache* characters and the three producers—this is no kind of *film à clef*—but there is a comparably urgent topical three-way tension at work at both levels, evoked in the austere triangular composition. Past, present, future.

One way of building cinematic tension, as Hitchcock frequently argued, and frequently demonstrated, is, of course, by exploiting the richly varied possibilities of cutting. Another is precisely by avoiding cutting, as he had also demonstrated from time to time, and does here, and was soon to do, very systematically, in the two major films of the Bernstein partnership: *Rope* and *Under Capricorn* (1949).

One way of studying, and teaching, film theory is to work successively through a range of topics like Authorship and Genre and Politics. Another, arguably more productive, is to do so by foregrounding history, focusing successively on three twentieth-century events in particular, and their formative impact on film culture and film theory: the Russian Revolution, the Second World War, and the upheavals of 1968 in Paris and beyond. Other influential factors have come into play at other times, but these three supply a robust framework for the major developments of, respectively, Soviet-based montage theory, the work of André Bazin and his associates, and (to use a shorthand term for a wider movement) the "*Screen* theory" that peaked in the decade after 1968.

Hitchcock's career spans all three of these landmarks. The same applies, naturally, to many others of his generation, the set of "old masters" who had their formation in silent cinema, made an assured transition into the synchronized medium, and stayed busy during and beyond the Second World War. Whether or not they were still active in the late 1960s, their work came to supply wonderfully rich material for post-1968 analysis, in the new era of "*Screen* theory" and its ramifications, closely linked to the growth of institutionalized film study. The great names include men—inevitably all of them men, *masters*—like John Ford and King Vidor and Raoul Walsh and Howard Hawks. New theory deconstructs their work, but does not diminish it.

Among these old masters, Hitchcock has a special place. This book is itself an affirmation: has there been, could there be, an equivalent for anyone else? Two related factors help to explain this, in both of which he goes beyond his peers, always so much more calculating and more articulate than any of them. First, his cosmopolitanism, moving repeatedly between Britain and America and Europe: aware of what he can pick up from all three, and aware, always, of the wider international audience, and the need to cater for their response too. Second, his fascination with film form, his constant readiness to experiment with it, and to discuss it, to an extent others may find no reason to.

Born in 1899, starting in films in the decade after 1917, Hitchcock was quickly receptive to the work of the first Soviet director-theorists, Lev Kuleshov and Vsevolod Pudovkin especially, and never forgot them. He worked intensively through the war and its aftermath, deeply marked by it in multiple ways, personal and professional; and he stayed active beyond 1968, coming closer than anyone of his generation to adapting directly to a film culture in process of transformation, as opposed to just supplying, by now, rich historic product for analysis. Biographers have recorded his response to seeing such films as Michelangelo Antonioni's *Blow-Up* (1966), a portent both for its new form of US-UK-Europe cosmopolitanism (MGM finance, British cast and setting, Italian director) and for its formal boldness: "These Italian directors are a century ahead of me in terms of technique. What have I been doing all this time?"[5] What is more, Hitchcock energetically followed through with his own ambitious project, innovative in form as in subject matter, known variously as *Kaleidoscope* and as *Frenzy*, a project that was, to his distress, after several weeks of trial shooting, aborted by the studio, but which confirmed his readiness, always, to push the boundaries of film form in shrewd response to wider social and cultural change.[6]

Aventure Malgache caught him at an exact moment of hesitation, transition, between countries, between producers, and between formal strategies. It pointed forward, where its twin film, *Bon Voyage*, pointed back. It seems possible, in fact, that *Malgache* was, for practical reasons, shot first, but it was planned later, being developed only after Hitchcock's arrival in London, out of discussions, held in his suite at Claridge's Hotel, with a range of well-informed French advisers. *Bon Voyage* had been planned in advance, one of a small number of script outlines sent to him in America that helped to secure his commitment: it would be fine-tuned after his arrival, making it an even more solid project, well calculated to reach its intended audience and to fulfill its purpose, as it most efficiently did, and as *Malgache*, with its altogether looser schedule, conspicuously did not. I don't think it is too cynical to imagine Hitchcock as having silently done a deal with himself: delivering one safely predictable success to the authorities, while allowing himself the risk of experiment, in form as in content, with the other project. The kind of deal that directors have been known to make: a box-office success, carried out in obedience to expectations, allows the license for something riskier and more personal. In the formula sometimes attributed to John Ford, "one for you, one for me."

Average Shot Length measurement (ASL) is in itself of limited value as an index of style, since long takes may (as in *Citizen Kane*, 1941) alternate with fast-edited passages, thus bringing the ASL close to normal; but the ASL figure can, judiciously used, be significant, as in the case of these two short films. The ASL of *Bon Voyage* is 13 seconds, of *Aventure Malgache* 23 seconds. Some of the establishing scenes of the former are played out economically in wide shot, but for major scenes of confrontation Hitchcock relies, very effectively, on close-up and shot–reverse shot—appropriately so for a narrative in which oppositions are clearly set up and resolved.

There is nothing in *Bon Voyage* comparable to the selected triangle image from *Aventure Malgache*, which is held for nearly 2 minutes. It starts by quickly pulling back from the entry of the two protagonists, as they take up their places at the table, and ends by moving forward as they depart; there is a brief exchange of close shots toward the end, but the wide shot is dominant, at the time and in memory—I had even forgotten those brief inserts, until a recent re-viewing. The frame-still is a true record of the dominant image and impact of the scene, like the multilevel image of the telephone scene in William Wyler's *The Best Years of Our Lives* in 1946 that was so famously dwelt upon by Bazin—even though Bazin had to admit, half-apologetically, that Wyler had used two brief inserts of closer shots to break up the purity of the master shot (see Figure 7.2).[7]

Figure 7.2 A multi-level image in the telephone scene in William Wyler's *The Best Years of Our Lives* (1946).

That widely seen 170-minute Oscar-winner, examining unsentimentally and movingly the raw experience of US veterans returning to civilian life, and Hitchcock's unshown half-hour short about mid-war conflicts in a French colony, unite in historical retrospect. They both play out before us diagrams of how things are, and leave us to take stock. Bazin is not afraid to invoke the term "democracy," in relation to the viewer's freedom.[8]

After shooting the two Resistance films in early 1944, Hitchcock returned to America, but came back to London in June 1945 to work on another project, again with Bernstein, again for the Ministry, a more ambitious one, a compilation film about the reality of the Nazi concentration camps. For a variety of reasons, mainly to do with politics, the project had to be shelved, though versions of it would, decades later, emerge from the archives. Hitchcock is credited, in retrospect, as "Treatment Adviser," and quite detailed evidence survives about the advice he gave, after viewing masses of footage, on how to handle the editing.

Unsurprisingly, he suggests a range of montage effects, for instance cutting back and forth "between the horrors of the camp and the charming German countryside." But more important, again in the words of the project's designated editor Peter Tanner, "Hitchcock's main contribution to the film was to try to make it as authentic as possible": this meant finding and using an abundance of camera records, protracted and uncut, with or without panning, of the stark reality of the camps, "so that there was no possibility of trickery . . . so that it couldn't be suggested that we were faking the film."[9] "Montage interdit" is the title of a celebrated Bazin essay: in certain contexts like these, whether documentary or fiction or something in between, *editing is forbidden*, out of respect to the material, and equally to the viewer, who can be trusted to engage with that screened material more directly than if it were mediated through the structures of the "classical" system, a system of which Bazin was himself an early definer and, indeed, in a limited way, admirer.[10]

I don't think one can overestimate the importance of Hitchcock's exposure, as consultant, to the Camps footage, in influencing the direction of his work in the second half of this decade. In personal terms, it reinforced the powerful impact on him of the war, not cocooned safely in California but anxious about the safety of family members back in England, and making some uncomfortable journeys back and forth across the Atlantic. In formal terms, it reinforced the movement he had already measured out between the two Resistance shorts, the safe *Bon Voyage* and the risky *Aventure Malgache*, and it looks ahead to his two feature films with Bernstein, based on longer-running unbroken shots than any other director ever attempted in those days of 35mm film, 10 minutes per reel.

Hitchcock had always been fascinated by the dialectic between quick cutting and long takes, as practiced with consummate assurance in, for instance, *The Skin Game* in 1931, where one-take dialogue scenes of several minutes contrast with the rapid montage of, notably, an auction scene that climaxes in a sequence of sixteen shots in 21 seconds.[11] That was primarily an exercise in adapting to the formal possibilities of the new synchronized medium. Now, the case for the long take has become more than simply a formal one.

Between them, in form and in content, *Aventure Malgache* and the aborted Camps project can be seen to point ahead to the two big Transatlantic features. But first, Hitchcock had to work out his Selznick contract. Editor Alan Osbiston was brought from England to Hollywood to consult on the fine-tuning of the Resistance films (described by him as "bloody good")— this journey, made at Hitchcock's request, being itself a testimony to the seriousness he brought to the shaping of these twin productions. According to Osbiston, *Notorious* (1946), a masterpiece of tight editing, with Cary Grant and Ingrid Bergman, was by then already in preparation; in fact, the film which he saw being planned was its predecessor *Spellbound* (1945), for which the role designed for Grant was in the event played, still opposite Bergman, by Gregory Peck.[12] After *Notorious* came *The Paradine Case*, again with Peck, where a number of Hitchcock's elaborate long takes were, to his frustration, chopped into pieces by his imperious producer, intensifying his determination to move on as early as possible to Bernstein and Transatlantic—and to indulge to the full his post-*Malgache* wish to challenge the postwar viewer with unfragmented takes and complex images to read, some of them triangular in construction.

I think it was plausible to claim, as do Kerzoncuf and Barr, in *Lost and Found* that:

> Hitchcock carries over into *Rope* the strategy that he had articulated so strongly in his advice to Tanner on the Camps film: use long takes where you can find them, to stop the possibility of any attempt by the perpetrators to avoid guilt for what is shown. Avoiding cuts for several minutes at a time, until the end of a reel makes one unavoidable, Hitchcock's camera in *Rope* tracks its offenders relentlessly until their guilt is uncovered.[13]

The two young killers are explicitly, in an updating of Patrick Hamilton's original text from 1929, linked in the dialogue to Hitler and Nazism. And in a pioneering essay on *Rope* in 1963, V. F. Perkins wrote that "Hitchcock likes to give his films a central compositional motif: in *Vertigo* [1958], the spiral; in *Psycho* [1960], the circle. Here he uses the triangle."[14]

A prime instance is the tight isosceles triangle of the protracted one-shot static-camera scene of the maid (Edith Evanson) clearing up after the meal, centerpiece of the small party thrown by the killers (see Figure 7.3). On the left is the chest on which the food was laid out; we know it holds the murdered youth's body. To the right we glimpse, and hear, the babble of the calculating hosts and the unwitting guests. From the triangle's apex, the maid moves back and forth, and we wait for her to complete the clearance and open the chest. It is a classic instance of how to build suspense without cutting. The shot is a strong aesthetic pleasure in itself, and morally complex in that it is hard to avoid feeling anxiety, as so often in Hitchcock, on behalf of the killers. For now, they get away with it.

Perkins also describes the strategy by which at other moments the triangle composition is left for a time incomplete, in such a way as "to presuppose the existence of a missing 'third point.'"[15] His essay, like the film, moves to the endpoint at which a triangle is consolidated, with Rupert (James Stewart) slotting himself in at its apex: the teacher who shares, from way back, some of the responsibility for his pupils' callous philosophy, but who is now bringing them to justice (see Figure 7.4). Perkins's caption for the still is "the completion of the triangle."

In the successor to *Rope*, *Under Capricorn*, shot at Pinewood in 1948, four technicians are credited as "operators of camera movement"—and clearly they were needed, to handle a task even more taxing, within a complex network of spaces, than that of *Rope*, with its single basic set. That staffing was the kind of luxury unavailable for *Malgache* at Welwyn in 1944, where Hitchcock still, with the help of his cinematographer Gunther Krampf (credited also for *Bon Voyage*), accomplished some effective fluid shots, notably one that runs two and a half minutes, shortly before the scene of Clarus and the lawyer. A member of the resistance group, on the eve of departure on a mission, comes to say a confidential, anxious *au revoir* to his fiancée in her bedroom. The camera picks him up as he enters; pans right to frame, and to hold, an evenly balanced two-shot as the pair argue; loses him frame left as he exits; and adjusts to the woman's movement as after long hesitation she phones

Figure 7.3 (See also Plate 2) Another triangle composition emerges through staging in Alfred Hitchcock's *Rope* (1948).

Figure 7.4 (See also Plate 3) A third triangle is consolidated by the position of Rupert (James Stewart) in *Rope*.

the police. This could be seen as, in Perkins's terms, an incomplete triangle, with Clarus as the missing third point, author of the scheme over which the couple argue, and victim of the eventual betrayal, as we shortly learn in the scene with the lawyer—the triangle this time completed by the presence of the guard, opening up new issues.

Doing anything like justice, in this context, to the riches of *Under Capricorn*, set in Australia in 1831, would require a separate essay.[16] Its fabulously swirling camera movements work continual variations on the "incomplete triangle" of Perkins's formulation, through a number of tête-à-tête scenes that refer, explicitly or implicitly, to a third party, before—sometimes—completing the triangle. The main thrust of the film is not only to "rescue" Lady Henrietta (Bergman) from drunken despair, but to restore dignity and confidence to her husband, Sam Flusky (Joseph Cotten), with whom she had eloped in Ireland, years ago, and whom she followed to Australia when he was deported as a convict, waiting till he served out his sentence. The trigger for change is the arrival, at the start, of two more members, like her, of the "English Ascendancy" in Ireland, the new governor (Cecil Parker) and his cousin Charles (Michael Wilding).

In Figures 7.5 and 7.6, we see Cotten intruding, belatedly, on scenes of harmony, based on the three other characters' shared family and class background. He in contrast is non-ascendancy Irish, working-class, the groom who eloped with the titled daughter of the house. But he wins through. At the end, the triangle is reworked: Charles takes the boat home, with the reconciled couple waving farewell. Flusky can be compared to the guard at the apex of the triangle in *Malgache*. This is the future of the country, as it would develop in growing independence from Europe. The original novel by Helen Simpson included much reference to Indigenous Australian peoples, who she calls "aboriginals." These have been stripped from the screenplay, other than through a shock effect involving a shrunken head (which of course is a mistaken representation of Australian Indigenous cultures).

Hitchcock and race

"No Blacks, no Irish": this was a notorious formula used by many twentieth-century English landladies when advertising rooms. Hitchcock himself had Irish roots, on his mother's side, but he soon came to disavow these roots.

Figure 7.5 (See also Plate 4) Sam Flusky (Joseph Cotten) intrudes on a conversation between Henrietta Flusky (Ingrid Bergman) and Sir Richard (Cecil Parker) in Alfred Hitchcock's *Under Capricorn* (1949).

Figure 7.6 (See also Plate 5) Sam forms the apex of a triangle between Henrietta and Hon. Charles Adare (Michael Wilding) in *Under Capricorn*.

Perhaps he saw an affinity between those two categories of the racial other, in the culture within which he was formed. His treatment of neither has, to my knowledge, been systematically analyzed, across his fifty-year directing career, though an enlightening start has been made by David Greven in a weighty essay focused on a single canonical film, *Vertigo*.[17] All I will attempt for now is to place the image of the Black Malagasy soldier, tentatively, in a wider context.

In his early British films, Hitchcock includes a few Black characters, in plausible settings. In the early scenes of *Blackmail* (1929), both the silent and sound versions, police visit a working-class area of London's East End, just a few miles inward from Leytonstone, where he himself was born and raised; children playing out of doors include Black as well as White. Before that, some of the all-silent films have Black actors—never credited—in small parts, again in settings that are true to the demographics of this time: cargo boat (*Downhill*, 1927), fairground and boxing ring (*The Ring*, 1927), and an American tycoon's office (*Champagne*, 1928).

Some of these roles are painfully servile, others not, least of all that of a member of the support team for the boxer played by the star of the film, Carl Brisson. The man is unobtrusively but consistently present in both the fight scenes and the domestic scenes, with no reference made to his color. No Black fighter is seen in action, but one of them is an off-screen opponent for Brisson's rival, as cited in an intertitle: "If you win this next fight with the nigger, you'll be in the running for the championship." This was a time of respect, already, for Black boxers, in the wake of champions like Jack Johnson; the unselfconscious wording of the title, within a popular film, supplies evidence about the society in which Hitchcock had his formation, and with which his films engage.

Further evidence is found in the two films of the 1930s with a significant racial element, *Murder!* (1930) and *Young and Innocent* (1937). The former, a rare "whodunit," hinges upon the revelation that a man played by a White actor (Esme Percy) has "Black blood": he killed the woman who might have given away his shameful secret. In a curious reversal of this, the killer in *Young and Innocent*, played by George Curzon, is White, but masquerading as Black, a drummer in a blackface band; the blackening agent has to be wiped off before, at the film's ending, he can be formally identified and charged. Neither film is moved to question the easy assumptions of the time: prejudice against the "half-caste," acceptance of the weird rituals of blackface performance.

At last, in *Lifeboat*, Hitchcock's sixth film in Hollywood, released in early 1944, a Black character has dramatic weight: Joe, played by a Black actor, Canada Lee, who is credited on screen, and on posters.[18] Joe is one of the small group stranded on a mid-Atlantic lifeboat, one of those who have to cope with the twin challenges of survival, and of working out how to respond, suddenly, to the presence among them of a Nazi, survivor from another wreck. Joe's response is at least as mature and sensible as any of the White characters. He is surprised at being given a vote in decisions—which is, again, true to the historical moment. Again, Hitchcock is, with his team, responding to that moment, as previously to the very different culture of interwar England. Black soldiers did, as on this lifeboat, microcosm of America at war, contribute indispensably to the defeat of Nazism. It was directly after *Lifeboat* that Hitchcock made *Aventure Malgache*, with its prophetic use of the Black soldier. As is well known, America soon lurched back. It took years for Black status, and rights, to be asserted effectively in civilian life. Again, Hitchcock can be seen to have gone on recording, accurately enough, the social and political realities of the time—with no featuring of non-menial Black characters in his postwar American films. Until 1959 and *North by Northwest*.

This epic of late 1950s America, a fantastic time capsule, travels from New York to Chicago to the iconic site of Mount Rushmore in South Dakota, home to the massive granite gallery of the heads of American presidents. Along the way, a range of Black characters are kept, with carefully measured consistency, in the background. They are present in the main public venues: hotels, train, and auction room. They serve, but scarcely speak. At the Ambassadors Hotel in Chicago, a Black employee silently collects Cary Grant's suit for cleaning, but a white man has checked him in at reception. At the auction that follows, Black staff members silently hold up the objects for display, while White men continue to make all the announcements and decisions. But one scene departs from this pattern. Thornhill is drawn to the United Nations building in his efforts to understand the nightmare into which he has been thrown. He is received there by a non-White female receptionist (Doris Singh), described in Ernest Lehman's script as "a lovely Indian." She at once has more agency than any non-white hitherto, setting up a meeting with a senior UN official Lester Townsend. He is paged, and quickly appears.

The image that follows is triangular, closely echoing the key image of *Aventure Malgache* (see Figure 7.7). On the left is Thornhill, calling himself George Kaplan, the role assigned to him by others, including the fake Townsend, played by James Mason. On the right is the real Townsend (Philip

Figure 7.7 (See also Plate 6) Roger Thornhill (Cary Grant) and Lester Townsend (Philip Ober) in Alfred Hitchcock's *North by Northwest* (1959), with unnamed West African characters positioned, out-of-focus, at the apex of the triangle.

Ober), strangely oblivious to what has been going on in his name: the spectacular takeover, in the cause of some kind of Cold War plot, of his house and his identity. In the background stand a group of Black visitors to the UN. The script describes them as "West African." They have been unobtrusively busy already, subjects of a flash-bulb photograph; now they are centered, at the apex of a flattened isosceles triangle, a triangle perfectly congruent with the one from *Malgache*. Just as a second photograph is being set up, a knife is thrown from the wings, killing Townsend. Grant is shown—after a small reframing movement—with the dead man in his arms, and with his hand on the knife. The photographer rapidly swings round to capture the image of "the UN Killer"—an image which will drive the next stage of the narrative, as Grant strives to escape his sudden notoriety and clear his name.

However many times one watches this UN sequence, the precision of its planning and execution remains dazzling. And the presence of the Africans—deep in the shot, never brought closer, never referred to, never identified further—is part of what makes it so memorable and so portentous. It may seem paradoxical to suggest the importance of an element that is so pointedly *not* emphasized, left in the background. But in a book like this, the case surely does not need to be argued. Projected on the big screen, as in 1959, in its Vistavision print—the same "Motion Picture High Fidelity" system as used in *Vertigo*—every detail is clear and sharp. Seen in the modern manner on viewer-controlled smaller screens, the same details stand up to scrutiny at length and in depth. We know how obsessively Hitchcock and his writers came to plan every detail of a film's narrative. The background action of the UN scene, and the way it explodes into the foreground via the action of the photographer, is a considered and integral part of the expert mechanism of *North by Northwest*.

Past, present, future. You could say that Townsend stands for an old complacent America, unaware of threats happening in his own personal backyard, and punished accordingly. The Grant character is the present, ducking and weaving all through the film to grapple, in the end successfully, with the ruthlessness of contemporary Cold War politics. And in the background, tip of the triangle, is the future, the UN, and Africa, at the start of the pivotal 1960s decade of the move to decolonization.

Hitchcock may very well have been deliberate in his echoing of the triangle from *Malgache*. Patrick McGilligan records that he "took considerable pride in *Bon Voyage* and *Aventure Malgache*. He was fond enough of the former that he later explored expanding it into a feature film, rescreening it as late as 1958."[19] That was the year in which he and Ernest Lehman were wrestling hard with the task of getting the narrative of *North by Northwest*—one of Hitchcock's rare original scripts—into shape. *Bon Voyage* was never remade, but was invaluable in helping to solve a scripting problem. At the Mount Rushmore café, toward the film's end, Eve Kendall (Eva Marie Saint) draws a gun and appears to shoot Thornhill dead, in front of Vandamm (James Mason) and Leonard (Martin Landau), clearing herself, for now, of any suspicion that she might be allied to Thornhill and to the United States rather than to them. Later Leonard realizes, and explains: "It's an old Gestapo trick: shoot one of your own people, to prove that you're not one of them. They just freshened it up a bit with blank cartridges." It's a direct echo of *Bon Voyage*, where the pilot, being debriefed in London, expresses puzzlement at the action, witnessed by us too, of the chief Gestapo agent in killing a fellow agent, likewise in a café: "But if Godowski was a spy, why would he kill a fellow-spy?" The officer duly tells him.

According to Lehman, reminiscing years later, he had a sudden mysterious inspiration in coming up, at a late stage, with the idea of the fake shooting.[20] But he had most likely been present at the screening of *Bon Voyage*, in line with Hitchcock's regular practice of screening relevant films for himself and his writers. Even if not, it was enough that Hitchcock himself had re-seen it and taken note. And if one of the French-language shorts was screened in 1958, why not the other? We know, anyway, that Hitchcock was thinking back to that pair of films of which he was justifiably proud. Lehman had wanted to help make "the Hitchcock picture to end all Hitchcock pictures," the essence of Hitchcock packaged in a single new drama. This aim was fulfilled both on a big scale—travel, mystery, romance, suspense, on the *39 Steps* (1935) model, now in spectacular Hollywood terms—and in crucial details like those drawn from the two modest short films: respectively the café shooting and the past-present-future triangle, both brought forward from 1944 to 1959, and seamlessly incorporated.

An eye to the future

The year of *North by Northwest* was the eve of Madagascar's independence, and a high point of the vision and influence of the UN, under its most dynamic secretary-general, the Swede Dag Hammarskjöld, who was in office from 1953 up to his death in a plane crash in Africa in 1961. Hitchcock was well aware of the UN and of its work, just as he had been well aware, in 1943/44, from urgent discussions with fully engaged Resistance workers, of the political realities of Madagascar. At the end of 1944 he was involved in plans for a short propaganda film, *Watchtower over Tomorrow*, celebrating the ideals behind the new UN organization: doing a few days of intensive scripting work in collaboration with a favored collaborator, Ben Hecht, although he was not in the end free to direct the result.[21] In 1964 he was one of a small number of directors invited to contribute to a set of high-profile one-hour films designed to promote UN ideals. He at once gave an enthusiastically affirmative response. For various reasons, the series never happened, but the episode is testimony, likewise, to his seriousness about embracing their progressive vision.[22]

After a further decade, Hitchcock returned to London for what turned out to be his penultimate film. *Frenzy* (1972) is a consciously nostalgic, old-fashioned production, but its opening scene does engage briefly with the vision of a progressive new city, cleaner and greener, before we are pulled back, via the discovery of a butchered corpse floating in the Thames, to the city of the historic serial killers, Jack the Ripper and John Christie, both of them referenced in an early pub conversation. No Black characters appear after this riverside opening, which features Hitchcock himself in his accustomed cameo appearance, along with two Black citizens, behind and ahead of him,

Figure 7.8 (See also Plate 7) A rare glimpse of multiculturalism in the opening scene of Alfred Hitchcock's *Frenzy* (1972).

Figure 7.9 (See also Plate 8) The last time a Black character is seen in *Frenzy.*

plus a third, closer to camera, in the following shot (see Figures 7.8 and 7.9). Such casting decisions, even of extras, are always calculated. Hitchcock may in *Frenzy* be making a sentimental return to the past—his own film past, his family's past in the Covent Garden market—but, as often, he has at least half an eye to the future. A post-imperial, postcolonial future, multicultural, which we now inhabit.

Notes

1. In this essay I draw here and there upon material used in *Hitchcock Lost and Found: The Forgotten Films*, a book I researched and authored jointly with the Parisian scholar Alain Kerzoncuf (Lexington: University Press of Kentucky, 2015). This is, however, emphatically not a rehash of the book's material but a sequel.

2. *Malgache* evidently functions in French both as adjective and noun, denoting the island and its language—an alternative term being *Malagasy*.

3. See ruling of October 7, 1963, by an official of the Central Office of Information, confirming the ban, quoted in Kerzoncuf and Barr, *Hitchcock Lost and Found*, 168.

4. For details of this "deserter" controversy, see Charles Barr, "Deserter or Honored Exile? Views of Hitchcock from Wartime Britain," in *The Hitchcock Annual Anthology*, ed. Sidney Gottlieb and Richard Allen (London: Wallflower Press, 2009), 82–96. The essay was first published in volume 13 of *The Hitchcock Annual* (2004–2005).

5. Hitchcock quoted in Donald Spoto, *The Dark Side of Genius: The Life of Alfred Hitchcock* (Boston: Da Capo, 1983), 495–496.

6. More details of the unfinished project are given in Dan Auiler, *Hitchcock's Secret Notebooks* (London: Bloomsbury, 1999), 545–550, and at greater length as a main component—along with *The Mountain Eagle*—of Dan Auiler, *Hitchcock Lost: The Lost Silent Hitchcock and Frenzy 67* (Kindle edition only, 2013). The title *Frenzy* was used later for a different project, shot in London, as discussed briefly below.

7. See the two essays, "L'Évolution du langage cinématographique" and "Montage interdit," first published in André Bazin, *Qu'est-ce que le cinéma?* 2 vols. (Paris: Cerf, 1958), vol. 1. Both were consolidated versions of earlier journalistic writings. English translations have followed, notably in Peter Graham and Ginette Vincendeau, eds., *The French New Wave: Critical Landmarks* (London: British Film Institute, 2009).

8. "Depth of field in Wyler aims at being liberal and democratic, like the conscience of both the American viewers and of the characters in." From Bazin's 1948 essay "William Wyler, or the Jansenist of Directing," included in Bert Cardullo, ed., *Bazin at Work: Major Essays and Reviews from the Forties and Fifties*, trans. Alain Piette and Bert Cardullo (London: Routledge, 1997), 9.

9. Testimony from Peter Tanner, editor of the aborted *Memory of the Camps* film, interviewed in the Granada TV production *A Painful Reminder* (broadcast on the ITV network, 1985), quoted more fully in Kerzoncuf and Barr, *Hitchcock Lost and Found*, 186–187.

10. See note 7 above.

11. Shot-by-shot details of these contrasting scenes in *The Skin Game* are given in Charles Barr, *English Hitchcock* (Moffat: Cameron & Hollis, 1999), 104–107.

12. For the Osbiston interview, see Cedric Belfrage, ed., *All Is Grist* (London: Parallax Press, 1997), 114. Osbiston's retrospective confusion of the two Hitchcock titles is understandable, but we should have put this right when quoting him in the *Hitchcock Lost and Found* book, 154.

13. Kerzoncuf and Barr, *Hitchcock Lost and Found*, 192.

14. V. F. Perkins, "*Rope* (1963)," in *V. F. Perkins on Movies: Collected Shorter Film Criticism*, ed. Douglas Pye (Detroit: Wayne State University Press, 2020), 151–161.

15. In fact, in the 2020 collection, a slightly different image of the three men is (as here) printed, this time with a frame still rather than a production still, and a slightly different caption: "The triangle is stabilised."

16. For an enlightening collection of new essays, see the essays published for the special issue "Under Capricorn: 70 Years On," *Movie: A Journal of Film Criticism*, https://warwick.ac.uk/fac/arts/film/movie/capricorn/.

17. David Greven, "The Dark Side of Blondeness, *Vertigo* and Race," *Screen* 59, no. 1 (Spring 2018): 59–79.

18. Greven plausibly suggests the influence here of "the original screenwriter John Steinbeck's social activist vision." Greven, "The Dark Side of Blondeness," 60.

19. Patrick McGilligan, *Alfred Hitchcock: A Life in Darkness and Light* (Chichester: John Wiley & Sons, 2003), 348.

20. Ernest Lehman, *North by Northwest* (London: Faber & Faber, 1999), vii, xi.

21. See the extensive research on this project by Sidney Gottlieb, "The Unknown Hitchcock: Watchtower over Tomorrow," *The Hitchcock Annual* 5 (1996–1997): 117–130. Also see Kerzoncuf and Barr, *Hitchcock Lost and Found*, 175–182.

22. Kerzoncuf and Barr, *Hitchcock Lost and Found*, 182.

8

Rope (1948)

Chromatic design and neon light

Sarah Street

> I never wanted to make a Technicolor picture merely for the sake of using color. I waited until I could find a story in which color could play a dramatic role, and still be muted to a low key. In *Rope* the sets and costumes are neutralized so that there are no glaring contrasts. The key role played by color in this film is in the background. I insisted that color be used purely as the eye received it.[1]

Rope (1948) was notable for launching two new technical departures for Hitchcock. The film famously showcased an experiment: the illusion of a full-length feature film being realized in a single shot. To create the illusion the film was staged on a meticulously constructed studio set of a New York apartment. Since the camera's film magazine capacity expired after 10 minutes, Hitchcock carefully masked the end of each segment by focusing on dark objects such as the back of a piece of furniture, or the lid of a wooden chest. In so doing, the camera's movement appeared to flow seamlessly between the discrete segments that made up the film. Hitchcock's daring experiment has deservedly attracted extensive critical and scholarly commentary, but this has tended to overshadow the film's second technical milestone, that *Rope* was Hitchcock's first Technicolor film. For this book I have chosen to focus on *Rope*'s penultimate segments when the film's overall color design, described by Hitchcock as "muted to a low key," is broken by the intrusion of a striking color effect that intensifies the drama's closing action, as the murderers realize their actions have been discovered.

Rope's narrative centers on the concealment of the body of David Kentley (Dick Hogan), a man strangled in a New York apartment by Brandon Shaw

Sarah Street, Rope *(1948)* In: *One Shot Hitchcock*. Edited by: Luke Robinson and Melanie Robson, Oxford University Press. © Oxford University Press 2024. DOI: 10.1093/oso/9780197682876.003.0008

(John Dall) and Phillip Morgan (Farley Granger). Brandon and Phillip strangle him for no apparent reason other than to execute an experiment about intellectual superiority, to commit the "perfect" murder of their former Harvard classmate. The film's timespan takes place over an evening during which Brandon and Phillip host a buffet dinner party, for which David arrived early. They strangle him and hide his body in a wooden chest, even serving food on the top of the chest when the party commences. The guests, who each have a connection to David, are of course oblivious, but the film's knowing audience is kept in constant suspense. The suspense is intense, especially when Rupert Cadell (James Stewart), one of the guests and Brandon and Phillip's former prep-school housemaster, grows increasingly suspicious when David apparently fails to arrive. The suspense increases even further when the "art of murder" is discussed and Phillip, in particular, appears increasingly nervous. At the same time that Phillip shows his nervousness at being caught, in his desire to impress Rupert, Brandon cannot conceal his excitement, as if he wants to reveal the fatal ingenuity that resulted in David's murder but, because of the consequences, is unable to fully articulate what has happened.

Toward the end of *Rope*, after the dinner party has ended and the guests have left, Rupert returns to Brandon and Phillip's apartment on the pretense of recovering his cigarette case (which he actually had with him). Rupert is suspicious because earlier, as he was leaving, he was accidentally handed the wrong hat that was monogrammed "D.K.," evidence that David had indeed been in the apartment. On his return, Rupert is offered a drink and the conversation turns to David's disappearance, with Brandon almost luring Rupert into hypothesizing how they might have got David "out the way" if he had arrived early for the party. The camera roves around the room as Rupert describes David's possible movements, how they could have knocked him out and taken him outside. Brandon interjects that they would have needed to hide him until after dark, causing Phillip to smash a glass on the floor, obviously disturbed that Rupert might have guessed their crime. Rupert admits he returned to the flat to discover what happened to David because Brandon and Phillip were behaving strangely, as if fearful of discovery. Rupert guesses Brandon has a gun in his pocket, which he takes out, saying he needs it for protection when they drive later that night to the country, and places it on top of the piano. There is a lull in the conversation, a moment of temporary relaxation when Rupert says he almost wishes he was leaving the city with them, that driving at night is "exciting."

He continues, with his back to them and says: "But driving with you and Phillip now might have an additional element of suspense." As Rupert turns around, he reveals that he has been hiding a rope in his pocket. We know David was strangled with a rope, which was then used to tie up piles of books Brandon and Phillip gave to David's father, Mr. Henry Kentley (Sir Cedric Hardwicke). Having noticed Phillip's anxiety over the rope, on his return to the apartment Rupert deliberately uses a rope to test the validity of his growing suspicions. The camera tilts upward, away from a close shot of Rupert holding the rope, moving toward the window. After the word "suspense," it slowly glides rightward to the window and we see the large first letter "S" of a neon sign outside that changes in a recurring sequence from white, to red, and to green (see Figure 8.1). As the camera's viewpoint pans across the windows that allow the neon to shine inside, Brandon and Phillip's profiles are in the foreground, with the neon "S" beaming vibrantly, changing from green to red at the moment when they appear most in danger of their secret being discovered (see Figure 8.2). Phillip cries out: "He's got it! He knows," before reaching for the gun on the piano, and a shot misfires as he struggles with Rupert. The glow from the sign pulsates

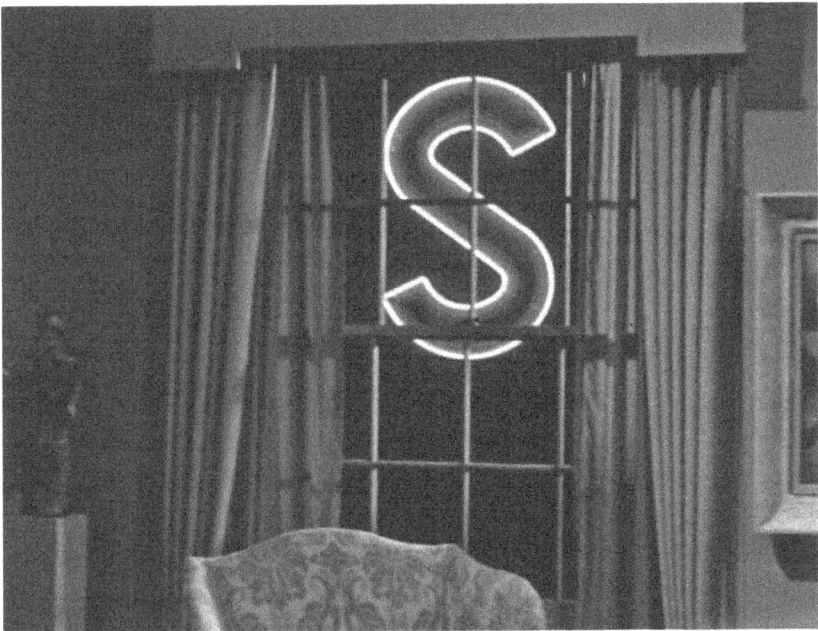

Figure 8.1 (See also Plate 9) The first letter "S" of the neon sign in *Rope*.

Figure 8.2 (See also Plate 10) Brandon (John Dall, left) and Phillip (Farley Granger, right) on the brink of discovery in *Rope*.

into the apartment for the rest of the film, underscoring the escalating drama of the closing action.

New York's skyline and the "cyclorama"

The key "shot," which I am taking as starting from the panning movement after Rupert's utterance of "suspense" and then showing the white, red, green sequence of colors emanating from the sign outside the window, technically ends when Phillip opens the chest. Here the real cut is masked by a completely dark frame as the lid opens, so the effect (what I am terming "the shot") continues just over five minutes longer to the end of the film. As Rupert lifts the lid, the red and green streaks are highly visible, especially when highlighting a white handkerchief he has wound around his hand following its injury when the gun was fired. The neon "S" has been seen earlier in the film outside the window as an innocuous signifier of the city in the daytime, but this now comes to life and color in the night. Brandon and

Phillip are about to close the curtains when they are disturbed by Rupert's return, ensuring that this particular feature becomes active and significant as the narrative climaxes toward closure. The shot announces the arrival of a new, obtrusive effect that thereafter collapses the distinction between exterior and interior. As noted above, this occurs at a crucial moment, as Brandon and Phillip realize that Rupert knows they murdered David. The changing sequence of lights beams its vivid colors inside the apartment as Rupert struggles with Phillip, retrieves the gun, and David's body is revealed to be in the chest. All this time the red and green lights can be seen reflected on surfaces inside the apartment. This effect is particularly obtrusive when Rupert, despairing at what they have done, stands with his back to the windows, which let in the neon's pulsating, glowing hues (see Figure 8.3). As he further discusses the severity of the crime, all three figures appear drenched in colors that shatter the previously unobtrusive, "subdued" design. Finally, Rupert alerts the police by firing shots out of the window.

The approach I am taking towards analyzing this shot is embedded within the history of color expression and theory. Hitchcock used artificial means

Figure 8.3 (See also Plate 11) Rupert (James Stewart) with the neon sign pulsating in the background in *Rope*.

of creating the Manhattan skyline view from Brandon and Phillip's apartment so that he could precisely create the impression of "real time" as the day progressed from sunset to darkness. The "cyclorama" made for *Rope* was an exact miniature reproduction of the New York skyline created "by 8,000 incandescent bulbs and 200 neon signs requiring 150 transformers."[2] Hitchcock proudly detailed how this complex device worked:

> In the 12,000 square feet of the cyclorama, the largest backing ever used on a sound stage, the spectator sees the Empire State, the Chrysler, and the Woolworth buildings; St. Patrick's, Radio City, and hundreds of other landmarks of the fabulous New York skyline. Each miniature building was wired separately for globes ranging from 25 to 150 watts in the tiny windows. (The electrician's eye level was at the 22nd story.) Twenty-six thousand feet of wire carried 126,000 watts of power for the building and window illumination—all controlled by a twist of the electrician's wrist, via a bank of 47 switches, as he sat at the light organ high up and far behind the camera. . . . That electrician who sat high on a parallel behind the camera manipulating the light organ controlled the lighting of the miniature like an artist at a console. He could illuminate an entire building or just one window at a time. He could, at the exact and rehearsed line of dialogue which gave him his cue, flood the Manhattan skyline with light from 200 miniature neon signs. By the time the picture went from the setting of the sun in the first reel to the hour of total darkness in the final denouement, the man at the light organ had played a nocturnal Manhattan symphony in light.[3]

This device showcased the film's expressive effects, enabling the dynamic neon "S" to function as a spectacular, graphic visual commentary on the developing narrative.

Hitchcock's decision to use a "light organ" effect recalls the 1920s, when experimentation with color constituted a vibrant and vital aspect of silent filmmaking and other arts. As Joshua Yumibe and I have documented, this was imbricated within a fertile cultural landscape in which many new color forms and techniques were developed across a range of media including film, architecture, theater, and advertising. The increasing incursion of color into people's everyday lives, fueled by the surge of newly available consumer products in Europe and the United States as a result of the increasing availability of synthetic dyes and materials, became a site of intense debate among contemporary artists, scientists, philosophers, and educationalists.[4] The "light organ" idea, for example, can be linked to Thomas Wilfred's demonstration of the "Claxilux" color organ for "lumina" (art created by light) performances in New York in the 1920s.[5] To contemporary audiences, Wilfred's recitals appeared as "the unfolding of a symphony," a comment that resonates with Hitchcock's later account of his own experiment with colored light for *Rope* as "a nocturnal Manhattan symphony in light." These approaches brought the affective power of color to the fore, emphasizing in particular its impact on mood and psychology.

Working in the UK and in Germany in the 1920s, Hitchcock was influenced by these developments, which can be seen in *The Lodger: A Story of the London Fog* (1926), a silent film that bears some striking resemblances to the design of *Rope*. In *The Lodger*, a studio-constructed set of a three-sided house anticipates *Rope*'s single apartment set, and in both contexts a distinction between interior spaces and the outside world is, at first, emphasized but subsequently collapsed as the narratives develop. The Victorian house in *The Lodger* is coded as a safe environment that is underscored by warm, amber tints, whereas the cooler, iron-blue tone exteriors are associated with modernity, the city, and danger. As the film progresses these differences, however, become less clearly delineated as we suspect that a serial killer in London might well be residing as a lodger in that very house. Color and lighting are used to convey this shift, for example through dual processing the blue tone with amber tinting.[6] As Thomas Connelly notes, *Rope* similarly presents Brandon and Phillip's apartment at first as an environment that protects them, and their secret, from outside interference. Although the window in *Rope*, with its panoramic views of the Manhattan skyline, is "both transparent and a barrier, providing spectacular views while protecting observers from exterior elements such as cold, wind, and rain," it also, as we see so vividly expressed in the film's final segments, disrupts that illusion by beckoning the outside in, coming "alive" with the pulsating neon sign that graphically underscores Rupert's exposure of the shocking crime that has taken place inside a "private" apartment.[7] For this effect Hitchcock clearly draws on the influence of German Expressionism by vivifying the mise-en-scène so that "the window visually transforms the penthouse into a state of unrest in order to visualize the film's narrative climax."[8] Steven Jacobs describes the set as "a virtuoso stage machine," an apt description of the techniques that allowed Hitchcock, a decade prior to *Vertigo* (1958), to experiment with the expressive possibilities of urban neon light.[9]

As a key feature of the cyclorama, neon lighting was by the 1940s a common signifier of a city's modernity. As an arresting advertising technique, neon signage had spread throughout US cities in the 1930s, and *Rope* was released a few years before the onset of its gradual decline as an illuminator.[10] Its brilliant colors were perfect for advertising products, and the neon signs on buildings in *Rope*'s cyclorama exploit this trend, most famously for Hitchcock's cameo appearance featuring his iconic facial profile as a red neon sign for "Reduco," a fictional weight-loss company, seen in the distance. The large neon "S" that is supposed to be much nearer the apartment, is the first letter of a sign that reads "STORAGE," perhaps as an ironic comment on the concealment of David's body in a wooden chest. Hitchcock commented that he "wanted the effect to add dramatic tension, much like the increasing crescendos of an orchestra at the climax of a symphony."[11] To gain the effect of enough light beaming into the room as the sign went through its color changes from white, to red, to green, an electrically timed switch was used to synchronize the alternate flashing with the opening and closing of shutters on three huge floodlights, which ensured enough light reached into the room. The ingenious idea to use a release switch was apparently James Stewart's, drawing on his knowledge of the bomb release switches used in heavy bombers during the war.[12]

Color and symbolism in *Rope*

Hitchcock's fascination with pulsating neon signage effects dates to the "Tonight . . . Golden Curls" neon seen flashing at the beginning of *The Lodger*. It associates artificial light with cities as places full of mystery and potential terror, and also as a symbol of modernity. This sign flashes each word at a time that constitutes another interesting precursor for the repetitive color cycle of *Rope*'s neon sign. Although the "STORAGE" sign is located outside the apartment, its unrelenting beam invades the interior, enabling it to function as an interrogatory force from which Brandon and Phillip cannot hide. Seen inside the apartment, the red and green color faces, bodies, and objects with an "unnatural" glow that brings out—quite literally—the strangeness of the murderous act that has taken place within its confines. This tendency, as noted by David Batchelor, is particularly common to artificially colored forms that appear to attach themselves to other surfaces:

Luminous colors, however old they are, appear to have a particular relationship with the world around them and with their beholders that is unlike that of other colors. First, these are colors that escape their containers and bleed into the street; they deliver what color always promises but doesn't always achieve: a release from the surfaces and materials that support it, a release that leads to the fleeting magic of the "fiery pool reflecting in the asphalt." This escape of color, this assertion of its autonomy and independence from the objects that lay claim to it, is momentous, in its way, but also momentary.[13]

By leaving it until the final two segments of the film, Hitchcock ensures that the neon effect is all the more impressive. This is in recognition of the power of artificial color to appear even more vibrant when seen in the dark. The lights are also shown off against lighter blocks of color when their presence is unexpected. The colors are first visible in the close-up of Rupert turning around with the rope; the red and green appear as intermittent glows of color reflected on the cream-colored couch beneath the apartment's panoramic window.

In terms of symbolic resonance, red and green are often associated with danger and death. Richard Allen has identified jade green as a color used by Hitchcock in *Rope*, *To Catch a Thief* (1955), and *Under Capricorn* (1949): "The jade-green light was derived from the London stage of his youth. . . . Perhaps jade is associated with ghostliness because it is close to the color of mold and hence evokes the presence of death."[14] In *Vertigo*, green similarly connotes otherworldliness and the film's uncanny resonances; green's recurrence suggests subtextual discourses. Such readings render the red and green neon as appropriate colors for the revelatory work they perform in *Rope*. The fact that the colors suffuse the appearance of all three characters is also significant in delineating the film's complex moral compass since both red and green can be connected symbolically to danger and death. This is articulated in the film's closing discussion of how at prep school Rupert introduced Brandon and Phillip to Nietzschean-influenced ideas concerning intellectual superiority and entitlement to commit actions outside the law. Rupert's strident rejection of any moral culpability in their crime is perhaps put into question by the colored light, while in addition exposing his horror that he may have unwittingly contributed to the "test case" of David's murder. Indeed, Ned Schantz has commented that the persistence of the light "casts Rupert's closing arguments in a rather perverse light," bringing him no relief at the revelations.[15] The ambiguities of the film's closure are thus underscored by the shafts of colored light his suspicions appear to have unleashed.

The color effect used in *Rope* has an interesting relation to Hitchcock's view that Technicolor should not be used for its own sake. While the neon light is part of the mise-en-scène that is embedded within the film's diegesis as a "natural" phenomenon occurring in a city, as previously mentioned, when night falls it is activated into something that subsequently exceeds its primary purpose as an object for advertising a storage service. The neon's dramatic role becomes something else as the red and green appear to attach themselves to the figures and objects inside the apartment. This changeable aspect of color was further developed by Hitchcock in later films, most markedly in *Marnie* (1964) in relation to red. As John Belton has observed, although the color is initially attached to certain objects, red is "repeatedly wrenched from these disparate and seemingly random objects and projected onto the face of the heroine herself in the form of red suffusions that fade in and out."[16] It is as if red has acquired "an independent existence . . . it has a meaning that transcends the objects with which it is associated."[17] In the case of *Marnie* this presents the color as profoundly enigmatic, as an intriguing manifestation of the heroine's trauma that is not resolved until the end of the film.

Color's tendency to "escape" from an object was discussed by Soviet filmmaker Sergei Eisenstein, who noted that color "assumes an endless multitude of forms and is bound up with a most complex set of phenomena."[18] This observation occasioned his oft-quoted remarks on how a color's meaning is influenced by context, as in red: "Red! The colour of the revolutionary flag. And the colour of the ears of a liar caught red-handed. The colour of a boiled crayfish—and the colour of a 'crimson' sunset. The colour of cranberry juice—and the colour of warm human blood."[19] So while the alternating red and green flashes of the neon sign in *Rope* in the first instance are designed to alert the viewer to the meaning of the "STORAGE" lettering, once inside the apartment they shatter the film's previously naturalistic color design. Even though there is a logical, "natural" explanation (the curtains have not been shut) for seeing beams of colored light invading the interior, these nevertheless mark the figures with "unnatural" hues that embody their strangeness and psychological disturbance in that particular context.

An important aspect of the colors is that although the neon sequence— white, to red, to green—is regularly timed, because the camera and figures move around the apartment the colors appear fleeting, to come and go, attaching themselves to different objects and figures once the lettering from which they emanate is no longer in view. It is as if Hitchcock is exploiting the momentary, temporary nature of artificially illuminated colors. This contributes to the mystique attached to neon, for its association with night-time and even illicit activities. Batchelor comments that "the knowledge of this sumptuous vividness could be gone in an instant is an integral part of its attraction. If these colours appear alive, after all, then they can also drop dead. That is the deal you do: a condition of this brilliance is its imperma-nence."[20] This tendency of neon light works perfectly to convey the wrought, tense atmosphere in *Rope*'s closing sequence, in particular Brandon's ina-bility to restrain himself from feeding Rupert's suspicions.

Color, taste, and psychology

The use of color to convey and explore mind-states, affective experiences, and psychological disturbance had been explored in previous Technicolor films such as *Blanche Fury* (1948) and *A Matter of Life and Death* (1946), but it was not until the 1960s when color films were more numerous that this was used more markedly in films such as in *The Ipcress File* (1965), when a character is "brainwashed" by being exposed to a barrage of flashing, artifi-cially colored lights. Even so, the use of color as an obtrusive effect tended to be carefully deployed in mainstream cinema, in keeping with Natalie Kalmus's guidelines for the application of Technicolor that warned against "a super-abundance of color," describing it as "unnatural, and has a most unpleasant effect not only upon the eye itself, but upon the mind as well."[21] She further stated that: "It is a psychological fact that the nervous system experiences a shock when it is forced to adapt itself to any degree of un-naturalness in the reception of external stimuli."[22] It is interesting that Brandon and Phillip do not close the curtains when the light throws its beams into the apartment. We get no sense that the glare disturbs their vi-sion even though its prominence might well, after a time, become bother-some. The escalation of the crisis is probably why the glare from the neon does not urge them to keep it out. The habit of drawing the curtains at night is, however, indicated when Rupert's unexpected return interrupts them from doing so. The proximity of the sign so near the luxury Manhattan penthouse apartment was, as Jacobs points out, probably in violation of New York's zoning laws.[23]

The theme of class and color is present in *Rope*, with its "tasteful" apartment decor of antique furniture, cream-colored couch and armchair with a pale green floral pattern, ceiling-high bookshelves, beige carpet, off-white walls and piano, contrasting with the neon's vibrant, bright colors. Neon was first seen in New York in the 1920s, exploding in the following decade for advertising signs that at first were not subject to regulation. When the "city beautiful" movement lobbied against neon, and zoning laws restricted the erection of advertising illuminations that were considered gaudy, neon's cultural identity became imbricated within judgments about taste and, by association, class. The fact that Fifth Avenue had few, if any, neon signs was due to zoning regulations, the implication of which was that neon was inappropriate for the parts of New York considered most elegant and expensive.[24] Brandon and Phillip's apartment is coded similarly, as an environment far removed from the commercialism represented by the neon signs that can be seen through the panoramic window in the evening. While the distance of most of the visible signs renders them attractive, like jewels twinkling in the distance, the proximity of the "STORAGE" sign is another matter; it is quite literally too close for comfort.

Discourses around color, taste, and class were long-standing by the time of *Rope*'s release. In the 1920s, educators, intellectuals, psychologists, and scientists urged consumers to be "color-conscious" about their choices for fashions, interior decors, and the array of newly available products. Neon's transformation of the urban skyline carried with it a number of associated trends including modernism and display of what Kirsten Thompson has referred to as "the technological sublime."[25] Neon's vibrant, glowing primary colors came to epitomize city life, a world highly networked by the intersecting flows of commerce, industry, consumerism, and mass entertainment. By contrast, the upper-middle-class social circles frequented by Brandon and Phillip, combined with the elitism implied in their philosophical debates about intellectual superiority, appear completely different. The apartment's expression of controlled, "tasteful" color—nothing brash, gaudy, or extreme—secludes them from the city's far brighter illuminated colors and what these represent in terms of zoning. The intrusion of the neon threatens their privacy, its beam acting as a panopticon from which they cannot hide. In addition, the "STORAGE" lettering becomes ironic when its unrelenting, flashing colors coincide with Rupert's opening the wooden chest where David's body has been hidden. Brandon and Phillip's anxiety not only relates to their crime but also to their homosexuality, a theme that creates another layer of secrecy in their unspoken gay relationship.[26] The neon thus symbolizes the outside world's scrutiny on their actions and sexuality, with "STORAGE" acquiring additional significance in perhaps alluding to Brandon and Phillip's closeted homosexuality.

So far from being an incidental embellishment, the neon in *Rope* is a highly significant bearer of meaning in terms of the film's color design. In presenting the effect, Hitchcock mobilized a stunning device to indicate the shift in temporality from early evening to nightfall. The choice to vary this by including the close "STORAGE" sign permitted it to exceed that function, to quite literally let the outside into the apartment with devastating consequences. Color and light were mobilized to perform a commentary on the film's closing action and to vivify the tense escalation of psychological intensity. Brandon's "cat and mouse" flirtation with danger as he feeds, almost deliberately, Rupert's suspicions, is accompanied by the intermittent beams of colored light as they flicker inside the apartment. Hitchcock went on to experiment further with color in later films, in particular suffusing the entire screen with a color as an expressive effect. Although otherwise his use of color was primarily to underscore character, action, and to embellish costume and mise-en-scène more generally, the experiment launched in *Rope* reconnected him with his earliest, formative years as a filmmaker when light and color encouraged the same kind of creative ingenuity that resulted in the "nocturnal Manhattan symphony in light."

Notes

1. Alfred Hitchcock, "My Most Exciting Picture (1948)," in *Hitchcock on Hitchcock: Selected Writings and Interviews*, ed. Sidney Gottlieb (Berkeley: University of California Press, 1995), 284.
2. Hitchcock, "My Most Exciting Picture," 276–277.
3. Hitchcock, "My Most Exciting Picture," 278.
4. Sarah Street and Joshua Yumibe, *Chromatic Modernity: Color, Cinema, and Media of the 1920s* (New York: Columbia University Press, 2019).
5. Street and Yumibe, *Chromatic Modernity*, 118–119.
6. Street and Yumibe, *Chromatic Modernity*, 213–216.
7. Thomas J. Connelly, *Cinema of Confinement* (Evanson, IL: Northwestern University Press, 2019), 32–35.
8. Connelly, *Cinema of Confinement*, 40.
9. Steven Jacobs, *The Wrong House: The Architecture of Alfred Hitchcock* (Rotterdam: 010 Publishers, 2007), 276–277.

10. Christoph Ribbat, *Flickering Light: A History of Neon* (London: Reaktion Books, 2011), 11.

11. Hitchcock, "My Most Exciting Picture," 282.

12. Hitchcock, "My Most Exciting Picture," 282.

13. David Batchelor, *The Luminous and the Grey* (London: Reaktion Books, 2014), 49.

14. Richard Allen, "Hitchcock's Color Designs," in *Color: The Film Reader*, ed. Angela Dalle Vacche and Brian Price (New York: Routledge, 2006), 137.

15. Ned Schantz, "Hitchcock's Shadow Scenes," *Camera Obscura* 25, no. 1 (2010): 17.

16. John Belton, "Color and Meaning in *Marnie*," in *Color and the Moving Image: History, Theory, Aesthetics, Archive*, ed. Simon Brown, Sarah Street, and Liz Watkins (New York: Routledge, 2013), 190.

17. Belton, "Color and Meaning in *Marnie*," 190–191.

18. Sergei Eisenstein, "On Colour," in *Color: The Film Reader*, 107.

19. Eisenstein, "On Colour," 107. Dash in the original.

20. Batchelor, *The Luminous and the Grey*, 49.

21. Natalie Kalmus, "Color Consciousness [1935]," in *Color: The Film Reader*, 25.

22. Natalie Kalmus, "Color Consciousness," 25

23. Steven Jacobs, "Color and Containment: Domestic Spaces and Restrained Palettes in Hitchcock's Color Films," in *Color and the Moving Image*, 182.

24. Thomas Rinaldi, *New York Neon* (New York: W. W. Norton, 2012).

25. Kirsten Moana Thompson, "Rainbow Ravine: Colour and Animated Advertising in Times Square," in *The Colour Fantastic: Chromatic Worlds of Silent Cinema*, ed. Giovanna Fossati et al. (Amsterdam: Amsterdam University Press, 2018), 168.

26. Viewers may have been aware of the real-life case of Leopold and Loeb, on which *Rope* was based.

9

Rear Window (1954)

Intermedialities of peeping in the plural

Martin P. Rossouw

Given the frequent kinship between Alfred Hitchcock's film titles and opening shots, it comes as no surprise that *Rear Window* (1954) opens—and famously so—with a view of a view. Hitchcock already sets the scene during the opening credits, with a shot of the eponymous rear window that overlooks an apartment courtyard (and thus also scenes *the set*: a humongous single set modeled on 1950s Greenwich Village, the largest that the Paramount studios had ever constructed at the time). Yet, it's only when the credits sequence-shot cuts to the *opening shot*, this chapter's object of analysis, that we're given an actual "*over*-view": a patient, winding long take presented in long shot, panning overall from screen right to left, showing the array of apartment windows and entrances that comprise the courtyard visible from L. B. "Jeff" Jeffries's (James Stewart) window (see Figure 9.1). (Jeff, by the way, is a busybody magazine photographer, who recently broke his leg, who is now not only stuck in a wheelchair but stuck in his apartment, and who therefore has nothing much to do other than to stare out from his rear window at the courtyard in the same way that the opening shot invites us to do. Right now, though, Jeff is still asleep—so let's not drift off with him.)

At this early point, most of the opposite apartments unveiled by the opening shot seem empty. But we'll get to know the main attractions soon enough. On the far right is the large bay window belonging to the Songwriter (Ross Bagdasarian), of which we only catch a partial glimpse when the crane shot starts its panoramic trajectory. Next in the gradual pan leftward, at a roughly one o'clock angle from our standpoint, come three crucial focal points: on the ground floor, the apartment windows of the sad spinster, Miss Lonelyhearts (Judith Evelyn); on the first floor, the windows of Lars Thorwald (Raymond Burr), the murderous jewelry salesman with

Martin P. Rossouw, Rear Window *(1954)* In: *One Shot Hitchcock*. Edited by: Luke Robinson and Melanie Robson, Oxford University Press. © Oxford University Press 2024. DOI: 10.1093/oso/9780197682876.003.0009

Figure 9.1 (See also Plate 12) Midway through Alfred Hitchcock's *Rear Window*'s (1954) opening pan across the courtyard as visible from L. B. "Jeff" Jeffries's (James Stewart) apartment.

a bedridden wife (spoiler: Thorwald owns a handsaw); and, on the second floor, the fire escape balcony where a quaint dog-coddling couple like to take their naps (spoiler: their dog eventually gets whacked by Thorwald too). A bit more toward the left, now at twelve o'clock directly opposite us, is a smaller section of apartments. Upstairs is the abode of the ever-stretching-and-dancing Miss Torso (Georgine Darcy), presently grooming herself in her bathroom; downstairs is the porch-cum-studio of the Sculptress (Jesslyn Fax), who acts as if the whole courtyard belongs to her. And, on the far left, before the crane shot finally retracts into the apartment to reveal Jeff's face, it passes over the window that will soon be occupied by the Newlyweds, for better or worse.

While the opening shot prefigures a number of similar shots throughout the film, it is worth also noting here the brief "sequel" sequence that follows *directly* thereafter. The sequence echoes the right-to-left surveyal of the opening shot, yet does so with a set of closer takes that cuts out specific segments of the space that was first surveyed in toto. By way of a leftward track, a cut, and downward tilt, that is, we get more up close and personal with the Songwriter, then one of the Dog-Coddlers, and then Miss Torso.

As will recur in the rest of the film, we're thus given a closer look at a sequence of sights picked out from the overall picture first presented in the opening shot.

With these opening moves Hitchcock sets up the most celebrated instance of *meta-cinema* in his oeuvre; cinema about cinema par excellence. Owing to the film being such a bold experiment in restricted point of view (for 99 percent of the film, the camera never leaves Jeff's apartment), the wheelchair-bound Jeff looking out his window becomes a metaphor for what *we* do. He is essentially a "spectator" in front of a "screen." In this way, *Rear Window* sets before its viewers an intensely self-reflexive examination: of the cinematic apparatus, the viewer within that apparatus, and spectatorial experience alike. Or, at least: this has been the predominant view that critics have expressed about the film ever since its release.

Jean Douchet led the meta-cinematic-way with his 1960 *Cahiers du cinéma* essay, in which he identifies James Stewart's lead character as a surrogate for the desiring, voyeuristic cinema spectator: "What he sees on the screen (and so what Stewart watches in the apartment on the other side of the courtyard) is the projection of his own self."[1] This metaphor of the spectator (Jeffries) and screen (the visible courtyard) sets the basic parameters for subsequent accounts of the film's self-reflexivity. For the likes of Eric Rohmer and Claude Chabrol, *Rear Window* quite simply "concerns the very essence of cinema, which is *seeing, spectacle*."[2] For Laura Mulvey, in her landmark reflection on the male gaze, Jeff's scrutiny of his apartment courtyard entails that "The audience is absorbed into a voyeuristic situation within the screen scene and diegesis which parodies his own in the cinema."[3] For Robert Stam and Roberta Pearson, moreover, this evocation of the cinema situation harnesses all "the diverse 'windows' of the cinema: the cinema/lens of the camera and projector, the window in the projection booth, the eye as window, and film as 'window on the world.'"[4] For this reason, they add, Jeffries-the-spectator can also be construed as the "director/auteur" of what happens on the "screen": kitted with his binoculars and telephoto lens, Jeff—as if playing Hitchcock—collects various sights, framings, and perspectives from his window-view, thus editing together *his* vision for spectators within, and of, the film.[5] And, speaking of whom, Hitchcock himself was of course just as outwardly smitten with *Rear Window* and its reflexive merits: among other choice phrases, he famously labeled his exploits in the film as "the purest expression of a cinematic idea."[6]

Yet for all this talk of cinematic purity and reflexivity, there is one discrepant feature of *Rear Window* "as cinema" that sticks out like a jewelry salesman who sawed up his wife: as the panoramic opening shot makes so clear, the courtyard-spectacle opposite Jeffries puts *more than one* sight on *simultaneous* display. While Jeffries's position as "spectator" is certainly singular and fixed, the plurality of sights established opposite him is anything but. Looking at it today, his view of the courtyard is far more reminiscent of a Zoom meeting or a security multicam monitor than it is of a unitary cinema screen. Certainly, Jeffries-the-spectator is a "peeping Tom." But his voyeurism is undeniably multi-windowed; the "view of the view" holds many views; Jeff is at once peeping *in the plural.*[7] As we'll see, critics who hold up *Rear Window* as an arch metaphor for cinema have not been entirely unaware of the challenges posed by its plural, multi-windowed sights—and, to be fair, some come up with interesting readings to neutralize their threat. But the fact remains that this plurality does pose a decided hindrance to the cinema metaphor. And by exposing the metaphor's limits, I propose, this plurality points up how Hitchcock's self-announced exemplar of cinematic purity actually cherishes a great deal of *impurity.* This shouldn't come as a surprise, not even to the "pure cinema"–parading Mr. Hitchcock: considering that cinema is the Seventh Art, a synthesis of arts, a paradigmatic *Gesamtkunstwerk,* the bastard art, André Bazin's mixed or "impure" cinema—call it what you like—it is simply inevitable that *Rear Window* will bear *intermedial* connections with other art forms and media.[8]

Jumping off (not from the balcony, but) from *Rear Window*'s celebrated opening sequence, then, this chapter considers the uses of intermediality theory as an approach to the analysis of screen narratives. Guided by the insights of two leading theorists of intermediality, Irina Rajewsky and Werner Wolf, the aim of this analysis is to show how a much-scrutinized classic exhibits its considerably less-scrutinized entanglement with other media. All of this is of course prompted by those plural sights that upset the meta-cinematic apple cart. An intermedial analysis helps us to come to grips with that plurality as a nexus, a generative crossover-point, which opens the door to *Rear Window*'s exchanges and connections with other responsive media. By tracing three connections with media that equally thrive on "peeping in the plural"—(*a*) multichannel television; (*b*) the comic book page; and (*c*) apartment architecture—readers should take away from this a better appreciation for how deeply other media can be invested in a film like *Rear Window*—in its visual style, the experiences that it affords, even its very premise. But, before any of that, we first need a quick peep at the business of intermedial analysis itself.

A view of intermediality

In the broadest sense, intermediality refers to "phenomena that (as indicated by the prefix *inter*) in some way take place *between* media."[9] Now—obviously—there is a multitude of ways in which this "taking place between" may play out, seeing that a given medium may inter alia join, birth, change, collaborate with, exchange with, fuse with, influence, incorporate, or react to another. Considering this complexity of options, many would insist that "intermediality" is in fact the condition of media *as such*, that *all* media are in one way or another constituted *in relation to* other media—as attested to by pronouncements like "all mediation is remediation"[10] and "all media are mixed media."[11] But how do we go about addressing a film like *Rear Window* against this sprawling big picture that is intermediality?

Rajewsky advises that, in order not to forgo intermediality's heuristic value as a category for concrete analysis, we split up this crazy cityscape into more manageable neighborhoods. To this end, she proposes three working subcategories of intermediality that help set apart distinct types of medial configurations and their specific qualities.[12]

The first subcategory, *medial transpositions*, refers to phenomena such as film adaptations and novelizations. Here intermediality understood as a general "occurrence" between media manifests in the stricter sense of the *transformation* of one media product *into* another medium.[13] The second subcategory concerns *media combinations*, phenomena that *join* at least two conventionally distinct media as a *composite whole*. Any constellation of so-called mixed, multi-, or plurimedia applies: films, theater performances, operas, ballets, music videos, installation art, illustrated texts, and beyond. The only qualification here is that each of the contributing media—as with the simultaneous *audio-visual* constitution of sound film—must retain a material presence within the overall combination.[14] But it is the third of Rajewsky's intermediality-hoods, the subcategory of *intermedial references*, that will be the focus of my attention. This is when one medium is used in a manner that "thematizes, evokes, or imitates elements or structures of another, conventionally distinct medium."[15] Essentially the *incorporation* of one medium or art form (the reference) *within* another (the referent), intermedial references materialize exclusively through means and devices that are native to, or associated with, the referring medium.

Intermedial references vary in kind and are therefore not all equally significant. Werner Wolf provides further guidance: the references at issue for my purposes here are not explicit references—that is, those that point to another medium in a denotative and non-imaginative way, as with the direct depictions of sculpture and dance and making music in *Rear Window*—but *implicit references* that primarily appeal to our imagination.[16] What I am essentially on the lookout for in *Rear Window*, therefore, are intermedial references that do the work of *formal imitation*, as Wolf puts it, the shaping of a medium's material "in such a manner that it acquires formal resemblance to typical features or structures of another medium."[17] And likewise in my viewfinder are instances where intermedial references do the related work of *evocation*. The latter, for Wolf, points to the fact that our imaginative grasp of one medium presented through another need not be restricted only to imitations of its *form*. It may just as much be grasped through imitations of the *effects* (typical perceptions or experiences) associated with that medium and its forms.[18] Take *Rear Window*'s intermedial relationship with theater. Its explicit references to theater are obvious (e.g., depicted dance routines, music rehearsals); and integral elements like acting and staging moreover underline the basic indebtedness that *any* fiction film has to theater; yet these factors do not preclude *Rear Window* from featuring *implicit* references to theater too. There is, for example, a distinct sense that Jeff's rear window functions as a proscenium, and that the panoply of windows opposite it, "like stages stacked one upon the other,"[19] open up "many small theatres, in which each actor is alone."[20] The clearest of these theater references already shows up in the opening credits, when the gradual rising of the window blinds both evokes and formally imitates a theatrical "opening of the curtains."

Both Rajewsky and Wolf are at pains for us not to lose sight of an important point, though: intermedial references operate by definition only within *one* materially present medium. It is for this reason that Rajewsky stresses the "as if" character of intermedial references: through formal imitations and evocations, the materials and means belonging to the referring host medium can at best generate an *illusion*, an approximation, of its absent referent.[21] The medium referred to—as with theater, by means of a window and blinds—is thus contacted in a *figurative* mode.

With especially the latter of these snapshots of downtown-intermediality in mind, then, we return to the question of the simultaneous plurality of sights staged in *Rear Window*: how can an intermedial analysis help to account for the nature, for the form and effects, of this peeping in the plural? Clearly, it is the formal centrality of the plural sights in *Rear Window* that opens the door (or window, if you like) to connections with a variety of media harboring similar formal affinities. Therefore, in what follows, I consider how *Rear Window* presents within the confines of its *own* medium a simultaneity of spectacles *as if* it had the formal properties and means of such other media at its disposal.

Channeled views

A first intermedial connection with *Rear Window* well worth a survey is its imbrication with multichannel television. In her intriguing analysis of the film, "Channeling *Rear Window*," Sue Brower never makes use of the term "intermediality"—but this is precisely what she proposes: that there are compelling reasons, both historical and formal, to take seriously the idea of television as a distinct intermedial influence on *Rear Window*.[22]

As far as historical exegesis in her argument goes, Brower approaches *Rear Window* as "a parable for the changes in American entertainment in the 1950s."[23] Her argument poses little to disagree with. It certainly is so that by the time of *Rear Window*'s production, television as a mass medium was booming in its popularity and cultural reach. Plus Hitchcock, as much the auteur as the market-savvy showman, was by no means unaware of its rapid development and potential. This is affirmed by the fact that, not long after *Rear Window*'s release, he himself ventured into the televisual domain with *Alfred Hitchcock Presents* (1955–1962) and *The Alfred Hitchcock Hour* (1962–1965). Against this background, Brower also makes evident how *Rear Window*'s narrative articulates the shifts in media consumption prompted by television. Important in her interpretation, for example, is the prominence of the domestic sphere: what makes Jeff much more of a television spectator than a cinema spectator per se is that he does his viewing from within a domestic setting—the newly conquered domain of television at the time—which turns out to make him not only a "domestic spectator" but a thoroughly "domesticated" spectator too. As Brower explains, Jeff forms part of "an interpretative community with Stella [Thelma Ritter] and Lisa [Grace Kelly]," female companions, tellingly, with whom he bonds through "their shared viewing experience."[24] Noticeably, their shared viewing out the rear window involves incessant verbal involvement, narrative speculation, even irrelevant chatter; blatant infringements of etiquette at the cinema, yes, but all quite natural when watching television at home.[25]

Still, the most decisive factor in Brower's intermedial account, taking us from historical considerations to also formal ones, is the ostensible *plurality* of the spectacle that *Rear Window* puts on display. This plurality is actually her stated point of departure. Noting the challenge that it poses to the prevailing perception of *Rear Window* as a metaphor for "the cinema situation," Brower first recounts some (quite admirable) attempts at reconciling our idea of the cinema with the splintered, pluralized spectacle set before Jeffries. One promising solution that she cites comes from John Belton, who proposes that the multiple spectacles at work in *Rear Window* can at least be seen as consonant with *early* cinema. Like pre-1906 films, that is, the various courtyard windows present a collection of exhibitions, acts, and displays—a sort of "montage of attractions"—and in this way also point to early cinema's non-narrative Vaudevillian roots.[26] A related solution noted by Brower comes from Stam and Pearson. They too are not oblivious to the simultaneous silent "tableau films" on display in *Rear Window*, but make peace with this plurality by portraying them as a reflexive index of classic Hollywood film genres.[27] And they do have a point: there is "the fifties social realist film" (Miss Lonelyhearts), "the murder mystery" (Thorwald), "the musical biopic" (the Songwriter), and "the musical comedy" (Miss Torso)—almost as if specimens, each behind its own glass.

But what if *Rear Window*'s reflexivity is essentially directed at *television*—not the cinema? This is Brower's response to the problem: that the plural spectacles on display in *Rear Window* are far better accounted for as "television channels." Her proposal makes many details fall into place. After all, Jeffries the "spectator"/voyeur is never bound to a singular "screen"/scene. In Brower's words, "As Jeffries looks out his window, he turns, repeatedly—one might say obsessively—not to *one* grand, cinematic spectacle, but to *many smaller* entertainments, little stories in lighted framed rooms."[28] His situation therefore much rather resembles the simultaneous offering of competing stories on television, where every micro-spectacle in a window acts as a channel to which Jeffries can turn at will.

So, let's channel these thoughts back to the opening of *Rear Window*. Admittedly, nothing about the opening shot and those that it anticipates really *looks like* television (barring perhaps a bunch of TVs stacked in a classic appliance store display). The film's intermedial referencing of television is thus not so much a matter of formal imitation. But what is clear from the opening shot and sequence is how they set up a totality of available views—the larger "multi-channel" template, a menu of options—that sets up the film's nevertheless powerful *evocations* of television. Though *Rear Window* might not formally resemble "television," watching Jeffries (and watching *with* Jeffries) does often have the *feel* of televisual experience. Browser points out in this regard the distinct sense of "channel-switching" that the film evokes. As others have likewise noted,[29] "Peeping into the apartments through the photographer's long-focus lens and binoculars is a bit like channel-swapping with a remote controller."[30] Yes, to bring the TV remote into the equation is anachronistic. But Brower rightly adds that manual switching between stations was already part and parcel of television consumption at the time, plus that the "switching" of Jeff's attention in any event captures how watching television is more generally "punctuated by interruptions."[31] So throw the remote out the window, if you like; the evocation of television seems more fundamental still. Even the most casual of Jeff's glances out the window are edited into a recurring "he looks"/"what he sees"/"he reacts" pattern—as in Jeff's early telephone conversation, where a frontal shot of him staring out the window is interspersed, Kuleshov-style, between a series of shots of what he respectively sees: sunbathers on the roof, a snooping helicopter above them, Miss Torso rehearsing her moves, the Sculptress below, the Songwriter, and finally Thorwald and his wife[32]— whereby the film cuts out specific views from the larger available totality and lines them up in a sequence of closer shots. More fundamentally than channel-switching, then, we have in these sequences the evocation of televisual "flow"[33]: the bringing together of a disparate assortment of views as a continuous stream of sights, with Jeffries-the-spectator (not unlike a multi-camera television mixer) as the common denominator that holds it all together.

Rear Window's evocation of television can thus be unfolded along a number of possible lines. But regardless of whether its "as if" staging of televisual experience comes down to a sense of channel-switching, interruption, or flow, what matters most is that these evocations can only play out against the larger backdrop of "viewing options" that Jeff is faced with (see Figure 9.2). All the cutting and switching and channel-hopping are intelligible "as television" only inasmuch as they are framed (often virtually, as a schema established in the viewer's mind) by the plurality of available sights first presented in the opening shot.

Figure 9.2 (See also Plate 13) Stills from *Rear Window Timelapse* (Jeff Desom, 2012), a large-scale projection composite that displays the panorama of "viewing options" on offer in the courtyard.

Paneled views

When Sue Brower looks at the opening shot of *Rear Window*, she sees television channels. But television is not the only medium that thrives on plural perspectives. A comics artist or comic book fan would no doubt look at the same courtyard setting and see the pluralizing stuff that strips are made off: grids, frames, thresholds, and by the same token what the insiders call "tiers," "panels," and "gutters" too (see Figure 9.3).

While comics were obviously a flourishing medium at the time, we have no hard evidence of Hitchcock drawing inspiration therefrom in making *Rear Window*. But an analysis of intermedial references need not, and really *should* not, be restricted to historically demonstrable influences alone. The obvious formal resemblances between *Rear Window* and comics give us more than enough reason to set the two in dialogue. To posit comic book form as a reasonable altermedial analogue to *Rear Window* can tighten our analytical grasp of the film regardless of whether it was directly influenced by comics. It's a matter of using one medium as a reservoir of concepts and motifs for examining formal particularities in another.[34] And, it turns out, there is a fascinating chapter in the afterlife of *Rear Window* that helps us to do just that.[35]

Figure 9.3 The *Rear Window* original US one-sheet, indicative of the film's formal affinities with comics.

In his recent *The Film Photonovel: A Cultural History of Forgotten Adaptations*, graphic narrative scholar Jan Baetens takes a brief but compelling look at the *cineromanzo*, "La Finestra sul cortile," the fifth issue of the *Star Cineromanzo Gigante* series, published in serial from March 15, 1955, to June 1956.[36] "La Finestra sul cortile" is a novelization of *Rear Window* (read: a *medial transposition*) in "photo comic" or photonovel form. This sort of hybridized second life of films was hugely popular in the 1950s and 1960s, particularly in Europe: since back then the public circulation of films had a definite expiry date, audiences were offered a token of the original film experience by reworking its photographic material into a comic book counterpart. Baetens's project is to show how the efficacy of such novelizations—of which its readers already know how the story will end—rests on a degree of refusal to directly compete with their original films. So he highlights in "La Finestra sul cortile" how aspects like page layout, panel sizes and compositions, as well as visual couplings, all contribute to a set of expressive resources, and readerly pleasures, that thrive on the medium's own terms.

Yet we need to do some reading between Baetens's lines. While not wanting to discount its distinctiveness as a medial transposition, "La Finestra sul cortile" does also bring to light the extent to which *Rear Window* was *already* invested in basic formal properties of comics to begin with. For all its medial autonomy, the film photonovel still seeks out in its cinematic source formal features that it *can* connect with. And those features in *Rear Window* that it *does* latch on to are telling—not the least because they revolve around the same central theme as in Brower's televisual reading: the inherent plurality of the view on display. As Baetens indeed observes first up:

> When Jeff and his visitors observe the neighborhood, what appears on screen is a multiply fragmented space: the courtyard wall is a surface that is divided into uniform floors, windows, bricks—in short, a space strictly divided along vertical and horizontal lines that transform it into a checkerboard of unequal squares that alternate light and dark colors.[37]

Baetens goes on to explain how "La Finestra sul cortile" expands upon these "grid-like motifs" in the film's mise-en-scène with various grids of its own.[38] Among other things, the film photonovel persists with a generally rigid page layout of identical tiers and similarly sized panels that echoes the "checkerboard" courtyard of its source. With such formal maneuvering, says Baetens, the film photonovel thus "translates the fictional setting of *Rear Window* into a set of fundamental page layout principles."[39] Yet this "translation," I would add, equally underlines *the film's* translatability into, and receptivity toward, comic book form. The plural sights at the core of *Rear Window* grants it a prior comic book–like quality that the photo comic version ultimately only amplifies by meshing this original "grid" with its own subsequent gridding in layout. This is a formal kinship to comics that *precedes*, and therefore stands apart from, the film's transposition into an actual comic.

Owing to *Rear Window*'s inherent imitations of the comic book page, the potential for evocation, for "bridging the phenomenological experience of reading comics and watching films,"[40] abounds. As we've seen, the idea of Jeffries as a cinema spectator has its shortcomings. So too Jeffries as TV spectator; as much as he and we might be doing "channel-hopping," actual television channels are rarely visible in the physically adjacent manner that the courtyard windows are. So how about the thought of Jeffries as a "comic book reader"?

It comes as no surprise that Baetens's account of the *readerly* experience of "La Finestra sul cortile" can also be mined for considerable insights into *viewing* experiences in, and of, the film. Baetens importantly notes how the reader of the photo comic can embrace and enact Jeff's way of looking, which is "*both* focused *and* multidirectional"[41]—or, he could have added, *both* sequential and global, *both* temporal and spatial, *both* concerned with a linear path across the page and the comic page overall. Emblematic of the "multidirectional" nature of the comic reader's gaze in *Rear Window* is, once again, the opening shot. The patient long-take pan of the courtyard can easily be read as unrolling the master "layout" in which multiple "panels" are (unlike TV channels) available for *simultaneous* view. This is why the long take is indeed also presented in long shot: for there to be, as on a comic page, no competition between the windows for room or attention within the film frame.[42] Hence, both the viewer and Jeff (once he wakes up) are free to "scan" this "page" in any direction they like. Yet if the opening shot is analogous to a comic page, then the earlier mentioned "sequel" sequence of closer shots thereafter is one of many that demonstrate how *Rear Window* also evokes the concurrently "focused" nature of the comic reader's way of looking. As much as comic panels are presented one *next to* another, the reader inevitably has to read them one *after* another.[43] Accordingly, the pan-cut-tilt by which we travel in closer shots from the Songwriter, via the Dog-Coddler, to Miss

Torso approximates the comics reader's moment-to-moment focus on individual panels ("traversed, crossed, glanced at, and analytically deciphered"[44]) in some sequence. Evocative of reading *through* a comic, then, this sequence after the opening shot shapes the initial *spatial* whole of the "page"/courtyard view into a *temporally* unfolding, linear experience of selected "panels"/windows.

To ask how Jeff's way of looking is "as if" reading a comic helps us to get at what peeping in the plural is essentially about: it is to take in the individual-in-sequence *while* never losing sight of the overall simultaneity of images in view. As preeminent comics theorist Thierry Groensteen would observe, "the focal vision never ceases to be enriched by peripheral vision."[45] Therefore, even as Jeff concentrates more and more on Thorwald, the murder mystery that plays out in that particular window is still surrounded, literally, by the stories of neighboring windows. *Rear Window*'s most memorable "multipanel" composition in this regard comes after Lisa Carol Fremont climbs up a fire escape and enters Thorwald's bedroom through a window (see Figure 9.4). The scenario amounts to the film's opening in miniature: a neat "page layout" with a "panel" in roughly every quadrant of the frame. Lisa is top-right, a by-now suicidal Miss Lonelyhearts bottom-right, while

Figure 9.4 (See also Plate 14) A "multipanel" composition of Lars Thorwald (Raymond Burr) and Miss Lonelyhearts's (Judith Evelyn) living spaces in juxtaposition in *Rear Window.*

Thorwald, at top-left, ominously turns the corner toward his front door. As a cinematographic composition, this can certainly be said to one-up comics in some respects—the characters actually *move within* their respective "panels," and even move *between* them (the snooping Lisa "jumps the gutter" on more than one occasion)—thus reminding us that intermedial imitations often expand representational modes of the medium imitated.[46] But, even so, the power of this composition ultimately derives from the same kind of "iconic solidarity" that is at work between comic book panels in juxtaposition.[47] As much as the impending confrontation between Thorwald and Lisa is the focus of our attention, we cannot watch that drama other than *in dialogue* with Miss Lonelyhearts's own little drama downstairs, as the two situations unavoidably enrich each other through irony, affect, and visual semblance.

So what is it that comics teach us about Jeff's plural viewing options? Simply put: the pictures at which we peep are bound to the company they keep.

Congregated views

This chapter has taken a glimpse at intermedial connections that can be drawn with *Rear Window* on account of the plurality of sights set before Jeffries, our fellow spectator-voyeur. Two clear contenders have emerged: the courtyard view as "television channels" and as "comic book layout." However, by way of drawing some conclusions, let us briefly consider what I take to be a rather more fundamental connection: *Rear Window*'s indebtedness to architecture. Reportedly, Hitchcock often spoke in the pre-production phase of his film about his interest in presenting a series of "little stories" in tandem.[48] And what better way to do so—what *other* way—than to put those stories together under a single proverbial roof? One of the key visual affordances of architecture, and apartment architecture in particular, is that the assembly of spaces in a building typically manifests also as an assembly of scenes, or "views." From this perspective, the built environment showcased by the opening shot invites something of an "archaeological" appraisal[49] of *Rear Window*'s juxtaposed pictures on view: namely, that one of the most primitive expressions of plural *sights* is to be found in the bringing together of distinct *sites*.[50]

An intermedial assessment of *Rear Window* in terms of architecture of course requires some loosening up of our concept of media, which needn't be restricted only to "mass media" like comics and television. A "medium" in the more elementary sense simply refers to something that enables us to *do* something, a medium as a *means*. And, in this sense, architecture clearly represents a medium for bringing together, juxtaposing, through windows and doors and alleys and passageways, diverse sights and perspectives within the same field of view. In fact, this juxtaposing capacity of architecture is why *Rear Window* and comics make for such cozy intermedial bedfellows, for comics themselves—with all that talk about tiers, panels, and gutters— are routinely conceived of in architectural terms. There is an undeniable "architectural unconscious" that gives the comics page its basic structure, its readability, and emotional power.[51] This architecture *of* comics has long been a reflexively depicted motif *in* comics, starting with Winsor McCay's *Little Nemo in Slumberland* (1905–1913), and arguably finding its apotheosis in Chris Ware's magisterial *Building Stories* (2012). Hitchcock, it seems, harnessed a similar reflexive awareness of architecture in his own "building" of little stories.

Some might however conclude that, by essentially *filming* buildings, Hitchcock merely gives us a direct, denotative depiction of architecture "nested" within film. What would be so intermedially special or interesting about that? Here it is worth bearing in mind that the particular architectural structure unveiled in the opening shot is still *a set*, one painstakingly designed by Hitchcock and his collaborators over many weeks. Most of the windows on display are implausibly large.[52] And the narrowed, even squashed, apartment spaces that the windows reveal are clearly laid out for the purpose of optimizing their visibility.[53] In short, "This movie could never have been accomplished on location with the same dramatic effect."[54] In the not-*exactly*-realistic courtyard replica, therefore, we have a definite distillation, almost a hyperbole, of the kind of plural sights that one would generally expect to encounter around apartment architecture—which suggests that the film is not just *making use of* the architecture, but is indeed also *imitating* one of its formal commonplaces in a mode of imaginative "as if" reference. Not that merely "making use" of another medium is so uninteresting in this case, though. More than any other medium covered in this chapter, *Rear Window* makes use of apartment architecture to the extent that it acts as a narrative and formal *infrastructure*. Take away the physical structures and spatial organization at the heart of this archetypal "apartment plot" film,[55] and what would be left? The set, this fake set of buildings, but buildings no less, is the "stage machine which produces the narrative."[56] It is the framework that

Figure 9.5 An apartment block cross-section with resultant pictorial tableaux: "L'électricité chez soi coupe d'une maison Parisienne," from *Le magasin pittoresque* (1891).

conglomerates the stories of many characters in one spot. And (much as you'd find in a dollhouse or the cutout diagrams of yore, as seen in Figure 9.5) it offers the basic means of also *displaying* their stories in simultaneous cross section: a collection of sights that Hitchcock himself called "a real index of individual behavior."[57]

So we have to conclude that *Rear Window* is not remotely as "pure" a cinema as Hitchcock might've wanted us to believe. There are palpable cues and reasons for us to view *Rear Window* "as" multichannel television, "as" a comic book, even "as" an apartment building, in addition to other con-temporary media like digital windows and split-screens, no doubt. But

these intermedial connections are certainly no mixed bag. I would suggest in closing that they stem from the same essential *spatial montage* that
constitutes *Rear Window*'s multi-windowed opening shot.[58] Spatial montage
itself is not exactly a medium. It is rather what the likes of Rajewsky would
label a transmedial phenomenon, a basic form or motif available for realization across various media[59]—in this case: multiple images that occupy the
same visual field at the same time, realizable as anything from cave paintings
and church windows to panels and TV channels. Spatial montage is the condition for the intermedial kinship between *Rear Window* and those media
considered here, because it is first of all the condition for the co-present plurality of sights that each of them realizes in its own medium-specific way. This
leads me to believe that the ultimately impure *Rear Window* at least retains
some manner of purity: montage rendered in its most primitively spatial and,
arguably, purest form.

Notes

1. Jean Douchet, "Hitch and His Public," in *Cahiers du Cinema, 1960–1968: New Wave, New Cinema, Reevaluating Hollywood*, ed. Jim Hillier (1960; Cambridge, MA: Harvard University Press, 1983), 150–151.

2. Eric Rohmer and Claude Chabrol, *Hitchcock: The First Forty-Four Films*, trans. Stanley Hochman (New York: Frederick Ungar, 1979), 124.

3. Laura Mulvey, "Visual Pleasure and Narrative Cinema," *Screen* 16, no. 3 (1975): 15.

4. Robert Stam and Roberta Pearson, "Hitchcock's *Rear Window*: Reflexivity and the Critique of Voyeurism," in *A Hitchcock Reader*, ed. Marshall Deutelbaum and Leland A. Poague (Ames: Iowa State University Press, 1986), 193.

5. Also see Robert Stam, *Reflexivity in Film and Literature: From Don Quixote to Jean-Luc Godard* (Ann Arbor, MI: UMI Research Press, 1992), 46.

6. François Truffaut with Helen G. Scott, *Hitchcock*, rev. ed. (1966; New York: Simon & Schuster, 1985), 214.

7. Of course, "peeping in the plural" is only possible where there is an "*image* in the plural." I am grateful to my colleague and friend Josef van Wyk for introducing to me the latter as a prominent theme in art history. See, e.g., Christopher S. Wood, "Painting and Plurality," *Yearbook of Comparative Literature* 56 (2010): 116–139.

8. For probably the most classical statement along these lines, see André Bazin, "In Defense of Mixed Cinema," in *What Is Cinema?*, trans. and ed. Hugh Gray, 2 vols. (1967; Berkeley: University of California Press, 2005), 1:53–75. For more recent insights on the topic, see Lúcia Nagib and Anne Jerslev, eds., *Impure Cinema: Intermedial and Intercultural Approaches to Film* (London: I. B. Tauris, 2014).

9. Irina O. Rajewsky, "Intermediality, Intertextuality, and Remediation: A Literary Perspective on Intermediality," *Intermédialités / Intermediality* 6 (2005): 46.

10. Jay David Bolter and Richard Grusin, *Remediation: Understanding New Media* (Cambridge, MA: MIT Press, 1999), 55.

11. W. J. T. Mitchell, "There Are No Visual Media," *Journal of Visual Culture* 4, no. 2 (2005): 260.

12. Rajewsky, "Intermediality," 51–53.

13. *Rear Window* as an example of medial transposition thus concerns the intermediality at its *origin*: although Hitchcock with screenwriter John Michael Hayes took many creative liberties with regard to its source material, *Rear Window* is nevertheless recognized as an adaptation—of Cornell Woolrich's 1942 short story, "It Had to Be Murder," republished in 1944 as "Rear Window"—and in this way represents, even if only to a degree, a transposition of a written text into the medium of film. See Pamela Robertson Wojcik, "The Author of This Claptrap: Cornell Woolrich, Alfred Hitchcock, and *Rear Window*," in *Hitchcock at the Source: The Auteur as Adapter*, ed. R. Barton Palmer and David Boyd (Albany: State University of New York Press, 2011), 213–227.

14. Certainly, media combinations are often so effective that they soon become conventionalized as an independent syncretistic "medium" in own right, which is indeed how in this chapter I approach the likes of film and theater. Cf. Werner Wolf, "Literature and Music: Theory," in *Handbook of Intermediality: Literature-Image-Sound-Music*, ed. Gabriele Rippl (Berlin: De Gruyter, 2015), 463.

15. Rajewsky, "Intermediality," 53. I should clarify that I am here interested not in the intermedial (i.e., across media borders) referencing of *individual* works, as one would normally speak of an "intertextual reference," but in the intermedial referencing of *more general* media systems, their formal qualities, and associated experiential features.

16. Wolf, "Literature and Music," 466.

17. Wolf, "Literature and Music," 466.

18. Wolf, "Literature and Music," 466.

19. Juhani Pallasmaa, *The Architecture of Image: Existential Space in Cinema* (Helsinki: Rakennustieto Oy, 2001), 155.

20. Michel Foucault quoted in Stam, *Reflexivity*, 46.

21. Rajewsky, "Intermediality," 54–57. Cf. Wolf, "Literature and Music," 465–467.

22. Sue Brower, "Channeling *Rear Window*," *Journal of Popular Film and Television* 44, no. 2 (2016): 89–98.

23. Brower, "Channeling," 97.

24. Brower, "Channeling," 94.

25. Brower, "Channeling," 96.

26. John Belton, "Introduction: Spectacle and Narrative," in *Alfred Hitchcock's Rear Window*, ed. John Belton (Cambridge: Cambridge University Press, 2000), 3.

27. Stam and Pearson, "Hitchcock's *Rear Window*," 201.

28. Brower, "Channeling," 94; emphasis mine.

29. Brower credits John Fawell for being the first to bring up this remote-control analogy.
30. Pallasmaa, *The Architecture of Image*, 152.
31. Brower, "Channeling," 94.
32. See Truffaut and Scott, *Hitchcock*, 214–216.
33. Raymond Williams, *Television: Technology and Cultural Form*, ed. Ederyn Williams (1975; London: Taylor & Francis, 2005), 71–111.
34. Cf. Wolf, "Literature and Music," 471
35. In what follows I'm making what I hope to be an uncontroversial assumption: that a *film photonovel*, owing to its sharing in basic properties like page layout and sequential images, at least, can serve as a tutor case on *Rear Window*'s dialogue with the medium of *comics* more broadly.
36. Jan Baetens, *The Film Photonovel: A Cultural History of Forgotten Adaptations* (Austin: University of Texas Press, 2019), 130–139.
37. Baetens, *The Film Photonovel*, 131.
38. Baetens, *The Film Photonovel*, 131–133.
39. Baetens, *The Film Photonovel*, 133
40. Dru Jeffries, *Comic Book Film Style* (Austin: University of Texas Press, 2017), 23.
41. Baetens, *The Film Photonovel*, 133; emphasis mine.
42. See Jeffries, *Comic Book Film Style*, 40.
43. Jan Baetens and Charlotte Pylyser, "Comics and Time," in *The Routledge Companion to Comics*, ed. Frank Bramlett, Roy T Cook, and Aaron Meskin (New York: Routledge, 2017), 303.
44. Thierry Groensteen, *The System of Comics*, trans. Bart Beaty and Nick Nguyen (1999; Jackson: University Press of Mississippi, 2007), 19.
45. Groensteen, *The System of Comics*, 29.
46. Rajewsky, "Intermediality," 57.
47. Groensteen, *The System of Comics*, 17–22.
48. Patrick McGilligan quoted in Brower, "Channeling," 93.
49. For an excellent overview of the field of media archeology, which frequently overlaps with that of intermediality, see Wanda Strauven, "Media Archaeology: Where Film History, Media Art, and New Media (Can) Meet," in *Preserving and Exhibiting Media Art: Challenges and Perspectives*, ed. Julia Noordegraaf et al. (Amsterdam: Amsterdam University Press, 2013), 59–80.
50. On various generative connections between the notions of "sight" and "site," see Giuliana Bruno, *Atlas of Emotion: Journeys in Art, Architecture, and Film* (New York: Verso, 2002).
51. Catherine Labio, "The Architecture of Comics," *Critical Inquiry* 41, no. 2 (2015): 317.
52. John Fawell, *Hitchcock's Rear Window: The Well-Made Film* (Carbondale: Southern Illinois University Press, 2001), 17.
53. Steven Jacobs, *The Wrong House: The Architecture of Alfred Hitchcock* (Rotterdam: 010 Publishers, 2007), 288.
54. Hal Pereira quoted in Jacobs, *The Wrong House*, 285.
55. Pamela Robertson Wojcik, *The Apartment Plot* (Durham, NC: Duke University Press, 2010).

56. Pallasmaa, *The Architecture of Image*, 167.

57. Truffaut and Scott, *Hitchcock*, 216.

58. On spatial montage distinguished from sequential montage, see Lev Manovich, *The Language of New Media* (Cambridge MA: MIT Press, 2001), 269–272.

59. Rajewsky, "Intermediality," 46n6.

10

To Catch a Thief (1955)

Stanley Cavell and the end of a conventional myth

Susana Viegas

Alfred Hitchcock's romantic thriller *To Catch a Thief* (1955) tells the story of John "The Cat" Robie (Cary Grant), a retired burglar and former member of the French Resistance during the Second World War, now expatriated to the French Riviera, and Frances Stevens (Grace Kelly), a young rich oil heiress vacationing in Cannes with her widowed mother, Jessie Stevens (Jessie Royce Landis). The film was shot following the immense success of the two mystery thrillers that Hitchcock directed in 1954, *Dial M for Murder* and *Rear Window*, both starring Grace Kelly in major performances and memorable female roles. It inaugurated a new era in Hitchcock's oeuvre, simultaneously influenced by certain European postwar art cinema filmmakers and artistically endorsed by the French film critics.[1]

Although generally regarded as a minor Hitchcock film,[2] *To Catch a Thief* contains many of his most famous narrative motifs: long driving scenes, unsuccessful police pursuits, dangerous rooftop clambering, characters hanging from tall buildings only to be saved at the last minute, informal conversations about food and gastronomy, the transference of guilt, the theme of "the wrong man," and an obsession with women's expensive jewelry. It is a film in which Grace Kelly plays the eternal sophisticated blonde and Cary Grant the charming, confident (wrong) man, the presence of both actors remaining a subject of fascination for Hitchcock's camera.

Film criticism generally gives significance not only to repeated narrative fragments and elements but to aspects that seem unusual. These are aspects that define Hitchcock's oeuvre, which is full of self-reflexive authorship features. This film departs in certain respects from other films directed by Hitchcock, the most evident of these being the role of Frances's mother. Contrary to other mother figures in Hitchcock's films, Jessie is neither terrifying nor disturbed; indeed, she flirts with John, vying for his attention

Susana Viegas, To Catch a Thief *(1955)* In: *One Shot Hitchcock*. Edited by: Luke Robinson and Melanie Robson, Oxford University Press. © Oxford University Press 2024. DOI: 10.1093/oso/9780197682876.003.0010 and thus competing with her own daughter. As a lively mother-in-law-to-be she is a decisive element of the humor of many of the film's comedic dialogues and situations. Key examples of this include the casino scene and the film's final moments, where, when agreeing to marry John (which the audience deduces from the ringing of church bells) and to live with him in his bachelor villa in the hills of the Côte d'Azur, Frances proclaims: "Oh, mother will love it up here!"

To Catch a Thief is also a story of deception and identity theft. Someone, a new "Cat," is pretending to be John, mimicking his signature burgling techniques. Although the robberies imitate his style, he insists he has been mistaken for someone else and that the French police are chasing the wrong man. John decides that the only way to prove his innocence is to catch this new Cat in the act, and, following the old adage that "it takes a thief to catch a thief," he determines that no one is better qualified for the job than he. It is in this context that a long shot of the unlikely couple, framed in a semi-dark room illuminated by an emerald green light, stands out (see Figure 10.1). On the left side of the shot we see Frances, wearing a white gown and exhibiting her diamond necklace, aiming to arouse John's desire to steal it (although, sipping his drink, he seems indifferent to the bait). The two are physically distant from each other, separated by the open

Figure 10.1 (See also Plate 15) Frances Stevens (Grace Kelly, left) and John "The Cat" Robie (Cary Grant, right) are so focused on each other they seem to ignore the background fireworks in Alfred Hitchcock's *To Catch a Thief*.

window, yet they are so focused on each other that they seem not to notice the impressive fireworks over the bay. Frances's confidence contrasts with John's hesitation. This transgression of gender roles and the couple's repeated sexual innuendos encapsulate Hitchcock's perspective on romantic love.

In *To Catch a Thief* the plot continually shifts from romantic comedy to lighthearted thriller. John meets the Stevenses as a result of his plan to expose the fake Cat, who is most likely planning to steal Frances's mother's jewelry. He devises his plan with the help of an insurance agent, H. H. Hughson (John Williams), and presents himself to the Stevenses disguised as Conrad Burns, an American lumberman from Oregon who is looking to purchase a villa. As François Truffaut observes, this is a film in which "Hitchcock remains absolutely faithful to his perennial themes: interchangeability, the reversed crime, moral and almost physical identification between two human beings."[3] In other words, the film is about the double. Indeed, on several occasions, the new Cat is visually associated with John: John has a black cat in his villa, similar to the one we see in the series of robberies, and he seems to be fit enough to climb his villa rooftop when hiding from the detectives. When he catches the bus to Monaco after outwitting the police, he behaves like a criminal. But the true identity of the new Cat is the last thing to be revealed in the film. We discover that John's copycat burglar is a teenage girl (a surprising twist in the expected transference of guilt), Danielle Foussard (Brigitte Auber), a character who bears a close physical resemblance to John, not just in terms of her short hair but also in the way she dresses, including her red and white striped T-shirt. John and Danielle are doppelgangers, each other's double, and opposites at the same time. This recurring exchange between characters will also be a topic in other scenes, such as the masquerade ball, where Hughson takes John's place—all this in addition to the fact that Conrad Burns does not exist and is but a charade. Imitation, farce, suspicion: the perfect elements of a modern comedy of errors.

A shared fantasy

To Catch a Thief also contains one of Hitchcock's most memorable scenes: the night Frances and John kiss passionately during a firework show. Frances is interested in John, either because she is in love with him, because she is intrigued about the identity of the new Cat, or, most likely, both. This is the scene in which the shot discussed in Figure 10.1 appears. The standard interpretation of this scene is that the fireworks are a metaphor for the sexual act itself, but the American film-philosopher Stanley Cavell gives us another perspective on it, contextualizing the film within a modernist film history and film criticism background. Along with French philosopher Gilles Deleuze, Cavell's serious philosophical approach to film is a major reference for the discipline. His interest in thinking philosophically about the Americans' "common cultural inheritance"[4] led him to classical Hollywood films, especially those made between 1934 and 1949, and to new cinematic genres that he coined the "remarriage comedy" and the "melodrama of the unknown woman."[5] In both genres, the focus is on the married couple, particularly the female protagonist.

Marriage and its breakdown (divorce or separation) are seen as the emblem of a society facing the moral and existential problems that separate the couple: dilemmas such as a woman's right to tell her story and to have a voice, the need for conversation, self-knowledge and acknowledgment, and moral skepticism. In *To Catch a Thief*, the single shot of the couple during the fireworks show in particular present aspects of the comedy's repeated narrative structure, along with the relevant derivations and compensations of the genre. For example, the couple is not yet married, and the woman leads the philosophical conversation. These deviations from the norm are even clearer in postwar films that do not pursue the conventional myths and figures that dominated in Hollywood. As Cavell observed a decade before in the first edition of *The World Viewed*,[6] *To Catch a Thief* is seen as the end of a conventional myth regarding the creation of woman, viewed as "the business of men."[7]

The scene begins with Frances and John finishing dinner at her hotel room, a privileged spot from which to watch the fireworks over the bay. Frances seems to flirt with John. She tries to attract him with her diamond necklace, but this is a trap. From the moment they met, she has suspected that his true name is not Conrad Burns but John Robie—"The Cat." In this scene, Frances is sure that she is right, and now her thoughts are on what she thinks is his plan to steal her mother's jewels. She tries to get him to admit his true intentions, but he remains deceptively passive, casually sipping his drink. Hitchcock breaks up the sequence into thirty-five shots. The sequence begins with a long shot that establishes the context: John has been invited to have dinner in Frances's hotel room. As the servers leave the room, Frances and John look outside at the fireworks through separate windows. The scene thus begins by presenting the couple as distant from each other, with their respective open windows framing them.

Sensing that John will not be fooled so easily, Frances turns off the lights, claiming that this will give them a better view of the fireworks. With a medium tracking shot, the camera accompanies Frances's delicate movements. "I have a feeling that tonight you're going to see one of the Riviera's most fascinating sights," she says. Recognizing the double sense of her own words, she adds, "I was talking about the fireworks!" to which he simply replies, "I never doubted it." John seems indifferent to Frances's double entendres and invites her for a drink, which she refuses. A faster lateral camera movement replicates John's movement. She sits on the couch, but the staged set only highlights her static pose, with her white strapless gown and necklace, as if to "reinforce Kelly's status as a fetish object."[8] While the visual emphasis of the film is on Kelly's fashionable wardrobe (with costumes by Edith Head), she does not wear jewelry until the moment the necklace itself becomes the center of the scene (and of the setup). Thus, although the dialogue provides important evidence for how to "read" the scene, equally important are Hitchcock's images: what the filmmaker shows without telling, as if talking directly to his audience.

"Give up John, admit who you are. Even in this light, I can tell where your eyes are looking." The medium shot is subjective (from John's point of view). In the semi-dark room, illuminated by a soft, emerald green light (when shooting night scenes, Hitchcock used a green filter to avoid blue tones),[9] he joins her on the couch. "You know as well as I do: this necklace is imitation," he replies. To which she responds: "Well, I'm not." While she says this, the counterfeited necklace is as artificial as France's innuendos. For this reason, François Truffaut described *To Catch a Thief* as "one of the most cynical films Hitchcock has ever made."[10] The couple initially apart from each other in the shot and then standing close together, they eventually kiss passionately on the couch. The final shots of the scene are close-ups of John and Frances kissing intercut with insert shots of the fireworks.

According to Hitchcock, "The fireworks scene is the orgasm,"[11] reinforcing a psychoanalytic description of his own narratives and motifs. This remains the standard interpretation of the scene. (To the fireworks' Freudian significance, we can also add the meaning of jewels and windows in the mise-en-scène.) Thus, according to Irving Singer, the filmmaker "develops the notion that the family jewels are attractive to a former thief like Cary Grant because they represent Grace Kelly's sexuality, as in the explosively orgasmic fireworks scene."[12] Critics often view the fireworks as a conventional meta-phor for the sexual act itself. To better understand this view (and to better comprehend how simplistic it may be), however, it is important to recall another scene from the film: Frances and John's first kiss.

On the first night they meet, in a "casual" encounter at the hotel (a plan that John orchestrated with the help of Hughson), Jessie Stevens spots John at the restaurant, where she remarks on his good looks. After objectifying him, she flirts with him at the casino, where he tries to catch her attention with a silly gag. Unlike her bejeweled mother, Frances is indifferent to his good looks and charm, as if her ice-cold attitude and unadorned fashion were an expression of her austere and modest feelings. But we know this is a pretense: she spotted him long before, at the beach, lying on the sand in his swimsuit. Preoccupied with escaping the police, he did not notice her at the time. And so, when John courteously offers to escort the mother and daughter to their rooms that evening, it is a great surprise when Frances kisses him goodbye. She is "a great believer of getting down to essentials," as she would admit the following day. For Hitchcock, "the kiss in the hallway is as if she unzipped his fly."[13] That kiss is a surprise without warning, the sensual spontaneity of an ice-cold blonde.[14] As Todd McGowan notes, "Hitchcock prolongs the time before the kiss in order to create suspense, but this suspense relies on the previous surprise kiss, which allows us to know what the result of the suspense sequence will be."[15]

On this standard interpretation, Kelly and Grant's real personalities have great importance. Kelly plays the role of the seductive woman, a sophisticated, rich, and naturally beautiful blonde, and Grant plays the role of the charming, confident man, a desirable bachelor living on the French Riviera. These roles suit them; they could not have been cast as villains. Their presence mesmerizes the camera and allures the audience: Kelly's clothing is immaculate, and Grant is "comically shown to be irresistible,"[16] dressed like a dandy in a simple, long-sleeved, blue and white striped T-shirt and a red and white polka-dot neckerchief. Indeed, when comparing Grant's performances in Hitchcock's films, Cavell highlights his role as an innocent man in *North by Northwest* (1959) and the need to "redeem" him from his role in *Notorious* (1946), "as if film actors and their characters get stuck to one another."[17]

A further detail that is relevant to understanding the audience's shared impression of the couple is the evidence suggested by the film's location, the French Riviera. It was the first film that Hitchcock shot in that location (although some scenes were shot in a Hollywood studio). The glamour and good taste that middle-class Americans associated with the two main female characters are a pure expression of the postcard scenery, as announced at the beginning of the film: the credits sequence overlaps a shot from a window of the French Government Tourist Office advertising some of the exclusive touristic sights of France and the Côte d'Azur. As Robert R. Shandley states, *To Catch a Thief* responds to a "tourist anxiety" (being accepted as having good taste) and expresses a "tourism-related trauma" (being robbed).[18]

In the postwar European situation, the South of France was widely regarded as a relaxing, easygoing place for the rich. But postwar Europe was also a site of innumerable crises, both from a social and from a cinematographic perspective.[19] Does this mean that the film is merely an obsolete fairy tale? When Cavell gave philosophical seriousness to the comedies of the 1930s, he "rescued" a genre that was generally thought to consist of fairy tales that alienated the audience from their real problems (during the years of the Great Depression).[20] *To Catch a Thief*'s plot can likewise be criticized for being light and unrealistic. It is a summer tale, after all; not only is the setting ideal for a romantic story, but the season in which the tale takes place reinforces its ontological superficiality: summer is an ideal season for flirtation and casual romance between (transient) tourists. Thus, when Frances says that her mother will love John's villa, the film itself humorously acknowledges that the summer romance is over and that married life will now begin. This intelligent way of ending a likely "fairy tale" strengthens the sense that the audience members "no longer grant, or take it for granted"[21] that marriage is the happy ending conveyed by conventional stories, thus revealing a crisis in their shared imagination.

"While a standard reading might interpret the fireworks as the successful achievement of the sexual relation," Angelo Restivo observes, "a close reading of the sequence would show rather the failure of the relation, as the abyss of *double-entendres* renders everything as fake as the jewels in the room, pure seductive surface."[22] Indeed, in the series of medium close-up shots of the two on the couch, the audience has a privileged perspective on the contrast between Frances's expression of excitement and wit (she feels she is living out a dangerous adventure, mingling with a potential criminal) and John's expression of disappointment and resentment (when he becomes aware of how society views him, the exciting orchestrator of a slew of robberies). Whereas Frances is confident that she has guessed correctly, John is unsure about her true feelings for him. Counterfeit affects are expressions of the artificiality of the moment.

On this first reading of the shot, the firework imagery is used to emphasize Frances and John's sexual tension, just as the necklace is used as a symbol of Frances's sexuality. Hitchcock was conscious of the visual cliché, and thus he decided to avoid the evident sexual innuendo in the scene by changing the score (composed by Lyn Murray), giving the scene a more comical interpretation as the sound grows louder each time the montage cuts to the insert shots of the fireworks (which move closer and closer). If, as Cavell writes, the audience members first "laugh at the laughability of the movie cliché," they soon realize that the filmmaker is exploring his own self-consciousness: "Hitchcock too is grinning."[23]

The end of the myth

For Cavell, the shot in Figure 10.1 is depicting a couple, distant from each other and in opposite states of mind (she is confident of her suspicions; he is trying to prove his innocence), and represents the end of a conventional myth, a "parody of the sharing of fantasy required in the marriage of true minds."[24] Society, marriage, and the risk of separation are connected with what Cavell considers to be one of philosophy's main issues: skepticism regarding the existence of the world and other minds. The philosopher claims that the photographic foundation of cinema allows the audience to experience and conceive of a world that is independent of, and exterior to, all subjectivity.[25] The world is ontologically present and absent at the same time. It is worth analyzing this memorable scene, separating out its elements and gathering the pieces within a wider interpretation, thus establishing a connection to Cavell's film-philosophical criticism. The standard interpretation of the shot is focused on the background fireworks and its psychoanalytic explanation, while Cavell's focus remains on the couple and how they (do not) pay attention to each other. What does the image show without telling? Guided by Cavell, we must first rethink the standard interpretation of this shot by inquiring into what we are seeing, what the evidence is, and the historical and social context in which the film was shot.

For Cavell, the standard psychoanalytic interpretation is reductive because *To Catch a Thief* is not a traditional movie that makes us believe in conventional myths or stories. But what does Cavell take these conventional myths to be (those that modernist films put an end to)? His inspiration is Charles Baudelaire's "The Painter of Modern Life" and his collection of terms, which,

Cavell argues, became a true "cinematic obsession,"[26] in particular the three major types of character to which Cavell calls our attention to: the Military Man (male comradeship asserting the myth of community), the Woman (interfering with male comradeship, thus threatening community), and the Dandy (the "lone wolf" who decides to remain outside of society).

The historical and geographic context in which Cavell wrote *The World Viewed* gives us clues as to what he thought about the world and its relation to cinema, especially postwar films. *The World Viewed* was written during a turbulent period in the United States, characterized by the civil rights movement and the Vietnam War, which made Cavell examine acritical shared fantasies that had been synthesized in conventional myths, such as the Military Man, the Woman, and the Dandy. The world was changing, as was the audience and the film philosopher. Cavell argues that films based on these conventional myths and figures are no longer taken seriously (the first edition of *The World Viewed* was published in 1971): "conviction in the movies' originating myths and geniuses—in the public world of men, the private company of woman, the secret isolation of the dandy—has been lost, or baffled."[27] The audience's shared convictions and myths, which supported the endurance of traditional genres such as war films and romantic comedies, have disappeared, the sense of community has dissolved, and, consequently, traditional movies from American cinema (from Hollywood, to be more precise) no longer connect to their audience. Why? Because with traditional movies, myths were essential to orienting the audience's relation to the world, which they presented as being there, independently, as a world *viewed* (hence the audience's ontological status of invisibility). The postwar situation changed this: the connection between the audience and the world viewed is no longer intelligible or trustworthy. Cavell focuses on the end of the myth of the Woman. As he says, "We no longer grant, or take it for granted, that stylish dumb women are as interesting as stylish intelligent ones; we don't even think they look alike."[28] The end of this myth is the end of stereotyped characters, since the audience does not share its collective fantasies; that is, each individual has his or her own fantasies. The modernist audience acknowledges its own conditions, bringing back the menace of skepticism and isolation as an ontological state.

Thus, in Cavell's view, the firework imagery embodies Frances's own imagination and desire to "be absorbed into [John's] fantasy."[29] She sets the stage according to a traditional story, driving the narrative (literally, just as she drove John along dangerous roads). "She made some small plans for the two of us," says John to Bertani (Charles Vanel), the restaurant owner. The plan was to make him admit that he had designs on her mother's jewels. She offers herself; the necklace may be an imitation, but she is not. But the way the film depicts the crisis of convictions (of myths and genres) is the expression of a transformation within the medium: it is how Frances imagines John's imaginary. Frances defies gender roles since she epitomizes the modern desire of the emancipated woman (thanks to Kelly's presence): of one who merely seems to hide herself behind traditional social and gender conventions (the white gown, her chastity and innocence, is a projection that is no longer aligned with reality). When both are at the beach and John swims alongside Danielle to speak to her privately, Frances pops up without warning and puts him in an awkward position, between her and Danielle, affirming that they were talking like old friends.

Regarding the prejudice about ice-cold blondes and sexuality, which explains the audience's surprise at Frances and John's first kiss, Michael Walker notes that "most of Hitchcock's more famous blondes are not virgins."[30] The fireworks are a laughable cliché of the sexual tension between Frances and John. Thus the necklace (a fake) may not be a symbol of Frances's sexuality after all; perhaps it, along with her white gown, is a symbol of her false chastity. The necklace is as fake as her supposed innocence (giving another meaning to Irving Singer's use of the expression "family jewels").

Modern love

Richard Allen was right to highlight the resonance between the films directed by Hitchcock and some of Cavell's philosophical themes:

the link between the theme of doubt and romance; the idea of love as a secular form of faith and its impact on knowledge; and the asymmetry between male and female in their capacities for attunement with the other. His films thus seem to provide an ideal test case for Cavell's view of the relationship between skepticism and romance.[31]

Indeed, it is possible to link Cavell's interpretation of the end of myths from *The World Viewed* with his future philosophical ideas on Hollywood narrative structures and the legitimation of marriage: including the comedy of remarriage (*Pursuits of Happiness*, from 1981) and the melodrama of the unknown woman (*Contesting Tears*, from 1996). Although we find some of the characteristics of the comedy of remarriage in many recent films, either by negation or derivation, the genre is based on myths that have also came to an end.[32]

Insofar as romantic comedies like *To Catch a Thief* are prone to raise questions about romantic love, marriage, doubt, skepticism, and false impressions (both for society and in private), it makes sense to redirect the analysis to one of Cavell's most significant philosophical projects: the "creation of a new woman" or "a new creation of the human."[33] His later paradigm of the creation of a new woman/human is based on a (heterosexual) couple's mutual recognition, successfully accomplished in the comedy of remarriage, and rejected in the melodrama of the unknown woman. The individual and existential process is led by the male protagonist (who educates the female protagonist in conversation): "In these comedies the creation of the woman . . . takes the form of the woman's education by the man. . . . This suggests a privileging of the male still within this atmosphere of equality."[34]

But this is not true of *To Catch a Thief*, a film that has a different narrative structure and that differs in important respects from comedies of remarriage, the most important being the fact that it does not feature a remarried couple. Frances and John do not have a common past; they did not grow up together. The first impressions of Frances are of a statuesque, unreachable, emotionally detached, sophisticated blonde. Unlike her mother, she does not wear jewels. This contrast is significant, not just for psychoanalytical reasons but also because she *has* a mother (an absent mother makes us wonder where a woman comes from).[35] One of Cavell's answers to this question has mythological roots (as in the case of the Book of Genesis): "the absence of the mother continues the idea that the creation of the woman is the business of men,"[36] another myth that is no longer sustained in this romantic thriller.

Cavell's efforts are based on the ideal of men's and women's mutual acknowledgment, which is a "battle between men and women for recognition of one another."[37] Yet doubt haunts the possibility of faith. In *To Catch a Thief*, the female protagonist does not have blind faith in the man's innocence, as she does, for example, in Hitchcock's *Rebecca* (1940); on the contrary, she shares the male lead's extreme skepticism and isolation. As we have seen, Frances is confident in her belief that John is the true author of the robberies; she is extremely cynical and incapable of love, but eventually, when she finally realizes how wrong she was about John, she is the one who wants to help him catch the thief at the masked ball. In a sense, she becomes responsible for his education (regarding marriage, but also regarding false accusations).

Thus the role reserved for the man is slightly different in this narrative; it lacks a pure sense of "gender asymmetry,"[38] as Cavell still finds in *North by Northwest*. Indeed, it seems that the male lead must be confronted with his emotional detachment and refusal to love (or at least to love someone besides himself) in order to better appreciate and recognize the female lead. Thus, while John is first seen as a lighthearted bachelor, an independent dandy—a role that suits a male character in any traditional movie—he eventually comes to understand himself better when he allows a woman like Frances into his life (and not a girl like Danielle—although, ironically, when he rescues Danielle, he is actually saving himself from public defamation). The narrative justifies his nonchalant attitude toward marriage. In the end, John finally acknowledges that he has found himself: "I needed the help of a woman. I guess I'm not the lone wolf I thought I was."

Why should a former thief and member of the French Resistance (that is, someone who used to live dangerously) prefer to live peacefully, tending to his roses, rather than being married? Why does he not believe in marriage? Apparently, Frances doesn't either. One of their long conversations is about marriage and money, and John accuses her of husband-hunting. She replies that all her suitors are interested in her money, which makes her insecure (one reason not to show off her jewels). At this point in the conversation, she has not yet told him that she knows he is not Conrad Burns, so in her mind he could be a con artist as well.

In this model, the man is "educated" by the woman, who was not "created" by him. This is a reversal of the film's social and psychoanalytic background, given how society viewed gender and gender roles. In Cavell's terms, this is a different form of skepticism, of uncertainty, concerning the existence of the other: John is mistaken for a thief, so he is the epitome of the wrong man, but there is the suspicion that he is more than he appears to be; Frances, on the contrary, is seen as a true believer, never doubting her conviction. Both fail to acknowledge the truth because each is isolated. The skeptical doubt concerns the fact that there is a lack of, or a failure to achieve, mutual acknowledgment. But both Frances and John overcome skepticism and achieve knowledge and self-knowledge.

A modernist film like *To Catch a Thief* can inspire significant philosophical and moral questions that echo other questions about social and economic class related to love and marriage, untrustworthiness and delusion, and the struggle to create a new woman/human. By reexamining Cavell's paradigm for the creation of the new woman/human through the lens of

Hitchcock's famous fireworks shot, we gain a different perspective on the nature of modern love and the role of women in Hitchcock's films.[39] In Cavell's view, the fireworks embody Frances's own imagination and represent the end of a conventional myth (one that involves the figures of the Dandy and the Woman) and, in particular, of the tales we tell ourselves—including the story that love between a man and a woman is not only earned but stolen.

Notes

1. This work is funded by national funds through the FCT-Fundação para a Ciência e a Tecnologia, I.P., under the Norma Transitória-DL 57/2016/CP1453/CT0031 and PTDC/FER-FIL/32042/2017. Richard Allen, "Hitchcock and the Wandering Woman: The Influence of Italian Art Cinema on *The Birds*," *Hitchcock Annual* 18 (2013): 149–194.

2. Joe McElhaney, "Hitchcock, Metteur-en-scène: 1954–60," in *A Companion to Alfred Hitchcock*, ed. Thomas Leitch and Leland Poague (West Sussex: Wiley-Blackwell, 2011), 329; William Rothman, *Hitchcock: The Murderous Gaze*, 2nd ed. (Albany: State University of New York Press, 2012), 258.

3. François Truffaut, *The Films of My Life* (New York: Touchstone, 1985), 80.

4. Stanley Cavell, *Pursuits of Happiness: The Hollywood Comedy of Remarriage* (Cambridge, MA: Harvard University Press, 1981), 9.

5. More than cinematic genres, the "remarriage comedy" and the "melodrama of the unknown woman" are new philosophical concepts as they disclosure the film's "craving for speculation" and the "portrayal of philosophical conversation" (see Cavell, *Pursuits of Happiness*, 14).

6. Stanley Cavell, *The World Viewed: Reflections on the Ontology of Film*, enl. ed. (Cambridge, MA: Harvard University Press, 1979).

7. Cavell, *Pursuits of Happiness*, 57.

8. Susan White, "A Surface Collaboration: Hitchcock and Performance," in *A Companion to Alfred Hitchcock*, ed. Thomas Leitch and Leland Poague (West Sussex: Wiley-Blackwell, 2011), 188.

9. François Truffaut with Helen G. Scott, *Hitchcock*, rev. ed. (1966; New York: Touchstone, 1985), 224.

10. Truffaut, *The Films of My Life*, 82.

11. Charlotte Chandler, *It's Only a Movie: Alfred Hitchcock, a Personal Biography* (New York: Simon & Schuster, 2005), 220.

12. Irving Singer, *Three Philosophical Filmmakers: Hitchcock, Welles, Renoir* (Cambridge, MA: MIT Press, 2004), 24.

13. Chandler, *It's Only a Movie*, 220.

14. Truffaut and Scott, *Hitchcock*, 226.

15. Todd McGowan, "Hitchcock's Ethics of Suspense: Psychoanalysis and the Devaluation of the Object," in *A Companion to Alfred Hitchcock*, 513.

16. Stanley Cavell, "North by Northwest," *Critical Inquiry* 7, no. 4 (Summer 1981): 763.

17. Cavell, "North by Northwest," 763.

18. Robert R. Shandley, *Runaway Romances: Hollywood's Postwar Tour of Europe* (Philadelphia: Temple University Press, 2009), 100–101.

19. This was the case with the crisis of the action-image that caused the transition to a new regime of signs, the time-image. Gilles Deleuze, *Cinema 1: The Movement-Image*, trans. Hugh Tomlinson and Barbara Habberjam (London: Continuum, 2009), ch. 12.

20. Cavell, *Pursuits of Happiness*, 6.

21. Cavell, *The World Viewed*, 63.

22. Angelo Restivo, "Hitchcock and the Postmodern," in *A Companion to Alfred Hitchcock*, 566.

23. Cavell, *The World Viewed*, 64–65.

24. Cavell, *The World Viewed*, 65.

25. Cavell, *The World Viewed*, 23.

26. Cavell, *The World Viewed*, 43.

27. Cavell, *The World Viewed*, 62.

28. Cavell, *The World Viewed*, 63.

29. Cavell, *The World Viewed*, 65.

30. Michael Walker, *Hitchcock's Motifs* (Amsterdam: Amsterdam University Press, 2005), 72.

31. Richard Allen, "Hitchcock and Cavell," *Journal of Aesthetics and Art Criticism* 64, no. 1 (2006): 52.

32. Cavell introduces the idea of "adjacent genres" to the genre of remarriage comedy in his essay on Hitchcock's *North by Northwest*.

33. Cavell, *Pursuits of Happiness*, 16.

34. Stanley Cavell, *Contesting Tears: The Hollywood Melodrama of the Unknown Woman* (Chicago: Chicago University Press, 1996), 5.

35. Cavell, *Pursuits of Happiness*, 57.

36. Cavell, *Pursuits of Happiness*, 57.

37. Cavell, *Pursuits of Happiness*, 18.

38. Allen, "Hitchcock and Cavell," 47.

39. While I am aware that the subject of women in Hitchcock's films has not been without controversy since Laura Mulvey's critique of classic Hollywood films as fetishizing women through the male gaze, my aim is to focus on the Cavellian reading of *To Catch a Thief* and on how gender roles are portrayed in the film. Laura Mulvey, "Visual Pleasure and Narrative Cinema," *Screen* 16, no. 3 (Autumn 1975): 6–18. As Tania Modleski puts it, one will either see Hitchcock's misogyny or his criticism of patriarchal society—see Tania Modleski, *The Women Who Knew Too Much: Hitchcock and Feminist Theory*, 3rd ed. (New York: Routledge, 1988)—but in either case the answer is not straightforward, and I do not wish to oversimplify the debate. For a well-sustained feminist take on the role of women in Hitchcock's films, see, e.g., Mary

Ann Doane's analysis of the trope of "paranoid woman's films" and Jacobowitz's analysis of the (im)possibility of female spectatorship, Mary Ann Doane, *The Desire to Desire: The Woman's Film of the 1940s* (Bloomington: Indiana University Press, 1987), 123–124; Florence Jacobowitz, "Hitchcock and Feminist Criticism: From *Rebecca* to *Marnie*," in *A Companion to Alfred Hitchcock*, ed. Thomas Leitch and Leland Poague (West Sussex: Wiley-Blackwell, 2011), 452–472.

Plate 1 Alfred Hitchcock's cameo in his film *To Catch a Thief* (1955).

Plate 2 Another triangle composition emerges through staging in Alfred Hitchcock's *Rope* (1948).

Plate 3 A third triangle is consolidated by the position of Rupert (James Stewart) in *Rope*.

Plate 4 Sam Flusky (Joseph Cotten) intrudes on a conversation in Alfred Hitchcock's *Under Capricorn* (1949).

Plate 5 Flusky forms the apex of a triangle in *Under Capricorn*.

Plate 6 Roger Thornhill (Cary Grant) and Lester Townsend (Philip Ober) in Alfred Hitchcock's *North by Northwest* (1959).

Plate 7 A rare glimpse of multiculturalism in the opening scene of Alfred Hitchcock's *Frenzy* (1972).

Plate 8 The last time a Black character is seen in *Frenzy*.

Plate 9 The first letter "S" of the neon sign in *Rope*.

Plate 10 Brandon (John Dall, left) and Phillip (Farley Granger, right) on the brink of discovery in *Rope*.

Plate 11 Rupert (James Stewart) with the neon sign pulsating in the background in *Rope*.

Plate 12 Midway through Alfred Hitchcock's *Rear Window*'s (1954) opening pan across the courtyard as visible from L. B. "Jeff" Jeffries's (James Stewart) apartment.

Plate 13 Stills from *Rear Window Timelapse* (Jeff Desom, 2012), a large-scale projection composite that displays the panorama of "viewing options" on offer in the courtyard.

Plate 14 A "multipanel" composition of Lars Thorwald (Raymond Burr) and Miss Lonelyhearts's (Judith Evelyn) living spaces in juxtaposition in *Rear Window*.

Plate 15 Frances Stevens (Grace Kelly, left) and John "The Cat" Robie (Cary Grant, right) are so focused on each other they seem to ignore the background fireworks in Alfred Hitchcock's *To Catch a Thief*.

Plate 16 Josephine "Jo" Conway (Doris Day) screams in *The Man Who Knew Too Much* (1956).

Plate 17 *Vertigo* (Alfred Hitchcock, 1958): the setup.

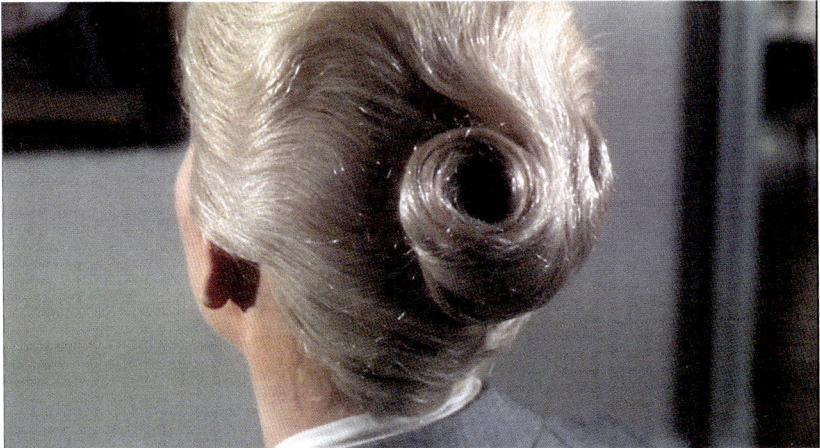

Plate 18 *Vertigo*: The first coil.

Plate 19 *Vertigo*: In between one and two.

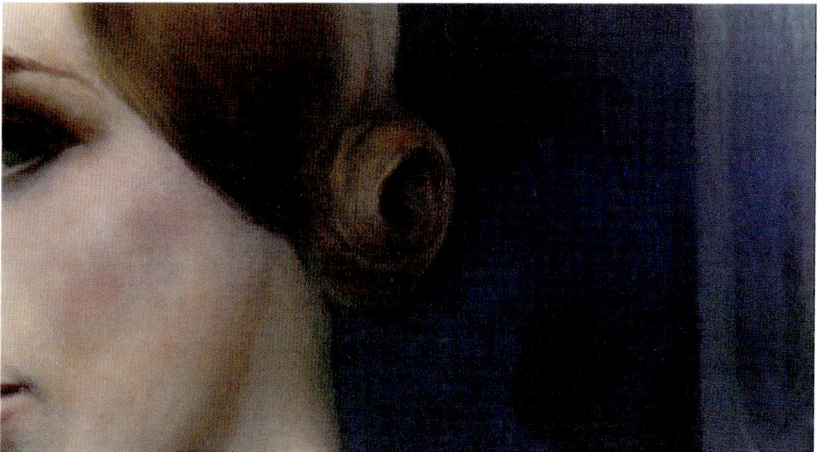

Plate 20 *Vertigo*: The second coil.

Plate 21 Close-up of Melanie Daniels (Tippi Hedren) on the couch in Alfred Hitchcock's *The Birds* (1963).

Plate 22 Bird's-eye view of Bodega Bay in *The Birds*.

Plate 23 Lydia (Jessica Tandy) in bed in *The Birds*.

Plate 24 Melanie attacked in phone booth in *The Birds*.

Plate 25 Cleaning out Rutland & Co. in Alfred Hitchcock's *Marnie* (1964).

Plate 26 Marnie (Tippi Hedren) waits, in *Marnie*.

Plate 27 A little rest room, in *Marnie*.

Plate 28 Barbara "Babs" Milligan (Anna Massey) leaves a Covent Garden pub in a medium shot in Alfred Hitchcock's *Frenzy*.

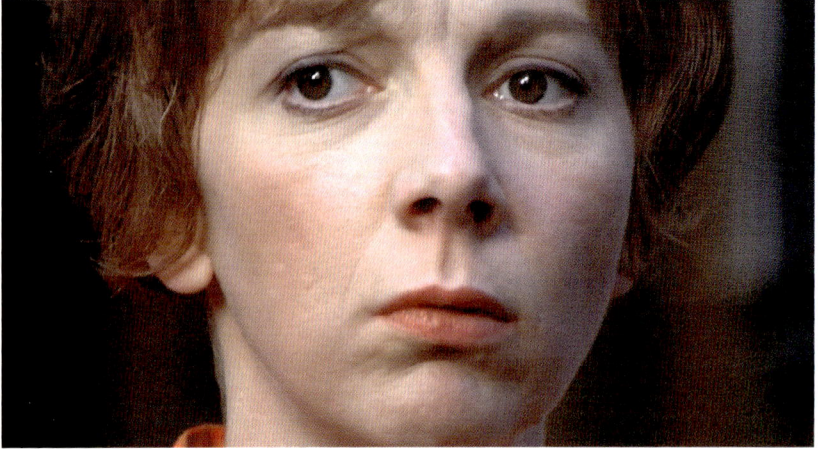

Plate 29 Extreme close-up of Babs in *Frenzy*.

Plate 30 Robert "Bob" Rusk (Barry Foster) invades Babs's close-up in *Frenzy*.

Plate 31 Babs and Bob walk off together in a medium-long shot featuring Covent Garden market sellers in *Frenzy*.

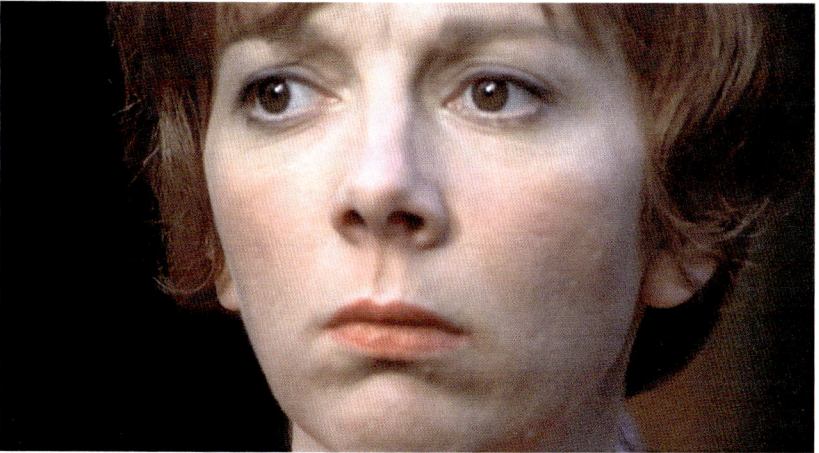

Plate 32 Extreme close-up of Babs in *Frenzy*.

Plate 33 Tracking shot of Babs and Bob walking up the stairs of Bob's building, with him leading from behind in *Frenzy*.

Plate 34 Tracking shot down the stairs of Bob's building, reminiscent of Jeff's view from Alfred Hitchcock's *Rear Window*.

Plate 35 Long shot of Bob's building, looking toward his apartment window with the Covent Garden market sellers in the foreground in *Frenzy*.

11

The Man Who Knew Too Much (1956)

Hitchcock remakes himself in Hollywood

Megan Carrigy

In 1956, Alfred Hitchcock directed a star-studded Hollywood remake of *The Man Who Knew Too Much*, a film he had first made in Britain in 1934. The 1956 version is the only one of Hitchcock's films that meets the clear and unambiguous definition of the remake provided by Constantine Verevis: it is "a particular case of repetition" that is "stabilised, or *limited*, through the naming and (usually) legally sanctioned (or copyrighted) use of a particular literary and/or cinematic source which serves as a retrospectively designated point of origin and semantic fixity."[1] Indeed, it is an example of what Michael B. Druxman and Harvey Roy Greenberg, in their different taxonomies, would consider a direct remake or an acknowledged, transformed remake: it retains the title and overall narrative structure of the original film but contains notable variations to aspects of the plot, script, characterization, casting, locations, politics, and cultural contexts.[2] Both versions of *The Man Who Knew Too Much* explore the dynamics of marriage and in each film a married couple must rescue their kidnapped child. The 1934 film, produced in Britain, begins with an English family, Bob Lawrence (Leslie Banks), Jill Lawrence (Edna Best), and their daughter Betty (Nova Pilbeam) on vacation in St. Moritz where they witness the murder of an acquaintance, French spy Louis Bernard (Pierre Fresnay), who offloads information about an impending assassination attempt on the ambassador in London. Betty is kidnapped by the assassins to blackmail Bob and Jill who return home to London to find their daughter, thwarting the assassination attempt during a performance of *The Storm Clouds Cantata* (composed by Arthur Benjamin) at Albert Hall. The remake engages with a different set of geopolitical circumstances. It begins with an American family, Dr. Benjamin "Ben" McKenna (James Stewart), Josephine "Jo" Conway McKenna (Doris Day), and their son Henry "Hank" McKenna (Christopher Olsen), on vacation in Morocco. Hank is kidnapped

Megan Carrigy, The Man Who Knew Too Much *(1956)* In: *One Shot Hitchcock*. Edited by: Luke Robinson and Melanie Robson, Oxford University Press. © Oxford University Press 2024. DOI: 10.1093/oso/9780197682876.003.0011 by the assassins, Mr. and Mrs. Drayton (Bernard Miles and Brenda de Banzie), to stop Ben and Jo from sharing information about a British ambassador's attempt to have his own prime minister assassinated, information that was imparted to them by the murdered French spy, Louis Bernard (Daniel Gelin). Rather than returning home to the United States, they travel to London, as the couple did in the original film, in search of their son, likewise thwarting the assassination attempt during a performance of *The Storm Clouds Cantata* at Albert Hall.

Of course, it is well known that many filmmakers have repeatedly taken inspiration from the challenge of remaking Hitchcock films. Gus Van Sant infamously produced a widely derided shot-for-shot remake of *Psycho* in 1998.[3] *The 39 Steps* (1935), adapted from John Buchan's 1915 novel, was even remade twice.[4] And while it is unusual for directors to remake their own films, Hitchcock, of course, is not the only director to do so. Howard Hawks, Raoul Walsh, and John Ford have all been identified as directors "given to authorial repetitions" within the Hollywood context whose careers predate and overlap with Hitchcock's.[5] Hitchcock's remake is an example of what Jennifer Forrest and Leonard R. Koos call—following Daniel Protopopoff and Michel Serceau—an "autoremake." Protopopoff and Serceau position a director's "auteurist reworking and re-interpretation" of his or her own material to be a legitimate artistic practice, distinct from what they describe as the "shameless plagiarism" of a remake that "copies the way the original's images are presented on the screen."[6] Several scholars have explored the ways in which the remake has been understood in relation to notions of authorship. As Forrest and Koos point out, Protopopoff celebrates Leo McCarey's remake of his film *Love Affair* (1939) as *An Affair to Remember* (1957) and Raoul Walsh's remake of *High Sierra* (1941) as *Colorado Territory* (1949), for example, as autoremakes that succeed in exploring evolving engagements with the generic conventions associated with the originals. For these scholars, following André Bazin, a director who engages in the practice of revising and reworking his or her own material "falls into established art and literary world practices, with the latest edition welcoming comparison not only with the earlier effort, but with the artist's entire oeuvre."[7] Verevis points to Steven Soderbergh as a more contemporary example of a director whose body of work has been understood in these terms.[8] But Stuart Y. McDougal goes so far as to argue: "The notion of a remake becomes complex with a filmmaker like Hitchcock because he was continuously and obsessively remaking his own work."[9]

McDougal's account of Hitchcock resonates with the sentiment expressed by Bazin and by Protopopoff and Serceau because he connects Hitchcock's approach to remaking his own work with the conceptualization of Hitchcock as an *auteur*. He proposes that the incessant refinement of ideas, themes, and techniques across Hitchcock's filmmaking career reflects Hitchcock's "exploration of the expressive potential of film," his "desire for technical perfection" and "obsession with the details of moviemaking," all of which contributed "to a sense of cohesion in his oeuvre."[10] The remake of *The Man Who Knew Too Much* embodies all these aspirations and preoccupations, representing the intensification of a process of continuous reworking that characterized Hitchcock's career. Andrew Horton and McDougal have together characterized the remake as a specific aspect of intertextuality, working to distinguish it from a more general conceptualization of "citation, plagiarism and allusion."[11] Verevis likewise positions the film remake as a "specific (institutionalised) aspect of the broader and more open-ended intertextuality" associated with "other types of repetition such as quotation, allusion and adaptation," drawing on the body of scholarship that has worked to conceptualize the remake in these terms.[12] Situating the remake of *The Man Who Knew Too Much* in relation to Hitchcock's repeated efforts to revisit and revise fits well with this approach to the remake.

Remaking, reworking, and doubling the scream

Significantly, as McDougal points out, Hitchcock not only returned compulsively to certain themes but also often remade single shots, transitions, and even whole sequences, driven by this endeavor to continually push the technical and expressive potential of cinema.[13] The remake of *The Man Who Knew Too Much* contains many explicit and comprehensive examples of this strategy. At the heart of this undertaking is the remake of the scene of the assassination attempt, which is punctuated in both versions by the climactic shot of the scream unleashed by the heroine. In both films, the parents' desperate search for their kidnapped child ultimately leads the heroine to a performance of *The Storm Clouds Cantata* at London's Albert Hall. In both films, the heroine comes to know that the assassin is preparing to fire a bullet at the very moment the percussionist performs a lone cymbal crash, which will drown out the sound of his gunshot. Having been warned that she may not see her child again if she reports the assassination plot, she struggles to stay silent throughout the performance, ultimately letting out a horrified scream as the gunshot is about to be fired, inadvertently saving the victim's life. In both versions, the shots of the heroines' scream, although very brief, mark the eruption of her dilemma. The scream releases the tension and suspense that has been built up and drawn out by the preceding shots. It initiates an abrupt shift in which dialogue erupts into the scene, piercing the soundtrack. By interrupting, indeed ending, the domination of the sound of the London Symphony Orchestra playing *The Storm Cloud Cantata*, the scream ruins the carefully orchestrated musical score as well as the carefully orchestrated assassination plot, with which it was intertwined. Notably, the screams in these two scenes also join numerous other examples of shots of women screaming from throughout Hitchcock's career, during which he experimented with a variety of different framings, juxtapositions, and transitions.

While the heroine's scream performs the same disruptive narrative function in both versions of *The Man Who Knew Too Much*, they are shot very differently. In the 1934 film, Jill's scream is represented by a wide shot. After a final close-up of the gun barrel angling out from behind a curtain and a brief close-up of the ambassador's face twitching in profile, we cut to the wide shot. Initially, for a brief second, it seems like an unexceptional shot of an unassuming section of the audience watching the performance unfold. Jill is camouflaged in this crowd, essentially invisible until she suddenly stands up from her seat at back of the stalls, a small figure in the center of the frame, grasping her head in her hands as she abruptly lets out a loud, shocking, piercing, high-pitched scream (see Figure 11.1). As soon as she screams, we cut abruptly to a reaction shot at the assassin's hideout, where her husband Bob is being held captive. The group visibly flinch at the sound of her scream, which is audible on the live radio broadcast they are listening to. The sound of Jill's scream functions as a sound bridge that connects the action taking place at Albert Hall with the assassin's hideout. It is followed immediately by the sound of the cymbal crash on the assassin's radio, a sound that makes them feel hopeful that the attempt has proceeded as planned, but they remain unsure of the outcome of the attack, as are the film's audience. The displacement of the scream from the concert hall to the hideout brings together the events happening in these two different locations and also propels the action toward the final shootout and the rescue of Jill's daughter. Cutting back to the concert hall, and the incessant chatter of the crowd trying to make sense of the chaos, the ambassador is shown slumped over in his chair, his eyes closed, his health status unclear. We see Jill run out of the hall to direct the officers to

Figure 11.1 Jill (Edna Best) stands up in the theater stalls and screams in Alfred Hitchcock's *The Man Who Knew Too Much* (1934).

the assassin's car. The shooter is subsequently shown arriving at the hideout where his conspirators hear an announcement on their radio:

> We have to apologize to listeners for the delay which has occurred in the broadcast of the concert from the Albert Hall. An attempt has been made to assassinate the distinguished European diplomat, Monsieur Ropa, who is attending the concert. We are happy to say, however, that the shot fired merely caused a slight flesh wound in Monsieur Ropa's shoulder and he has been able to return home.

One of the assassins declares, "It must have been that damned woman screaming." Upon realizing that the shooter was followed, the conspirators prepare for the siege.

McDougal points out that the strategy employed in the 1934 version of *The Man Who Knew Too Much*, in which the shot of the scream functions as a sound bridge between action taking place in different locations, had been tried out previously and Hitchcock's experimentation with this strategy continued in subsequent films. In *Blackmail* (1929), for example, the scream of the heroine, Alice, at the sight of the outstretched arm of an anonymous homeless man is juxtaposed with the scream of her victim's landlady as she discovers the victim's outstretched arm behind a curtain in his apartment. In this instance, the same scream appears to be shared across the two shots, making it hard to work out which woman the scream belongs to. In a later example in *The 39 Steps*, the shot of the scream of Hannay's landlady on discovering Annabella's dead body in his flat is juxtaposed with a shot of the train Hannay is traveling on coming out of a tunnel, which reveals what first appeared as the landlady's scream actually to be the sound of the train whistle.[14]

In the remake of *The Man Who Knew Too Much*, in contrast to the original, Jo's scream is shot in close-up. And we remain at Albert Hall for the duration of the performance, watching the attack unfold at close range without ever cutting to the assassin's hideout. As the camera gets closer to Jo during a series of reaction shots that precede the cymbal crash, she becomes more alert, her mouth open in horror, her head moving from side to side. Shots of Jo's face with her mouth open as she anticipates the impending attack are juxtaposed with shots of several women in the London Philharmonic Choir singing, their mouths similarly open, the color of their lipstick matching hers. The musical score, reworked and expanded for the remake by Bernard Herrmann, is longer and the scene more elaborately choreographed. The tension and suspense are tangibly ramped up through this expansion and elaboration of the scene, which delays the outcome even longer than in the original. Jo's scream continues to be delayed as the percussionist stands up, his cymbals poised on either side of his face. Following a shot as if looking down the barrel of the gun as the assassin takes aim, we cut to the pronounced horror on Jo's face in a final, brief, tight close-up of her disembodied head as she finally opens her mouth wider and belts out a loud, terrified scream (see Figure 11.2). As soon as her scream is unleashed, we cut to a close-up of the assassin. Her scream continues to reverberate as he stares down the barrel of his gun, trailing off as we cut back to the percussionist holding the cymbals in front of his face. He smashes the cymbals together violently, staring directly at the camera, framed in mid-shot, the shot explicitly standing in for the gunshot. As in the original, we never hear the gunshot since it is masked by the sound of the cymbals, which continue to reverberate as we cut to a wide shot showing the Prime Minister as he stands, his eyes bulging, grasping his arm. The sound of the scream and the cymbals unite the four shots—three close-ups and one wide shot—that represent the unsuccessful assassination attempt, rapidly connecting the actions of Jo, the assassin, the percussionist,

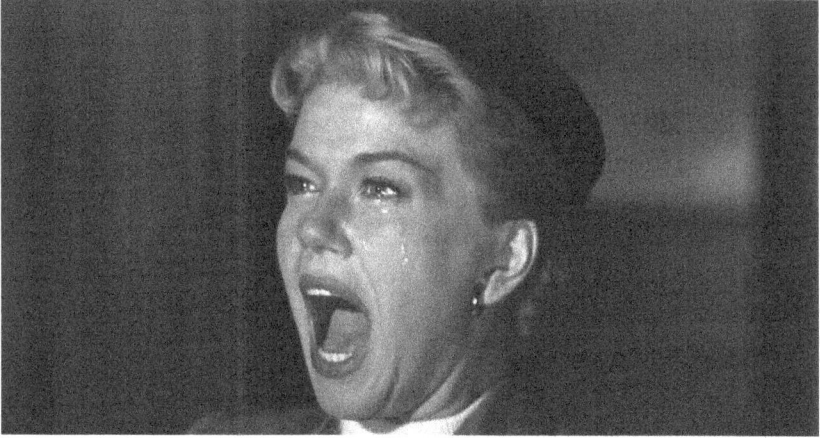

Figure 11.2 (See also Plate 16) Josephine "Jo" Conway (Doris Day) screams in *The Man Who Knew Too Much* (1956).

and the Prime Minister, who are spread across different locations inside the concert hall.

The decision to use a close-up shot of Jo's scream in the remake is not a new strategy for Hitchcock, either. We can go back, for example, to the close-up of the inaudible scream of the victim at the opening Hitchcock's much earlier silent film *The Lodger: A Story of the London Fog* (1927). Later, in *Psycho* (1960), Hitchcock gets much closer with the infamous extreme close-up of Marion's screaming mouth as she is murdered in the shower at the Bates Motel. Susan Smith describes Jo's scream in the remake and Marion's screams in *Psycho* as "aural *punctums*" that "punctuate and disturb the general tonal field of the soundtrack."[15] But their functions, she points out, are very different. The juxtaposition of Marion's multiple screams and the shrieks of the strings in *Psycho* work together to prolong our sense of shock and surprise. On the other hand, Jo's single, preemptive scream is deftly embedded in the complex construction of suspense and its cathartic release.[16] Indeed, it is the superior manipulation of suspense in this scene that most notably distinguishes the remake from the original.

The decision to change the shot of the heroine's scream to a close-up in the remake is significant. This close-up is part of a tighter imbrication of reaction and point-of-view shots. We get closer to the face of the shooter and share his point of view as his peers through his opera glasses, and later down the barrel of his gun. Hitchcock explains that his "power over the audience" comes from using framing and editing to bring them into a situation and control their attention:

> You gradually build up the psychological situation, piece by piece, using the camera to emphasize first one detail, then another. The point is to draw the audience right inside the situation instead of leaving them to watch it from outside, from a distance. And you can do this only by breaking the action up into details and cutting from one to the other, so that each detail is forced in turn on the attention of the audience and reveals its psychological meaning.[17]

This approach to the construction of the action is already embedded in the original version of the Albert Hall scene, and close-ups and reaction shots are a dominant feature of this version too. But in the remake, Hitchcock doubles down on this strategy and keeps us close to the action across the different locations in the concert hall and close to our female protagonist as the build-up intensifies and the suspense is repeatedly drawn out. It is only once the Prime Minister is shown grasping his arm in shock that we return to a wide shot of the stalls, the patrons getting up from their seats and turning in confusion toward the sound of Jo's scream. Only then does Jo, standing at the top of the stairs, become framed as a tiny figure reminiscent of the shot of Jill's scream in the original.

Hitchcock, transnational remakes, and the "Golden Age" of Hollywood

During François Truffaut's lengthy interviews with Hitchcock conducted in 1962, both filmmakers agreed that the remake of the Albert Hall scene was "far superior to the original." "The first version is the work of a talented amateur," Hitchcock explains to Truffaut. "The second was made by a professional."[18] This apparently straightforward distinction suggests that the second version reflects some of the major developments that characterized the intervening years in Hitchcock's long, transnational career. Of the variety of frameworks and debates that have emerged in screen studies to explain the scope and significance of film remakes, there are several perspectives that are particularly useful for interrogating the significance of the remake of the shot of the heroine's scream in *The Man Who Knew Too Much*. First, there is much discussion in the existing scholarship about the myriad of implications of the ways that remakes, as Forrest and Koos put it, necessarily "reflect the different historical, economic, social, political and aesthetic conditions that made them possible."[19] Indeed, Robert Eberwein argues that a remake provides the opportunity to "return to the original and reopen the question of its reception," bringing with it the potential for new insights into how we might contextualize the original film in light of subsequent economic, social, political, and aesthetic developments.[20] Second, scholarly interrogations into the transnational dimensions of film remakes, particularly Hollywood remakes, have highlighted the ways in which these various conditions play out in relation to particular eras in Hollywood.[21] These date back at least to Bazin's discussions of Hollywood remakes from the early 1950s.[22] When the activity of remaking foreign films in Hollywood ramped up in the 1980s, critical discussion about how this practice related to the industry's commercialism and imperialism intensified.[23]

Juxtaposing the two versions of this shot here, and the sequences to which they belong, highlights how the remake offered Hitchcock an opportunity to exploit the very different economic and industrial conditions in which he was working in 1956 to successfully refine the technical and thematic concerns of the original. Most notably, Hitchcock's approach to remaking this scene reflects the maturing of his relationship with Hollywood cinema, his extensive experimentation with the thriller genre, and his ongoing refinement of the workings of cinematic suspense. The significant gap in time between the making of the two versions marks a period during which Hitchcock made more than twenty-five films, most of them after he had left Britain and established his career in Hollywood. The original film, produced in Britain, had achieved notable critical and popular acclaim. It marked an important turning point in Hitchcock's career. It represented his return to producer Michael Balcon and Gaumont-British Picture Corporation after nine years working for John Maxwell and British International. The 1934 version of *The Man Who Knew Too Much* heralded his return to the thriller—the genre in which had had enjoyed early success with *The Lodger* and *Blackmail*—after an intermittent hiatus. It became the first of six British spy thrillers directed by Hitchcock between 1934 and 1938, now known as the "classic thriller sextet."[24] It was followed by *The 39 Steps*, *The Secret Agent* (1936), *Sabotage* (1936), *Young and Innocent* (1937), and *The Lady Vanishes* (1938), signaling a notable consolidation of his association with the genre before he made *Rebecca* (1940), yet another thriller and his first American production, under contract with David O. Selznick.

According to Donald Spoto and McDougal, Selznick raised the idea of remaking *The Man Who Knew Too Much* when he was negotiating a contract with Hitchcock for *Rebecca* and bought the rights to the film *The Lodger* as well.[25] As such, the idea of remaking *The Man Who Knew Too Much* was initially entangled with Hitchcock's move to Hollywood. However, when in 1941 Selznick asked the producer John Houseman to collaborate with Hitchcock on the remake, Hitchcock became displeased with the reimagining of the politics and characterizations in the version developed with Houseman and dropped the project. It was Hitchcock's honeymoon at the luxurious St. Moritz resort in Switzerland in 1926 that had inspired the 1934 version of *The Man Who Knew Too Much* and his subsequent return to St. Moritz with his wife, Alma, in 1954 sparked the idea of remaking it to fulfill a contractual obligation to Paramount Pictures.[26]

Hitchcock and Truffaut's discussion about the improvements of the remake position it as what Thomas M. Leitch calls a "true remake." In Leitch's taxonomy, true remakes are those which are framed as "just like their originals only better."[27] In Leitch's taxonomy, the *true remake* "seeks to make the original relevant by updating it."[28] Leitch worked to emphasize that technological innovations, such as the introduction of color, new types of special effects, new sound systems, are often a significant aspect of the economic and aesthetic conditions associated with the decision to undertake a remake.[29] This is relevant to the remake of *The Man Who Knew Too Much* since aesthetics of the two versions are unmistakably different. Most obviously, of course, the original was shot in black and white and was distributed in the academy ratio while the remake utilizes Technicolor and VistaVision, a high-resolution widescreen format released by Paramount Pictures in 1954. Evidently, as Peter Wollen argues, Hollywood provided Hitchcock with "money, professionalism, and technology," his engagement with "the gloss, sophistication and technical polish of Hollywood" contributing to the "overall look" of his "American" films including the remake of *The Man Who Knew Too Much*.[30] Another commonly identified impetus to produce a remake has been the intention to address new developments and changes in particular film genres. John Frow even proposes that "Every remake simultaneously refers to and remakes the genre to which that intertext belongs."[31] The abundant permutations of the thriller provided Hitchcock with a wealth of resources through which to continuously hone his craft. He delved deep into a spectrum of possibilities, exploring its overlapping subgenres from psychological to horror, mystery, crime, political, and spy thrillers. The influence of his films on the evolution of the genre is unparalleled.

We can certainly consider the 1956 version of *The Man Who Knew Too Much* as a transnational Hollywood remake of what was originally a British production. It is not unprecedented for directors to undertake a Hollywood remake of a film they made in a different national and industrial context. And it is typical, even in cases where directors are remaking their own work, for such films to undergo substantial makeovers during the remake process to accommodate the expectations of the new industry and tastes associated with its audiences, as is the case with *The Man Who Knew Too Much*. More recent examples include George Sluizer, who directed a Hollywood remake of the Dutch thriller *Spoorloos* (1988) as *The Vanishing* (1993), and Ole Bornedal, who directed a remake of his Danish thriller *Nattevagten* (Denmark 1994) as *Nightwatch* (1997). Michael Haneke's insistence on remaking his 1997 German-language film *Funny Games* shot-for-shot in Hollywood in 2007 is in some respects an attempt to resist this trend.[32] While examples of transnational autoremakes like *Spoorloos* and *Nattevagten* were critical and commercial failures, Hitchcock's much earlier autoremake of *The Man Who Knew Too Much* was a success. Unlike these other examples, the remake reflects Hitchcock's already long-standing relationship with the Hollywood industry and his successful engagement with Hollywood conventions and genres. Indeed, as John Belton points out, Hitchcock's filmmaking has often been characterized "as paradigmatic of classical Hollywood cinema."[33] What is more, the coincidence between the last decades of Hollywood's "Golden Age" and Hitchcock's so-called golden period during the 1950s and 1960s— the era to which the remake *The Man Who Knew Too Much* belongs—was characterized by the intensification of his exploration of suspense, point of view, and identification in thrillers like *Strangers on a Train* (1951), *Rear Window* (1954), *Vertigo* (1958), *North by Northwest* (1959), and *Psycho*.[34] This period of intensification gives weight to Belton's argument that Hitchcock's filmmaking practice "defines itself, more than others do, through a self-reflexive relation with that paradigm."[35] It is precisely the intensification of this self-reflexivity, characteristic of his films during this era, that makes the remake, as Hitchcock himself put it, "far superior to the original."

With James Stewart and Doris Day cast in the leading roles, the remake is also notably distinguished from the original by its engagement with

Hollywood stardom and celebrity. This brings additional layers of inter-textual self-reflexivity characteristic of the films of this "golden period" to the remake. Of course, Stewart, known as one of Hitchcock's favorite alter egos, had previously starred in *Rear Window* and subsequently starred in *Vertigo*, two films that have regularly been interpreted as self-reflexive commentaries on identification and film spectatorship. Significantly, Day's performance in *The Man Who Knew Too Much* functions as an important intertextual reference point for *Vertigo* too. Wendy Lesser points out, when Judy Barton (Kim Novak) is remade to look like Madeleine Elster, first by Gavin Elster (Tom Helmore) and then again by Scottie (James Stewart), her costume mirrors almost exactly the outfit that Jo wears throughout her time in London in *The Man Who Knew Too Much*: a tailored gray suit, white shirt, blonde hair tied in a low bun.[36] As Lesser puts it, "Kim Novak is haunted by the figures of Hitchcock's other blonde heroines, and in par-ticular by the nearly adjacent Doris Day."[37] So in *Vertigo*, Stewart's widely discussed status as a surrogate for Hitchcock's obsession with controlling his blonde heroines is connected to his co-starring role with Day in *The Man Who Knew Too Much*.

In *Vertigo*, too, the heroine's scream is also central to the representation of the crime. It is yet another example of the experimentation with shots of women screaming that are spread across Hitchcock's body of work. Judy, dressed as Madeleine (dressed as Day), is dragged up the infamous bell tower twice. The second time she is made up to look like Madeleine/Day, Scottie has realized he was set up as the "made-to-order witness" for the staged su-icide of the real Madeleine Elster and narrates the scenario he has restaged with the new knowledge he has ascertained. In the original version of these events, the sound of a woman's horrified scream plays over a close-up shot of Scottie as he clings to the belltower stairs, unable to move, followed by a point-of-view shot through a bell tower window as a blonde woman dressed in the tailored gray suit and white shirt plummets by. Upon restaging the event, having realized it was Judy's scream he had heard and not Madeleine's, he asks Judy why she screamed when Madeleine was pushed from the tower, and she tells him desperately, "I wanted to stop it, Scottie." But her scream did not prevent Madeleine's murder, instead becoming part of Scottie's and the audience's deception. When she reaches the top of the tower a second time, Judy screams again upon being frightened, losing her balance, and plunging off the top of the tower to her death, just as the actual Madeleine had done. In Scottie's attempt to remake Judy as Madeleine/Day and to restage the scene of Madeleine Elster's death, he inadvertently stages Judy's own demise, her scream again echoing over a close-up of Scottie's distressed face.

Self-reflexivity, suspense, and excessively obvious cinema

The Man Who Knew Too Much engages in a different self-reflexive exploration of the constellation between suspense, point of view, and identification than *Vertigo*. Both versions of the scene inside Albert Hall are organized around the cultivation and manipulation of audiences' anticipation of the impending assassination attempt. Suspense builds primarily through an intricate exchange of shots alternating between the mother of the kidnapped child, the assassin, the politicians, and the musicians from the London Symphony Orchestra and the Covent Garden Chorus performing Andrew Benjamin's *The Storm Clouds Cantata*. Both versions are designed to build audiences' expectations about the impending dangerous situation in which they are powerless to intervene. Audiences are positioned to identify with the heroine, who also anticipates the attack, facing an intense emotional conflict, making her emotional journey central to our experience of suspense. Embroiled in an increasingly urgent dilemma, she is suspended between the desire to thwart the assassination plot that she is watching unfold and the fear that doing so would threaten the life of her kidnapped child. We watch the heroine caught between her desires and fears—wrestling with what Smith calls an "interior form of suspense" common to the thriller—and we are simultaneously confronted with our own conflicting expectations and desires about what might happen.[38] Here suspense not only involves being suspended between question and answer but also conflicting emotions and sympathies. As Martin Rubin argues, it is common in the thriller for nonprofessional or victim protagonists to find themselves swept up in unfamiliar situations that foster in protagonists and audiences "a strong sense of being carried away, of surrendering oneself," generating "a remarkable degree of passivity on the part of the heroes with whom we as spectators identify."[39]

It is the concert hall setting in both versions of *The Man Who Knew Too Much* that gives this a dynamic its heightened reflexivity because of the explicit the role that the music plays in generating suspense. The heroine becomes "spectator-like," as Smith puts it, watching and listening to the performance and the action unfolding before her from the audience. She compelled to warn the character under threat about the pending attack but feels unable to do so, becoming "a surrogate for the spectator" who is unable to intervene.[40] As the diegetic performance of the music appears to drive the action, it also becomes the mechanism that animates and expresses the heroine's suspense and turmoil. As Smith explains:

> While the concert scene would seem to provide a most powerful demonstration of music's ability to draw the audience into an extremely close bond of empathy with the character, it is also, simultaneously, exposing the very apparatus used to construct such an effect.[41]

The musical score dominates the soundtrack in both versions of the scene, the action unfolding without dialogue. As the musicians are shown plowing through the score, oblivious to the impending attack that their performance enables, the music becomes a "ticking clock," as McDougal describes it, that propels the action toward its anticipated conclusion.[42] At the same time, the focus on the unfolding of musical performance helps to drag out the suspense by repeatedly focusing on specific details of the performances of the orchestra, choir, and the conductor.

This reflexive engagement with spectatorship already apparent in the original is deepened further in the remake. The remake emphasizes the mechanics of the production of the music more explicitly and repeatedly, incorporating of a much wider variety of shots of the musical score being followed by the conductor, the musicians, and the assassin's accomplice. As well, composer Bernard Herrmann's cameo in the remake as the orchestra's conductor has typically been understood to function as surrogate for Hitchcock's direction and control of the scene and of Jo's emotions. What is more, Jo's character is given the status of a celebrated singer, drawing on Day's celebrity, which was already closely tied to her reputation as a commercially successful singer. Jo/Day's scream evokes her singing voice, furnishing the remake with a greater thematic and narrative consistency and the Albert Hall scene a greater self-reflexivity. As well, her status a singer in the remake significantly changes the film's conclusion. While in the original, Jill saves her daughter during a shootout at the assassin's hideout, in the remake, Jo's scream plays a more coherent narrative function, prompting the gratitude of the Prime Minister and his invitation to sing at the ambassador's residence, where Hank is being held captive. Jo sings "Que Sera Sera" ("Whatever Will Be, Will Be," 1955) for Hank who recognizes her voice, and the song they had sung together in Morocco before he was kidnapped. He responds by whis-tling the tune loudly, with encouragement from his captor, Mrs. Drayton, making it possible for Ben to find and save him. As Ben breaks down the door, Mrs. Drayton, fearing it is her husband coming to kill Hank, screams "No!", her cry also echoing Jo's horrified scream at Albert Hall.

The self-reflexivity of this scene is intensified further because, as Hitchcock himself points out, the role of the cymbals in the assassination attempt is preempted during the opening credits.[43] The credits are projected over an ominous-sounding musical overture, performed at Albert Hall, the camera framing the percussion and brass sections of the London Symphony Orchestra. The camera begins to slowly zoom toward the percussion section. At first, the camera seems to be moving towards the beating of the timpani drums, positioned at the center of the frame and a dominant force in the unfolding musical score. But it slowly shifts toward the musician standing next to the drummer, who stands still, staring straight ahead, his hands by his sides, not holding any instruments. As the camera slowly tracks toward him, he reaches behind him to pick up a set of cymbals. The camera settles into a mid-shot of a percussionist positioned in the center of the frame as holds the cymbals either side of his body. He crashes them together and opens them to face the camera, holding these two large circles that fill the frame, his small head peering from behind them. As the sound of the cymbals reverberates, a single sentence appears superimposed over the shot: "A single crash of cymbals and how it rocked the lives of an American family." The screen fades to black and a mid-shot of a couple sitting at the back of a bus appears, their son perched between them, launching us into the story. The audience is primed to anticipate the cymbal well before the actual buildup to the heroine's scream, although they do not yet know what role they will play.

The addition of this opening scene reflects Hitchcock's evolving relation-ship with one of the basic principles that David Bordwell, Janet Staiger, and Kristin Thompson associate with the narrative style of classical Hollywood as an "excessively obvious cinema": the idea that "film should be comprehen-sible and unambiguous."[44] It is a concept that Hitchcock expressly articulates in his discussions with Truffaut about what makes the remake superior to the original. "I've often found that a suspense situation is weakened because the action is not sufficiently clear," he explains to Truffaut. "So, it's important to be explicit, to clarify constantly." The new opening, Hitchcock explains, reflects a refinement of his approach to working with suspense:

We had to do that so that the audience would participate completely. In the audience, there are probably many people who don't even know what cymbals are, and so it was necessary not only to show them but even to spell out the word. It was also important that the public be able not only to recognize the sound of the cymbals but to anticipate it in their minds. Knowing what to expect, they wait for it to happen. This conditioning of the viewer is essential to the build-up of suspense.[45]

This insight into the kind of thinking that helped to make Hitchcock's reputation as a master of classical Hollywood cinema and a master manipulator of the audience is crucial to the buildup and release of the heroine's scream which is inescapably connected with the cymbals.

Hitchcock's successful refinement of *The Man Who Knew Too Much* can be attributed to the ways in which his career trajectory is marked by his persistent and sustained interrogation of the conventions of the paradigms he inhabited, which included those associated with era of Hollywood in which he worked. As I have discussed, the remake of *The Man Who Knew Too Much* participates in a long, identified pattern of remaking and reworking shots of women screaming. This is but one example of the emphasis on repeated, self-reflexive interrogation that characterized Hitchcock's filmmaking practice and contributes significantly to his status as an *auteur*. Significantly, it also resonates with some of the long-standing commercial principles and enduring negotiation between repetition and innovation long associated with the Hollywood industry and, of course, the vicissitudes of genre, especially the thriller, the genre in which Hitchcock was most influential. Verevis argues that when remakes are industrial products, one of the perspectives that emerges focuses on how remakes can "satisfy the requirement that Hollywood deliver reliability (repetition) and novelty (innovation) in the same production package."[46] From this perspective, he explains, remakes can be understood in relation to what he describes as "the repetition effects which characterize the narrative structure of Hollywood film" and broader practices of repetition that have helped to manage audience expectations.[47] Situating the remake of the heroine's scream within the broader emphasis on remaking in Hitchcock's filmmaking serves to highlight how successfully Hitchcock's *auteurism*, as explained by McDougal, overlaps with, and provides insight into, the complexities of the evolving and multivalent industrial and commercial phenomenon associated with Hollywood cinema, as outlined by Verevis. In this respect, we can even think about Hitchcock's work as prescient of what Iain Robert Smith and Verevis describe as an "increasing emphasis on reworking existing material within global film (and screen) culture" in the twenty-first century,[48] a trend that has only served to intensify the range of circumstances in which filmmakers and screen artists continue to remake and rework aspects of Hitchcock's oeuvre.

Notes

1. Constantine Verevis, *Film Remakes* (Edinburgh: Edinburgh University Press, 2015), xii.
2. Harvey Roy Greenberg, "Raiders of the Lost Text: Remaking as Contested Homage in *Always*," *Journal of Popular Film and Television* 18, no. 4 (1991): 170; Michael B. Druxman, *Make It Again, Sam: A Survey of Movie Remakes* (South Brunswick, NJ: A. S. Barnes, 1975).
3. See Megan Carrigy, "Re-staging the Cinema: *Psycho*, Film Spectatorship and the Redundant New Remake," *Screening the Past* 34 (2012), http://www.screeningthep ast.com/issue-34-untimely-cinema/re-staging-the-cinema-psycho-film-spectators hip-and-the-redundant-new-remake/.
4. Thomas M. Leitch, "How to Steal from Hitchcock," in *After Hitchcock: Influence, Imitation, and Intertextuality*, ed. David Boyd and R. Barton Palmer (Austin: University of Texas Press, 2006), 251–270; Verevis, *Film Remakes*.
5. David Desser "'Crazed Heat': Nakahira Ko and the Transnational Self-Remake," in *Transnational Film Remakes*, ed. Iain Robert Smith and Constantine Verevis (Edinburgh: Edinburgh University Press, 2017), 164.
6. Cited in Jennifer Forrest and Leonard R. Koos, "Reviewing Remakes: An Introduction," in *Dead Ringers: The Remake in Theory and Practice*, ed. Jennifer Forrest and Leonard R. Koos (Albany: State University of New York Press, 2002), 20–22.
7. Forrest and Koos, "Reviewing Remakes," 22. André Bazin, "Remade in USA," *Cahiers du cinéma* 2, no. 11 (1952): 54–59.
8. Verevis, *Film Remakes*, 10.
9. Stuart Y. McDougal, "The Director Who Knew Too Much: Hitchcock Remakes Himself," in *Play It Again Sam: Retakes on Remakes*, ed. Andrew Horton and Stuart Y. McDougal (Berkeley: University of California Press, 1998), 52–53.
10. McDougal, "The Director Who Knew Too Much," 52–53.
11. Andrew Horton and Stuart Y. McDougal, "Introduction," in *Play It Again, Sam: Retakes on Remakes*, ed. Andrew Horton and Stuart McDougal (Berkeley: University of California Press, 1998), 3.
12. Verevis, *Film Remakes*, 1, 21.
13. McDougal, "The Director Who Knew Too Much," 52–53.
14. See McDougal, "The Director Who Knew Too Much," 52–53.
15. Susan Smith, *Hitchcock: Suspense, Humour and Tone* (London: BFI Publishing, 2000), 38–39.

16. Smith, *Hitchcock*, 38–39.
17. Cited in Marilyn Fabe, *Closely Watched Films: An Introduction to the Art of Narrative Film Technique* (Berkeley: University of California Press, 2014), 144–145.
18. François Truffaut, *Hitchcock* (1966; London: Faber & Faber, 2017), 94.
19. Forrest and Koos, "Reviewing Remakes," 3.
20. Robert Eberwein, "Remakes and Cultural Studies," in *Play It Again Sam, Retakes on Remakes*, ed. Andrew Horton and Stuart McDougal (Berkeley: University of California Press, 1998), 15–16.
21. See Iain Robert Smith and Constantine Verevis, "Introduction: Transnational Film Remakes," in *Transnational Film Remakes*, ed. Iain Robert Smith and Constantine Verevis (Edinburgh: Edinburgh University Press, 2017), 1–18.
22. See Bazin, "Remade in USA," 54–59.
23. See Forrest and Koos, "Reviewing Remakes." This discussion about Hollywood remakes of foreign films has played out, in particular, in discussions about remakes of French films. See Carolyn A. Durham, *Double Takes: Culture and Gender in French Films and Their American Remakes* (Hanover, NH: University Press of New England, 1998); Lucy Mazon, *Encore Hollywood: Remaking French Cinema* (London: BFI, 2000); and David I. Grossvogel, *Didn't You Used to Be Depardieu?: Film as Cultural Marker in France and Hollywood* (New York: Peter, 2002).
24. See Robert E. Kapsis, *Hitchcock: The Making of a Reputation* (Chicago: University of Chicago Press, 1992), 22; McDougal, "The Director Who Knew Too Much."
25. Donald Spoto, *The Dark Side of Genius: The Life of Alfred Hitchcock* (Boston: Little, Brown, 1982), 248; McDougal, "The Director Who Knew Too Much," 58.
26. Spoto, *The Dark Side of Genius*, 248; McDougal, "The Director Who Knew Too Much," 58.
27. Thomas M. Leitch, "Twice-Told Tales: Disavowal and the Rhetoric of the Remake," in *Dead Ringers: The Remake in Theory and Practice*, ed. Jennifer Forrest and Leonard R. Koos (1990; Albany: State University of New York Press, 2001), 45.
28. Leitch, "Twice-Told Tales," 49.
29. See Forrest and Koos, "Reviewing Remakes"; Druxman, *Make It Again, Sam.*
30. Peter Wollen, "Hitch: A Tale of Two Cities London and Los Angeles," in *Hitchcock: Past and Future*, ed. Richard Allen and Sam Ishii-Gonzeles (London: Routledge, 2004), 21.
31. John Frow, "Review: *Play It Again, Sam: Retakes on Remakes*," *Screening the Past* (1999), http://www.screeningthepast.com/issue-7-reviews/play-it-again-sam-retakes-on-remakes/.
32. See Kathleen Loock, "Remaking Funny Games: Michael Haneke's Cross-Cultural Experiment," in *Transnational Film Remakes*, 181.
33. John Belton, "Hitchcock and the Classical Paradigm," in *After Hitchcock: Influence, Imitation, and Intertextuality*, ed. David Boyd and R. Barton Palmer (Austin: University of Texas Press, 2006), 237, 245.
34. See Martin Rubin, *Thrillers* (Cambridge: Cambridge University Press, 1999), 80, 113.
35. Belton, "Hitchcock and the Classical Paradigm," 237, 245.
36. Wendy Lesser, *His Other Half: Men Looking at Women through Art* (Cambridge, MA: Harvard University Press, 1991), 142.

37. Lesser, *His Other Half,* 143.

38. Smith, *Hitchcock,* 21.

39. Rubin, *Thrillers,* 6–7, 35.

40. See Smith, *Hitchcock,* 20–21; McDougal, "The Director Who Knew Too Much," 56.

41. Smith, *Hitchcock,* 40–42.

42. McDougal, "The Director Who Knew Too Much," 65.

43. See Truffaut, *Hitchcock,* 92.

44. David Bordwell, Janet Staiger, and Kristin Thompson, *The Classical Hollywood Cinema: Film Style and Mode of Production to 1960* (1988; London: Routledge, 2019), 1–2.

45. Truffaut, *Hitchcock,* 92–93

46. Verevis, *Film Remakes,* 4–5.

47. Verevis, *Film Remakes,* 4–5.

48. Smith and Verevis, "Introduction," 2–3.

12

The Wrong Man (1956)

Towards singularity

Noa Steimatsky

For Tom Gunning

It is, in a way, telling that one of Alfred Hitchcock's most celebrated shots—the shot that immediately presents itself to my imagination in response to the prompt of a "one-shot Hitchcock"—is in fact not a single but, inherently, a double.[1] Commonly referred to as "the superimposition scene" in *The Wrong Man* (1956), the single/double shot/s is a unique manifestation that stands out against the film's realist fabric, while at the same time epitomizing its narrative conceit, its deeper existential thematic of the double, and its probing the irrecoverable gap between seeing and knowing—a set of concerns shared with other Hitchcock films. That I'm compelled to signal the singular/plural ambiguity of this shot/s even through the graphic slash mark (following which verb agreement becomes problematic) may itself be construed as a challenge to the present volume's prompt, even as it is stimulated by it. How to isolate such a basic unit, the single shot, in the work of a director whose engagement with construction and montage inflects each and every instance of his work? Quasi-cubist in orientation, inclined to chop up the world into little pieces before rebuilding the parts exactly as he wishes, framing, blocking, and juxtaposing facets in ways that so often depart from a straight "realist" perception, Hitchcock is nevertheless grounded in mainstream narrative cinema and its illusionist continuity techniques. When compared with certain postwar realisms—to which *The Wrong Man* gestures in other respects—the single shot does not seem to hold integral, organic unity and value for him. And when a particular shot is singled out in Hitchcock, it is often determined not only by editing but by assertive framing or the unsettling play of planes and parts of the mise-en-scène, which—we shall see—infuse the shot with tension and blow it open, as it were, beyond its own limits. Namely, the Hitchcockian single shot tends to be an always-already complex entity that

Noa Steimatsky, The Wrong Man *(1956)* In: *One Shot Hitchcock.* Edited by: Luke Robinson and Melanie Robson, Oxford University Press. © Oxford University Press 2024. DOI: 10.1093/oso/9780197682876.003.0012 can be said—as Sergei Eisenstein's late films and theory put it—to incorporate montage, in its broad sense of duality and contradiction, *within* the shot which thus emerges—even preceding the editing of successive units—as a "montage-image."[2]

The climactic shot/s at the heart of the sequence with which I'm concerned is composed, then, of two different shots, evidently filmed in different spaces and moments, and involving two different men. It consists, in brief, of a big close-up of Henry Fonda's beautiful features, invaded by another shot.[3] The latter is more complex and dynamic, first discernible as an extreme long shot down a nocturnal urban street, from which depth a man emerges walking toward the camera and into his own big close-up. One soon senses this development as a buildup toward a climactic instance in which the two men's faces converge for an instant, to then be re-differentiated as the second man turns his face toward screen-left, by which point Fonda's face fades away. The camera now pans left following the second man's movement, then stays put as he turns his back and walks toward the door of a grocery store. Two shots are stamped into one even as we recognize, by this point, the transition to a new sequence, and a narrative turning point. The transition between the two shots, and sequences, capitalizes on the formal similarity and convergence of two faces, yet there is a way in which the shot/s, glued by the protracted double-exposure in the lap-dissolve, are experienced (and remembered) as a single, powerful impression of superimposition, economically clarifying all that had passed. Interfering with the realist linear thrust of film, the shot/s further solicits our turning back to revise and realign events up to this point in the diegesis.

By coincidence—or a sort of deus ex machina, appearing to emerge from another plane of existence—in this pivotal moment, when all seems lost, the protagonist's fate suddenly turns by no act of his own. The nocturnal scene, at once interior and exterior, seems to flare suddenly and to illumine an otherwise bleak, gray, quotidian universe. We are its sole witnesses, and thus we feel addressed by a kind of apotheosis, a spectacular revelation effected not simply through narrative suggestion but as a striking visual experience. This must account for François Truffaut's calling it Hitchcock's most beautiful shot and the summation of his work.[4] Its movie-magic—by technical prowess that still impresses viewers—its range of visual, symbolic, and cultural connotations, and what it signals, or even *generates*, when all else fails, all add up to a singular vision as if inspired by divine intervention, a "miracle."[5] Hitchcock seems to have regretted the extent of its interference in the film's prevailing factual simplicity as an error of his own judgment and rejected, in retrospect, such overt "fictitiousness" of style within "a documentary type picture."[6] But even such fiction, such divine or authorial intervention that appears to explain the mystery and usher its resolution, does not altogether repair the damage or efface the terror that lurks in *The Wrong Man*. For the film, and the superimposition shot/s in particular, profoundly disturbs our confidence in the perceived uniqueness of human beings, and in our own frail singularity. Reflecting on the deep ambiguities of the shot, and working through close analysis of the sequence that culminates in the superimposition, we confront the uncanny play of appearances, the crux identification, and the terrifying porosity and instability of identity at the heart of Hitchcock's film.

It is not, then, an end-to-end, full-fledged double-exposure shot, but a passage from one shot, and from one scene, to another through lap-dissolve wherein the overlapping of the two swells at a climactic point toward the shot's conclusion when graphic elements—the position of the head, eyes, and mouth in the frame—converge for an instant. The climax is then released such that the second man "carries" us into the sequence that follows. Building toward, then slipping away from, the climactic formal matching, a dynamic play of surface and depth, transparency and opacity, singularity and multiplicity transpires before our eyes. Since spatial co-presence strikes us as phantasmic, and since temporal simultaneity remains questionable, the cinematographic coinciding of elements introduces perhaps more doubt than certainty—a profound instability. What is actually going on here? Does this apparition constitute definite proof? The spatiotemporal parameters of the double-as-single shot/s thus inform the disturbing, and not-altogether-resolved, questions of identity and the definition of self—its limits, its permeability, its relation to visuality—evolving through the film. The displacement and contamination of guilt, the implication of the greater guilt within the minor crime, the doubling (or is it splitting?) of identity—these are the moral and existential dimensions of Hitchcock's engagement with the power and the deceptiveness of appearances, in this as in other films, and even as it regards the beautiful but opaque face of the movie star. It is particularly striking to consider the ways in which this seemingly modest film is rehearsing, in effect, for the mind-spinning orchestration of visual and psychic constructions, of deceptions and doublings and doubling-back in Hitchcock's subsequent film, *Vertigo* (1958)—a work so different in other respects. The closely related musical beat shared by the superimposition scene and Carlotta's theme in *Vertigo* interlaces anticipation and unresolved mystery, even mystical suggestion. And also in the latter film, the superimposition effect in Judy's flashback—in some ways a more conventional use of the device—reveals the mystery to our eyes only. Indeed, double exposure properly pertains to cinematic vision, removed from natural perception and workaday experience. Such privileged vision is not granted to *Vertigo's* male protagonist, intent on further embellishing the woman's image to return it to its earlier, immaculate perfection, with disastrous consequences. And while the catastrophic loss in *Vertigo* is extreme and irreversible, twice over, it is distressing to recognize that, also in *The Wrong Man*, there is no going back to "before the fall"—no recovery of primal innocence and unity that precede, as it were, the self-alienating knowledge of identity.

In the gap between seeing and knowing lie questions of identity, identification, and recognition.[7] Christopher Emmanuel Balestrero, played by Henry Fonda, is first misidentified at the offices of a life-insurance agency as the criminal who had held up the place. Subsequently misidentified in a police line-up, he finds himself caught in the machinations of the law and state apparatuses. All the elements conspire against him: from the inadequacy of criminological methods and police procedures to the obtuseness of bureaucracy and the maddening indifference of institutions, and beyond this the contingencies and errors of daily life and other people's circumstances—including their own mistakes and misfortunes. In the turning point signaled by the superimposition scene, the disastrous string of chance happenings that has tripped Balestrero is resolved by another coincidence—the criminal's return to action—and is literalized by the *coinciding* of faces. But while, by strict reference to plot causality or motivation, the surfacing of the "right man" is mere chance, the scene's incorporation of the prayer to the Christ icon, and the apparition of the facial coinciding as such, translates (for our imagination) spatiotemporal coinciding and succession to causality, and imbues coincidence with meaning, even a sense of providence.

Particularly against the film's realist fabric—itself notable when compared to other Hitchcock films of the period—the superimposition scene stands out for the grand symbolic resonances of doubling, the mysterious workings of fate that has joined the two men, as for the extraordinary visual spectacle that it presents. In addressing itself to our eyes only, the scene leaps out of the film, as it were, exceeding any perception or knowledge internal to the diegesis at this point. Having lamented his helplessness and despair that the actual criminal might never materialize, Fonda is urged by his mother to pray for strength. He goes to the bedroom to dress for work, whereupon we see him in the semi-darkness, putting on his dress shirt. The shot is peculiarly framed such that the camera seems perched just behind that same toiletry-table mirror that cracked when Vera Miles—in the role of the wife descending into mental breakdown—threw a hairbrush at her husband, bruising his fore-head before hitting the mirror. It was also in that earlier scene that we might have first glimpsed the icon on the wall. In the later scene, with which we are concerned, the mirror's upper edge stubbornly blocks the lower left of the frame, such that the camera seems perched in an impossible space between the wall and the mirror that is ostensibly set directly against it—introducing the play of two- vs. three-dimensional forms that will be developed in what follows (see Figure 12.1). It is the sort of quasi-inarticulate visual disturbance that Hitchcock incorporates elsewhere in the film, as in other work, creating an interference that viewers sense even when—or precisely because—they might not consciously account for it.[8] Why do this, since it does not seem to signify anything in particular, but rather to underscore the reality of the set *as set*? On some level this intrusion effects a sense of the camera peeking clandestinely onto a private space, encroaching, almost ominously, upon the protagonist. With just a bit of a stretch, the peculiar "behind-the-mirror," or rather "over-the-mirror" (as in "over the shoulder"), camera position can also be read symbolically, in covert allusion to the theme of the double: we

Figure 12.1 A Hitchcockian visual disturbance in Alfred Hitchcock's *The Wrong Man* (1956).

might infer that, in the diegetic world, and at this point, Fonda glimpses his reflection in the mirror opposite that he distractedly dresses, so that his own "double" prepares him, as it were, for what's to come. We might wonder, in fact, if the mirror is still cracked—mirrors are pricy to replace, and the Balestreros are short on cash. If so, does his broken Picasso-esque countenance in the mirror still shock as in the earlier dramatic breakdown scene? Even assuming that, in routine film-viewing, this "over-the-mirror" position is not fully and consciously registered by the common viewer, at the very least a certain tension is introduced into the situation with this eclectic mise-en-scène. It is as if an alien dimension has thus invaded the scene as something hovering, though not fully conscious or integrated, on the edge of one's field of vision.[9]

As he puts on his shirt Fonda's eyes are initially downcast, but then he looks up. The Christ icon appears to return his look from the reverse-field shot, where it occupies the center of the frame (see Figure 12.2). To the right we glimpse part of a framed painting; to the lower left the curved edge of the mirror initially occupies roughly the same area where previously we've seen the mirror's shadowy backside. Fonda's own large shadow is cast on the wall and on part of the mirror, and is thus tightly nested between it and the icon. The shadow's two-dimensionality rhymes with the allusion to mirror

Figure 12.2 Opening to an altered dimension? The Christ icon, Christopher "Manny" Balestrero's (Henry Fonda) shadow, and the mirror's edge in *The Wrong Man*.

reflections—even as none are seen in this sequence while other forms of doubling dominate. In this way the shadow also prefigures the overlapping optical play of surfaces in the cinematographic superimposition. In all, different dimensions—physical and, in a sense, metaphysical—intrude at this point upon the film's realist fabric. The camera now dollies forth toward the icon, suggesting a shift and concentration of Fonda's attention—from inner contemplation, nudged perhaps by a glimpse of his own mirror image, then past his shadow, on to the icon.

Epiphanic devices

The iconography is conventional: Christ's left hand points to the epiphanically flamed, beaming Sacred Heart, while his right is raised in benediction. The heart seems to hover over the robed chest as if, externalized, it floats toward the picture plane, suspended between different spatial orders. Everything about the icon is addressed outward, to the viewer's look and his supplication. An anything-but-realistic image, instantly identifiable, heavily coded and formulaic, Christ's image and the icon's mode of address make a claim to the sacred. The realism of *The Wrong Man* is overtaken here by the icon's mystical-magical suggestion, leading to the purely filmic event of the superimposition. Insofar as succession suggests (even as it might not prove) causality, the superimposition could thus seem prompted by the man's encounter with the icon. We are not, however, in St. Peter's cathedral, nor even in the quasi-auratic presence of original art works in the Metropolitan Museum, a subway ride away. This is the lowly setting of a modest row house in Jackson Heights, Queens, of the 1950s, and the icon is nothing more than a cheap, mass-produced reproduction of a popular rendering of Christ and the flaming heart.

What auratic power, what agency, can such an image carry? By the Catholic doctrine of the incarnate image, in fact, a reproduction is just as potent as an original by a power that derives from the ultimate "original model": Christ's earthly, human form as itself incarnation of the divine. The claim of icons rests on this presumed identity with the original, and this identity transfers— as by way of André Bazin's photographic ontology—also to any and all of its replicas.[10] This is why it is legitimate to approach even such a common, naïve, mass-produced and mass-disseminated image as object of prayer and supplication. Like a miracle, the incarnate image only requires faith—but nothing less. Hitchcock's film assumes at this point the position of the believer—like the Catholic Italian-American protagonist—and extends the icon's power of address to the domain of cinema.[11] The dissonance between the icon's archaic-sacral claim and its popular rendering for mass reproduction might be labeled kitsch, but is not its charge the same as that of the cinema? How *can* the cinema restore our human faith—I mean faith in the human—in a desacralized world of popular replicas and simulations on the one hand, and random contingencies of the urban crowd on the other—all of which the cinema instantiates and perpetuates? What meaning or value can it inspire in the leveling grids of modern industrial technologies, classifications, and institutions? Its challenge is to negotiate the original, unique subject and the mass-produced and replicated image, the powers and complexities of art, and the common culture. Surely, this challenge is among the great concerns of film history, and we find it evolving through post-classical American cinema in the era of Cold War late capitalism with which some of Hitchcock's best films are concerned.

The brief shot–reverse shot between Fonda and the icon further suggests that the human eyes meet the Christ icon's gaze head-on: eye-to-eye, face-to-face. Since the man's lips move in prayer, one might also say that there is a sort of conversation taking place here. While such face-to-face "sacred conversation" with a holy figure does not imply that the two parties are on the same order of being, a sense of reciprocity, transference, doubling (or twinning), even identity, surfaces here.[12] One can imagine an almost physical manifestation of the icon's inspiration (as in a "transfer of spirit") through the trajectory of lights: from the starry-night iconic backdrop to the big close-up of Fonda, wherein two bright pin-lights reflect in his eyes as if responding to the icon. Seconds later, as the superimposition begins to unfold, these twinkling little lights seem to leap into the splatter of streetlights and neon punctuating the nocturnal urban scene from which the criminal emerges (see Figure 12.3). Subsequently, with the matching of faces in the superimposition, even Christ's halo seems to be mirrored, flashing for an instant before our eyes when the criminal's hat, optically translucent by the double exposure, hovers momentarily over Fonda's head (see Figure 12.4). The icon's naïve pictorial play of inner and outer—the artifice of floating surfaces and painted lights, the pointing to the hovering heart and the address to the viewer—thus finds a sort of equivalence in the piece of heightened filmic artifice that follows: the optical joining of the superimposition, with its own play of transparency and surface, interiors and exteriors, its matching and joining of disparate forms, its odd, magical spatiality.

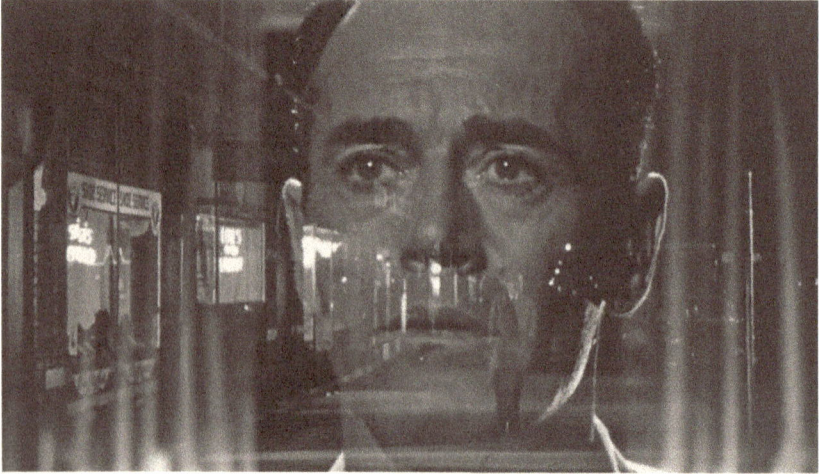

Figure 12.3 The play of interior and exterior, surface and depth, solidity and transparency, the real and the phantasmic effected by the double exposure in *The Wrong Man*.

Figure 12.4 The criminal's hat endows Fonda with a kind of halo in *The Wrong Man*.

Are we too familiar with superimpositions, too jaded by such special effects—seminal to the very medium of film—to really pay attention, to perceive and still to marvel at what the technique can accomplish? In this scene, diametrically opposed mise-en-scènes, involving distinct image-planes, collide: Fonda's big close-up in the dark interiors, against a window curtain, is so shallow that it almost functions, in its entirety, like a screen upon which the second image is projected. The latter's prominent perspectival depth in the urban location is underscored by the criminal's movement from the depth of the image toward us, perpendicular to the image-plane, from extreme long shot toward his own big close-up—as if now claiming the screen as his own.[13] But at the height of the superimposition, illusionistic depth appears altogether negated, summoning quite another order of surface effects: suddenly each of the two images becomes a ghostly, transparent reflection. It is such tension of the real and the phantasmic, of presence and absence, in superimposition that Bazin considered to be paradigmatic of the way in which the cinema's realistic powers and its capacity to invoke the unreal are joined.[14] One recalls the quaint tricks of early "ghost photography" that claimed to manifest and prove the reality of spirit visitations and other sorts of supernatural phenomena. Such photography routinely exploited multiple exposure techniques to effect an uncanny meeting of the singular and the plural, the solid and the transparent, the material and the immaterial, the supernatural and the real. Phantasmic bodies, "visible, yet seen through," writes Tom Gunning, in this way also recalled "the transparent nature of film itself, its status as a filter of light, a caster of shadows, a weaver of phantoms."[15]

Similar techniques and effects were also employed in the service of pseudo-scientific claims. Most prominent, in this context, is Francis Galton's use of multiple exposures to support his eugenics system, devising a quasi-statistical photography (foreshadowing, incidentally, certain digital imaging) that involved the graphic alignment of numerous individual likenesses, superimposed. The resulting image was a ghostly composite, seemingly depicting a representative physiognomic type. Galton's technique resulted in the effacement of singular features and idiosyncrasies, preserving on the photographic plate only the recurring basic features, and giving rise to a synthetic portrait grasped as visual equivalent, and as proof, of an abstract statistical average: a type whose features are then posited as a measure against which to evaluate and classify actual individuals. The leap from visual impression, or imprint—the perceptual, the imaginative, and the photographic should all echo here—to knowledge and proof is in fact tested several times over in *The Wrong Man*.[16] And while we condemn such hasty leap on the part of the clerk at the life insurance agency who has triggered the chain of misidentifications, we ourselves rehearse some version of it in view of the superimposition: to a point it explains the clerk's error, but does it offer proof? In comparing the two men, which the superimposition begs us to do, we too might jump to conclusions, imagining that we can now definitively read innocence in Fonda's face vs. malice in the other man's features. Does the film endorse such readings or throw them all into doubt?

Contingency; recognition

In a sense, the superimposition is an *event*: it is construed as something that happens *to* the protagonist, like a kind of visitation. But primarily it is a cinematographic event, inviting ways of seeing and hosts of possible meanings, committing to none. On the one hand it seems to come at Fonda from the outside, to meet the interiority (as in, occurring indoors *and* inhabiting an inner life) of the scene of prayer. On the other hand, the way in which the criminal's figure emerges from the depth of "his" shot—the second shot—to then be fully revealed at the fore, but from an initial frame position which appears to be located "inside" Fonda's head (in the first shot), also effects a sense of something "bursting," as it were, from a point of origin *within* the protagonist. It is, indeed, an overdetermined shot/s, and we are pressed to see it on several levels simultaneously. First, and at the simplest level (which cannot be dismissed), as a sort of catechistic lesson literalized by the special effect: *if* you pray, you will be saved. Second, reinforcing some such pious wish-fulfilment, but also distinguishable from it, is the basic narrative syntax of parallel action: *while* he prayed at home, this transpired down the street. Third, it is a reiteration of Fonda's overall passivity in the film—worlds away from the protagonist's energetic pursuit in other Hitchcock films (e.g., *North by Northwest*, 1959) to correct a mistaken identity, leading to an exhilarating realization of one's own. Fonda, by contrast, is motionless and, in fact, impassive in his close-up, and it is the active criminal who walks forth into the matching of faces to then take over the scene. Fourth, it transpires as the exteriorizing of the protagonist's presumed thought—his wish that the right man materialize. Fifth (and conversely), it could also suggest a way of unconsciously receiving, or interiorizing, a miraculous event qua act of Grace—namely an act independent of any human will or act. Sixth, one considers the magical suggestion of superimposition: not, in this case, by way of representing ghost visitations, but as a conjuring of quasi-magical *sympathy* between the two men. Their coinciding, merging features bring them into contact *via* their images—sympathetic magic, as Frazer considered, is predicated on contact and similarity—and imply a deeper level in which they

are joined, and by which some magical exchange, or contagion, occurs between them. Guilt can thus seem to pass back and forth from one to the other,
its existential dimensions increasing in the process, engulfing both, and even
as they are to be re-differentiated as self and other, identity and difference,
through a vision that is proper to the cinema.[17]

Finally, one considers the intellectual and reflexive possibilities of superimposition as a mode of *cinematic thought*, along the lines that Daniel
Morgan explores in reference to Bazin's essay on "The Life and Death of
Superimposition," and to Jean-Luc Godard's film-historiographic and ana-
lytic deployment of the device in the *Histoire(s) du cinema*.[18] Godard's abundant use of superimposition qua montage of simultaneity, Morgan suggests,
reinforces the possibilities of the device not only as a way of visually signaling
a fiction of inner thoughts or memories, but as a way for the cinematic medium to think *itself* through two (or more) images together. The composite
image in this way emerges as an image of thought, and it posits the cinematic device, as such, as a mode of thinking. Godard's video manipulation
of film in the *Histoire(s)* brings superimposition to yet another, historio-
graphic order. A sequence devoted to Hitchcock in episode 4A culminates,
precisely, with the shot/s with which we are concerned. Upon the already-
superimposed faces of the wrong and the "right" man, Godard superimposes
a third man's face, that of Hitchcock himself, controller of the universe—as
that section's title suggests.[19] Hitchcock's spectral face is itself abundantly familiar while, physiognomically, it is as dissimilar as can be when compared
with the two matching faces that concern us—one a major Hollywood star,
the other anonymous as character and unknown as actor. Godard's way of
citing *The Wrong Man* shot/s, yoked with Hitchcock's own countenance, thus
associates questions of identity and responsibility (a variant of guilt?) with
that of authorial agency—Hitchcock's and, by extension, Godard's own. It is
the filmmaker who frames and blocks the shot, who holds the threads and
stitches images together, assuming responsibility for the result. Hitchcock's
unique face hovers in the Godard sequence as a sort of presiding consciousness, a power that joins and distinguishes the elements at will, turning technology into magic, contingency into form, and reality into meaning.

Avoiding his playful cameo-signature, Hitchcock adopts instead, in *The
Wrong Man* prologue, a direct frontal personal imprint—nothing coy about
it. The presentation of self and the claim to truth are bound in his pledge of
responsibility to historical events, face-to-face with the camera. Committing
to a "true story, every word of it," a story that he has not invented or

manipulated, Hitchcock nevertheless holds all the powers of suggestion and implication. This is radicalized in the superimposition shot/s that he later disavowed—ostensibly, because it "never happened in the real story."[20] But even if "unreal," is it not, nevertheless, "true"? That the prologue's remarkable statement on veracity and authenticity is itself staged as a geometrical play of shadows and light in what appears to be a vast movie studio soundstage— so distinct from the film's showcasing of authentic location shooting—itself teases our notions of the "real" and the "true," disturbing simple oppositions of location and set, actor and role, identity and appearance. One must be able to join things together, to associate and link people—since their stories, and their fates, are intertwined. But one must also tell them apart, not lump them in a crowd—this is how the superimposition scene concludes, as facial contours converge, break down into distortion, and are re-differentiated.

The porosity of identity, the terror of doubling, the circulation and contamination of guilt are translated into thought through the workings of the cinematographic device. Even to us jaded viewers, the shot/s—with its escalating tension in the movement of the anonymous man's approach and our dawning recognition—still appears astonishingly choreographed, a cinematographic feat, a wonder to behold. Its intensity projects past the sociohistorical setting, past the gray everyday world of toothaches and insurance agencies and police precincts, pointing toward more mysterious riddles of selfhood—of the unique being, alone in his uniqueness. It translates the social, imaginary, and miraculous correspondences of identity, at the uncertain intersection of seeing and knowing, for our human eyes. It encapsulates in a single/double shot—in the cinematic gesture—the film's exploration of ways in which it is always for one person looking at another to negotiate contingency—the fleeting glance, the limits of perception—with recognition, appearance with insight. Not only the coinciding of the two men—their visual matching in the shot, the intersecting of their fates—but also, for each one of them, as for each and every one of us, the coinciding of what is seen and what is known, of the face in the crowd and the singular person is only, at most, asymptotic.[21]

Notes

1. Excited by the present volume's prompt of the "one shot Hitchcock," this essay revisits and expands an earlier discussion of the relevant scene in my book, *The Face on Film* (New York: Oxford University Press, 2017), 172–176. I underscore here the essayistic

mode of my contribution to this anthology, even hoping to associate its happy invitation to dwell on a single shot with creative interventions along the lines of *24 Hour Psycho* (Douglas Gordon, 1993). These sections of my previous chapter have been reproduced by permission of Oxford University Press.

2. See Yuri Tsivian's gloss on Eisenstein's ecstatic "montage-image" in *Ivan the Terrible* (London: British Film Institute, 2002), 51.

3. Apart from the obvious fact that it *is* Fonda's face with which we are confronted in this close-up, I take the common liberty to dub the protagonist Fonda, since the star's fame transpires so clearly through his role, while most other parts are securely designated by their screen roles, along with the anonymous participants, some drawn from life, that populate the film, including the "right" man.

4. François Truffaut, *The Films in My Life*, trans. Leonard Mayhew (New York: Simon & Schuster, 1978), 86.

5. Eric Rohmer and Claude Chabrol, in *Hitchcock: The First Forty-Four Films*, trans. Stanley Hochman (1957; New York: Frederick Ungar Publishing, 1979), 145–152, were perhaps the first to dwell on the miracle as Hitchcock's "privileged, perfected form" in the film. Jean-Luc Godard further embellished this idea—I address his treatment of the scene below.

6. Anthony Macklin and Alfred Hitchcock, "'It's the Manner of Telling': An Interview with Alfred Hitchcock (1976)," in *Hitchcock on Hitchcock*, Vol. 2: *Selected Writings and Interviews*, ed. Sidney Gottlieb (Berkeley: University of California Press, 2015), 49–58.

7. In "I Saw, Therefore I Know? Alfred Hitchcock's *The Wrong Man* and the Epistemological Potential of the Photographic Image," *Film Criticism* 41, no. 1 (2017), Sabrina Negri maps the epistemological questions relating to photographic evidence by which this film can be said to reflect on a longer visual culture. She extends to *The Wrong Man* Tom Gunning's interrogation of such terms in "In Your Face: Physiognomy, Photography, and the Gnostic Mission of Early Film," *Modernism/Modernity* 4, no. 1 (1997): 1–29, especially as relating to the thematic of police interrogation and the detective genre, and further elaborates on my own probing of the gap between seeing and knowing throughout *The Face of Film* (New York: Oxford University Press, 2017).

8. A notable instance in which Hitchcock's camera seems perched in such non-space is the kiss on the train in *North by Northwest* (1959). But for another sort of uncanny visual intrusion into the diegetic space it suffices to rewind *The Wrong Man* back to the first police station sequence, where a conspicuous formless stain on the wall recurs in several shots. See my discussion of this stain in *The Face on Film*, 169–170. In *Hidden Hitchcock* (Chicago: University of Chicago Press, 2016), D. A. Miller works through the film with a fine-toothed comb to pick out a surprising number of continuity errors: perhaps the most notable involves the substitution of a mirror by a painting in the hallway to the Balestrero home. These are in some ways consistent with the visual disturbances I describe above, and partake in what Miller discusses as a diegetic "universe of misrecognitions and false continuities" (p. 121).

9. Stephen Heath discusses in comparable terms Hitchcock's use of a Picasso-esque painting in *Suspicion* (1941), but even if not fully integrated, that painting is at least

attended to in the earlier film, while in *The Wrong Man* the back of the mirror, as well as some framed pictures in the darkened room, hover on the edge of visibility and might escape conscious attention even as their intrusion on the scene is carefully calculated. Stephen Heath, *Questions of Cinema* (London: Macmillan, 1981), 69n1.

10. Apart from André Bazin, the suggestiveness of the doctrine of the icon in relation to photography and film has been discussed by scholars of Byzantine art, e.g., Hans Belting, *Likeness and Presence: A History of the Image Before the Era of Art*, trans. Edmund Jephcott (Chicago: University of Chicago Press, 1994), 4, 11, 53.

11. See Dudley Andrew's recent discussion, "The Effect of Miracles and the Miracle of Effects: Bazin's Faith in Evolution," in *Special Effects on the Screen: Faking the View from Méliès to Motion Capture*, ed. Marc Furstenau and Martin Lefebvre (Amsterdam University Press, 2022), 451–474, on the film's opening to chance and miracle against its realist grain, comparing it productively with Carl Theodor Dreyer's *Ordet* (1955) and Robert Bresson's *A Man Escaped* (1956).

12. The twinning of man and Christ is already intimated by the protagonist's name, Christopher Emmanuel—names of Christ both. That this was in fact the name of the actual person whose life experience inspired Hitchcock's film does not cancel this suggestiveness—one could not have invented better, and it's even possible that it inspired Hitchcock's decisions relating to the Christ icon scene in the first place.

13. In his essay "*Notorious*," in *Everything You Always Wanted to Know about Lacan (But were Afraid to Ask Hitchcock)*, ed. Slavoj Žižek (London: Verso, 1992), 151–154, Pascal Bonitzer describes the movement from distance into close-up as Hitchcock's characteristic device, which also carries erotic connotations. Here it is handled not by a camera or lens movement but via a character's movement, and even as a close-up shot is, in a sense, both its point of origin and its destination. Thanks to Joe McElhaney for his input on this point.

14. André Bazin, "The Life and Death of Superimposition," in *Bazin at Work: Major Essays and Reviews from the Forties and Fifties*, trans. Alain Piette and Bert Cardullo, ed. Bert Cardullo (New York: Routledge, 1997), 73–76.

15. I quote from Tom Gunning, "To Scan a Ghost: The Ontology of Mediated Vision," *Grey Room* 26 (Winter 2007): 98. Gunning's other essays on the topic include the seminal "Phantom Images and Modern Manifestations: Spirit Photography, Magic Theater, Trick Films, and Photography's Uncanny," in *Fugitive Images: from Photography to Video*, ed. Patrice Petro (Bloomington: Indiana University Press, 1995), 42–71.

16. See examples of composite photography in my *The Face on Film*, and in Negri's "I Saw, Therefore I Know?"

17. Rohmer and Chabrol were the first to discuss the transfer and interchangeability of guilt as a Hitchcockian idea, culminating in this film. James George Frazer developed the idea of sympathetic magic, as predicated on similarity (or imitation) and contact (or contagion), in *The Golden Bough: A Study of Magic and Religion* (1890; Floating Press e-book, 2009), 36–120.

18. Daniel Morgan, "The Afterlife of Superimposition," in *Opening Bazin: Postwar Film Theory and Its Afterlife*, ed. Dudley Andrew (New York: Oxford University Press, 2011), 127–141. Godard's graphic play in the title *Histoire(s)* resonates nicely with the traversing of singular/double (or multiple) that I have been exploring.

19. Rick Warner elaborates on this sequence, and the notion of a cinematic "control of the universe," in "Difficult Work in a Popular Medium: Godard on 'Hitchcock's Method,'" *Critical Quarterly* 51, no. 3 (2009): 63–84.

20. Arthur Knight, "Conversation with Alfred Hitchcock," in *Alfred Hitchcock: Interviews*, ed. Sydney Gottlieb (Jackson: University Press of Mississippi, 2003), 169.

21. This should echo, of course, Bazin's notion of cinema as "the asymptote of reality," in "*Umberto D*: A Great Work," in *What Is Cinema?* trans. and ed. Hugh Gray, 2 vols. (Berkeley: University of California Press, 1971), 2:82.

13

Vertigo (1958)

Labor in a single shot

Domietta Torlasco

It is an iconic scene and almost an art installation in its own right: John "Scottie" Ferguson (James Stewart) enters the Palace of the Legion of Honor and stands behind Madeleine Elster (Kim Novak) as she is sitting— composed and motionless—in front of Carlotta Valdes's portrait. He looks at her looking, or so he believes. The scene is part of a series, a string of "tailing" episodes that lead Scottie to the Podesta Baldocchi flower shop, the Mission Dolores cemetery, and the McKittrick Hotel. Yet it is this scene that stands out as the most formidable setup—the setting in place of an apparatus or *dispositif* that aims at harnessing and orienting Scottie's conjectural thinking (see Figure 13.1).[1]

That such reasoning realizes itself through intensely visual means cannot surprise the Hitchcock spectator, whose attention and cunning have been re- peatedly teased by an array of minor details across his films: keys, eyeglasses, a glass of milk, a bottle of wine, a handbag, an emerald ring. Unremarkable in themselves, these objects are suddenly brought to the fore—often by virtue of a camera movement—and made to stand out as hints of past or future crimes. They become clues or symptoms, to borrow from Carlo Ginzburg's famous article on Giovanni Morelli, Sigmund Freud, and Sherlock Holmes, in a universe that pivots around conjectural reasoning. For Ginzburg, the latter constitutes nothing less than a method—a paradigm for the pursuit of knowledge that is "indirect, based on signs and scraps of evidence, conjec- tural" and that, since the nineteenth century, has tied together the figures of the detective, the analyst, and the art historian.[2] Hitchcock shows us that this kind of reasoning can be made visible—that, indeed, it occurs in the midst of the visible world as much as it does in the mind of the thinker. *Rear Window* (1954) sets the standard in this respect, and films such as *Suspicion* (1941),

Domietta Torlasco, Vertigo *(1958)* In: *One Shot Hitchcock.* Edited by: Luke Robinson and Melanie Robson, Oxford University Press. © Oxford University Press 2024. DOI: 10.1093/oso/9780197682876.003.0013

Figure 13.1 (See also Plate 17)   *Vertigo* (Alfred Hitchcock, 1958): the setup.

Shadow of a Doubt (1943), *Notorious* (1946), *Strangers on a Train* (1951), and *Dial M for Murder* (1954) offer other remarkable examples of Hitchcock's treatment of details.

It is in *Vertigo* (1958), however, that we encounter the most concise cinematic instantiation of conjectural thinking as a method that spans multiple fields of inquiry. At the museum, Scottie is at once a working detective, hired to keep track of Madeleine's erratic behavior; an aspiring analyst, determined to demystify her mystery; and a provisional art historian, confronted with the likeness of her ancestor. He occupies the position of the "subject supposed to know" and, accordingly, enjoys the privileges of the autonomous point of view, commanding the camera and scanning the scene—except that the scene is a setup. This essay will reassess the terms of this setup—and point to ways of escaping it—in light not only of Hitchcock's treatment of spectatorship, but also of our current predicament as screen viewers. What can *Vertigo* still show us, now that we find ourselves in a "screen-sphere," living "primarily in and through screens, rather than merely on or with them?"[3]

The shot I am returning to consists of a virtuoso camera movement, a dolly-in that leads the eye in two different directions: first, down and toward Madeleine's spiral-shaped hair and then up—across the distance separating the bench from the wall—toward Carlotta's hair similarly coiffed. In both cases, the camera pauses on the whorls for a few moments. The shot appears seamless and yet the spectator can feel a hesitation, even a sense of exertion where the look reorients itself, as if the camera had to put in more work to forge its own path. Indeed, the shot goes well beyond bringing about a comparison between details (for which a standard editing cut would have sufficed)—it expresses what Tom Gunning has called "the force of a look."[4] This force is already manifest in the preceding shot, as the camera slides from the floral bouquet lying next to Madeleine to the one resting in Carlotta's hands, and it will impose itself again a number of times in the film—most notably at the Empire Hotel, when Scottie finally sees the ruby necklace, first in Judy Barton's (also Kim Novak) mirror reflection and then, all of a sudden, in a flashback of Carlotta's portrait (see Figures 13.2–13.4).

However, while repeating and foreshadowing other sequences, our shot possesses a singular complexity. To begin with, the camera movement is of a more convoluted kind, as it attempts to mime the forms it highlights, to retrace the twirls in the women's hair by other means. It also lasts longer and veers off along the way, deliberately forging its own path. Last but not least, it brings to the fore an indistinction between shot and montage. There is no cut separating the "shot" of Madeleine's hair from the "shot" of Carlotta's hair. It might be tempting to suggest that this is but a kind of analytical editing that, pace André Bazin, makes use of duration to tell the spectator where to look and, concomitantly, how to look. This is not my wager. What I find at work here is that indeterminacy of articulation that Gilles Deleuze posits as a trait of modern cinema. For Deleuze, in the cinema of Robert Bresson, Jean-Luc Godard, and Jean Rouch, the discontinuity of montage and the continuity of the sequence shot are "reconciled" through the constitution of a new system, one that allows for the emergence of "non-chronological time relationships."[5] It is at this juncture that the subject of conjectural thinking and the spectator might part ways. Scottie, the detective/analyst who is called to investigate a disturbance in time, that is, the ghostliness of Madeleine's present, will want to put present and past back in chronological order. On the other hand, the dolly-in offers some spectators a line of flight, the possibility to see time otherwise. This is because, in its internal redoubling, the dolly-in does not unfold as an alternative to editing—it is itself a mode of editing, and one that upsets the continuity of the scene.

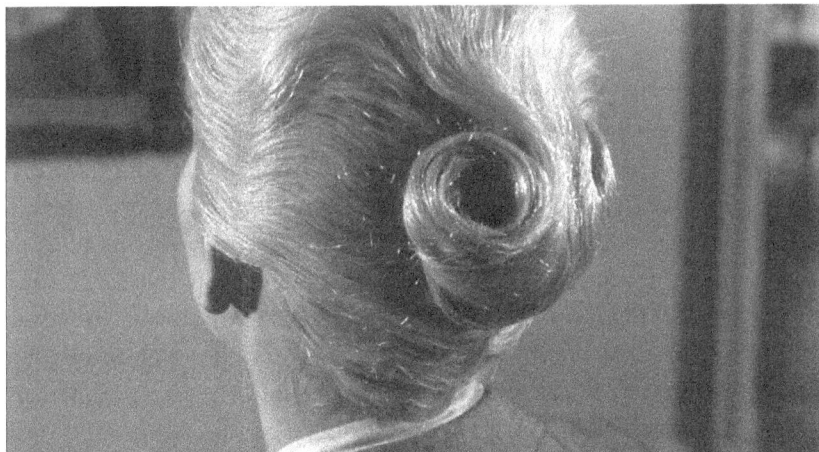

Figure 13.2 (See also Plate 18) *Vertigo*: The first coil.

Figure 13.3 (See also Plate 19) *Vertigo*: In between one and two.

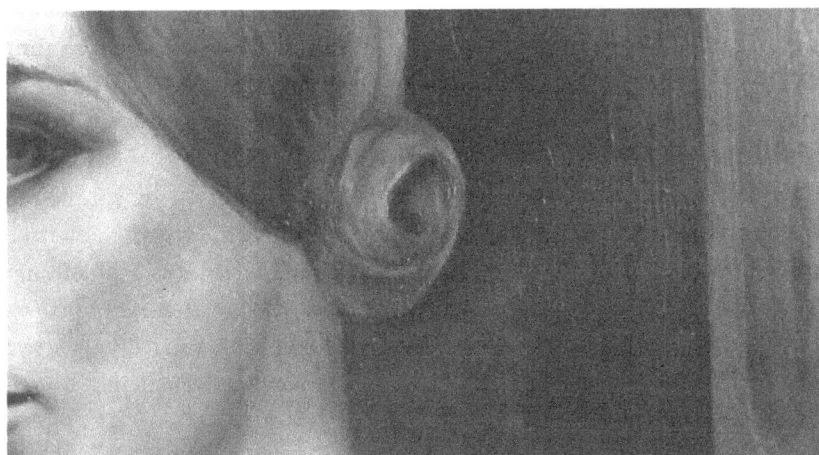

Figure 13.4 (See also Plate 20) *Vertigo*: The second coil.

I already knew *Vertigo* by heart when the German filmmaker Harun Farocki directed my attention toward this shot. I was working on a film essay that included a still of Madeleine's hairdo and Farocki suggested that I try to produce a similar camera movement, this time tracking on the still itself. The suggestion was offered offhandedly, in keeping with his advising style, and it took me by surprise. Nothing came of it. What I could not reconcile was the gap I perceived between Farocki's minimalist approach and Hitchcock's ostentatious gesture. Moreover, Farocki had devoted his career to critiquing image production and consumption under capitalism. At the time of our exchange, in the late 1990s, he had already made dozens of films investigating the "function of the eye" across the fields of artisanal and industrial labor, warfare, surveillance, advertising, pornography, and professional and life training. Later, he would move his practice into the gallery and the museum and focus on the role that new audiovisual technologies play in our post-Fordist economy, especially at the intersection of the military, carceral, and entertainment industries.[6] Throughout his career, his vision remained thoroughly analytical, combining detached observation, and the capacity to let things unfold in their own time, with a mode of editing that never tired of juxtaposing and distancing images of all kinds.

In an extreme case of deferred action—an *après-coup* that is not alien to *Vertigo*'s own dynamics—it took me years to realize why an artist like Farocki would be captivated by such a shot. Seeing takes time and this time does not progress along a straight path. Rather, it coils and uncoils, engulfing and turning us around. What I failed to see, perhaps in my bias for the more subtle gestures, was precisely the time of this shot—the time it takes for the shot to unfurl, to remain suspended in an uncertain zone, rather than to simply reach its destination. In the present chapter, I will attend to this time and the potential it releases, which might be nothing less than the potential for the world of the film to be different from what it is; or, at least, for the stories shaping it to take a different course. I wrote about this other world in the *Heretical Archive: Digital Memory at the End of Film*, where I theorized the film cut as a fold, less an erasure than a twisting of the visible upon itself and, as such, the site of a creative residue.[7] There I indicated that editing-as-folding could also occur in a sequence-shot, though I concentrated on actual edits. Among others, I attended to the edit separating *Vertigo*'s two main parts (the Madeleine/Carlotta story and the Judy/Madeleine story, if you will), looking for a line of flight in the interval between shots. The museum dolly-in offers me the opportunity to further elaborate on this excess of perception as it emerges within the same shot, as if hiding in plain sight, thanks to a masterful exercise in false continuity.[8] I propose this reading as a response to Farocki's suggestion—that is, as the attempt to develop a collaborative interpretation across time, rather than to guess what Farocki might have thought, which I will never learn.

Immaterial labor (after Harun Farocki)

If placed next to Farocki's work, the museum scene acquires a new kind of visibility. The dolly-in that leads from Madeleine to Carlotta stands out not only as an instance of conjectural thinking but also as a form of labor. Conjointly, it becomes possible to look at the scene itself as an image of labor—the portrayal of a process that is at once perceptual, cognitive, and affective. We enter here the controversial domain of immaterial labor, which contemporary Marxist authors have defined as "the labor that creates immaterial products, such as knowledge, information, communication, a relationship, or an emotional response."[9] In the post-Fordist regime, this kind of labor has inherited the centrality once occupied by mass factory production and pressed theorists to expand their definition of "productive labor" (labor that secures surplus-value) to include, for instance, service work. Michael Hardt and Antonio Negri distinguish between two key forms of immaterial labor: "intellectual or linguistic" and "affective." The former fabricates "ideas, symbols, codes, texts, linguistic figures, images," while the latter "produces or manipulates affects such as feeling of ease, well-being, satisfaction, excitement, or passion."[10] It is important to note that these two forms intermingle in the reality of work; that they are habitually accompanied by material forms; and, most important, that the labor necessary for the production of immaterial commodities remains stubbornly *material*, as it occurs in and through our bodies and minds. Hardt and Negri would later propose the expression "labor of the head and heart" in order to disambiguate the question of immateriality.[11] Indeed, such an expression helps us with our reframing of the scene in *Vertigo*: isn't it precisely this kind of labor—of the head and heart—that Scottie is performing in his quest to solve the Carlotta mystery and save Madeleine?

Let's consider the diegesis, to start with. At the museum, as in the city's other landmark sites, both Scottie and Madeleine are covertly at work, charged with tasks that in due course will allow for a drastic reallocation of wealth. A former police detective, Scottie is now trying his hand as a private eye and, in pure hard-boiled tradition, will not be able to avoid getting involved. Madeleine's occupation, on the other hand, or rather, the job that Judy is carrying out while impersonating Madeleine, is harder to pin down: model, muse, actress, haunted lover. . . . In any case, she is a "virtuoso performer," one who, like a dancer, musician, or orator, requires the "'presence of others'"—the audience—as "both the instrument and the object of labor."[12] That product and process remain inseparable does not exclude her activity from the domain of surplus-value. Rather, it renders it all the more supple, capable of generating that excess—of knowledge and affect—that the system is eager to exploit. It also renders this work much more precarious, dependent, and disposable, as will become clear after the murder of Gavin Elster's wife. All this is not to turn Judy into a pioneer of the new economy. However, by recasting the museum scene from the viewpoint of labor, it becomes easier to see how the play of voyeurism and exhibitionism for which *Vertigo* is renowned takes place within a mesh of relations that are at once productive and social.[13]

Farocki meticulously recorded the vicissitudes of this other kind of labor, which is much harder to see. We might call it invisible for two interlocking reasons: it is often denied public recognition (let's think of housework, for instance) and it defies the tendency to think of process in terms of chronological succession. In fact, the duration of immaterial forms of labor cannot be clearly accounted for quantitatively, that is, divided up and counted.[14] It resists modernity's will to measure time by means of clocks, timetables, and a certain use of film and photography. Immaterial labor can take up the whole of life while not leaving immediately visible traces. In *Leben, BRD* (*How to Live in the Federal Republic of Germany*, 1990), for instance, Farocki reassembles thirty-two scenes shot in everyday settings. Each scene features specific groups (schoolchildren, expecting couples, midwives, bank employees, police officers, soldiers, car safety instructors, strip club dancers, etc.) as they train for—rehearse—situations they are bound to encounter in view of their occupation or life predicament. Farocki does not present these scenes in an orderly sequence. Instead, he cuts each scene into segments and then edits together, intersperses segments from different scenes. This break in continuity meddles with the linear instructional pathways that each scene is supposed to provide and further exposes the artificiality of the setup. As the subjects in the scenes practice against the odds of unpredictability, they "become actors who play themselves."[15]

Is it too farfetched to envision Judy undergoing a similar kind of life training? In fact, we do not need to imagine—in the film, we see her recalibrating her gait, speech, and overall demeanor, if only the second time around, and this time we do the work with her. At the department store, the beauty salon, and, soon after, in her motel room, Judy reluctantly accepts becoming Madeleine once again, by means of a makeover that repeats the one she undertook with Gavin Elster. Now we are asked not only to witness this process but also to affectively partake in the effort she makes to bear herself in a rarefied, distant fashion. This is another way of saying that Scottie's voyeurism/sadism and Judy's exhibitionism/masochism—the focus of many psychoanalytic readings—interlock within a field that is primed for and by immaterial labor. They emerge in a domain where the relationship between activity and passivity has mutated vis-à-vis novel conditions of production and consumption.

Other examples of Farocki's works can help us shed new light on the museum scene and the way it connects to the changing vicissitudes of production and consumption. At this juncture, let me mention *Stilleben* (*Still Life*, 1997), which he had just completed at the time of our conversation at the end of the 1990s, as it foregrounds the labor performed not only by the characters or the filmmaker, but also by the viewers. In *Still Life*, Farocki engages with the aesthetics of seventeenth-century Dutch paintings and, through a voice-over, places the inanimate objects they portray within a network of commercial, scientific, and colonial relations. These readings punctuate longer sequences documenting the production of commercial photographs, which he posits as the inheritors of the still-life tradition. The cinematography, by Farocki's longtime collaborator Ingo Kratisch, is unhurried and relentless in exposing what is, at the very least, a double process of image production. We come to see not only the process that turns mundane artifacts (a cheeseboard, beer glasses, and a luxury watch) into tokens of commodity fetishism, but also the process through which we, the viewers, are asked to labor in order to become consumers of image-commodities, if not commodities ourselves. In other words, Farocki foregrounds what remains hidden in everyday transactions, as we turn the pages of glossy magazines or click on pop-up windows.

Now, the setup that Hitchcock activates in the museum scene recalls the type of setup that Farocki is upsetting, but with some differences. On the one hand, the dolly-ins focus not only on perfectly composed objects (floral bouquets and spiral hairdos), but also on the very process that leads us to perceive them as interlocked or even identical. These shots put us to work in a particular way, together with Scottie and Judy themselves. On the other hand, Hitchcock does not show us the process through which these objects were initially produced, nor does he give us the time to really become aware of our labor as co-producers of both the images we consume and ourselves as consumers. In the end, we are meant to remember the objects. As Godard proclaims, it is by virtue of his control of these objects that "Alfred Hitchcock succeeded where Alexander, Julius Caesar and Napoleon failed: to become master of the universe."[16] Or so it seems. Yes, Hitchcock installs the scene in the film so as to leave us little room for play and yet, perhaps in a gesture of ultimate·control, he also hides in plain sight the device through which the setup might be upset.

Perhaps it is the way we are used to translating images into words that seals our entrapment. By calling the hairdos and the bouquets "identical," which is what happens by default in most critical literature, we are already falling into the trap. The trap, I will maintain, is that of a mode of symbolic production that privileges similarity or, better, the tendency to produce associations on the basis of similarity. Faced with objects that are uneven in terms of materials, dimensions, and time periods, Scottie—and the spectator he is supposed to stand in for—sees the *same* bouquet and the *same* hairdo. The problem is not that Scottie detects certain resemblances, but that he au-tomatically prioritizes them and, in fact, makes them serve the story he is compelled to desire. In this narrative, which the film shares with several noirs and melodramas, Romantic and Gothic elements spill over into modern life only to be ultimately brought to reason.[17] Portraits of beautiful women (an ancestor or predecessor of the beloved or the beloved herself, as in Otto Preminger's *Laura* [1944], or in Hitchcock's own *Rebecca* [1940]) are often key in this respect; neither dead nor alive, the marker of life's own ghostliness, they hold a power that the modern detective needs to neutralize. How does this neutralization occur? *Vertigo* offers two solutions to the disturbance of time introduced by the portrait—Scottie's and Marjorie "Midge" Wood's—but only the former gains narrative currency. When Midge (Barbara Bel Geddes) invites Scottie to her studio apartment and uncovers the portrait that she has painted in response to the mystery of Madeleine/Carlotta, Scottie recoils in a mix of horror, revulsion, and profound disappoint-ment. A more subtle detective and an analyst who better understands the interplay of condensation and displacement, Midge has copied the portrait while painting her own face in place of Carlotta's. This other, demystifying image will soon disappear from the film, as will Midge herself. On the other hand, Scottie returns to the image of Madeleine/Carlotta over and over, always implementing a logic predicated on identity or equivalence. It is only after measuring the two spiral hairdos (or the bouquets) against a third term, an ideal of perfection that remains external to them, that he can deem them alike. After all, this is the secret of the Hitchcock blonde, at once eternal and interchangeable to the very extent that she is manufactured in relation to a general equivalent—gold or phallus, to borrow from Luce Irigaray's critique of the value-form under patriarchy.[18] It is this very logic of exchange that sustains Scottie's conviction that Judy can be turned into Madeleine without any significant remainder.

In this context, the time it takes Scottie to develop his evaluation of the two hairdos should strike us as curious, at the very least. The detective feels particularly slow, and so does the camera. This kind of appraisal occurs by default in our culture, and a cut would have been enough to mark not only the outcome but also the process. Yet it would be a mistake to dismiss the effects caused by Scottie's privileging of similarity. Because they are nearly identical, the hair whorls can be substituted for one another with little remainder, and so can the women who showcase them. During her spells, Madeleine is possessed, taken over by Carlotta, becoming one with her. Scottie's rationalizing account rejects this tale but does not undermine its logic; because they are equivalent (via a third term), the two women do not need each other and can be kept apart. Indeed, they are rendered mutually exclusive in their very individuality. Madeleine cannot be "herself" and Carlotta or, rather, the interspersing of the two. Scottie, who is trying to overcome his vertigo, would find himself undone in this spiral image of the beloved, rather than recomposed and grounded. So, he coerces Madeleine to see the truth as it lies in the details of another setup (the tower, the bell, the livery stable . . .), an old Spanish mission south of the city that has been preserved as a museum. We know this half of the film ends in murder and insanity, but the cost of Scottie's logic will prove to be immeasurable in the second half of the film too. To be loved, Judy needs to undergo her training anew and become Madeleine once again, seam by seam, curl by curl. And, once again, there can be no room for imperfection, even less for contamination: either Madeleine is herself, only and fully herself, or she is "nothing." At the end, Judy meets her death even before falling off the tower, as she is violently denied the possibility of being herself "and" Madeleine, Madeleine "and" Carlotta, or, rather, a hybrid, self-differing being, a being of the in-between.

It goes beyond the scope of this essay to elaborate on the conditions that render this crossing of traits impossible to realize or accept. Feminist thinkers have repeatedly emphasized how the symbolic economy of patriarchy privileges "abstraction, generalization, rationalization" and marginalizes what exceeds the scaffolding of its systems of classification: "body, experience, nature, contingency, pleasure."[19] The messiness of materiality needs to be cleared up, its forms refashioned: Madeline is made to showcase an ideal of femininity that demands purity of line, rarefaction, and weightlessness (note, for instance, the near disappearance of color in favor of impeccably drawn lines in her clothing, the triumph of geometry in her hairdo, and the way she appears to glide over the ground). This is the ideal of White, upper-class femininity that Hitchcock pursued throughout his career, an ideal that here he exposes as a masquerade. What haunts the performance of rarefied White femininity is precisely what has been excluded or repressed, the materiality not of the body in general but of specific bodies—female, Black and Brown, working-class.[20] Carlotta Valdez, a Mexican American woman who worked in a cabaret, does not fit the template of the perfect blonde. Neither does Judy, who comes from Salina, Kansas, and is now employed in a department store. Madeleine and Carlotta need to be kept apart, and so do Madeleine and Judy, as their touching or mixing would awaken "fears of miscegenation, passing, and queer sexuality."[21] But, of course, this kind of anxiety signals that such a contact has already occurred and, most important, that Scottie feels an intense desire for it, a craving that turns into repulsion, if not murderous hatred.[22] In this symbolic universe, the woman named Judy has no chance of survival.

And

Let's return to the double dolly-in, this camera movement that is not required, that reads as "excessive," even "useless" from the viewpoint of a tight narrative economy.[23] Ostensibly positioned outside the scene, Scottie finds in it a relationality that threatens to become superimposition—a mingling between the two figures and their contexts. A threat to the White, upper-class order of which he partakes, the convoluted line traced by this camera movement will thus need to be put in order, divided into autonomous segments (here versus there, now versus then). But the camera does not quite match this directionality, even if it clearly prompts it, relying on shared viewing habits and the pleasures of the inspecting eye. The shot's two phases unfold at the threshold of continuity and discontinuity, as if they constituted interdependent and yet distinct takes, neither joined nor disjointed. This is part of what Farocki might have seen or intuited. In the 1990s, he was beginning to experiment with "soft montage": the use of a split or double screen that enables two images to be shown side by side, more or less simultaneously, and to be edited in relation to each other. In soft montage, which he first discusses with regard to Godard's *Numéro deux* (*Number Two*, 1975), "what is at issue is a general relatedness, rather than a strict opposition or equation." In a gesture of openness that bears on the viewer's own labor, "*Number Two* does not predetermine how the two images are to be connected; we must build up the associations ourselves in an ongoing way as the film unfolds."[24] Following this example, we can return to *Vertigo* and begin to see the two phases of the museum dolly-in as existing side by side, if only intermittently.

But isn't the plasticity described by Farocki antithetical to the rigidity of the Hitchcockian universe? My wager is that, far from being canceled out, this plasticity remains active as the shot's hidden counterpart. The laboriousness of the dolly-in, as it heads toward the painting, disturbs the smoothness of the transition from Madeleine to Carlotta. In place of a cut, we have a hinge that is overwrought and unstable so that the coils—of the two bodies and of the two stories—appear not only in succession but also in simultaneity. They linger next to each other for a prolonged moment. Yet, it is this very flaw in the suturing of the shot that we end up bypassing. We feel it, perhaps by virtue of the hesitation and the sense of exertion accompanying the transition between phases; but we do not have the time to clearly see it. So, I am ready to admit that what I have just described might be an effect of a hybrid viewing experience. In *Death 24x a Second*, Laura Mulvey adopts the expression "delayed cinema" to identify the temporal displacement brought about by video technologies. By delaying the film's progression, the playback and slow-down functions on our screens allow for the deferred emergence of latent details.[25] My interaction with Farocki's films might have worked along these lines. However, my findings would not be any less real for this reason. It even adds to the wicked intricacy of the film to imagine that Hitchcock was already playing (with) us, and Scottie, by offering us a break that we could not really enjoy.

What is it, more precisely, that we (almost) miss in the articulation of the shot? We might have guessed it already, as I have detailed the effects produced by Scottie's associative logic, but let me now present it in a more direct fashion. What we overlook, as the camera forges its path, is that the relation between the hair whorls is primarily one of contiguity rather than similarity. In the scene's perceptual field, these "cut-outs" exist in a relation of material proximity, proximity to the bodies of which they are a part and to each other. If we privilege this unpretentious relation, we might come to perceive the difference between the two figures or to notice the way they touch each other "without passing through identity or equivalence."[26] Displacement from one image to the other, and vice versa, takes priority over substitution (of one image for the other, after their connection has been established via a third term). The camera becomes here a medium less of comparison than of "contact or contagion," not only between the women, but also between them and the viewers.[27] In this other scene, Madeleine can be herself without being "one"—whole, indivisible, original—or the opposite: just a copy, a double, an impostor. And Judy, who is Madeleine without being just her, can get a chance at life, as morally dubious as she is for her complicity in both fraud and murder.

Let me be clear: I am not suggesting that, once we upset a way of making sense of things—of doing intellectual labor—that relies on identity or equivalence, everything will fall into place and bliss will be restored. On the contrary, if we start from difference, we find ourselves facing the complexity of lived experience, an entanglement of histories and desires for which no readymade account is available. In place of family triangles and lines of inheritance, we come to see arrangements that have no clear contour or texture, that struggle with the return of a repressed or unlived past and the moral ambiguity of the present. I am also not suggesting that Judy be considered the "sum" of herself and the roles she has played, as if we could lay out her real identity on one side and her assumed personas on the other, and then decide to combine them. Rather, in the space and time of contiguity, she can live as the difference, the discrepancy between her official and assumed identities, in a performance of the self that remains open to becoming. Having moved from the domain of transcendence to that immanence, she can perform the difference that she will have been. The possibility of being herself and Madeleine—Madeleine and Carlotta—emerges from a process not of addition (accumulation or incorporation) but of differentiation. In fact, not even

Madeleine and Carlotta exist "in themselves." Rather, they materialize as they do in and through the encounters precipitated by the film's plotting.

It is then a matter of inhabiting the interval that opens up between the two phases of the dolly-in, rather than bridging or suturing it. Soft montage, as practiced by Farocki and Godard, produces a third uncertain zone—the site of a potential—and so does our "delayed" disarticulation of the museum shot. When we modify our viewing habits and come to see according to an interval, rather than a linkage, we upset the setup—in this case, we take on a mode of symbolic production that leaves room for exploring what has no fixed place or outline, perhaps even what is yet to be invented. Or, to dovetail with the beginning of this essay, we begin to do immaterial labor otherwise, against the grain of the general economy that is putting us to work. Feminist thinkers have long supported a mode of production that aligns itself with metonymy, which is indeed a figure of contiguity, and opposes itself to metaphor and its logic of substitution.[28] But the metonymic principle that they theorize, and which I attempt to recover in the museum scene, is not the metonymic lock of narrative cinema. *Rear Window* provides us with a remarkable dramatization of the latter, to the point that its protagonist (James Stewart), a photographer and amateur detective, has been said to stand in for the twentieth-century film spectator. On the other hand, in my counter-reading of *Vertigo*, which aligns itself with what Deleuze writes about Godard's method of disjunctive montage, "it is not a matter of following a chain of images, even across voids, but of getting out of the chain or the association."[29]

Yet *Rear Window* can be helpful in other ways. It reminds us that we, too, find ourselves living not only "in front of" but also "in and through" multiple windows, albeit of the digital kind, doing free labor as viewers, even when we are not officially at work.[30] It is digital labor that Farocki would investigate in *Counter Music* (*Gegen-Musik*, 2004), a twenty-first-century city film in which we ultimately realize that we are all becoming screen workers of sorts, called upon to decode images in a 24/7 economy. In this context, to read the *Vertigo* dolly-in against itself—against the continuity it seems to impose—can constitute a sort of "re-training" for the contemporary viewer. As we relentlessly shift from window to window, and from screen to screen, following preordained associative paths, counter-readings of older media forms might train us to see according to an interval or potential; rather than generating yet more associations, these older forms show us how to look for what lies in-between, what cuts across our ordinary screen-sphere.

Notes

1. Giorgio Agamben, *"What Is an Apparatus?" and Other Essays*, ed. Werner Hamacher, trans. David Kishik and Stefan Pedatella (Stanford, CA: Stanford University Press, 2009).

2. Carlo Ginzburg, "Morelli, Freud and Sherlock Holmes: Clues and Scientific Method," *History Workshop Journal* 9, no. 1 (March 1980): 5–36.

3. Vivian Sobchack, "From Screen-Shape to Screen-Sphere: A Meditation in Media Res," in *Screens*, ed. Dominique Chateau and José Moure (Amsterdam: Amsterdam University Press, 2016), 158.

4. Tom Gunning, "In and Out of the Frame: Paintings in Hitchcock," in *Casting a Shadow: Creating the Alfred Hitchcock Film*, ed. Will Schmenner, Corinne Granof, and David Alan Robertson (Evanston, IL: Mary and Leigh Block Museum of Art, Northwestern University Press, 2007), 33. See also Brigitte Peucker, "The Cut of Representation: Painting and Sculpture in Hitchcock," in *Alfred Hitchcock: Centenary Essays*, ed. Richard Allen and S. Ishii-Gonzalès (London: BFI Publishing, 1999), 141–156.

5. Gilles Deleuze, *Cinema 2: The Time-Image*, trans. Hugh Tomlinson and Robert Galeta (Minneapolis: University of Minnesota Press, 1997), 181.

6. See Thomas Elsaesser, ed., *Harun Farocki: Working on the Sightlines* (Amsterdam: Amsterdam University Press, 2004).

7. Domietta Torlasco, *The Heretical Archive: Digital Memory at the End of Film* (Minneapolis: University of Minnesota Press, 2013).

8. See D. A. Miller, *Hidden Hitchcock* (Chicago: University of Chicago Press, 2016).

9. Michael Hardt and Antonio Negri, *Multitude: War and Democracy in the Age of Empire* (New York: Penguin Press, 2004), 108. See also Maurizio Lazzarato, "Immaterial Labor," in *Radical Thought in Italy: A Potential Politics*, ed. Paolo Virno and Michael Hardt (Minneapolis: University of Minnesota Press, 1996), 133–147, and Paolo Virno, "Virtuosity and Revolution: The Political Theory of Exodus," 189–212, in the same volume.

10. Hardt and Negri, *Multitude*, 108.

11. Michael Hardt and Antonio Negri, *Commonwealth* (Cambridge, MA: Belknap Press of Harvard University Press, 2009), 132.

12. Virno, "Virtuosity and Revolution," 193.

13. Laura Mulvey, "Visual Pleasure and Narrative Cinema," *Screen* 16, no. 3 (1975): 6–18. See also Kriss Ravetto-Biagioli, "*Vertigo* and the Vertiginous History of Film Theory," *Camera Obscura* 25, no. 3 (2011): 101–141.

14. My approach to labor and cinematic time keenly distinguishes itself from the one proposed by Salomé Aguilera Skvirsky in *The Process Genre: Cinema and the Aesthetic of Labor* (Durham, NC: Duke University Press, 2020).

15. Gerhard Richter, "Miniatures: Harun Farocki and the Cinematic Non-Event," *Journal of Visual Culture* 3, no. 3 (2004): 368.

16. *Histoire(s) du cinéma*, directed by Jean-Luc Godard (1988; France and Switzerland: Artificial Eye, 2009), DVD.

17. See Gunning, "In and Out of the Frame."

18. Luce Irigaray, "Women on the Market," in *This Sex Which Is Not One*, trans. Catherine Porter and Carolyn Burke (Ithaca, NY: Cornell University Press, 1985), 170–191.

19. Ida Dominijanni, "The Contact Word," in *Another Mother: Diotima and the Symbolic Order of Italian Feminism*, ed. Cesare Casarino and Andrea Righi, trans. Mark William Epstein (Minneapolis: University of Minnesota Press, 2018), 33–65.

20. See David Greven, "The Dark Side of Blondeness: *Vertigo* and Race," *Screen* 59, no. 1 (2018): 59–79.

21. Greven, "The Dark Side," 60.

22. See J. M. Coetzee, "The Mind of Apartheid: Geoffrey Cronjé (1907–)," *Social Dynamics* 17, no. 1 (1991): 1–35.

23. See Gunning, "In and Out of the Frame," and Stephen Heath's chapter "Narrative Space," in *Questions of Cinema* (London: Macmillan, 1981).

24. Kaja Silverman and Harun Farocki, *Speaking about Godard* (New York: New York University Press, 1998), 142.

25. Laura Mulvey, *Death 24x a Second: Stillness and the Moving Image* (London: Reaktion Books, 2006), chapter 1.

26. Luisa Muraro, "To Knit or to Crochet: A Political-Linguistic Tale on the Enmity between Metaphor and Metonymy," in *Another Mother: Diotima and the Symbolic Order of Italian Feminism*, ed. Cesare Casarino and Andrea Righi, trans. Mark William Epstein (Minneapolis: University of Minnesota Press, 2018), 76.

27. Muraro, "To Knit or to Crochet," 115.

28. See, as examples, Muraro, "To Knit or to Crochet," and Irigaray, "Women on the Market."

29. Deleuze, *Cinema 2*, 180. Godard's method, he writes, is "the method of BETWEEN, 'between two images' . . . the method of AND, 'this and then that.'"

30. See, as an example, Tiziana Terranova, "Free Labor: Producing Culture for the Digital Economy," *Social Text* 18, no. 2 (2000): 33–58.

14

The Birds (1963)

Trauma and the right of reply

Julian Murphet

It won't be the first shot you think of when calling to mind *The Birds* (1963), and there are certainly more eligible favorites to list in a "best shot" competition for the film: the famous bird's-eye overhead matte shot of Bodega Bay ablaze;[1] the final composite shot, "the most difficult single shot I've ever done," said Alfred Hitchcock, of a crack in the dawn sky over thousands upon thousands of roosting avian predators;[2] the jungle gym outside the schoolhouse festooned with feathered black death; the lovebirds in Melanie Daniels's (Tippi Hedren) car swaying as she takes the hard bends on the coastal highway; the triple-barrel cuts of Dan Fawcett with his eyes plucked out; the close-up of the bloodstain on Melanie's suede fawn glove; the starring of the phone-booth glass as one beaked attacker sends shards into Melanie's cheek; the dolly shot that discloses the sprawled bloody corpse of Annie Hayworth (Suzanne Pleshette) on her stoop; and various other famous exposures. Even more remarkable, though perhaps less successful aesthetically, are the various sodium vapor optical shots that allowed the filmmakers to visualize the film's central fact: the attacks on humans by swooping birds.

But there is no question as to what shot I find most moving, not only in this astonishing masterwork, but in the great director's entire body of work. Indeed, I would have to say that no other shot in American cinema leaves me so shaken, overwhelmed by affective agitation, as the shot in which, from a hovering overhead angle, we find Melanie recumbent, unconscious, blissfully unaware of what has just happened to her in the attic room upstairs at the Brenner's Bodega Bay residence; and then silently watch her awaken, rapidly remember her brutal assault, and, with devastating implication, look directly into the camera, at us, as we bear down with the director's relentless gaze upon her, and she flails her arms in self-defense and mutely, all alone in the tightening mise-en-scène, pushes us away. In what follows I will do my

Julian Murphet, The Birds *(1963)* In: *One Shot Hitchcock.* Edited by: Luke Robinson and Melanie Robson, Oxford University Press. © Oxford University Press 2024. DOI: 10.1093/oso/9780197682876.003.0014 best to unpack this moment, this camera movement, this performance, for what it is, precisely, that I find so appallingly effective in its power to shake and move the viewer.

It must be said that this shot has left barely a tremor in the vast critical literature on the film. It doesn't rate a mention in the book-length study *The Making of Hitchcock's The Birds* by Tony Lee Moral, or Kyle Counts's and Steve Rubin's 1980 "making of" article, or William Rothman's or Robin Wood's copious writings on the topic.[3] Camille Paglia, whose critical eye misses little, gives it a short sentence in which much is coiled: "Eyes wide, she sees us and flails wildly at the camera, which jumps back to give her space: Hitchcock and we are yet more hungry birds."[4]

It is, for me, the great emotional climax of this horrific film, following hard upon the film's most violent, and the director's second-most notorious scene as its traumatized aftermath, its coda, and its (as I hope to show) "right of reply" from the actor forced to endure it. It is as if here, all that concentrated violence and horror, which we have suffered as an in-suck of air held tightly in our lungs, is granted its release; the super-charged emotional valence of what has happened in the Brenner home and elsewhere in Bodega Bay now seizes hold of the film's star, whose inarticulate, spasmodic gestures—seemingly spontaneous and quite unpremeditated—is a warding-off of the camera's complicity and ours in all this senseless assault.

The shot

The shot in question is broken into four segments, obviously the same frame-up and performance, into which are cut low-angle inserts of Rod Taylor's and Veronica Cartwright's reactions on either side of the couch. It begins as a dimly lit, tight Cinemascope close-up of Hedren's unconscious semi-profile facing right, just where she has been lowered onto the couch by Rod Taylor (in a pan that takes him down the stairs and across the room with her body in his arms). I think it would be fair to say that, in context, we expect her to remain unconscious somewhat longer than she does, perhaps until Mitch Brenner (Rod Taylor) tries to ply her with the brandy that Cathy Brenner (Veronica Cartwright) has just brought him. But with dramatic suddenness, the head swivels to a forward-facing close-up and the eyes snap open, darting rapidly from Mitch to Cathy and then, wide-eyed and terrified, to us, and we hold her gaze until Mitch eventually wins it back.

Top light, subdued and spectral, dwells on Melanie's brow, where a huge red gash is surrounded by splotches of blood, and blood is visible on either cheek. The coif has come undone, and blonde curls and ringlets create a corona around the face. The jacket that she has worn for the last four days, a cool celadon green, is in tatters; ends are torn and frayed, and blood besmirches the collar; underneath, the matching sleeveless Chanel-style dress comes right up to her chin, instead of showcasing her elegant neck. The mouth is numb, drawn, and expressionless. Melanie's cherry lipstick and line of cerulean eye shadow are gone: the face appears raw and pale apart from the blood and the great white accusations of those unblinking eyes. The hazel corneas, getting no side-light, are sunk into the black of her pupils. They catch two sources of light, neither diegetic: one a rectangular diffuser, the other a piercing bulb, both arranged around the camera, which, briefly but distinctly, we feel as a presence in those optic depths.

The left hand with its prominent shell-style pinky ring (a luminous band of silver in this oppressive gloom) launches directly up at the camera, and catches its heavy, diegetically inexplicable shadow as it comes dangerously close to the lens. As if instinctively, the camera pulls upward and the shot rapidly adjusts to a higher position above the couch, of which we now see more—as we do of her jacket, down to the breast-line. Both Melanie's arms are wheeling, batting away at the camera's eye, whose stare she has held unbroken, as she raises herself slightly from recumbency to press the advantage and force its flight still further away. Here comes the first insert of Mitch's and Cathy's reactions, after four seconds of this distressing close-up. It catches Melanie's flailing arms from an angle just to her right and at sofa-height, strengthening the continuity, but focuses on Mitch to right and Cathy to left. These reaction shots are vital to the meaning of the shot in question, and work to subdue its meta-cinematic force, coaxing it (and its subject) back into the flow of narrative. Mitch is holding a glass of brandy, which he has to put down to hold the wildly swinging arms, as Cathy turns quietly away behind the couch to cry (triggering the same emotional release in the viewer); and articulate dialogue enters with Mitch's soft-spoken appeals, "No, it's alright, no, it's alright, it's alright, it's alright."

It isn't. We cut back to our shot of Melanie, into which Mitch's hands now enter, attempting to restrain her arms by the wrists. But her face has grown more frenzied, her teeth clenched, lips parted in aggressive fight-mode, eyes still staring directly at us—not, significantly, at Mitch, whom she has not yet recognized. She is panting, grunting, with the exertion of her gestures, which have become panicked and extreme, for the moment overriding Mitch's efforts at containment. She is a wild beast, sunk completely out of the civilized poses, games, and frames that have hitherto held her at such an elevation above the rest of Bodega Bay. The camera has steadied at its higher perch, but what it captures for these two terribly intense seconds is anything but a compliant subject; it is a dervish of adrenaline-fueled energy, head pressing upward, face kept in focus, but the arms cutting frantically into and blurring the composition with abandon. There is a second, brief insert, and then a cut back to our shot, which finally allows Melanie to register Mitch as she begins to calm down and breathe again. Color returns to the eyes; the light has crept up in luminosity within the frame, and the shadows are more defined on her face. The body stills, the arms are crossed across her chest as in a straitjacket, the eyes are glued to Mitch's, and the storm has passed. A final shot–reverse shot brace of cuts establish Mitch as the dominant force in the scene and Melanie as the subdued recovering hysteric, allowing the film to resume its narrative operations.

Analysis

What have we just watched? In the immediate context of the film's story, of course, it is a delayed aftershock of the terrible scene in the attic that has immediately preceded it. Melanie is still "seeing" the birds that had assailed her almost to death; her arms are automatically protecting herself from this attack, which has assumed a continuous present tense in her traumatized psyche. Her brief moment of unconsciousness as she was carried downstairs has not released her from that experience; indeed, she seems more powerfully terrified and gripped by the assault than while it was happening. The immediate reason for the power of this shot is that it allows the audience to "feel" what it has just seen and heard. That is to say, the shot is the affective distillate, the pure unmodified emotional kernel, of the sensational attic sequence, which at a technical and diegetic level, is perhaps just too complex, too much of a barrage, to have done anything but register as shock. It is in Melanie's delayed reaction on the couch that we truly come to terms with this shock and understand it as trauma (see Figure 14.1). Something has breached the psychic defenses, as Sigmund Freud might say, and sent its depth charges into the psychic substance, but it cannot be reduced to any one of the shots of birds upstairs as they tore Melanie's clothes and pecked at her

Figure 14.1 (See also Plate 21) Close-up of Melanie Daniels (Tippi Hedren) on the couch in Alfred Hitchcock's *The Birds* (1963).

flesh. It all happens too quickly, and too disjointedly; there is no center of experience. Rather, it is only once the birds have been removed from the frame that we can come face to face with their brutal attack, in the form of Melanie's astonishing "affection-image."[5]

Here, we can draw a relation to a previous shot, also in the Brenner home, after the first invasion by the smaller passerine birds down the chimney. Hitchcock had staged that sequence not as it was scripted, around the plodding policeman's dogged disbelief, but around Melanie's observations of Lydia Brenner's (Jessica Tandy) obviously traumatized clean-up operation. The camera doggedly follows Mrs. Brenner along the floor as she collects broken bits of crockery and attempts to restore order, cutting away regularly to shots of Melanie's silent watching. It is a powerful sequence, orchestrating an unspoken emotional realization about our protagonist, and it culminates on a particular shot: Lydia, discovering that her dead husband's portrait has been knocked askew by the birds, hastens to level it and in so doing dislodges a dead finch from atop the picture frame. With an audible gasp, and both arms jerking up, she finally loses all her composure, and reverts to a state of illness from which she will not properly recover until Melanie's own collapse. Here, too, it is a question of a delayed response, an emotional aftershock in a moment of calm; the birds (like any traumatic incident) are best felt in the quiet that follows their violence.

More pointedly, returning to our key shot, it is only once *we assume the point of view of the birds* that we really see and feel the extent of the damage being done to Melanie. What works most dramatically in this shot is precisely our "becoming-bird" in it. Melanie discovers us, our gaze, hovering in the empty air and recognizes it as the source of her trauma; we are called away from our cinematic invisibility and impunity, hailed into the space, by the electricity of her stare. We must be made to answer for it, to embody the bird's eye of ambient scopophilia, in this silent moment of traumatic aftermath. And we are subject to a violent resistance, a brief, deeply disturbing accusation that our viewing pleasure has not been without consequence. A fight to the death has been, however ephemerally, declared, and Melanie's combative stance, her gritted teeth, her snarling grunts and growls, the seething animosity of her stare and the animal strength of her pushes and shoves, are all directed at us and our proxy the camera, which (as nowhere else in this film) here becomes a physical, moral presence in the scene.

It is not the only occasion on which our look has been identified with the carnivorous gaze of the avian army. During the various assaults, there are brief moments when what we see is indistinguishable from what the assailants are seeing: bleeding hands thrust out at the lens, screaming faces averted from our hypothetical beaks, in momentary shots sutured into the montage of horror. But the crucial moment is of course the well-known high-altitude shot of the whole township (in a composite matte shot painted by the great Albert Whitlock), with the gas station aflame and panicked citizens running in every direction (see Figure 14.2). The perfectly still frame-up comes with a chilling disappearance of all the sounds of panic and terror at street level and the emergence of a whistling wind sound, as all the merely human concerns fade rapidly away, then one, two, three, four, half a dozen gulls enter the frame in close proximity, hovering alongside us, welcoming us into their flock and now, all at once, their squeaky inhuman cries begin to be heard.

This great image makes an explicit aesthetic association between the camera's eye and the swooping rapacity of these winged avengers, and carries with it a dim echo of Norman Bates's infamous peephole, at the moment that previous film suddenly pivots from "victim" to "predator."[6] The film's invitation to share the optical point of view with a non-human agent intent on harming humankind is perverse in the extreme but reminds us that our proxy on set is also a non-human agent transforming flesh-and-blood human beings into bloodless shadows.

Figure 14.2 (See also Plate 22) Bird's-eye view of Bodega Bay in *The Birds*.

Our shot also brings with it an association with other images in *The Birds* of actresses shot from a distinctly high angle, to establish a conventional image of dominance over the female subject. For instance, after Lydia's confinement to bed, the camera takes the opportunity to lord it over her in a manner that clearly suggests her submission to the authority of the story: rogue nature, the suddenly inexorable Melanie, dawning old age, all seeming to have suddenly diminished her power over her family (see Figure 14.3). Or again, when Melanie is trapped in the phone booth, we get a particularly claustrophobic overhead shot of her confinement that differs qualitatively from the more action-driven shots at eye level: Melanie is isolated, powerless, and almost touchingly vulnerable here (see Figure 14.4). These "unmotivated" high-angle shots (unlike, say, the ones where Melanie is in dialogue with Mitch while he looms over her car) prepare us for the shot on the couch, where what is exceptional is (of course) the violation of the rule never to look into the camera.

Even this has a precedent in the film, at the Tides restaurant when Mitch returns with Melanie after the phone booth episode to discover an eerie silence and emptiness, explained only when their ingress discovers a phalanx of women cowering in the corridor to the kitchen. Their spokesperson, the hysterical mother (Doreen Lang), stands to make the inevitable accusation that it is Melanie herself who has brought the birds down in anger upon the town. She walks to camera in what changes from a medium shot to a close-up,

Figure 14.3 (See also Plate 23) Lydia (Jessica Tandy) in bed in *The Birds*.

Figure 14.4 (See also Plate 24) Melanie attacked in a phone booth in *The Birds*.

speaking to Melanie but, critically, looking straight into the camera lens. The inserts of Melanie's reaction shots show her looking just to right of camera, but the mother's gaze into the lens is relentless, helping to justify Melanie's violent reaction, a slap in the face, forcing her accuser back, her eyes dropping and closing behind her hand.

In a complex network of associations and resonances, then, our shot builds upon and exceeds an emerging grammar of film language specific to *The Birds*. It accepts the idea that the camera can be an active agent in a shot by identifying it with an attacking bird, even when that bird is absent. It works within the established convention that women shot from high angles are relatively powerless and prey to elements and forces beyond their control. It "answers" a singular previous shot in the film, in which the camera was identified with Melanie's point of view, and which precipitated the violent use of her arm and hand against the invasive to-camera stare. And it builds on an earlier idea, set in the same domestic space, that trauma is best felt in the aftermath of an assault, through a woman's delayed reaction in the relative calm of a receding wave of violence. In all these ways, we can tease out the aesthetic meaning of the shot in terms of a deliberate tissue of signification worked out purely cinematically (without explanation or dialogue). But what remains exceptional about it is its power of excess: the woman rises up to the bird's-eye view, to attack it; she returns its malevolent, murderous gaze with unblinking tenacity; she manifests in every fiber of her body the desire not to go down without a struggle; and, critically, it is really as if the blistering affective surcharge here is *in excess* of the trauma suffered in the attic. There is more to this shot than meets the eye, and it is precisely that "more" that elevates it above the diegesis. It is meta-cinematic in a number of ways, not least in that it can be said directly to "answer" Laura Mulvey's hypothesis of woman's "to-be-looked-at-ness" in patriarchal cinema (she writes on *Vertigo* [1958], *Psycho* [1960], *Rear Window* [1954], and *Marnie* [1964] in this context, but not *The Birds*), which here begins to look like a traumatic experience for the woman.[7] But the most vital of these is its relationship to the production of the film itself, which I am now going to suggest that it draws into itself like a lethal cipher.

Context

Since Donald Spoto's revisionist exposé of the real conditions under which Hedren was obliged to work on this, her first motion picture, it has become increasingly clear that this production was stained by an unconscionable exercise of power by Hitchcock over his thirty-two-year-old leading actor.[8] Describing it as a commercial "monopoly," Spoto details how the "exclusive, seven-year contract to producer-director Alfred Hitchcock" that Hedren signed rapidly became the albatross around her neck, on set and off.[9] As Hedren puts it, she, "a woman who'd never even had a passing thought about becoming an actress," appealed to Hitchcock for everything she lacked: "Actors under contract were no longer required to take classes in singing, dancing, diction, poise and movement, horseback riding, and countless other skills that would prepare them for a wider variety of roles and groom them for stardom."[10] And this was just as Hitchcock wanted it: a blank canvas, his own, which he could fill out as required at his own discretion. In his interview with Truffaut, he explains that "I took an unknown girl and taught her to act. She knew nothing about acting, at all. So, fortunately, she had nothing to unlearn."[11]

Hitchcock never supplied "inner" kinds of direction. Actors must simply abide by one single law, outlined by Janet Leigh (in his voice): "The one requisite, absolute, is that you have to move when I tell you to move with my camera, because my camera is the most important."[12] Behaviorism, not expressionism; exteriority, not interiority; the camera, not the soul, governed his understanding of film performance. When Hedren explains that she had "the two best acting teachers in the business," Hitchcock and Alma Reville, she is ironically suggesting that thespian redundancies like "motivation" and "psychology" were ruthlessly subordinated to blocking, gestures, and facial expressions during her training; that acting was doing exactly what you were told.[13] But when it came to molding Hedren to his will for this film, something unexpected entered into the picture.

In his interview with Truffaut, Hitchcock's voice wavers and hesitates before telling the translator, "I'd like to explain to François the emotions I went through." It is a commonplace of criticism on the film, of course, but the specific reasons he gives are redacted from the published version of the interview:

> I ran into some emotional problems. I was pouring myself into The Girl, doing Svengali, you know. Because it needed so much, every . . . I taught her every expression, never a wasted one, you see. And I got very, in a state of distress, which is very unusual for me. Because for me I always laugh my way through a picture, and for the first time my crew around me said, "What's wrong with him?"[14]

In small part, this was a mediated expression of his financial stresses: putting a good deal of his own money into the production, he was under considerable pressure from Universal brass over the casting of a complete unknown in the starring role.[15] But the stakes were equally high on Hedren's end, who was made to feel increasingly guilty and responsible for this novel burden on Hitchcock's conscience and the dictates of the bottom line. "I overcompensated by working too hard, by sometimes being too accommodating to the crueller demands of the business of movie-making."[16] The more completely she relied on him, the more "Svengali"-like he had to become with his contracted employee. While she was "intensely focused on holding up my end of it and doing my damnedest to rise to the extraordinary expertise of my castmates," Hitchcock created a powerful protective ring around his protégée on set, including paying spies to follow her after hours, and barking "Do not touch The Girl!" at Rod Taylor.[17] He had her driven, always alone with him, in his limo to the locations and soundstage for shooting, and she began to notice him watching her on set: "this was an expressionless, unwavering stare, no matter where he was or what he was doing."[18] Eventually, she says, he forced an unwanted kiss on her outside a hotel, began stalking her off-set, and "in a relatively private corner of the soundstage, away from the set while we were shooting, he'd asked me to touch him."[19]

The culmination of the protracted, difficult shoot happened in the month of May 1962. The climactic attack on the Brenner house, "the imposing home of the established Gothic patriarchy," and the week-long ordeal of the infamous attic sequence all converged at this time, two distinct lines of emotional crisis intersecting with explosive violence.[20] On the one hand, Hedren's mounting trauma as a victim of sexual harassment by her employer ("pouring himself" into her); and on the other, Hitchcock's "emotional siege" by his own dissociated sexual drives, now as always mediated by his proxy, the camera, the "most important" element on set.[21] The outcome was thoroughly psychotic.[22] "I always believe in following the advice of the playwright Sardou," Hitchcock remarked. "He said, 'Torture the women!' . . . The trouble today is that we don't torture women enough."[23] The shooting of the attic sequence, one of Hollywood's darkest episodes, was the last significant stretch of principal photography, and took an excruciating week, during which Hitchcock was nervously confined to his hotel room and Hedren suffered a major nervous collapse, pelted by live animals in a frenzy of professional assault. But it is also during this final period that Hitchcock took time to shoot *our* shot, of Hedren reacting to the attack a moment after it is all over.

Let's be clear that there is nothing quite like our shot in the second, revised shooting script of the film by Evan Hunter (March 2, 1962). The episode in question reads, rather:

As they go downstairs:

MITCH: Cathy! Get a blanket and some bandages!

CATHY (at the foot of the stairs, on the verge of tears): Is she all right?

CLOSE SHOT—MELANIE cradled against Mitch's shoulder, her face bleeding profusely.

MELANIE: I'm . . . I'm . . .

FULL SHOT—MITCH as he carries her into the living room, [puts] her down on the couch.

MITCH: Just lie there and keep still.

Cathy rushes to them with a roll of bandages and a blanket. By the light of the lantern, Mitch drapes the blanket over Melanie and then begins unrolling the bandage. But his hands are trembling and he drops it.

LYDIA: Let me do that, Mitch.

She picks up the bandage.[24]

Hitchcock takes this bland scene and transforms it into a devastating affection-image, obviously improvising around a perceived fault in the script and finding something poetically true and searing. He dispatches Lydia entirely; introduces the brandy (which returns us to a very fine scene at Annie Hayworth's); and gives Hedren her extraordinary *contretemps* with the camera itself.

Improvisation was, indeed, the unexpected artistic result of what Hitchcock described as his "emotional siege" by unacknowledged desire on set. Turning his unique "state of distress, which is very unusual for me," into a new artistic opportunity, "an additional creative sense in me," Hitchcock found himself doing the unimaginable: turning away from the script and storyboards, rejecting months of preparation in a moment's misgiving, and allowing himself the freedom to extemporize on set.[25] Moved by un-precedented emotional surges, "I began to improvise."[26] Hitchcock lists an amazing number of distinct improvisational pivots away from the script, as "doubts about other passages in the movie" mounted and multiplied: partic-ularly the passage during which Lydia collects the broken crockery under Melanie's watchful eyes; the blocking of Lydia and Cathy during the final at-tack; and the hysterical mother shouting "you're evil!" to camera in the Tides restaurant.[27] To this list we are obliged to add *our* shot, in which the spirit of improvisation is at its most meta-cinematic, most dangerous to the diegetic consistency of the film, and comes closest to a "confession" by the filmmaker of his crimes against his leading actor.

As an aesthetic improvisation, shot in the immediate lead-up to or after-math of what the director knew would be the extremely grueling real-life torture of his star in the attic scene, this shot bears within it an unequaled, unprocessed surcharge of contextual affectivity and seething moral energy. For the first and last time in the film, his actor is directed to do everything his "Svengali" training has prepared her not to do: to stare, unblinking, into the camera, with little make-up and no smile, and attack it with the same frenzy that it has just attacked her with, thus abolishing the fourth wall and establishing a momentary, but electrifying, exchange of gazes between the camera's authoritative lens and Hedren's traumatized eyes. We are caught in this transfer of looks like skulking voyeurs hauled into the light, exposed to the blinding radiation of an incandescent "to-be-looked-at-ness" that has collapsed on its own weight and gone supernova. These few seconds undo decades of the commercial cinema's patriarchal gaze and the film is never fully able to stitch it back together again, despite the diegetic retreat of the protagonist into infancy and debility.[28] For a moment, an entire cinematic mode of production is presented with its own X-ray and a parlous bill of health.

Under siege

The classic interpretive accounts of *The Birds* are these: that nature is in re-volt against the treacherous stewardship of humankind, upending millennia of relatively docile subservience by launching a concerted attack on the very epicenter of late-modern capitalism; that Melanie is a spoiled heiress whose sexually liberated entitlements and presumptions come up against a stern moral barrier in small-town USA, where they translate as so many aerial bombardments from the animal kingdom; that Lydia Brenner's incestuous relationship with her eldest son has created a vortex of libidinal energy around her, and a protective force-field around her son, which wards off the sexual attentions of biddable women in the form of vast flocks of carnivorous birds; and that female sexual appetite itself is monstrous and punishable within a conventional Catholic frame of reference. But the now well-known story of the off-screen context of the film's production, a cut-and-dried case of sexual harassment and professional abuse, surely provides the most plausible hermeneutic framework for analysis. "Hitchcock abused his power as brand-name director and television star to mistreat the inexperienced actor Hedren, both on and off the set, during the making of the film," as Joy Schaeffer puts it unequivocally.[29] That mistreatment amounts to an oppressive sexual extortion of the lead actor, which we see traced through every frame of the film's unfolding, and which realizes itself as "bird attacks" on the protagonist she plays—a character created largely by Hitchcock himself to answer the requirements of his obsessive emotional and sexual predations upon Hedren.

Everything here was wrong. Hitchcock was "under siege" to his own sexual appetites, which he projected as a literal siege (an abuse, a betrayal, a crime) on to his leading actor, an ingenue with no power or reputation in Hollywood, and a metaphorical siege on his film's protagonist. In his words, he "played Svengali" with Hedren; in hers, he sexually assaulted her and destroyed her career. "It was sexual, it was perverse, and it was ugly."[30] Melanie, meanwhile, is unmade, stripped of her accoutrements and style and rendered mutely submissive. The entire film can be read as an allegory of its own conditions of production; its story, its making, its metaphorical logic all circle around the same intractable knot of manipulation, obsession, and the oppressive encroachment of director upon star. Birds dart unpredictably out of the air and create an omnipresent force-field of hanging threat. A camera records every look, word, movement, gesture that a man, an employer, has coerced from a first-time screen actor with a checkbook and a threatened assault. "Dealing with it by not dealing with it"; "becoming a master of getting out of the room," as well as of her own body, while being in every scene: this is how Hedren accounts for her ordeal, in language that is familiar from trauma theory.[31] Trauma scoops out a person's inside, turns her into an automaton, which is just what Hitchcock wanted Hedren to be. Cary Grant called her, on set, the bravest woman he had ever met, during a perceptive visit. It is this stupendous bravery, this immense courage in the midst of trauma, that we see, glaring us down, arraigning us before its white fire, in the shot I have singled out as perhaps the most moving in American cinema. It clinches an entire mode of cinematic production; a system of exploitation, of pitiless and shameless sexual subordination, by which men employ women to enact their fantasies, and in the meantime prey on their bodies, creating entertainment out of the results. If *The Birds'* heroine is not "totally defeated by a patriarchy implacably reinscribing itself,"[32] then that is in good measure due to the space afforded her performer in a single improvised shot where, for once, Hitchcock's emotional unease, his culpable, ambivalent artistry, seems to have granted a right of reply to his tormented star.

Notes

1. This shot was hailed by Camille Paglia as "one of the most startlingly memorable shots in the history of film." *The Birds* (London: BFI Publishing, 1998), 18.
2. See Kyle B. Counts and Steve Rubin, "The Making of Alfred Hitchcock's *The Birds*," *Cinefantastique* 10, no. 2 (Fall 1980): 33.
3. See William Rothman, *Must We Kill the Thing We Love?: Emersonian Perfectionism and the Films of Alfred Hitchcock* (New York: Columbia University Press, 2014); and Robin Wood, *Hitchcock's Films Revisited* (New York: Columbia University Press, 1965).
4. Paglia, *The Birds*, 84.
5. Gilles Deleuze, *Cinema 1: The Movement-Image*, trans. Hugh Tomlinson and Barbara Habberjam (London: Continuum, 2001), specifically chapters 6 and 7.
6. For further discussion of Bates's transformation from victim to villain during the peephole scene in *Psycho*, see Melanie Robson's chapter in this volume.
7. Laura Mulvey, "Visual Pleasure and Narrative Cinema," *Screen* 16, no. 3 (Fall 1975): 6–18.
8. The now notorious story provides the substance for a made-for-TV drama, *The Girl* (BBC/HBO, 2012), and at least one poem: see Dawn Marie Kresan, "*The Birds* (1963): Tippi Hedren's Response," *Queen's Quarterly* 120, no. 3 (Fall 2013): 464–466.
9. Donald Spoto, *The Dark Side of Genius: The Life of Alfred Hitchcock* (Boston: Da Capo Press, 1999), 449. For more on the links between *The Birds* and Coleridge's "Rime of the Ancient Mariner," see John P. McCombe, "'Oh, I see . . .': *The Birds* and the Culmination of Hitchcock's Hyper-Romantic vision," *Cinema Journal* 44, no. 3 (Spring 2005): 64–80.
10. Tippi Hedren, *Tippi: A Memoir* (New York: William Morrow, 2016), 45, 38.
11. This extract is not in the published version of François Truffaut's interviews with Hitchcock, *Hitchcock/Truffaut* (1966); it can be found as an audio file of the original tape recordings included as "Hitchcock-Truffaut Interview Excerpts" on the 2013 Blu-ray release of *The Birds* (Universal Studios, 1963).

12. Greg Garrett et al., "Hitchcock's Women on Hitchcock: A Panel Discussion with Janet Leigh, Tippi Hedren, Karen Black, Suzanne Pleshette, and Eva Marie Saint," *Literature/Film Quarterly* 27, no. 2 (1999): 79.

13. Hedren, *Tippi*, 39.

14. Alfred Hitchcock, "Hitchcock-Truffaut Interview Excerpts," *The Birds*, Blu-ray edition (Universal Studios, 2013). Ellipses in the original.

15. See John Billheimer, *Hitchcock and the Censors* (Lexington: University Press of Kentucky, 2019), 248.

16. Spoto, *Dark Side*, 450.

17. Hedren, *Tippi*, 47.

18. Hedren, *Tippi*, 50.

19. Hedren, *Tippi*, 53.

20. Kyle William Bishop, "The Threat of the Gothic Patriarchy in Alfred Hitchcock's *The Birds*," *Rocky Mountain Review* 65, no. 2 (Fall 2011): 137.

21. François Truffaut with Helen G. Scott, *Hitchcock*, rev. ed. (1966; New York: Touchstone, 1985), 290.

22. Though see the special pleading on Hitchcock's behalf in Tony Lee Moral, *The Making of Hitchcock's The Birds* (Harpenden: Oldcastle, 2013): "Contrary to popular opinion in the press, he didn't unleash the fury of the birds on Tippi out of sadism or spite. He was getting the job done and, in doing so, secured Tippi cinematic immortality just like he did for Janet Leigh in the shower scene in *Psycho*. After two days of shooting, the strain on Tippi was beginning to show. . . . Hitchcock himself seemed anxious directing the scene and wouldn't come out of his office until Bob Burks was ready to film the scene, perhaps feeling twinges of guilt having to put his inexperienced actress through such an ordeal" (p. 140).

23. Quoted in Spoto, *Dark Side*, 458. Ellipses in the original.

24. Evan Hunter, *The Birds* (1962), 2nd ed., *Daily Script*, www.dailyscript.com/scripts/The_Birds.html, accessed May 4, 2023.

25. Truffaut and Scott, *Hitchcock*, 290.

26. Truffaut and Scott, *Hitchcock*, 290.

27. Truffaut and Scott, *Hitchcock*, 290.

28. For Bishop, Melanie is "destroyed as an independent subject" by the film's close ("Threat of the Gothic Patriarchy," 36); and Judith Halberstam describes her as "completely under [Mitch's] power" in *Skin Shows: Gothic Horror and the Technology of Monsters* (Durham, NC: Duke University Press, 1995), 131.

29. Joy C. Schaeffer, "Must We Burn Hitchcock? (Re)Viewing Trauma and Effecting Solidarity with *The Birds* (1963)," *Quarterly Review of Film and Video* 32, no. 4 (2015): 330.

30. Hedren, *Tippi*, 72.

31. Hedren, *Tippi*, 78, 53.

32. Hildy Miller, "Refiguring *The Birds* as Modern Female Gothic in the Kennedy Era," *Rocky Mountain Review* 74, no. 2 (Fall 2020): 152.

15

Marnie (1964)

Restroom

Jodi Brooks

In her 2018 essay "Remastering the Master: Hitchcock after Feminism," Tania Modleski raises the question of "how hospitable Hitchcock scholarship has been to women in our postfeminist age."[1] Quoting and addressing what Ned Schantz calls the "still open question of whether Hitchcock, or Hitchcock scholarship, can fully welcome women into their abodes," Modleski analyzes and challenges what she describes as a recent turn in Alfred Hitchcock scholarship in which "the ground staked out by some queer critics, as well as feminist critics, has been increasingly evacuated by those who can't bear to find fault with the master."[2] Of all of Hitchcock's films, this question of "whether Hitchcock, or Hitchcock scholarship, can fully welcome women into their abodes" resounds particularly loudly in relation to *Marnie* (1964), a film in which the status of women's voices both in and on the film has been a site of contention (see Figure 15.1).

Marnie has had both an unsettled and an unsettling place in Hitchcock's work. A critical and commercial failure on its release, the film was frequently and famously ridiculed for what was regarded as its clunky and outdated use of rear projection and its theatrical, painted backdrop matte shots. Arguably one of Hitchcock's most experimental films in terms of both form and visual style, *Marnie*'s unsettled place in Hitchcock's oeuvre was long tied to its debated standing—masterpiece or misfire. In the decades since its release, the earlier charges of technical sloppiness have largely been dismissed and the film's aesthetic merits widely recognized, so much so in fact, that as Joe McElhaney would write in 2006, "finding a Hitchcock aficionado who is not fond of this obviously artificial production and postproduction work is increasingly difficult today."[3] The spatial disjunctions that result from the "glaringly artificial rear projections"[4] and the "hybrid space-time"[5] they produce have now long been recognized as part of the film's aesthetic design.[6] But if the film's

Jodi Brooks, Marnie *(1964)* In: *One Shot Hitchcock*. Edited by: Luke Robinson and Melanie Robson, Oxford University Press. © Oxford University Press 2024. DOI: 10.1093/oso/9780197682876.003.0015

Figure 15.1 (See also Plate 25)   Cleaning out Rutland & Co. in Alfred Hitchcock's *Marnie* (1964).

unsettled status in Hitchcock's oeuvre was for many years tied to the poor reception and disputed merits of its aesthetic innovations, *Marnie*'s place in and for the Hitchcock canon has also been unsettled by its star's account of the sexual harassment she experienced from Hitchcock during the film's production and its impact on her career in the years and decades that followed.[7]

Writing a few years before Donald Spoto's 2008 book *Spellbound by Beauty* was published but well after some of Tippi Hedren's experiences of harassment had been raised in Spoto's earlier book *The Dark Side of Genius* (1983), McElhaney writes that "Much of the discourse surrounding *Marnie* . . . is defensive in tone, alternately extolling the work's power and beauty while also feeling the need to construct a wall around the film, protecting it from any further hostile invasions."[8] And *Marnie*'s checkered history and troubled place in the Hitchcock canon has certainly generated some impassioned proclamations regarding its value. Robin Wood famously claimed early on that "if you don't like *Marnie*, you don't really like Hitchcock," a claim that William Rothman has more recently taken up a key or two, saying that "if you don't love *Marnie,* you don't really love cinema."[9] Rothman then adds a qualifier and an extension to his claim: "The truth is, though, that *Marnie* can be difficult to love even if you *do* love cinema. Thus I would slightly revise Robin Wood's formulation to say that you *cannot* love *Marnie*, you cannot *know* what makes it worthy of love, if you don't really love cinema."[10] While compelling in their theater and passion, these kinds of declarations or provocations leave little room for those more everyday questions and feelings that one might face in the classroom, the loungeroom, or indeed while reading some of the Hitchcock scholarship on the film—questions around how to love *Marnie* and at the same time recognize the injury done to its star, Hedren, in the film's making, or even simply leaving some room for relations to the film that might be fueled by something other than reverence.

To home in on one shot in *Marnie* that might open the film anew or provide insights into the discussions and critical debate that have already happened through and around this film is no small task. After all, key shots from the film have already, and frequently, been analyzed and celebrated. The matte shots and rear projections with their seams on show that were once the subject of "smug disdain"[11] have since been attended to and celebrated: Margaret "Marnie" Edgar (Hedren) atop her beloved Forio joyously riding nowhere in front of a rear projection (what Laura Mulvey called a "clumsy sublime"[12]), the shot of the mother's street with the painted backdrop that pushes forward as if threatening to drop Marnie back into her repressed trauma—these shots, with their shots within shots, have already been extensively discussed in terms of how they contribute to the claustrophobia of Marnie's world. Even the lengthy shot in the car when Mark Rutland (Sean Connery) has tracked down Marnie and blackmails her into marriage, clunky rear projection playing through the car's back window through the long and uncomfortable drive back to his estate, has been analyzed at length.[13]

In turning to *Marnie* in and through one shot, I want to take my cue from Modleski and be attentive to the female "counter voices" that might be audible in or through the film. Answering and extending Schantz's question about whether Hitchcock and Hitchcock scholarship can fully welcome women into their abodes, Modleski draws attention to the wide range of women, both on screen and off, that much recent Hitchcock scholarship concerned with "remastering the master" has failed to recognize, ignored, or marginalized—the female secondary characters, the women that Hitchcock regularly worked with in production roles, the work of feminist scholars and critics, and female and feminist spectators. How is it, she asks, that so much recent Hitchcock criticism has managed to marginalize or dismiss the place and roles of women in Hitchcock's work and in Hitchcock scholarship and has paid such little attention to questions of gendered spectatorship? "Feminist theory," Modleski writes, "has insisted on the presence of *female* spectators, female gazers, in the film audience, who may well bring a different perspective to the film, may see things unintended by the director and unseen by male viewers and critics."[14] Rather than turning to one of the film's more celebrated, signature, or frequently discussed shots, my focus here will be on a shot that might speak of and indeed enable allegiances beyond the film's visible world. That this shot unfolds through, and as, Marnie's silence, also opens a space in and through which women's voices and silences might have a longer throw.

Restroom

As Marnie prepares to break into the Rutland & Co. safe at the workday's end, she waits for the office to empty in a cubicle in the women's restroom (see Figure 15.2). In a strikingly lengthy shot that runs at close to a minute, Marnie remains behind the toilet door as other women from the office enter and leave. Composed and at ease—one might even say content—she waits while the sounds of doors opening and closing and the women's chatter about future dates and past disappointments peak and then fade. Marnie remains in the cubicle until the restroom is emptied of sound and fills with silence, waiting, it seems, until the quietness of the room is one with her own steady, calm silence.

This scene in the Rutland & Co. women's restroom launches the only sequence in the film where we get to see Marnie, our troubled but accomplished thief, execute one of her robberies in full. The audience has known, of course,

Figure 15.2 (See also Plate 26) Marnie (Tippi Hedren) waits, in *Marnie*.

that Marnie is a serial and itinerant thief from the very beginning. After all, the film's first spoken word is "robbed," a word spluttered by the apt-named and bespectacled Mr. Strutt (Martin Gabel) who is reporting the crime to two male police officers and fuming at finding that his own designs on the attractive young woman he employed without references have been well and truly trumped by her plans for the job and her assessment of him. And even before the film has begun, the film's original trailer (playing now, half a century later, on YouTube) had already shown Marnie busy at work, clearing a safe of its cash, as Hitchcock's voice drolly intones: "Marnie was going about her own business like any normal girl. Happy, happy, happy." Prior to the sequence in which Marnie robs Rutland & Co., the film—and its trailer—has presented the viewer with glimpses and souvenirs of Marnie's thefts and has done so in tones of smug amusement and naughty fascination. In the restroom, however, the audience is set up to be with her.

In one of the few extended critical engagements with the restroom scene, Victor Perkins discusses how this scene serves to intensify audience identification with the film's protagonist:

> The image of Marnie, leaning against the wall and listening, is held for much longer than might seem justified by its apparent content. But that is just the point. The picture is deliberately boring. Once we have seen that Marnie is waiting and listening, there is nothing more for us to look at. Instead we do what she does. We wait. We listen. The longer we listen, the more concentrated and alert our ears become, picking up snatches of distant conversation, predicting the all-clear of total silence. By restricting his heroine to an activity which the audience can share on completely equal terms, Hitchcock involves us more closely with her. We enter into her situation and become to some extent accomplices to her theft.[15]

"We enter into her situation," Perkins writes, and in the process of entering her situation, we come to wait as she waits and hear as she hears. But we do not share this activity "on completely equal terms" for the simple reason that we follow and learn from, rather than simply share, Marnie's auditory perception and rhythms. After the restroom has been emptied of sounds and the viewer is ready to move on, Marnie remains behind the door—still at ease, still composed, still content. And then, after more slow-stretched seconds have passed, there is the faintest wisp of an exchange, coming from some other place in the building seen neither now nor later—a sound barely audible and that the viewer seems to catch just behind or after Marnie has received it. Only then does Marnie leave the cubicle. "Any silence makes us feel exposed," Michel Chion writes in an oft-quoted passage, "as if it were laying bare our own listening, but also as if we were in the presence of a giant ear, tuned to our own slightest noises. We are no longer merely listening to the film, we are as it were being listened to by it as well."[16] The point of audition sound here—we come to hear as Marnie hears—means the viewer leaves the restroom and re-enters the Rutland office space with their senses realigned, tuned to the act and art of listening and to Marnie's—and now, too, our own—composed silence.

With rare exception, discussion usually focuses on how the scene in the restroom fuels and enables what follows on the other side of the door—the theft itself—by attuning the viewer to Marnie's heightened listening. And there is no question that the scene in the restroom does this. As has been well discussed, the restroom scene sets the audience up for one of the most celebrated scenes in the film, a scene in which Marnie must make her getaway right under the nose of a cleaner who has entered the office unexpectedly and now makes her weary way along a parallel path to Marnie. Elisabeth Bronfen has described Hitchcock's dual mode of narration as "predicated on fusing the emotional identification elicited by suspense with the ironic distance afforded by the director's implicit presence as the presiding intelligence of the film,"[17] and it is in full force here. The scene in the office space is organized around a tightly composed wide shot that creates a split-screen effect, requiring the viewer to toggle their attention from one side of the frame and screen to the other. With Hitchcock's dual narration in full swing, the shot functions as something of a visual joke. The symmetry of the shot with its frames within frames, boxes within boxes, sets the two women beside each other visually, but also socially. In a shot hushed of all sound other than the barely audible opening of a drawer and closing of the safe door, the two women are shown going about their business, side by side, unaware of each other. As we cut to a close-up of Marnie as she prepares to leave, she catches sight of the older woman, now shockingly near and bent over the mop on the other side of a glass partition. The two women are so close that they appear to brush past each other as Marnie makes her tiptoed dash to the stairs to escape, the steady swish-slop sounds of the mopping, amplified in the empty office, both feeding and soothing away the tension.

As Perkins and others have commented, this striking scene—perhaps the most celebrated scene in the film—with the split-screen effect shot that seems to lock parallel editing into the very same moment and the very same view at its center, is launched by Marnie waiting in the restroom. "Who but Hitchcock, arranging for theft, would set up the scene here?" Murray Pomerance asks admiringly in his BFI book on *Marnie*.[18] Rather than focusing on the scene that the restroom sets the viewer up for, I want to stay with, and linger in, the restroom itself. While the restroom scene sets the viewer up for what will soon take place on the other side of the door, unlike most of the other interior spaces in the film—the bedrooms, offices, parlors, and honeymoon suites in which Marnie has been or will be trapped physically, psychically, or both—the scene in the restroom offers one of the few interior spaces where Marnie has, and retains, full control of entry and exit. "Who but Hitchcock," Pomerance asks, "arranging for theft, would set up the scene here?" And where else but a women's restroom, a feminist spectator might ask, might a woman with no home of her own, and who changes and discards identities in hotel rooms and railway stations, prepare for a theft and an escape? After all, we have known from the film's start that Marnie has no home and that she is a woman who composes herself anew in transitory spaces so that she can pass unnoticed.

Rest room

The restroom scene takes place in one of the few locations, and offers one of the few extended moments, where Marnie is free from what Michele Piso has described as the "modern fluorescence that exposes her every move."[19] In this respect, however much the restroom scene sets up the scene that follows, it also gives Marnie, and the viewer, some *rest room* (see Figure 15.3). And in *Marnie* a little rest room is no small thing.

Piso has highlighted the central place of gendered poverty and women's financial insecurity in *Marnie*'s story and mise-en-scène—Marnie's "grindingly poor" childhood, the mother's sex work that supports the pair before "the accident" ended even that meager income source, the weary, working-poor cleaner at Rutland & Co. who drags her worn-out body and mop through the Rutland & Co. office, pushing herself to work faster so that she can get home to bed, the teenage virginity of the mother Bernice (Louise Lathan) that was exchanged for a sweater and a moment's attention and resulted in the girl-child Marnie. *Marnie*'s story is full of women who are just keeping afloat, or (if not bleak-street born) whose money is never fully their

Figure 15.3 (See also Plate 27) A little rest room, in *Marnie*.

own. As Piso argues, "Marnie's problems are both Oedipal and Capital— her world inhabited by those who can be entertained by suffering, like the hunters swarming around the wounded fox, elite dinner guests by night and, we might infer, corporate executives by day."[20]

As the place where the itinerant Marnie can hide out unnoticed, the lengthy shot of Marnie behind the cubicle door attunes the viewer to her relationship to this public space of private refuge and her ease in it. In his book *Intimate Violence: Hitchcock and Queer Theory*, David Greven writes that *Marnie* "frequently and palpably conveys her loneliness, most affectingly in the shots of Marnie isolated even when in contact with, or at least in physical proximity to, others: when, as business shuts down for the day, she hides in the bathroom stall at Rutland's, preparing to steal the money from the safe, as the chatter of the cheerfully loquacious office workers gradually dies down."[21] But I would contend that it is not with the other women that work in the office in the daylight hours that Marnie might have or find affinity, but with the cleaner Rita (Edith Evanson). It is not only Marnie that catches sight of the cleaning woman as she heads off with her takings. The cleaner too, for a split second (perhaps no more than a few frames, frames kept or included here by whom?), seems to also catch sight of Marnie, and for a fraction of a second, so quick you could miss it, we see the older woman's gaze flick up just before the cut, her view seemingly directed across the other side of the glass partition, before looking down again at the mop. The two women go about their business, silently, separately, and together (and it is worth remembering that while the first word spoken in the film is *robbed*, the next words Strutt splutters are "cleaned out"). The cleaner may well be hard of hearing, but the film leaves it open as to whether this weary woman who just wants to get home and go to bed is aware of Marnie's presence or not, and whether, perhaps, she might also be quite happy for Rutland & Co. to be cleaned out.

"Marnie's project is to undermine the power of money; yet in the end her class is crushed, her mother is marginalized, and Mark's capital and aggression are victorious," writes Piso in her beautiful essay on the film.[22] But before the end, there is the restroom, and rest room. Here in the restroom scene and its long-held shot of Marnie behind the cubicle door, Marnie is neither hounded by the demands of her repressed past or by the constraints and threats of her present; nor is she buffering the casual cruelty and pained ambivalence of the mother who requires the past to stay past and who, we later learn, has kept Marnie at a distance to protect Marnie from a memory that might break her or lose her. Calmly waiting in a toilet cubicle, her face brushed by a triangle of light that falls, like a projector's beam, across the top of the cubicle door, Marnie is both at ease and like a radar, a giant but weary ear, tuned to off-screen female voices—fragments of conversation that come from an elsewhere that the viewer never sees. In this respect, Marnie and the cleaner, Rita, are connected not only because they are both "cleaning out" Rutland & Co. after hours, but also because of how each woman uses and occupies her senses: both women fill the film with their knowing silences—Marnie hears beyond what the viewer can hear; Rita uses her reduced hearing to play at not seeing. But importantly, each of these women uses and is connected through their silences—for each, silence is respite and freedom. By shifting our attention from Rita's hearing or lack thereof (the "reveal" that serves to declare and seal Hitchcock's mastery of both the scene and the robbery) to Rita's *silence*, the cleaning out of the Rutland safe can also be seen as a scene where Marnie is not alone and has an ally. If the restroom scene sets the viewer up for a heightened identification with Marnie by aligning us with her listening and her silence (as Perkins writes, "We enter into her situation and become to some extent accomplices to her theft"), it also aligns us with and enables us to hear *Rita*'s silence. The restroom scene opens the possibility of other affinities, allegiances, and witnesses for Marnie.

"To perceive Marnie's marriage to Mark as a cure, in my view, is to deny the social misery in the bleak street and cast-off mother imaged at the film's end," writes Piso. "It is to accept a melancholic and merely subjective discovery as the salvation of modern life."[23] In a film in which all the women either lose or are broken by the end, the affinities and alliances that are evoked or forged through Marnie's silence in the restroom and the robbery that follows are significant. Marnie, of course, is frequently silent in the film, holding her tongue to better pass, infiltrate, or go unnoticed (and of course we first see Marnie silent—yellow purse clutched firm and center, walking down the train platform and the center of the shot, but there her silence serves to further anchor our gaze to her neat-trim form, a body that will be measured up and stripped down when Strutt makes his statement to the police in the very next shot). In the restroom scene, however, Marnie's silence is something we actively listen and attend to, and it is a silence we also listen *with*.

The restroom scene faces, and gives silent voice to, the social misery and the broken cast-off mother left behind in the painted backdrop street at the film's end (and in the novel by Winston Graham on which the film was based, Marnie's mother was a cleaner). Staying for a while with Marnie in the restroom and the silences it invites us to hear can sharpen our ear to the currents and sites of sadness within the film. *Marnie* is a film that is most loved—by those that love the film—for its sadness, though the location, nature, and course of that sadness are not the same for all. To return for a moment to the essay that I used to open this discussion of *Marnie*, Modleski identifies and examines what she describes as a recent turn in Hitchcock scholarship in which cinefeminism is appropriated "by male critics who want to re-master the master."[24] *Marnie* is a film in which the stakes of remastering the master have been high for Hitchcock scholars who have been affronted by suggestions that Hitchcock made unwelcome moves on the film's star and that such claims were being accommodated in commentary on Hitchcock and his work. The defensive tone that McElhaney describes as characterizing much of the discourse surrounding *Marnie* has perhaps been most evident in those studies that directly or indirectly take issue with Hedren's complaint and that regard both it, and the feminist analyses of and attention to the sexual violations and entrapments within the film, as causing injury to both Hitchcock and the film itself. Most striking is that in some of the recent pushback work on *Marnie*, the site and nature of the film's often recognized "profound sadness" has been relocated from what Piso eloquently describes as a study of "communal alienation and lost rapport"[25] to the sadness of the director himself as an injured party, unfairly harmed by a misunderstood or poorly received work and (then) by its star's account of sexual harassment gone public, the two "events" collapsed into one: "The film's failure was a catastrophe from with Hitchcock never fully recovered," writes Rothman. As if bearing witness to injury endured, Rothman continues, "As an artist, he was never the same again. Never again was he to probe so deeply the mysteries of love and the avoidance of love. Never again was he to bring to the screen a woman with whom he identified so profoundly."[26] By choosing the restroom—and rest room—I hope to return the film's eloquent sadness to its story (the communal alienation, the gendered poverty, Marnie's losses) and also leave some room for Hedren's losses. There is a certain poignancy in choosing the restroom shot for a discussion of *Marnie*. For while Marnie might have had a moment's peace and freedom in her restroom, in Hedren's accounts of the harassment she received from Hitchcock during the production, she had no such privacy in her dressing room. Marnie, at least, had control of this space.

Silence's long throw

The shot in the restroom cubicle and the silent allegiance and affinities it serves to anchor has long resonated for me with another shot from another—and very different—film in which a woman waits behind a door at night and has a moment to herself. That film is Chantal Akerman's *Toute une nuit* (1982), a film that unfolds over one hot summer night in Brussels and in which various couplings form, separate, pass time, reunite—none with backstory, always bodies finding or losing each other. And within this night there is one shot, one scene, in which a middle-aged woman steps out at night and leans against a white door (perhaps a back fence, perhaps the back door of a house) and has a cigarette. The shot is more than a minute in duration but less than two, a medium-long shot that stays and waits with the woman while she smokes and has a moment to herself, stepping out to have some private time in a public space. A girl's voice can be heard calling out to her from somewhere in the distance behind the wall, wanting something perhaps. After the third call the woman relinquishes the rest of her cigarette and her moment and goes back through the door. Many years after I first saw the film, I learned that the woman was in fact Akerman's mother—Natalia Akerman—and the voice, that of Chantal Akerman herself.[27] *Marnie* and *Toute une nuit* have so little in common that to place them alongside each other, even momentarily, is somewhat disorienting, *and yet* these two shots—the shot of Marnie behind the cubicle door, waiting past waiting, and that of the unnamed woman behind the back door who takes a moment for herself—each give these women some time and space that is presented as both precious and fragile, and in each shot these women's private moments are in public spaces, and each is orbited by or in touch with other distant female voices or bodies. The off-screen voice of the girl calling her mother draws an invisible line over this space; Marnie's silent waiting seeds a long throw of affinity to both Rita and to the mother left behind a door, speechless, at the film's close. Each shot, in different ways, is remarkable.

In her translator's notes for Chantal Akerman's book *My Mother Laughs*, Corina Capp talks about a word that "almost slipped her by" in Akerman's text—*décalage*. It is a word, Capp writes, that is commonly used by French speakers for jet lag and time difference. But finding this word appear twice in Akerman's text—in the writing of a filmmaker who "wanted people to *feel the experience of time passing*," and whose work is shaped and defined by "its intimate relationship to a spectator's sense of herself in time"[28]—was significant and posed questions for translation. As Capp writes, *décalage* refers to "a 'gap' in time *or* space that allows for a particular voice to construct and, importantly, reconstruct itself."[29] It seems to me that the shot in the restroom might also function and offer a form of *décalage*. Different in style, composition, and aesthetic from so much else in the film, emptied of suspense by the length of time Marnie remains behind the door, it also links Marnie to other women in the film and beyond it. Staying with and in the restroom for a little time provides a way to attend to some of the feminist scholarship on this film and some of the women's voices that can be heard in, around, and through it.

Notes

1. With thanks to Olivia Khoo for her generous feedback on an earlier draft of this essay. Tania Modleski, "Remastering the Master: Hitchcock after Feminism," *New Literary History* 47, no. 1 (2016): 135.
2. Modleski, "Remastering the Master," 140.
3. Joe McElhaney, *The Death of Classical Cinema: Hitchcock, Lang, Minnelli* (Albany: State University of New York Press, 2006), 98.
4. Michele Piso, "Mark's Marnie," in *A Hitchcock Reader*, ed. Marshall Deutelbaum and Leland Pogue (Ames: Iowa State University Press, 1986), 292.
5. Elisabeth Bronfen, "Screening and Disclosing Fantasy: Rear Projection in Hitchcock," *Screen* 56, no.1 (2015): 9.
6. Robin Wood, one of the film's early champions, argued that the overt artificiality of the rear projections and painted backdrops highlighted how "the constrictedness of Marnie's life belongs essentially to the world of unreality." Robin Wood, *Hitchcock's*

Films Revisited (London: Faber & Faber, 1989), 175. Tom Gunning describes *Marnie* as Hitchcock's "last great film." Tom Gunning, "A Hand for Hitchcock," *Crisis & Critique* 7, no. 2 (2020): 124.

7. Hedren's accounts of her experiences working with Hitchcock on *Marnie* and *Birds* are now well known and part of popular discourse about the director and about these two films in particular. Spoto's *Spellbound by Beauty: Alfred Hitchcock and His Leading Ladies* (London: Arrow, 2009) was inspiration for the 2012 film *The Girl* (Julian Jarrod, HBO/BBC2), with Hedren consulting on the script, and Hedren's own book, *Tippi: A Memoir* (New York: William Morrow, 2016), was published in 2016. Hedren's claims have been met with patronizing irritation or quick dismissal from some Hitchcock critics and seem to have motivated more disputes about the forms of sexual violence and entrapment *within* the film. A number of critics have produced complex and labyrinthine arguments as to why the film's marriage consummated in rape was not in fact a rape, as if disputing the form and place of sexual violence and entrapment in the film's *story* might deflate or undermine the accounts of sexual harassment in its *production*. In his BFI book on *Marnie*, Murray Pomerance concludes his discussion of this much-discussed scene with a startling series of propositions: "What precisely can Mark take her to mean when Marnie bellows, 'No!? I don't want to have sex with you'?—this she has said before, proclaims as a motto, notwithstanding the current of experience. This woman in extremis, whose every statement has been a lie, who has lived a life of masquerade: is she suddenly to be taken at face value because she has negated, of all things, sex?" and then further, "Could the 'No!' be for someone else? Could the 'No!' be emanating, totally acousmatic, from another Marnie?" Murray Pomerance, *Marnie* (London: BFI/Palgrave Macmillan, 2004), 34–35. Meanwhile in the introduction to his chapter on *Marnie*, William Rothman writes that "Unfortunately, *Marnie*'s reputation has been tarnished by the assertion, endlessly repeated, that the film contains an offensive rape sequence, that definitively exposes Hitchcock as an arch misogynist; and by Donald Spoto's claim, which many take to be proof of Hitchcock's egregious sexism, that near the end of production there was an incident in Tippi Hedren's trailer in which the director said or did something inappropriate to his star." William Rothman, *Hitchcock: The Murderous Gaze*, 2nd ed. (Albany: State University of New York Press, 2014), 351. It is unclear which of these three claims (that the film contains an "offensive rape sequence," that Hitchcock was "an arch misogynist," or that Hitchcock sexually harassed Hedren) is the primary focus of Rothman's palpable affront in this passage. Rothman "does not speculate on what may or may not have happened between director and star. That is none of my business," he writes (see p. 352), nor does he engage with much feminist scholarship on the film. Rothman devotes more than six pages of his revised edition of *The Murderous Gaze* to the rape scene (see pp. 411–418). There is something both unsettling and fascinating about the lengthy and often labored arguments that have been made to refute the film's marital rape as rape and/or qualify it through a cascade of hypotheticals that tend to come down to the same thing: there is nothing to see here except Mark's love for Marnie and Hitchcock's love of cinema.

8. McElhaney, *The Death of Classical Cinema*, 91.

9. Rothman, *Hitchcock*, 351.

10. Rothman, *Hitchcock*, 351.

11. Piso, "Mark's Marnie," 288.

12. Laura Mulvey, "A Clumsy Sublime," *Film Quarterly* 60, no. 3 (2007): 3.

13. See, e.g., Adrian Danks, "Being in Two Places at the Same Time: The Forgotten Geography of Rear Projection," in *B Is for Bad Cinema: Aesthetics, Politics, and Cultural Value*, ed. Claire Perkins and Constantine Verevis (Albany: State University of New York Press, 2014).

14. Modleski, "Remastering the Master," 150.

15. V. F. Perkins, *Film as Film: Understanding and Judging Movies* (New York: Da Capo Press, 1993), 142.

16. Michel Chion, "The Silence of the Loudspeakers; or, Why with Dolby Sound It Is the Film That Listens to Us," in *Soundscape: The School of Sound Lectures, 1998–2001*, ed. Larry Sider, Diane Freeman, and Jerry Sider (London: Wallflower Press, 2003), 151.

17. Bronfen, "Screening and Disclosing Fantasy," 3.

18. Pomerance, *Marnie*, 20.

19. Piso, "Mark's Marnie," 294.

20. Piso, "Mark's Marnie," 300.

21. David Greven, *Intimate Violence: Hitchcock, Sex, and Queer Theory* (New York: Oxford University Press, 2017), 194.

22. Piso, "Mark's Marnie," 302.

23. Piso, "Mark's Marnie," 289.

24. Modleski, "Remastering the Master," 140.

25. Piso, "Mark's Marnie," 292.

26. Rothman, *Hitchcock*, 352.

27. For a discussion of this scene see Mateus Araujo, "Chantal Akerman, between the Mother and the World," trans. Mark Cohen, *Film Quarterly* 70, no. 1 (2016): 32–38.

28. Corina Capp, "A Translator's Note," in Chantal Akerman, *My Mother Laughs*, trans. Corina Capp (Brooklyn: The Song Cave, 2013), 170–172.

29. Capp, "A Translator's Note," 172.

16

Frenzy (1972)

Pulling focus between a woman's face and a face of death

Luke Robinson

Alfred Hitchcock's penultimate film *Frenzy* (1972) could (or perhaps *should*) have been called "The Frenzy" for how it depicts violence as an intrinsic condition of patriarchy for women.[1] While the face of Brenda Blaney (Barbara Leigh-Hunt) being strangled to death by a necktie is the main image on many of the film's posters, in this chapter I turn my attention to one of Hitchcock's most fascinating and disconcerting shots—a facial close-up of Barbara "Babs" Milligan (Anna Massey) standing on a Covent Garden street in London as the diegetic sounds of the market activity around her become mute. This is the first time in the film that Babs has been given such a prominent close-up and it is the first time that the diegetic sounds of the film fade away within a single shot. In the facial close-up of Babs, the screen is hers—her face dominates the frame. At the same time, because the diegetic sounds fade away to the point where they have vanished, Babs is positioned in a bracketed space from the people and the life that is going on around her. Like a shift in a camera lens, this close-up, virtually if not actually, pulls focus between a thinking woman's face and a space of fading and disappearance that is deathly in its silence. While initially this silence, this soundlessness, might not be ominous for all viewers, when this silence is broken a few seconds later by the voice of Robert "Bob" Rusk (Barry Foster)—a man who violently kills women, including that of Brenda, the wife of Richard "Dick" Blaney (Jon Finch)—the implication of the muting of sounds, and the resultant soundlessness, is clear: a metaphorical grave has been dug around Babs's face—from the moment that the sounds begin to vanish, Babs is a dead woman walking.[2]

Babs is the star of my analysis, the story I am telling, even though she is not the main protagonist of *Frenzy* itself. While she is one of the most sympathetic and likeable characters in Hitchcock's film, the film's actual protagonist and the antagonist, and the three top-billed actors, are men. The film is

Luke Robinson, Frenzy *(1972)* In: *One Shot Hitchcock.* Edited by: Luke Robinson and Melanie Robson,
Oxford University Press. © Oxford University Press 2024. DOI: 10.1093/oso/9780197682876.003.0016

centered on the protagonist Dick, who is accused of committing a series of murders, including that of his ex-wife Brenda. Then there is a detective (Alec McCowen) who is investigating the crimes. And then there is the antagonist, the real serial killer Bob, the so-called necktie murderer, one of the market sellers that Dick and Babs are acquainted with. Babs, like Brenda before her, is attracted to Dick despite his often-misogynistic behavior. And, even though all the evidence points to Dick as being the necktie murderer, Babs believes Dick's innocence and wants to help him. After defending Dick with her boss, a publican (Bernard Cribbins), Babs quits her job and leaves the pub, jobless and homeless. The shot that am I focusing on in this chapter begins the moment Babs steps out from the pub and ends with her and Bob walking off together. In this shot, Babs becomes the protagonist of the scene, if not the film.

The Hitchcock shot: Up close with Babs

Leaving the pub with some determination, Babs steps onto a cobblestone street of London's Covent Garden market. After she has taken a few steps, the camera speedily tracks forward from a medium shot of Babs's upper body and handbag to an extreme close-up of her face (see Figures 16.1 and 16.2). Throughout the shot Babs's eyes maintain their position in the top third of the frame—she is looking right and then, when the camera stops moving, she

Figure 16.1 (See also Plate 28) Barbara "Babs" Milligan (Anna Massey) leaves a Covent Garden pub in a medium shot in Alfred Hitchcock's *Frenzy*.

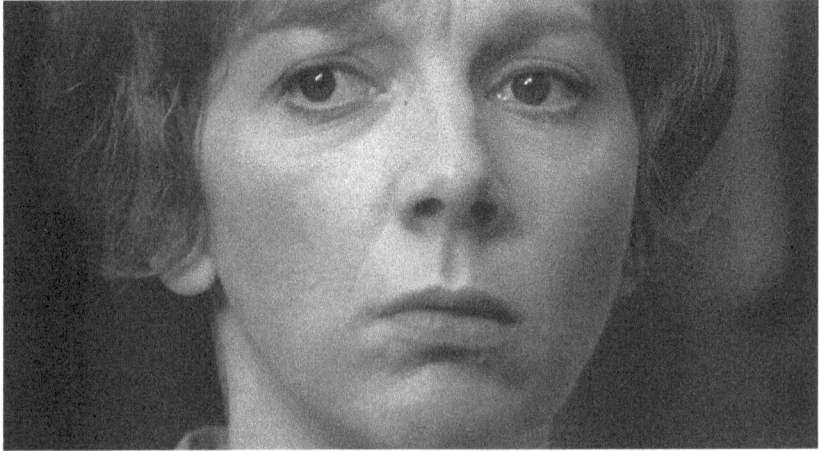

Figure 16.2 (See also Plate 29)   Extreme close-up of Babs in *Frenzy*.

looks to the left. Here, like in many Hitchcock films, the cinematic apparatus is aligned with one of the film's principal characters. For one, the speed of the camera tracking movement after Babs leaves the pub—and the abruptness of its halt when her face is in close-up—mimics Babs's own hasty retreat and her sudden stop outside. For another, the way that the camera maintains its focus on Babs's moving eyes throughout the shot gives the impression her next movement could also determine where the camera will move. And, in addition, the muting of sounds, at least to some extent, implies that she is taking some time to stop and think. The close-up of Babs is thus an example of an introspective gaze, which for Edward Branigan is when "a character instead of glancing at an object, glances *inward* and becomes introspective."[3] So, while Babs might not be the main protagonist of *Frenzy*, these techniques work together so that the story—at this point in the film—is hers.

While the silence gives Babs and the spectator a pause for thought, there is also something distinctly uncomfortable about the way the muting of sounds isolates Babs from the other people around her. When we consider that *Frenzy* is about a serial killer who strangles women to death using his necktie, the gradual fading of the diegetic sounds—their suffocation, and the shot's eventual soundlessness—has distinct sinister implications. Tania Modleski argues that the world represented in *Frenzy* "is a world from which women are altogether excluded, having been expelled from it mostly by brutal means, their power throttled. Throughout the film, the specter of this power has been continually evoked and subsequently choked off."[4] The moment of soundlessness is a moment in the film where the diegetic sounds are themselves literally "choked," indicating that Babs's agency, and her power, is being throttled in the same moment that she has command of the screen. So, while in the tracking shot and close-up Babs is momentarily the protagonist of the shot and the film, the muting of the diegetic sounds signals to the spectator that this story is already coming to a violent end.

Babs's story indeed does not last that long. After a few moments of silence from somewhere off-screen, Bob asks, "Got a place to stay?" Since Babs was only just fired from her job and made homeless Bob's question is telling—he was watching Babs and saw her having an argument with her former boss. The close-up swiftly changes from being about Babs, and what Babs is looking at, to being about a man that was observing Babs. If, as Laura Mulvey argues, the male gaze is constituted through the look of the camera, the look of the viewers in the audience, and looks of characters at each other on-screen in a film's diegesis,[5] then the shift of the spectator's focus from what Babs is looking at to Bob and his look is an instance where the male gaze violently supplements the female gaze. Prior to *Frenzy*, Massey had played Helen Stephens in Michael Powell's 1960 serial killer film *Peeping Tom*.[6] In a scene from that film, Helen looks into a mirror that is attached to a camera. Also attached to the camera is a sharp spike that is pointing toward her throat. Because of this spike, when Helen looks into the mirror, she sees her face at the moment of her own (probable) death, an image that the diegetic camera apparatus attempts to record.[7] In Powell's film Helen is forced to view her face as a face of death, a distorted view that the spectator and her potential murderer also sees. In the tracking to close-up of Babs from *Frenzy*, the man who wants to murder Babs is watching her from a place behind her offscreen. In contrast to the scene in *Peeping Tom*, it is Bob's face that is representative of the pointy spike that is coming for Babs's neck from behind.

In horror films off-screen spaces are often charged. It is from the spaces we do not see that murderers and monsters strike unsuspecting protagonists who are in view. Through Bob's voice the horror that was off-screen strikes and then invades a close-up that was originally for Babs. When he speaks, Bob's voice initially echoes within the same aural register as the soundlessness of the muted sounds. Like an aural line of graffiti, his voice tags the close-up as his. Responding to his voice, Babs turns to face him and, in so doing, she leaves the close-up allowing Bob's face to take its place (see Figure 16.3). With Bob's face now in view, the shot continues by tracking backward

Figure 16.3 (See also Plate 30) Robert "Bob" Rusk (Barry Foster) invades Babs's close-up in *Frenzy*.

and panning right, showing Babs and Bob walking off together. In this new framing, Covent Garden fruit market sellers can be seen working around them (see Figure 16.4). Babs's determined expression gives the appearance that she has agency throughout the shot; however, as the camera tracks backward away from his face, Bob moves himself into a position so that Babs is encouraged to turn around and face a different direction from where she was

Figure 16.4 (See also Plate 31) Babs and Bob walk off together in a medium-long shot featuring Covent Garden market sellers in *Frenzy*.

previously looking. Bob then lightly touches and interlocks her arm with his, guiding Babs in the direction they should walk. This lengthy shot begins with Babs having agency, and at least some control over the cinematic apparatus, to being a shot where her agency is hijacked by a murderous man. By this point in the film the spectator has been a witness to Bob's violent and lengthy rape and murder of Brenda. That Bob guides Babs at the end of the shot signals to the spectator that Babs is likely to be Bob's next necktie victim.

When Babs leaves the shot, and we see Bob is standing behind her, the camera pulls focus so that his face is visible. "Pulling focus" is a term for when the camera lens shifts its focal point of view from the background to the foreground, and/or vice versa. The theorization of a shot or scene can also be a type of pulling focus, with the theorist choosing to identify and describe, and pull forward and push backward, different elements of a shot to discuss. It is imperative that the act of pulling focus does not cloud one part of a shot over another. For example, it would be wrong to ignore the threat of death that casts its shadow on Babs in this shot since it is crucial that we identify, name, and challenge the forces of violence that structure and give power to patriarchy. In the shot described, the violence of patriarchy can be identified in Bob's gestures that control and manipulate women, in the changing intonations of Bob's voice that are covert in their meanings, in the blocking and spatial relationships between Bob and Babs both on- and off-screen, and, most important, in the ways sound, or the lack of sound, signals the presence of a murderous man whom we initially cannot see. At the same time, to focus purely on the forces of death and violence that threaten Babs in her close-up at the expense of discussing her agency would, in turn, only give voice to this violence, and potentially make this violence an *attraction*, and even something attractive (at least for some). Therefore, for the remainder of this chapter, I continue to pull focus between the close-up of Babs's face, and the agency that she has, and the face of death that threatens her life and her agency as a thinking, self-determining woman. I take this approach with the aim of giving more voice to the former—Babs's agency—over the latter—the face of death and the invisible and inaudible modes of patriarchal violence that it represents.

Pulling focus: Babs's thinking face

To pull focus to Babs's thinking face and her introspective gaze, I will begin by looking at the close-up itself. The close-up of Babs's face is an extreme

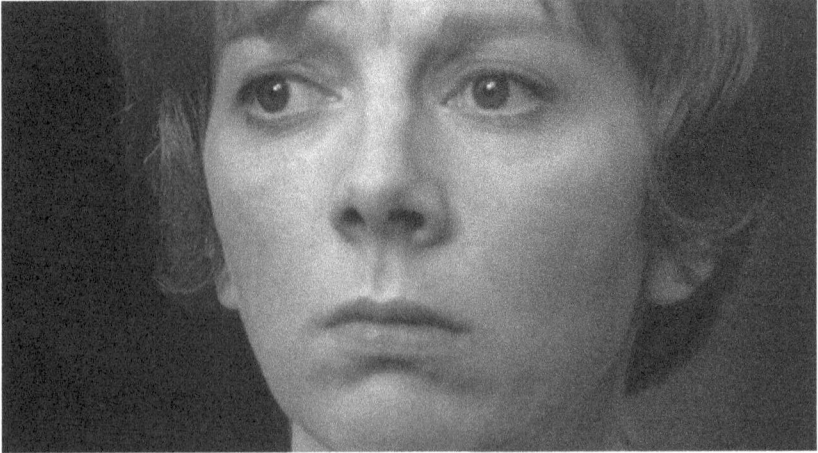

Figure 16.5 (See also Plate 32) Extreme close-up of Babs in *Frenzy*.

close-up since her face also extends beyond the frame, with her chin and the top of her head cut off. This, combined with the fact that the sounds are muted and that all activity that occurs behind her is distinctly out of focus, draws attention to the close-up as a means of cinematic articulation (see Figure 16.5). In a passage that could have been used to describe this close-up, Béla Balázs argues in his *Theory of the Film*:

> The facial expression on a face is complete and comprehensible in itself and therefore we need not think of it as existing in space and time. Even if we had just seen the same face in the middle of a crowd and the close-up merely separated it from the others, we would still feel that we have suddenly been left alone with this one face to the exclusion of the rest of the world.[8]

In Babs's close-up we can see her face and her facial expression; however, this is not exactly what Balázs means when he argues that the defining feature of a facial close-up is "the expression of the face."[9] Balázs provides examples of what this facial expression might instead be, examples that make it clear that for him a new dimension is produced by a facial close-up, a dimension that is neither spatial nor visible. Balázs argues that in a close-up of the face:

> we see emotions, moods, intentions and thoughts, things which although our eyes can see them, are not in space. For feelings, emotions, moods,

intentions, thoughts are not themselves things pertaining to space, even if they are rendered visible by means which are.[10]

When a film viewer looks at a character's (or documentary subject's) face in a close-up, they often think they can see, or read, what a person might be feeling or thinking by the way the character's, or subject's, emotions, moods, intentions, and/or thoughts seem to be rendered visible by the face. However, for Balázs, this is not all that a close-up does. For him, the film viewer can also "see" feelings, emotions, moods, intentions, and/or thoughts in, and for, themselves, and it is these feelings, emotions, moods, intentions, and thoughts that are seen in, and for, themselves that constitutes a facial expression.

The different dimension that is being produced in a close-up—the facial expression—is also related to the character, or subject, who is feeling or thinking them. These feelings, emotions, moods, intentions, and thoughts are of a different temporal order to the space and time of the physical face that is visible in the shot. It is thus possible to "see" thought without knowing what these thoughts are. It is also possible to "see" thinking, as something that a character is doing, but also to "see" thinking as a process, with its own properties, its own materiality, as having its own spatial and temporal order that is being produced by the thinking subject. Crucially, when we "see" thinking in this way, we are seeing a process that is the product of an-*other*'s agency. In his discussion of the mental images of Hitchcock's films in *Cinema 1: The Movement-Image*, Gilles Deleuze argues: "With Hitchcock, a new kind of 'figures' appears which are figures of thoughts."[11] Using Deleuze's terminology, in the close-up of Babs's face it is a figure of her thought that appears—it is her thoughts that are being projected, and rendered as something to "see," even if the spectator is not precisely sure what Babs might be thinking about when they look at her during her close-up.

Films often present a character's thoughts through flashbacks or voice-over techniques, but this is not taking place in this close-up of Babs. Here we can learn from Noa Steimatsky, who argues that Hitchcock's mode of "cinematic articulation," which for her is "the shot–reverse shot regime," reflects on "the gap between seeing and knowing."[12] In Babs's close-up there is a gap between seeing and knowing because we both know, and do not fully know, what Babs is thinking about during her close-up. To put it differently, in her close-up her agency extends beyond the ability of a spectator to identify or understand her as a thinking woman. The gap between seeing and knowing in this shot is productive as it represents thinking as a process and demonstrates agency—these are Babs's thoughts and not the thoughts of the spectator. At the same time, there is another "gap" that we need to be attentive to in this close-up, the gap of soundlessness that is produced when the diegetic sounds fade away and then return. It is now time to pull focus to this other gap, and toward forces of violence and death that confronts Babs's face—a gap that, as we will see, takes the form of an inactive and soundless void.

Pulling focus: The face of death

To pull focus to the face of death, I will begin with the soundlessness of the void that frames Babs's face. In the tracking movement to Babs's face the sound fades to the point of its becoming mute, and since to erase something is to rub something out, or to make something fade, the fading of sound can be considered a type of erasure. In her discussion of how death is represented on-screen, Mulvey argues: "The silence of 'The End' duplicates the silence of death itself but it also signifies total erasure, the nothing that lies beyond it."[13] The soundlessness of the close-up of Babs's face conjures up the silence Mulvey identifies with "The End" of a film, which is also total erasure and the nothing beyond. If, as Jacques Aumont argues, a "threat of death" is "always implicitly and metaphorically proffered from beyond the frame,"[14] then in this close-up of Babs's face the threat of death—in the form of a soundless void—has, implicitly and metaphorically, encroached within the framing of this shot. In *Cinema 1*, Deleuze argues that "The facial close-up is both the face and its effacement."[15] In her close-up, Babs's face is visible—it is Babs's thinking face that fills the screen. At the same time, the diegetic sounds have been erased. It is therefore a close-up of a face, and an instance of effacement—the effacement of diegetic sounds, an effacement that is representative of a death of threatens her off-screen. That Babs's face is literally replaced by a man who later will kill her in the *same* close-up, also means that her face is effaced, and when we consider that originally it was Babs's close-up—*defaced*, by a face of a man that murders women. We can thus understand that in the facial close-up of Babs a void is given facial form—a face of death—and that it is this void that shares the close-up of Babs's face before it eventually replaces hers.

The isolation of Babs's face from her surrounds allows her thoughts to be projected in the close-up of her. In *Cinema 1*, Deleuze argues that facial close-ups can produce what he identifies as an "any-space-whatever."[16] For him an any-space-whatever is a when a "Space is no longer a particular determined space." And then, in his discussion of the films of Robert Bresson he argues that it can be "an equivalent of space and the affect expressed as pure potentiality."[17] To one extent, the space of Babs's close-up gives the potential for her thoughts to be projected, even if these thoughts, in themselves, remain largely unknown. At the same time, because the sounds have been, to use Modleski's phrase, "choked off," they are representative of death and the male gaze that is itself structured as, and by, a lack. The space of Babs's close-up is therefore not a space of pure potentiality, since it is also a space where the power of the potential is rendered void by the invading male gaze. Instead of Babs being purely in an any-space-whatever, a space without a particular determination, the space that Babs is positioned is also a *no-space-whatever*—a space that is momentarily *nowhere* and in *no time*, a space of death that is being projected by the serial killer from behind her.

Deleuze might not give a name to the type of no-space-whatever I am identifying in this shot, although he does refer to the void in his account of another postwar European film. In his account of the facial close-ups in Ingmar Bergman's films, with a particular focus on *Persona* (1966), Deleuze argues: "Bergman has pushed the nihilism of the face the furthest, that is its relationship in fear to the void or the absence, the fear of the face confronted with its nothingness."[18] In Babs's close-up she is unaware that her face is confronted with its nothingness—the void is not something that she sees or hears. Instead, the void is something that is made "audible" for the spectator—it is a void that frames, but does not yet consume, Babs's face.

In another of Deleuze's books that he coauthored with Félix Guattari, the two of them refer to the films of Josef von Sternberg. Regarding Sternberg's films, they argue that the facial close-up can "emphasize its shadows to the point of engulfing it 'in pitiless darkness.'"[19] There are no shadows to be seen in the close-up of Babs; rather, what the film spectator is presented with is Babs's thinking face and a void of sound, both which divide and share the one shot. Shortly after they make their argument about faces being engulfed by shadows in Sternberg's films, they argue: "*A horror story, the face is a horror story.*"[20] In her close-up, Babs is not aware that she is in this void—the shot up until this point has been aligned with Babs, but the eventual soundlessness of the close-up is not her experience of horror (which is to come later in the scene). Rather, the muted sounds and their soundlessness are representative of a void that *is facing her*—at least in the sense that it is confronting her, since the agent of this void—the literal face of death—is actually behind her when she is in the close-up. In Babs's close-up, one type of void—the spaceless space that is without sound, a space without acoustics—an acoustic void, signals and is indexical to another type of void—the void that is representative of violence that empowers patriarchy when it remains as something that cannot be seen nor heard.

The muted sound is a face of death that is confronting Babs's face; at the same time, the muted sound could also be a temporal index to the dead women that Bob has already killed since we know that Babs could die because Bob has already killed so many women. If a bullet hole is an index,[21] and if a bullet hole points to a scene of previous violence, then the muted sound is the temporal and audible (inaudible) equivalent of this form of indexical sign. The muted sounds are an example of what Michel Chion calls *en creux*, when we understand that "*En creux properly refers to negative space—the shape of the space in a sculptor's mold, defined by the mold*."[22] In *Frenzy*, the muted sound acts as an instance of this void that metaphorically frames Babs's face as if it were an iris frame or the mold of a bullet hole. Bob's face is therefore both the face of murderer and the face of a mass grave, the grave of the women he has already murdered. In this regard, that his face appears in the close-up of Babs is even more disturbing than one of the famous faces of death that features in a Hitchcock film, the close-up of Norman Bates at the end of *Psycho* (1960), that cross-dissolves to the face of his dead mother.

The close-up of Babs being replaced by Bob foreshadows and doubles the later frequently discussed long tacking shot where Babs is murdered off-screen, a shot that has been discussed by Sebastian Smoliński in an earlier chapter of this book. As she walks through the Covent Garden market with Bob, we hear how Bob manages to convince Babs to stay with him in his home. Later in the same scene Babs walks up some stairs to Bob's apartment. In this shot Babs is leading the way, but unbeknownst to her she is being directed by Bob from behind (see Figure 16.6). After Babs enters through Bob's front door, there is a long tracking shot down the stairs that she previously climbed. As the camera tracks down and passes a staircase landing, a window that looks onto the buildings behind enters vision. The view through the window is reminiscent of the opening shot of *Rear Window* (1954), as discussed by Martin P. Rossouw in this volume (see Figure 16.7). As *Rear Window* meticulously stages, it is in such views that murders are "witnessed" by spectators, sight unseen. In *Rear Window* we never see Lars Thorwald (Raymond Burr) murder his wife (Irene Winston), but like Jeff Jeffries (James Stewart) the spectator is encouraged to believe Thorwald killed her. Similarly,

Figure 16.6 (See also Plate 33) Tracking shot of Babs and Bob walking up the stairs of Bob's building, with him leading from behind in *Frenzy*.

Figure 16.7 (See also Plate 34) Tracking shot down the stairs of Bob's building, reminiscent of Jeff's view from Alfred Hitchcock's *Rear Window*.

in *Frenzy* we never see Bob murder Babs; however, we know that her murder is taking place even though we cannot see or hear it.

As the camera passes the landing and tracks further down the stairs and along a corridor to the street outside, the diegetic sounds of traffic and people slowly rise in volume (see Figure 16.8). Here we have a reversal of the close-up that I have been discussing—in this shot the diegetic sounds slowly

Figure 16.8 (See also Plate 35)   Long shot of Bob's building, looking toward his apartment window with the Covent Garden market sellers in the foreground in *Frenzy*.

become louder, an act that draws attention to the deathly silence that had been previously accompanying the long tracking shot down the stairs. As the camera tracks away from the crime scene, the horror of the scene that we are encouraged to imagine is of *Babs's* death. Even though the diegetic sounds are increasing in volume, the soundlessness of the acoustic void, at least virtually, accompanies the emerging sounds of a busy London scene. The soundlessness that is representative of Babs's death, and the violence and death that gives power to patriarchy, is something we are encouraged to imagine as the sounds of Covent Garden begin to dominate the film's soundtrack.

Pulling focus: Resisting erasure

In her essay on *Frenzy*, Modleski argues: "I do mean to insist on the importance of the fact that woman is never completely destroyed in these films— no matter how dead Hitchcock tries to make her appear, as when he inserts still shots in both *Psycho* and *Frenzy* of the female corpse. There are always elements resistant to her destruction or assimilation."[23] In the close-up of Babs, she is the protagonist of the scene, and it is her thoughts—her introspective gaze—that is given their own dimension, even at the same time as she is being marked for death by the film's serial killer. In the close-up of Babs, she has agency, and she has thoughts that are beyond what a spectator can share. It is her story that resists complete destruction or assimilation even when the tragedy of her death is, in our imagination, being invisibly and inaudibly projected as the camera tracks away from Bob's apartment. In our imagining, we know that Babs has been a victim not only of a serial killer, but of a force of violence that structures and gives power to patriarchy. While Babs does not survive much longer after her close-up, her close-up recalls many other facial close-ups in Hitchcock's films where thinking women populate the picture. It is with this idea I wish to end my chapter and this coedited collection, a volume that has been examining and theorizing single shots from Alfred Hitchcock's films.

Notes

1. Thank you to Jodi Brooks, Colin Campbell Robinson, and Melanie Robson for their editorial suggestions. Jodi Brooks suggested to me in conversation that the film should have been called "The Frenzy." My opening sentence, and my argument in this chapter, is indebted to Tania Modleski's chapter on *Frenzy* in *The Women Who Knew Too Much: Hitchcock and Feminist Theory*, 3rd ed. (New York: Routledge, 2016), 103–115.
2. Thank you to one of my anonymous peer-reviewers for giving me the phrase "a dead woman walking."
3. Edward Branigan, *Point of View in the Cinema: A Theory of Narration and Subjectivity in Classical Film* (New York: Mouton Publishers, 1984), 80. Italics in the original.
4. Modleski, *The Women Who Knew Too Much*, 112.
5. Laura Mulvey, "Visual Pleasure and Narrative Cinema," *Screen* 16, no. 3 (Autumn 1975): 17.
6. Jodi Brooks raised this point at Bruce Isaacs, "Aural Abstraction in Hitchcock and De Palma," paper presented at the Sydney Screen Studies Network Seminar Program: Across Screens and Borders, University of New South Wales, Sydney, September 2019.
7. Carol J. Clover, *Men, Women, and Chain Saws: Gender in the Modern Horror Film* (Princeton, NJ: Princeton University Press, 1992), 170.
8. Béla Balázs, *Theory of the Film: Character and Growth of a New Art*, trans. Edith Bone (1952; New York: Dover, 1970), 61.
9. Balázs, *Theory of the Film*, 61.
10. Balázs, *Theory of the Film*, 61.
11. Gilles Deleuze, *Cinema 1: The Movement-Image*, trans. Hugh Tomlinson and Barbara Habberjam (Minneapolis: University of Minnesota Press, 1986), 203.
12. Noa Steimatsky, *The Face on Film* (New York: Oxford University Press, 2017), 152.
13. Laura Mulvey, *Death 24x a Second: Stillness and the Moving Image* (London: Reaktion Books, 2007), 79.

14. Jacques Aumont, "Griffith—The Frame, The Figure," trans. Judith Ayling and Thomas Elsaesser, in *Early Cinema: Space, Frame, Narrative*, ed. Thomas Elsaesser with Adam Barker (London: BFI Publishing, 1990), 354. Aumont's argument is made with reference to D. W. Griffith's Biograph film *An Unseen Enemy* (1912).

15. Deleuze, *Cinema 1*, 100.

16. Deleuze, *Cinema 1*, 109. Deleuze notes that he sources the term from Pascal Augé.

17. Deleuze, *Cinema 1*, 109.

18. Deleuze, *Cinema 1*, 100.

19. Gilles Deleuze and Félix Guattari, *A Thousand Plateaus: Capitalism and Schizophrenia*, trans. Brian Massumi (London: Continuum, 1987), 186. Deleuze and Guattari cite Josef von Sternberg, *Fun in a Chinese Laundry* (New York: Macmillan, 1965), 324.

20. Deleuze and Guattari, *A Thousand Plateaus*, 186; my emphasis.

21. Charles Sanders Peirce, *Peirce on Signs: Writings on Semiotic by Charles Sanders Peirce* (Chapel Hill: University of North Carolina Press, 1991), 239–240.

22. See Claudia Gorbman's translator's commentary at the beginning of the endnote section for chapter 6, "Phantom Audio-Vision," in Michel Chion, *Audio-Vision: Sound on Screen*, trans. Claudia Gorbman, with a foreword by Walter Murch (New York: Columbia University Press, 1994), 218. Italics in the original.

23. Modleski, *The Women Who Knew Too Much*, 113.

Bibliography

Abel, Richard. *French Film Theory and Criticism*, Vol. I: *A History/Anthology 1907–1939*. 2 vols. Princeton, NJ: Princeton University Press, 1993.

Agamben, Giorgio. *"What Is an Apparatus?" and Other Essays*. Edited by Werner Hamacher. Translated by David Kishik and Stefan Pedatella. Stanford, CA: Stanford University Press, 2009.

Aguilera Skvirsky, Salomé. *The Process Genre: Cinema and the Aesthetic of Labor*. Durham, NC: Duke University Press, 2020.

Allen, Richard. "Hitchcock and Cavell." *Journal of Aesthetics and Art Criticism* 64, no. 1 (2006): 43–54.

Allen, Richard. "Hitchcock and the Wandering Woman: The Influence of Italian Art Cinema on *The Birds*." *Hitchcock Annual* 18 (2013): 149–194.

Allen, Richard. "Hitchcock's Color Designs." In *Color: The Film Reader*, edited by Angela Dalle Vacche and Brian Price, 131–144. New York: Routledge, 2006.

Allen, Richard. "*The Lodger* and the Origins of Hitchcock's Aesthetic." *Hitchcock Annual* 10 (2001): 38–78.

Araujo, Mateus. "Chantal Akerman, Between the Mother and the World." Translated by Mark Cohen. *Film Quarterly* 70, no. 1 (2016): 32–38.

Atanasov, Svet. "The Lodger: A Story of the London Fog / Downhill Blu-ray Review." Blu-ray.com, May 27, 2017, https://www.blu-ray.com/movies/The-Lodger-A-Story-of-the-London-Fog-and-Downhill-Blu-ray/122277/#Review.

Auiler, Dan. *Hitchcock Lost: The Lost Silent Hitchcock and Frenzy 67*. Kindle edition, 2013.

Auiler, Dan. *Hitchcock's Secret Notebooks*. London: Bloomsbury, 1999.

Aumont, Jacques. "Griffith—The Frame, the Figure." Translated by Judith Ayling and Thomas Elaesser. In *Early Cinema: Space, Frame, Narrative*, edited by Thomas Elsaesser with Adam Barker, 348–359. London: BFI Publishing, 1990.

B., O. "Advance Monologue." *Close Up* 7, no. 2 (August 1930): 146–147.

Baetens, Jan. *The Film Photonovel: A Cultural History of Forgotten Adaptations*. Austin: University of Texas Press, 2019.

Baetens, Jan, and Charlotte Pylyser. "Comics and Time." In *The Routledge Companion to Comics*, edited by Frank Bramlett, Roy T Cook, and Aaron Meskin, 303–311. New York: Routledge, 2017.

Balázs, Béla. *Theory of the Film: Character and Growth of a New Art*. Translated by Edith Bone. New York: Dover, 1970; London: Dennis Dobson, 1952.

Bantman, Constance. *Jean Grave and the Networks of French Anarchism, 1854–1939*. London: Palgrave, 2021.

Barr, Charles. "Amnesia and Schizophrenia." In *All Our Yesterdays: 90 Years of British Cinema*, edited by Charles Barr, 1–29. London: British Film Institute, in association with the Museum of Modern Art, New York, 1986.

Barr, Charles. "Before *Blackmail*: Silent British Cinema." In *The British Cinema Book*, edited by Robert Murphy, 145–154. London: British Film Institute, 2009.

Barr, Charles. "Deserter or Honored Exile? Views of Hitchcock from Wartime Britain." In *The Hitchcock Annual Anthology*, edited by Sidney Gottlieb and Richard Allen, 82–96. London: Wallflower Press, 2009.

Barr, Charles. *English Hitchcock*. Moffat: Cameron & Hollis, 1999.

Barr, Charles. "Hitchcock and Early Filmmakers." In *A Companion to Alfred Hitchcock*, edited by Thomas Leitch and Leland Poague, 48–66. Chichester: Wiley-Blackwell, 2011.

Batchelor, David. *The Luminous and the Grey*. London: Reaktion Books, 2014.

Bazin, André. "An Aesthetic of Reality: Cinematic Realism and the Italian School of Liberation." In *What Is Cinema?*, translated and edited by Hugh Gray, 2:16–40. 2 vols. Berkeley: University of California Press, 1967.

Bazin, André. "In Defense of Mixed Cinema." In *What Is Cinema?*, translated and edited by Hugh Gray 1:53–75. 2 vols. Berkeley: University of California Press, 1967; 2005.

Bazin, André. "The Life and Death of Superimposition." In *Bazin at Work: Major Essays and Reviews from the Forties and Fifties*, translated by Alain Piette and Bert Cardullo, edited by Bert Cardullo, 73–76. New York: Routledge, 1997.

Bazin, André. *Qu'est-ce que le cinéma?* 2 vols. Paris: Cerf, 1958.

Bazin, André. "Remade in USA." *Cahiers du cinéma* 2, no. 11 (1952): 54–59.

Bazin, André. "*Umberto D*: A Great Work." In *What Is Cinema?*, translated and edited by Hugh Gray, 2:79–82. 2 vols. Berkeley: University of California Press, 1967; 1971.

Bazin, André. "William Wyler, or the Jansenist of Directing." In *Bazin at Work: Major Essays and Reviews from the Forties and Fifties*, edited by Bert Cardullo, translated by Alain Piette and Bert Cardullo, 1–22. London: Routledge, 1997.

Belfrage, Cedric, ed. *All Is Grist*. London: Parallax Press, 1997.

Belting, Hans. *Likeness and Presence: A History of the Image before the Era of Art*. Translated by Edmund Jephcott. Chicago: University of Chicago Press, 1994.

Belton, John. "Color and meaning in *Marnie*." In *Color and the Moving Image: History, Theory, Aesthetics, Archive*, edited by Simon Brown, Sarah Street, and Liz Watkins, 150–159. New York: Routledge, 2013.

Belton, John. "Hitchcock and the Classical Paradigm." In *After Hitchcock: Influence, Imitation, and Intertextuality*, edited by David Boyd and R. Barton Palmer, 235–247. Austin: University of Texas Press, 2006.

Belton, John. "Introduction: Spectacle and Narrative." In *Alfred Hitchcock's Rear Window*, edited by John Belton, 1–2. Cambridge: Cambridge University Press, 2000.

Bennett, Charles. *Hitchcock's Partner in Suspense: The Life of Screenwriter Charles Bennett*. Lexington: University Press of Kentucky, 2014.

Billheimer, John. *Hitchcock and the Censors*. Lexington: University Press of Kentucky, 2019.

Bishop, Kyle William. "The Threat of the Gothic Patriarchy in Alfred Hitchcock's *The Birds*." *Rocky Mountain Review* 65, no. 2 (Fall 2011): 135–147.

Bolter, Jay David, and Richard Grusin. *Remediation: Understanding New Media*. Cambridge, MA: MIT Press, 1999.

Bonitzer, Pascal. "*Notorious*." In *Everything You Always Wanted to Know about Lacan (But were Afraid to Ask Hitchcock)*, edited by Slavoj Žižek, 151–154. London: Verso, 1992.

Bordwell, David. "Classical Hollywood Cinema: Narrational Principles and Procedures." In *Narrative, Apparatus, Ideology: A Film Theory Reader*, edited by Philip Rosen, 17–34. New York: Columbia University Press, 1986.

Bordwell, David. *Narration in the Fiction Film*. Madison: University of Wisconsin Press, 1985; London: Routledge, 1987.

Bordwell, David, and Kristin Thompson. *Film Art: An Introduction*. 5th ed. New York: McGraw Hill, 1997.

Bordwell, David, Kristin Thompson, and Janet Staiger. *The Classical Hollywood Cinema: Film Style and Mode of Production to 1960*. New York: Columbia University Press 1985; London: Routledge, 2019.

Borthwick, A. T. *Daily News*, London ed., December 3, 1936, 9.

Branigan, Edward. *Point of View in the Cinema: A Theory of Narration and Subjectivity in Classical Film*. New York: Mouton Publishers, 1984.

Brill, Lesley. *The Hitchcock Romance: Love and Irony in Hitchcock's Films*. Princeton, NJ: University of Princeton Press, 1988.

Bronfen, Elizabeth. "Screening and Disclosing Fantasy: Rear Projection in Hitchcock." *Screen* 56, no. 1 (2015): 1–24.

Brooks, Peter. *The Melodramatic Imagination: Balzac, Henry James, Melodrama, and the Mode of Excess*. 2nd ed. New Haven, CT: Yale University Press, 1995.

Brower, Sue. "Channeling *Rear Window*." *Journal of Popular Film and Television* 44, no. 2 (2016): 89–98.

Bruno, Giuliana. *Atlas of Emotion: Journeys in Art, Architecture, and Film*. New York: Verso, 2002.

Buchanan, Barbara J. "Women Are a Nuisance: An Interview with Barbara J. Buchanan (1935)." In *Hitchcock on Hitchcock: Selected Writings and Interviews*, edited by Sidney Gottlieb, 79–81. Berkeley: University of California Press, 1997.

Capp, Corina. "A Translator's Note." In Chantal Akerman, *My Mother Laughs*. Translated by Corina Capp, 170–172. Brooklyn: The Song Cave, 2013.

Carlson, Matthew. "Conrad's *The Secret Agent*, Hitchcock's *Sabotage*, and the Inspiration of 'Public Uneasiness.'" In *Hitchcock and Adaptation: On the Page and Screen*, edited by Mark Osteen, 79–94. Lanham, MD: Rowman & Littlefield, 2014.

Carrigy, Megan. "Re-Staging the Cinema: *Psycho*, Film Spectatorship and the Redundant New Remake." *Screening the Past*, no. 34 (2012). http://www.screeningthepast.com/issue-34-untimely-cinema/re-staging-the-cinema-psycho-film-spectatorship-and-the-redundant-new-remake/.

Cavell, Stanley. *Contesting Tears: The Hollywood Melodrama of the Unknown Woman*. Chicago: University of Chicago Press, 1996.

Cavell, Stanley. "*North by Northwest*." *Critical Inquiry* 7, no. 4 (Summer 1981): 761–776.

Cavell, Stanley. *Pursuits of Happiness: The Hollywood Comedy of Remarriage*. Cambridge, MA: Harvard University Press, 1981.

Cavell, Stanley. *The World Viewed: Reflections on the Ontology of Film*. Enl. ed. Cambridge: Harvard University Press, 1979.

Chandler, Charlotte. *It's Only a Movie: Alfred Hitchcock, a Personal Biography*. New York: Simon & Schuster, 2005.

Chion, Michel. *Audio-Vision: Sound on Screen*. Translated by Claudia Gorbman, with a foreword by Walter Murch. New York: Columbia University Press, 1994.

Chion, Michel. "The Silence of the Loudspeakers; or, Why with Dolby Sound It Is the Film That Listens to Us." In *Soundscape: The School of Sound Lectures, 1998–2001*, edited by Larry Sider, Diane Freeman, and Jerry Sider, 150–154. London: Wallflower Press, 2003.

Clover, Carol J. *Men, Women, and Chain Saws: Gender in the Modern Horror Film*. Princeton, NJ: Princeton University Press, 1992.

Coetzee, J. M. "The Mind of Apartheid: Geoffrey Cronjé (1907–)." *Social Dynamics* 17, no. 1 (1991): 1–35.

Coffin, Lesley L., *Hitchcock's Stars: Alfred Hitchcock and the Hollywood Studio System*. Lanham, MD: Rowman & Littlefield, 2014.

Cohen, Paula Marantz. "The Ideological Transformation of Conrad's *The Secret Agent* into Hitchcock's *Sabotage*." *Literature Film Quarterly* 22, no. 3 (1994): 199–209.

Connelly, Thomas J. *Cinema of Confinement*. Evanson, IL: Northwestern University Press, 2019.

Conrad, Joseph. *The Secret Agent*. 1907; London: Collector's Library, 2005.

Cook, Pam, and Mieke Bernink, ed. *The Cinema Book*. 2nd ed. London: BFI Publishing, 1999.

Cotten, Joseph. *Vanity Will Get You Somewhere: An Autobiography*. 2nd ed. San Jose, CA: toExcel, 2000.

Counts, Kyle B., and Steve Rubin. "The Making of Alfred Hitchcock's *The Birds*." *Cinefantastique* 10, no. 2 (Fall 1980): 14–35.

Danks, Adrian. "Being in Two Places at the Same Time: The Forgotten Geography of Rear Projection." In *B Is for Bad Cinema: Aesthetics, Politics, and Cultural Value*, edited by Claire Perkins and Constantine Verevis, 65–84. Albany: State University of New York Press, 2014.

Deleuze, Gilles. *Cinema 1: The Movement-Image*. Translated by Hugh Tomlinson and Barbara Habberjam. 1983; Minneapolis: University of Minnesota Press, 1986; London: Continuum, 2009.

Deleuze, Gilles. *Cinema 2: The Time-Image*. Translated by Hugh Tomlinson and Robert Galeta. 1985; Minneapolis: University of Minnesota Press, 1997.

Deleuze, Gilles, and Félix Guattari. *A Thousand Plateaus: Capitalism and Schizophrenia*. Translated by Brian Massumi. 1980; London: Continuum, 1987.

Desser, David. "'Crazed Heat': Nakahira Ko and the Transnational Self-Remake." In *Transnational Film Remakes*, edited by Iain Robert Smith and Constantine Verevis, 164–176. Edinburgh: Edinburgh University Press, 2017.

Doane, Mary Ann. *The Desire to Desire: The Women's Film of the 1940s*. Bloomington: Indiana University Press, 1987.

Dominijanni, Ida. "The Contact Word." In *Another Mother: Diotima and the Symbolic Order of Italian Feminism*, edited by Cesare Casarino and Andrea Righi, translated by Mark William Epstein, 33–65. Minneapolis: University of Minnesota Press, 2018.

Douchet, Jean. "Hitch and His Public." In *Cahiers du Cinéma, 1960–1968: New Wave, New Cinema, Reevaluating Hollywood*, edited by Jim Hillier, 150–157. 1960; Cambridge, MA: Harvard University Press, 1983.

Druxman, Michael B. *Make It Again, Sam: A Survey of Movie Remakes*. South Brunswick, NJ: A. S. Barnes, 1975.

Dudley, Andrew. "The Effect of Miracles and the Miracle of Effects: Bazin's Faith in Evolution." In *Special Effects on the Screen: Faking the View from Méliès to Motion Capture*, edited by Marc Furstenau and Martin Lefebvre, 451–474. Amsterdam: Amsterdam University Press, 2022.

Du Maurier, Daphne. *Rebecca*. 1938; London: Virago, 2015.

Durham, Carolyn A. *Double Takes: Culture and Gender in French Films and Their American Remakes*. Hanover, NH: University Press of New England, 1998.

Dyer, Richard. *Lethal Repetition: Serial Killing in European Cinema*. London: British Film Institute, 2015.

Eberwein, Robert "Remakes and Cultural Studies." In *Play It Again Sam: Retakes on Remakes*, edited by Andrew Horton and Stuart Y. McDougal, 15–33. Berkeley: University of California Press, 1998.

Eisenstein, Sergei. "On Colour." In *Color: The Film Reader*, edited by Angela Dalle Vacche and Brian Price, 105–117. New York: Routledge, 2006.

"L'électricité chez soi." Illustration. *Le magasin pittoresque*, May 31, 1891, 155.

Elsaesser, Thomas, ed. *Harun Farocki: Working on the Sightlines*. Amsterdam: Amsterdam University Press, 2004.

Fabe, Marilyn. *Closely Watched Films: An Introduction to the Art of Narrative Film Technique*. Berkeley: University of California Press, 2014.

Fairfax, Daniel. *The Red Years of Cahiers du Cinéma (1968–1973)*, Vol. II: *Aesthetics and Ontology*. Amsterdam: Amsterdam University Press, 2021.

Fawell, John. *Hitchcock's Rear Window: The Well-Made Film*. Carbondale: Southern Illinois University Press, 2001.

Florin, Bo. *Transition and Transformation: Victor Sjöström in Hollywood 1923–1930*. Amsterdam: Amsterdam University Press, 2013

Forrest, Jennifer, and Leonard R. Koos, eds. *Dead Ringers: The Remake in Theory and Practice*. Albany: State University of New York Press, 2002.

Frazer, James George. *The Golden Bough: A Study of Magic and Religion*. 1890; Floating Press e-book, 2009.

Frow, John. "Review: *Play It Again, Sam: Retakes on Remakes*." *Screening the Past*, July 1, 1999. http://www.screeningthepast.com/issue-7-reviews/play-it-again-sam-retakes-on-remakes/.

Garrett, Greg, Janet Leigh, Tippi Hedren, Karen Black, Suzanne Pleshette, and Eva Marie Saint. "Hitchcock's Women on Hitchcock: A Panel Discussion with Janet Leigh, Tippi Hedren, Karen Black, Suzanne Pleshette, and Eva Marie Saint." *Literature/Film Quarterly* 27, no. 2 (1999): 78–89.

Ginzburg, Carlo. "Morelli, Freud and Sherlock Holmes: Clues and Scientific Method." *History Workshop Journal* 9, no. 1 (March 1980): 5–36.

Gottlieb, Sidney. "Early Hitchcock: The German Influence." In *Framing Hitchcock: Selected Essays from the Hitchcock Annual*, edited by Sidney Gottlieb and Christopher Brookhouse, 35–58. Detroit: Wayne State University Press, 2002.

Gottlieb, Sidney. "Introduction." In *Framing Hitchcock: Selected Essays from the Hitchcock Annual*, edited by Sidney Gottlieb and Christopher Brookhouse, 13–32. Detroit: Wayne State University Press, 2002.

Gottlieb, Sidney. "The Unknown Hitchcock: Watchtower over Tomorrow." *The Hitchcock Annual* 5 (1996–1997): 117–30.

Graham, Peter, and Ginette Vincendeau, eds. *The French New Wave: Critical Landmarks*. London: British Film Institute, 2009.

Greenberg, Harvey Roy. "Raiders of the Lost Text: Remaking as Contested Homage in *Always*." *Journal of Popular Film and Television* 18, no. 4 (1991): 164–172.

Greven, David. "The Dark Side of Blondeness: *Vertigo* and Race." *Screen* 59, no. 1 (2018): 59–79.

Greven, David. *Intimate Violence: Hitchcock, Sex, and Queer Theory*. New York: Oxford University Press, 2017.

Groensteen, Thierry. *The System of Comics*. Translated by Bart Beaty and Nick Nguyen. 1999; Jackson: University Press of Mississippi, 2007.

Grossvogel, David I. *Didn't You Used to Be Depardieu?: Film as Cultural Marker in France and Hollywood*. New York: Peter Lang, 2002.

Gunning, Tom. *The Films of Fritz Lang: Allegories of Vision and Modernity*. London: BFI Publishing, 2000.

Gunning, Tom. "A Hand for Hitchcock." *Crisis & Critique* 7, no. 2 (2020): 105–127.

Gunning, Tom. "In and Out of the Frame: Paintings in Hitchcock." In *Casting a Shadow: Creating the Alfred Hitchcock Film*, edited by Will Schmenner, Corinne Granof, and David Alan Robertson, 29–48. Evanston, IL: Mary and Leigh Block Museum of Art, Northwestern University Press, 2007.

Gunning, Tom. "In Your Face: Physiognomy, Photography, and the Gnostic Mission of Early Film." *Modernism/Modernity* 4, no. 1 (1997): 1–29.

Gunning, Tom. "Phantom Images and Modern Manifestations: Spirit Photography, Magic Theater, Trick Films, and Photography's Uncanny." In *Fugitive Images: From Photography to Video*, edited by Patrice Petro, 42–71. Bloomington: Indiana University Press, 1995.

Gunning, Tom. "To Scan a Ghost: The Ontology of Mediated Vision." *Grey Room* 26 (Winter 2007): 94–127.

Halberstam, Judith. *Skin Shows: Gothic Horror and the Technology of Monsters*. Durham, NC: Duke University Press, 1995.

Hansen, Miriam Bratu. *Cinema and Experience: Siegfried Kracauer, Walter Benjamin, Theodor Adorno*. Berkeley: University of California Press, 2012.

Hansen, Miriam Bratu. "The Mass Production of the Senses: Classical Cinema as Vernacular Modernism." *Modernism/Modernity* 6, no. 2 (1999): 59–77.

Hansen, Miriam Bratu. "Vernacular Modernism: Tracking Cinema on a Global Scale." In *World Cinemas, Transnational Perspectives*, edited by Natasa Ďurovičová and Kathleen A. Newman, 287–314. New York: Routledge, 2010.

Hardt, Michael, and Antonio Negri. *Commonwealth*. Cambridge, MA: Belknap Press of Harvard University Press, 2009.

Hardt, Michael, and Antonio Negri. *Multitude: War and Democracy in the Age of Empire* New York: Penguin Press, 2004.

Hark, Ina Rae. "Keeping Your Amateur Standing: Audience Participation and Good Citizenship in Hitchcock's Political Films." *Cinema Journal* 29, no. 2 (1990): 8–22.

Harris, Thomas. "The Building of Popular Images." In *Stardom: Industry of Desire*, edited by Christine Gledhill, 41–45. London: Routledge, 2005.

Heath, Stephen. *Questions of Cinema*. London: Macmillan, 1981.

Hedren, Tippi. *Tippi: A Memoir*. New York: William Morrow, 2016.

Hitchcock, Alfred. "Direction." In *Hitchcock on Hitchcock: Selected Writings and Interviews*, edited by Sidney Gottlieb, 253–261. Berkeley: University of California Press, 1997.

Hitchcock, Alfred. "Let 'Em Play God (1948)." In *Hitchcock on Hitchcock: Selected Writings and Interviews*, edited by Sidney Gottlieb, 113–115. London: Faber & Faber, 1995.

Hitchcock, Alfred. "My Most Exciting Picture (1948)." In *Hitchcock on Hitchcock: Selected Writings and Interviews*, edited by Sidney Gottlieb, 275–284. Berkeley: University of California Press, 1995.

Hitchcock, Alfred. "On Style (1963)." In *Hitchcock on Hitchcock: Selected Writings and Interviews*, edited by Sidney Gottlieb, 285–302. Berkeley: University of California Press, 1997.

Hitchcock, Alfred. "Search for the Sun (1937)." In *Hitchcock on Hitchcock: Selected Writings and Interviews*, edited by Sidney Gottlieb, 250–252. London: Faber & Faber, 1995.

Hoberman, J. "The Twinned Evils of *Nosferatu*." *Tablet*, May 19, 2020. https://www.tablet mag.com/sections/arts-letters/articles/nosferatu-hoberman-murnau.

Horton, Andrew, and Stuart Y. McDougal. "Introduction." In *Play It Again Sam: Retakes on Remakes*, edited by Andrew Horton and Stuart Y. McDougal, 1–11. Berkeley: University of California Press, 1998.

Hunter, Evan. *The Birds* (1962). 2nd rev. *Daily Script*, http://www.dailyscript.com/scripts/ The_Birds.html.

Irigaray, Luce. "Women on the Market." In *This Sex Which Is Not One*. Translated by Catherine Porter and Carolyn Burke, 170–191. Ithaca, NY: Cornell University Press, 1985.

Isaacs, Bruce. *The Art of Pure Cinema: Hitchcock and His Imitators*. New York: Oxford University Press, 2020.

Isaacs, Bruce. "Aural Abstraction in Hitchcock and De Palma." Paper presented at the Sydney Screen Studies Network Seminar Program: Across Screens and Borders, University of New South Wales, Sydney, September 2019.

Jacobowitz, Florence. "Hitchcock and Feminist Criticism: From *Rebecca* to *Marnie*." In *A Companion to Alfred Hitchcock*, edited by Thomas Leitch and Leland Poague, 452–472. West Sussex: Wiley-Blackwell, 2011.

Jacobs, Lea. *The Decline of Sentiment: American Film in the 1920s*. Berkeley: University of California Press, 2008.

Jacobs, Steven. "Color and Containment: Domestic Spaces and Restrained Palettes in Hitchcock's Color Films." In *Color and the Moving Image*, edited by Simon Brown, Sarah Street, and Liz Watkins, 179–189. New York: Routledge, 2013.

Jacobs, Steven. *The Wrong House: The Architecture of Alfred Hitchcock*. Rotterdam: 010 Publishers, 2007.

Jagose, Annamarie. *Inconsequence: Lesbian Representation and the Logic of Sexual Sequence*. Ithaca, NY: Cornell University Press, 2002.

Jeffries, Dru. *Comic Book Film Style*. Austin: University of Texas Press, 2017.

Kalmus, Natalie. "Color Consciousness." In *Color: The Film Reader*, edited by Angela Dalle Vacche and Brian Price, 24–29. New York: Routledge, 2006.

Kapsis, Robert E. *Hitchcock: The Making of a Reputation*. Chicago: University of Chicago Press, 1992

Kerzoncuf, Alain, and Charles Barr. *Hitchcock Lost and Found: The Forgotten Films*. Lexington: University Press of Kentucky, 2015.

Knight, Arthur. "Conversation with Alfred Hitchcock." In *Alfred Hitchcock: Interviews*, edited by Sydney Gottlieb, 160–185. Jackson: University Press of Mississippi, 2003.

Kresan, Dawn Marie. "*The Birds* (1963): Tippi Hedren's Response." *Queen's Quarterly* 120, no. 3 (Fall 2013): 464–466.

Labio, Catherine. "The Architecture of Comics." *Critical Inquiry* 41, no. 2 (2015): 312–343.

Laine, Tarja. *Feeling Cinema: Emotional Dynamics in Film Studies*. London: Continuum, 2011.

Langlands, Rebecca. "Britishness or Englishness? The Historical Problem of National Identity in Britain." *Nations and Nationalism* 6, no. 1 (1999): 53–69.

Lazzarato, Maurizio. "Immaterial Labor." In *Radical Thought in Italy: A Potential Politics*, edited by Paolo Virno and Michael Hardt, 133–147. Minneapolis: University of Minnesota Press, 1996.

Lehman, Ernest. *North by Northwest*. London: Faber & Faber, 1999.

Leitch, Thomas M. "How to Steal from Hitchcock." In *After Hitchcock: Influence, Imitation, and Intertextuality*, edited by David Boyd and R. Barton Palmer, 251–270. 1990; Austin: University of Texas Press, 2006.

Leitch, Thomas M. "Twice-Told Tales: Disavowal and the Rhetoric of the Remake." In *Dead Ringers: The Remake in Theory and Practice*, edited by Jennifer Forrest and Leonard R. Koos, 37–62. Albany: State University of New York Press, 2001.

Lejeune, C. J., "One for all, and all for one." *Sunday Observer*, London ed., December 6, 1936, 14.

Lesser, Wendy. *His Other Half: Men Looking at Women Through Art*. Cambridge, MA: Harvard University Press, 1991.

Loock, Kathleen. "Remaking Funny Games: Michael Haneke's Cross-Cultural Experiment." In *Transnational Film Remakes*, edited by Iain Robert Smith and Constantine Verevis, 177–194. Edinburgh: Edinburgh University Press, 2017.

Lowndes, Marie Belloc. *The Lodger*. Chicago: Academy Chicago Publishers, 2010.

Macklin, Anthony, "'It's the Manner of Telling': An Interview with Alfred Hitchcock (1976)." In *Hitchcock on Hitchcock, Vol. 2: Selected Writings and Interviews*, edited by Sidney Gottlieb, 49–57. Berkeley: University of California Press, 2015.

Manovich, Lev. *The Language of New Media*. Cambridge, MA: MIT Press, 2001.

"*The Manxman*." *Bioscope*. January 1929, 38.

Massumi, Brian. *Parables for the Virtual: Movement, Affect, Sensation*. Durham, NC: Duke University Press, 2002.

Mazon, Lucy. *Encore Hollywood: Remaking French Cinema*. London: BFI Publishing, 2000.

McCay, Winsor. "Little Nemo in Slumberland." Cartoon (series). *New York Herald*, 1905–1914.

McCombe, John P. "'Oh, I see . . .': *The Birds* and the Culmination of Hitchcock's Hyper-Romantic Vision." *Cinema Journal* 44, no. 3 (Spring 2005): 64–80.

McDougal, Stuart Y. "The Director Who Knew Too Much: Hitchcock Remakes Himself." In *Play It Again Sam: Retakes on Remakes*, edited by Andrew Horton and Stuart Y. McDougal, 52–69. University of California Press, 1998.

McElhaney, Joe. *The Death of Classical Cinema: Hitchcock, Lang, Minnelli*. Albany: State University of New York Press, 2006.

McElhaney, Joe. "Hitchcock, Metteur-en-scène: 1954–60." In *A Companion to Alfred Hitchcock*, edited by Thomas Leitch and Leland Poague, 329–346. West Sussex: Wiley-Blackwell, 2011.

McGilligan, Patrick. *Alfred Hitchcock: a Life in Darkness and Light*. Chichester: John Wiley & Sons, 2003.

McGowan, Todd. "Hitchcock's Ethics of Suspense: Psychoanalysis and the Devaluation of the Object." In *A Companion to Alfred Hitchcock*, edited by Thomas Leitch and Leland Poague, 508–528. West Sussex: Wiley-Blackwell, 2011.

McLaughlin, James. "All in the Family: Alfred Hitchcock's Shadow of a Doubt." In *A Hitchcock Reader*, edited by Marshall Deutelbaum and Leland Poague, 145–155. Malden, MA: Wiley-Blackwell, 2009.

Miller, D. A. *Hidden Hitchcock*. Chicago: University of Chicago Press, 2016.

Miller, Henry K. *The First True Hitchcock*. Oakland: University of California Press, 2022.

Miller, Hildy. "Refiguring *The Birds* as Modern Female Gothic in the Kennedy Era." *Rocky Mountain Review* 74, no. 2 (Fall 2020): 133–155.

Mitchell, W. J. T. *Picture Theory*. Chicago: University of Chicago Press, 1994.

Mitchell, W. J. T. "There Are No Visual Media." *Journal of Visual Culture* 4, no. 2 (2005): 257–266.

Modleski, Tania. "Remastering the Master: Hitchcock after Feminism." *New Literary History* 47, no. 1 (2016): 135–158.

Modleski, Tania, "Suspicion: Collusion and Resistance in the Work of Hitchcock's Female Collaborators." In *A Companion to Alfred Hitchcock*, edited by Thomas Leitch and Leland Poague, 162–180. Chichester: Whiley-Blackwell, 2011.

Modleski, Tania. *The Women Who Knew Too Much: Hitchcock and Feminist Theory*. 3rd ed. 1988; New York: Routledge, 2016.

Monaghan, Whitney, Belinda Glynn, and Kate Warren eds. "About." *Peephole Journal*. http://peepholejournal.tv/about/.

Moral, Tony Lee. *The Making of Hitchcock's "The Birds."* Harpenden: Oldcastle, 2013.

Morgan, Daniel. "The Afterlife of Superimposition." In *Opening Bazin: Postwar Film Theory and Its Afterlife*, edited by Dudley Andrew, 127–141. New York: Oxford University Press, 2011.

Mulvey, Laura. "A Clumsy Sublime." *Film Quarterly* 60, no. 3 (2007): 3.

Mulvey, Laura. *Death 24x a Second: Stillness and the Moving Image*. 2006; London: Reaktion Books, 2007.

Mulvey, Laura. "Visual Pleasure and Narrative Cinema." *Screen* 16, no. 3 (1975): 6–18.

Muraro, Luisa. "To Knit or to Crochet: A Political-Linguistic Tale on the Enmity between Metaphor and Metonymy." In *Another Mother: Diotima and the Symbolic Order of Italian Feminism*, edited by Cesare Casarino and Andrea Righi, translated by Mark William Epstein, 67–120. Minneapolis: University of Minnesota Press, 2018.

Nagib, Lúcia, and Anne Jerslev, eds. *Impure Cinema: Intermedial and Intercultural Approaches to Film*. London: I. B. Tauris, 2014.

Negri, Sabrina. "I Saw, Therefore I Know? Alfred Hitchcock's *The Wrong Man* and the Epistemological Potential of the Photographic Image." *Film Criticism* 41, no. 1 (2017). https://quod.lib.umich.edu/f/fc/13761232.0041.107/--i-saw-therefore-i-know-alfred-hitchcocks-the-wrong-man?rgn=main;view=fulltext.

Osteen, Mark. "'It Doesn't Pay to Antagonize the Public': Sabotage and Hitchcock's Audience." *Literature and Film Quarterly* 28, no. 4 (2020): 259–268.

Osteen, Mark, ed. *Hitchcock and Adaptation: On the Page and Screen*. Lanham, MD: Rowman & Littlefield, 2014.

Paglia, Camille. *The Birds*. London: BFI Publishing, 1998.

Pallasmaa, Juhani. *The Architecture of Image: Existential Space in Cinema*. Helsinki: Rakennustieto Oy, 2001.

Peirce, Charles Sanders. *Peirce on Signs: Writings on Semiotic by Charles Sanders Peirce*. Chapel Hill: University of North Carolina Press, 1991.

Perkins, V. F. *Film as Film: Understanding and Judging Movies*. New York: Da Capo Press, 1993.

Perkins, V. F. "*Rope* (1963)." In *V. F. Perkins on Movies: Collected Shorter Film Criticism*, edited by Douglas Pye, 151–161. Detroit: Wayne State University Press, 2020.

Petersen, Christina G. "Impossible Spaces: Gothic Special Effects and Feminine Subjectivity." In *Gothic Heroines on Screen: Representation, Interpretation, and Feminist Inquiry*, edited by Tamar Jeffers McDonald and Frances Kamm, 57–69. London: Routledge, 2019.

Petrie, Duncan. "Innovation and Economy: The Contribution of the Gainsborough Cinematographer." In *Gainsborough Pictures*, edited by Pam Cook, 118–136. London: Continuum, 1997.

Peucker, Brigitte. "The Cut of Representation: Painting and Sculpture in Hitchcock." In *Alfred Hitchcock: Centenary Essays*, edited by Richard Allen and S. Ishii-Gonzalès, 141–156. London: BFI Publishing, 1999.

Piso, Michele. "Mark's Marnie." In *A Hitchcock Reader*. Edited by Marshall Deutelbaum and Leland Pogue, 288–303. Ames: Iowa State University Press, 1986.

Plamper, Jan. *The History of Emotions: An Introduction*. Translated by Keith Tribe. Oxford: Oxford University Press, 2017.

Pomerance, Murray. *Marnie*. London: Palgrave Macmillan, 2014.

Pomerance, Murray. "Some Hitchcockian Shots." In *A Companion to Alfred Hitchcock*, edited by Thomas Leitch and Leland Poague, 237–252. Chichester: Wiley-Blackwell, 2011.

Prince, Stephen. *Digital Visual Effects in Cinema: The Seduction of Reality*. New Brunswick, NJ: Rutgers University Press, 2012.

Pudovkin, V. I. *Film Technique*. Translated by I. Montagu. 2nd ed. London: Geo. Newnes, 1933.

Rajewsky, Irina O. "Intermediality, Intertextuality, and Remediation: A Literary Perspective on Intermediality." *Intermédialités / Intermediality* 6 (2005): 43–64.

Ravetto-Biagioli, Kriss. "*Vertigo* and the Vertiginous History of Film Theory." *Camera Obscura* 25, no. 3 (2011): 101–141.

Restivo, Angelo. "Hitchcock and the Postmodern." In *A Companion to Alfred Hitchcock*, edited by Thomas Leitch and Leland Poague, 555–571. West Sussex: Wiley-Blackwell, 2011.

Ribbat, Christoph. *Flickering Light: A History of Neon*. London: Reaktion Books, 2011.

Richter, Gerhard. "Miniatures: Harun Farocki and the Cinematic Non-Event." *Journal of Visual Culture* 3, no. 3 (2004): 367–271.

Rinaldi, Thomas. *New York Neon*. New York: W. W. Norton, 2012

Rivette, Jacques. "De l'abjection." *Cahiers du cinéma* 120 (June 1961): 54–55.

Rohmer, Eric, and Claude Chabrol. *Hitchcock: The First Forty-Four Films*. Translated by Stanley Hochman. Paris: Classiques du cinema, 1957; New York: Frederick Ungar Publishing, 1979.

Rothman, William. *Hitchcock: The Murderous Gaze*. 2nd ed. Albany: State University of New York Press, 2014.

Rothman, William. *The "I" of the Camera: Essays in Film Criticism, History, and Aesthetics*. 2nd ed. Cambridge: Cambridge University Press, 2004.

Rothman, William. *Must We Kill the Thing We Love?: Emersonian Perfectionism and the Films of Alfred Hitchcock*. New York: Columbia University Press, 2014.

Rubin, Martin. *Thrillers*. Cambridge: Cambridge University Press, 1999.

Ryall, Tom. *Alfred Hitchcock and the British Cinema*. London: Athlone Press, 1996.

Salt, Barry. "From Caligari to Who?" *Sight and Sound* 48, no. 2 (1979): 119–123.

Sawicki, Mark. *Filming the Fantastic: A Guide to Visual Effects Cinematography*. Waltham, MA: Focal Press, 2011.

Schaeffer, Joy C. "Must We Burn Hitchcock? (Re)Viewing Trauma and Effecting Solidarity with *The Birds* (1963)." *Quarterly Review of Film and Video* 32, no. 4 (2015): 329–343.

Schantz, Ned. "Hitchcock's Shadow Scenes." *Camera Obscura* 25, no. 1 (2010): 1–27.

Schatz, Thomas. "Hitchcock and the Studio System." In *The Cambridge Companion to Alfred Hitchcock*, edited by Jonathan Freedman, 25–39. New York: Cambridge University Press, 2015.

Shandley, Robert R. *Runaway Romances: Hollywood's Postwar Tour of Europe*. Philadelphia: Temple University Press, 2009.

Silverman, Kaja, and Harun Farocki. *Speaking about Godard*. New York: New York University Press, 1998.

Singer, Irving. *Three Philosophical Filmmakers: Hitchcock, Welles, Renoir*. Cambridge, MA: MIT Press, 2004.

Smith, Iain Robert, and Constantine Verevis. "Introduction: Transnational Film Remakes." In *Transnational Film Remakes*, edited by Iain Robert Smith and Constantine Verevis, 1–18. Edinburgh: Edinburgh University Press, 2017.

Smith, Steven C. *A Heart at Fire's Center: The Life and Music of Bernard Herrmann*. Berkeley: University of California Press, 2002.

Smith, Susan. *Hitchcock: Suspense, Humour and Tone*. London: British Film Institute, 2000.

Sobchack, Vivian. "From Screen-Shape to Screen-Sphere: A Meditation in Media Res." In *Screens: From Materiality to Spectatorship*, edited by Dominique Chateau and José Moure, 157–175. Amsterdam: Amsterdam University Press, 2016.

Solomon, Vlad. *State Surveillance, Political Policing and Counter-Terrorism in Britain 1880–1914*. Woodbridge: Boydell Press, 2021.

Spoto, Donald. *The Dark Side of Genius: The Life of Alfred Hitchcock*. 1983; Boston: Da Capo Press, 1999; London: Collins, 1983. The London edition's title is *The Life of Alfred Hitchcock: The Dark Side of Genius*.

Spoto, Donald. *Spellbound by Beauty: Alfred Hitchcock and His Leading Ladies*. London: Arrow, 2009.

Staiger, Janet. "Creating the Brand: The Hitchcock Touch." In *The Cambridge Companion to Alfred Hitchcock*, edited by Jonathan Freedman, 40–56. New York: Cambridge University Press, 2015.

Stam, Robert. *Reflexivity in Film and Literature: From Don Quixote to Jean-Luc Godard* Ann Arbor, MI: UMI Research Press, 1992.

Stam, Robert, and Roberta Pearson. "Hitchcock's *Rear Window*: Reflexivity and the Critique of Voyeurism." In *A Hitchcock Reader*, edited by Marshall Deutelbaum and Leland A. Poague, 193–206. Ames: Iowa State University Press, 1986.

Steimatsky, Noa. *The Face of Film*. New York: Oxford University Press, 2017.

Strauven, Wanda. "Media Archaeology: Where Film History, Media Art, and New Media (Can) Meet." In *Preserving and Exhibiting Media Art: Challenges and Perspectives*, edited by Julia Noordegraaf, Cosetta G. Saba, Barbara Le Maître, and Vinzenz Hediger, 59–80. Amsterdam: Amsterdam University Press, 2013.

Street, Sarah. *British National Cinema*. New York: Routledge, 2009.

Street, Sarah, and Joshua Yumibe. *Chromatic Modernity: Color, Cinema, and Media of the 1920s*. New York: Columbia University Press, 2019.

Stefano, Joseph. *Psycho* (1959). *Screenplays for You*. https://sfy.ru/?script=psycho.

Tallents, Stephen. "The Projection of England." In *Public Relations and the Making of Modern Britain*, edited by Scott Anthony, 206–235. Manchester: Manchester University Press, 2012.

Terranova, Tiziana. "Free Labor: Producing Culture for the Digital Economy." *Social Text* 18, no. 2 (2000): 33–58.

Thompson, Kirsten Moana. "Rainbow Ravine: Colour and Animated Advertising in Times Square." In *The Colour Fantastic: Chromatic Worlds of Silent Cinema*, edited by Giovanna Fossati, Victoria Jackson, B. G. Lameris, Elif Rongen-Kaynakci, Sarah Street, and Joshua Yumibe, 161–177. Amsterdam: Amsterdam University Press, 2018.

Torlasco, Domietta. *The Heretical Archive: Digital Memory at the end of Film*. Minneapolis: University of Minnesota Press, 2013.

Truffaut, François. *The Films in My Life*. Translated by Leonard Mayhew. 1978; New York: Simon & Schuster/Touchstone, 1985.

Truffaut, Francois. *Hitchcock/Truffaut: The Definitive Study of Alfred Hitchcock*. Rev. ed. New York: Simon & Schuster, 1984.

Truffaut, François, and Helen G. Scott. *Hitchcock*. 1966; London: Faber & Faber/A Panther book, 1969, 2017; New York: Simon & Schuster/Touchstone, 1985, rev. ed.

Tsivian, Yuri. *Ivan the Terrible*. London: British Film Institute, 2002.

Turnock, Julie. *Plastic Reality: Special Effects, Technology, and the Emergence of 1970s Blockbuster Aesthetics*. New York: Columbia University Press, 2015.

"*Under Capricorn*: 70 Years On." *Movie: A Journal of Film Criticism*. Special collection. 2019. https://warwick.ac.uk/fac/arts/film/movie/capricorn/.

Van Eynde. Laurent. *Vertige de l'image: L'esthétique reflexive d' Alfred Hitchcock*. Paris: Presses Universitaires de France, 2011.

Verevis, Constantine. *Film Remakes*. Edinburgh: Edinburgh University Press, 2005.

Virno, Paolo. "Virtuosity and Revolution: The Political Theory of Exodus." In *Radical Thought in Italy: A Potential Politics*, edited by Paolo Virno and Michael Hardt, 189–212. Minneapolis: University of Minnesota Press, 1996.

Walker, Michael. *Hitchcock's Motifs*. Amsterdam: Amsterdam University Press, 2005.

Ware, Chris. *Building Stories*. New York: Pantheon, 2012.

Warner, Rick. "Difficult Work in a Popular Medium: Godard on 'Hitchcock's Method.'" *Critical Quarterly* 51, no. 3 (2009): 63–84.

Waugh, Norah. *The Cut of Men's Clothes*. New York: Theatre Arts Books, 1964.

Wear. Review of *The Woman Alone*, directed by Alfred Hitchcock. *Variety*, March 3, 1937, 14.

Webster, Walter. "Bombs and Villainy in London." *Sunday Pictorial*, London ed., December 6, 1936, 16.

Whissel, Kristen, and Charlie Keil. "Introduction." In *Editing and Special/Visual Effects*, edited by Kristen Whissel and Charlie Keil, 1–21. New Brunswick, NJ: Rutgers University Press, 2016.

White, Patricia. *Rebecca*. London: British Film Institute, 2021.

White, Susan. "A Surface Collaboration: Hitchcock and Performance." In *A Companion to Alfred Hitchcock*, edited by Thomas Leitch and Leland Poague, 181–197. West Sussex: Wiley-Blackwell, 2011.

Wilder, Thornton. *Our Town*. 1938; New York: HarperPerennial, 2013.

Williams, Linda. "Discipline and Fun: *Psycho* and Postmodern Cinema." In *Alfred Hitchcock's Psycho: A Casebook*, edited by Robert Kolker, 164–204. 2000; New York: Oxford University Press, 2004.

Williams, Raymond. *Television: Technology and Cultural Form*. Edited by Ederyn Williams. 1975; London: Taylor & Francis, 2005.

Wojcik, Pamela Robertson. *The Apartment Plot*. Durham, NC: Duke University Press, 2010.

Wojcik, Pamela Robertson. "The Author of This Claptrap: Cornell Woolrich, Alfred Hitchcock, and *Rear Window*." In *Hitchcock at the Source: The Auteur as Adapter*, edited by R. Barton Palmer and David Boyd, 213–227. Albany: State University of New York Press, 2011.

Wolf, Werner. "Literature and Music: Theory." In *Handbook of Intermediality. Literature–Image–Sound–Music*, edited by Gabriele Rippl, 459–474. Berlin: De Gruyter, 2015.

Wollen, Peter. "Hitch: A Tale of Two Cities London and Los Angeles." In *Hitchcock: Past and Future*, edited by Richard Allen and Sam Ishii-Gonzeles, 15–21. London: Routledge, 2004.

Wood, Christopher S. "Painting and Plurality." *The Yearbook of Comparative Literature* 56 (2010): 116–139.

Wood, Robin. *Hitchcock's Films Revisited*. New York: Columbia University Press, 1965/1989/2002; London: Faber & Faber, 1989.

Yacowar, Maurice. *Hitchcock's British Films*. 2nd ed. Detroit: Wayne State University Press, 2010.

Mediography

Akerman, Chantal, director. *Toute une nuit* (*A Whole Night*). Paradise Films, 1982.

Allégret, Marc, director. *Blanche Fury*. Cineguild, 1948.

Antonioni, Michelangelo, director. *Blow-Up*. Carlo Ponti Productions, 1966.

Barron, Craig. "New Interview with Craig Barron on *Rebecca*'s Visual Effects." *Rebecca*. Sony Criterion Collection Blu-ray, 2017.

Benjamin, Arthur, composer. "Cantata / The Storm Clouds." London Symphony Orchestra, 1956. Re-recorded on Bernstein, Elmer, conductor. *Bernard Herrmann Film Scores (From Citizen Kane to Taxi Driver)*. Royal Philharmonic Orchestra. Milan Records, 1993.

Bornedal, Ole, director. *Nattevagten* (*Nightwatch*). Thura Film, 1994.

Bornedal, Ole, director. *Nightwatch*. Dimension Films, 1997.

Bresson, Robert, director. *A Man Escaped*. Gaumont, 1956.

Buñuel, Luis, director. *Un Chien Andalou* (*An Andalusian Dog*). 1929.

Carpenter, John, director. *Halloween*. Compass International Pictures, 1978.

Clair, René, director. *Entr'acte*. Les Ballets Suédois, 1924.

Cromwell, John, Harold F. Kress, and Alfred Hitchcock. *Watchtower over Tomorrow*. US Office of War Information, 1945.

Crosland, Alan, director. *The Jazz Singer*. Warner Bros., 1927.

Day, Doris. "Que Sera Sera" ("Whatever Will Be, Will Be"). Written by Jay Livingston and Ray Evans. Recorded 1956. Columbia.

Desom, Jeff. *Rear Window Timelapse*. 2012. Art installation and online video, https://jeffdesom.com/portfolio/hitch.

Dreyer, Carl Theodor, director. *Ordet*. Palladium Film, 1955.

Duvivier, Julien, director. *Lydia*. Alexander Korda Films, 1941.

Eisenstein, Sergei, director. *Battleship Potemkin*. Mosfilm, 1925.

Farocki, Harun, director. *Counter-Music* (*Gegen-Musik*). Harun Farocki Filmproduktion, 2004.

Farocki, Harun, director. *Leben, BDR* (*How to Live in the Federal Republic of Germany*). Harun Farocki Filmproduktion, 1990.

Farocki, Haryn, director. *Stilleben* (*Still Life*). 3Sat, 1997.

Furie, Sidney J., director. *The Ipcress File*. The Rank Organisation, 1965.

Godard, Jean-Luc, director. *Histoire(s) du cinéma*. Canal+, 1989.

Godard, Jean-Luc, director. *Numéro deux* (*Number Two*). Anne-age-Bela, 1975.

Gordan, Douglas. *24 Hour Psycho*. 1993. Video art installation. Tramway, Glasgow.

Griffith, D. W., director. *An Unseen Enemy*. Biograph Company, 1912.

Griffith, D. W., director. *Way Down East*. D. W. Griffith Productions, 1920.

Hand, David, director. *Who Killed Cock Robin*. Walt Disney Productions, 1935.

Haneke, Michael, director. *Funny Games*. Filmfonds Wien, 1997.

Haneke, Michael, director. *Funny Games*. Celluloid Dreams, 2007.

Harrison, Joan, and Alfred Hitchcock, creators. *Alfred Hitchcock Presents*. Alfred J. Hitchcock Productions, 1955–1962.

Herrmann, Bernard. *Music from the Great Movie Thrillers*. Recorded 1968, 1969. Decca. Liner notes.

Hitchcock, Alfred. "Hitchcock-Truffaut Interview Excerpts." In *The Birds* [2013 Blu-ray]. Universal Studios, 1963.

Hitchcock, Alfred, director. *The 39 Steps*. Gaumont British Picture Corporation, 1935.

Hitchcock, Alfred, director. *Aventure Malgache*. Ministry of Information (UK), 1944.

Hitchcock, Alfred, director. *The Birds*. Alfred J. Hitchcock Productions, 1963.

Hitchcock, Alfred, director. *Blackmail*. British International Pictures, 1929.

Hitchcock, Alfred, director. *Bon Voyage*. Ministry of Information (UK), 1944.

Hitchcock, Alfred, director. *Champagne*. British International Pictures, 1928.

Hitchcock, Alfred, director. *Dial M for Murder*. Warner Bros., 1954.

Hitchcock, Alfred, director. *Downhill*. Gainsborough Pictures, 1927.

Hitchcock, Alfred, director. *Easy Virtue*. Gainsborough Pictures, 1927.

Hitchcock, Alfred, director. *The Farmer's Wife*. British International Pictures, 1928.

Hitchcock, Alfred, director. *Foreign Correspondent*. Walter Wanger Productions, 1940.

Hitchcock, Alfred, director. *Frenzy*. Alfred J. Hitchcock Productions, 1972.

Hitchcock, Alfred, director. *Jamaica Inn*. Renown Pictures Corporation, 1939.

Hitchcock, Alfred, director. *The Lady Vanishes*. Gainsborough Pictures, 1938.

Hitchcock, Alfred, director. *Lifeboat*. Twentieth Century–Fox, 1944.

Hitchcock, Alfred, director. *The Lodger: A Story of the London Fog*. Gainsborough Pictures, 1927.

Hitchcock, Alfred, director. *The Man Who Knew Too Much*. Gaumont British Picture Corporation, 1934.

Hitchcock, Alfred, director. *The Man Who Knew Too Much*. Paramount Pictures, 1956.

Hitchcock, Alfred, director. *The Manxman*. British International Pictures, 1929.

Hitchcock, Alfred, director. *Marnie*. Alfred J. Hitchcock Productions, 1964.

Hitchcock, Alfred, director. *The Mountain Eagle*. Gainsborough Pictures, 1926.

Hitchcock, Alfred, director. *Murder!* British International Pictures, 1930.

Hitchcock, Alfred, director. *North by Northwest*. Metro-Goldwyn-Mayer, 1956.

Hitchcock, Alfred, director. *Notorious*. RKO Radio Pictures, 1946.

Hitchcock, Alfred, director. *The Paradine Case*. Selznick International Pictures, 1947.

Hitchcock, Alfred, director. *The Pleasure Garden*. Münchner Lichtspielkunst AG (Emelka) and Gainsborough Pictures, 1925.

Hitchcock, Alfred, director. *Psycho*. Shamley Productions, 1960.

Hitchcock, Alfred, director. *Rear Window*. Patron Inc., 1954.

Hitchcock, Alfred, director. *Rebecca*. Selznick International Pictures, 1940.

Hitchcock, Alfred, director. *The Ring*. British International Pictures, 1927.

Hitchcock, Alfred, director. *Rope*. Warner Bros., 1948.

Hitchcock, Alfred, director. *Sabotage*. Gaumont British Picture Corporation, 1936.

Hitchcock, Alfred, director. *Saboteur*. Frank Lloyd Productions, 1942.

Hitchcock, Alfred, director. *The Secret Agent*. Gaumont British Picture Corporation, 1936.

Hitchcock, Alfred, director. *Shadow of a Doubt*. Universal Pictures, 1943.

Hitchcock, Alfred, director. *The Skin Game*. British International Pictures, 1931.

Hitchcock, Alfred, director. *Spellbound*. Selznick International Pictures, 1945.

Hitchcock, Alfred, director. *Stage Fright*. Warner Bros., 1950.

Hitchcock, Alfred, director. *Strangers on a Train*. Warner Bros., 1951.

Hitchcock, Alfred, director. *Suspicion*. RKO Radio Pictures, 1941.

Hitchcock, Alfred, director. *To Catch a Thief*. Paramount Pictures, 1955.

Hitchcock, Alfred, director. *Under Capricorn*. Transatlantic Pictures, 1949.

Hitchcock, Alfred, director. *Vertigo*. Alfred J. Hitchcock Productions, 1958.

Hitchcock, Alfred, director. *The Wrong Man*. Warner Bros., 1956.

Hitchcock, Alfred, director. *Young and Innocent*. Gaumont British Picture Corporation, 1937.

Jarrold, Julian, director. *The Girl*. HBO/BBC2, 2012.

Keaton, Buster, and Clyde Bruckman, directors. *The General*. Buster Keaton Productions and Joseph M. Schenck Productions, 1926.

Lang, Fritz, director. *Metropolis*. UFA, 1927.

Leni, Paul, director. *Waxworks*. Neptune-Film A.G., 1924.

Lloyd, Norman, creator. *The Alfred Hitchcock Hour*. Shamley Productions, 1962–1965.

McCarey, Leo, director. *An Affair to Remember*. Jerry Wald Productions, 1957.

McCarey, Leo, director. *Love Affair*. RKO Radio Pictures, 1938.

Murnau, F. W., director. *Nosferatu*. Jofa-Atelier Berlin-Johannisthal and Prana-Film GmbH, 1922.

Murnau, F. W., director. *Sunrise: A Song of Two Humans*. Fox Film Corporation, 1927.

Pontecorvo, Gillo, director. *Kapò*. Cineriz, 1960.

Powell, Michael, director. *Peeping Tom*. Michael Powell (Theatre), 1960.

Powell, Michaell, and Emeric Pressburger, directors. *A Matter of Life and Death*. The Archers, 1946.

Preminger, Otto, director. *Laura*. Twentieth Century–Fox, 1944.

Reed, Carol, director. *The Third Man*. London Film Productions, 1949.

Reisz, Karel, director. *Saturday Night and Sunday Morning*. Woodfall Film Productions, 1960.

Richardson, Tony, director. *A Taste of Honey*. Woodfall Film Productions, 1961.

Robison, Arthur, director. *Warning Shadows*. Pan-Film, 1923.

Sjöström, Victor, director. *The Scarlet Letter*. Metro-Goldwyn-Mayer, 1926.

Slan, John, and Michael Sloan, creators. *Alfred Hitchcock Presents*. NBC, 1985–1989.

Sluizer, George, director. *Spoorlos* (*The Vanishing*). Argos Films, 1988.

Sluizer, George, director. *The Vanishing*. Twentieth Century–Fox, 1993.

"A Talk with Alfred Hitchcock." *Telescope*. CBC, 1964.

Van Sant, Gus, director. *Psycho*. Universal Pictures, 1998.

Walsh, Raoul, director. *Colorado Territory*. Warner Bros., 1949.

Walsh, Raoul, director. *High Sierra*. Warner Bros., 1941.

Welles, Orson, director. *Citizen Kane*. RKO Radio Pictures, 1941.

Welles, Orson, director. *The Magnificent Ambersons*. RKO Radio Pictures, 1942.

Wiene, Robert, director. *The Cabinet of Dr. Caligari*. Decla-Bioscop AG, 1920.

Wyler, William, director. *The Best Years of Our Lives*. Samuel Goldwyn Company, 1946.

Index

For the benefit of digital users, indexed terms that span two pages (e.g., 52–53) may, on occasion, appear on only one of those pages.

Figures are indicated by *f* following the page number